The 25 Most Influential Aircraft of All Time

Walter J. Boyne and Philip Handleman

LYONS
PRESS

Essex, Connecticut

*To the dreamers and doers of the aerospace future—
the designers, engineers, and builders of as yet unimagined platforms and to
the crews who will fly and maintain them*

An imprint of Globe Pequot, the trade division of
The Rowman & Littlefield Publishing Group, Inc.
4501 Forbes Blvd., Ste. 200
Lanham, MD 20706
www.rowman.com

Distributed by NATIONAL BOOK NETWORK

British Library Cataloguing in Publication Information available

Library of Congress Cataloging-in-Publication Data available

ISBN 978-1-9430-6638-4 (paperback)
ISBN 978-1-4930-2631-9 (ebook)

♾™ The paper used in this publication meets the minimum requirements of American National
Standard for Information Sciences—Permanence of Paper for Printed Library Materials, ANSI/
NISO Z39.48-1992.

CONTENTS

Contents

Section 3   Sky Warriors: Military Platforms

Section 4   Fun Flying: Trainer/Sport Platforms

ACKNOWLEDGMENTS

In basic ways, artistic and literary endeavors, indeed, the creative processes in general, are inescapably collaborative in nature. For us as pilots writing about planes and the people who made and flew them, the beginning point is the understanding that comes from our own time manipulating controls in cockpits, which only could have happened with the guidance and encouragement—the collaboration—of mentors who passed along their knowledge of the science of flight. From our first instructor pilots, who introduced us to underlying principles, to recurrency and refresher course instructors, who honed our technique, we owe a debt of gratitude.

Words are one thing, but illustrations often go further than text in explaining a subject, event, or phenomenon, especially when the circumstances leave language shorthanded for the occasion. Fortunately, friends in the aviation artist community have contributed stunning paintings that depict most of the aircraft chosen for inclusion in our book. These images convey the drama and beauty, the unmitigated allure of great planes.

Sam Lyons, himself a pilot of charming antique taildraggers, has spent much of his life perfecting the feel for old-time aviation, as is apparent in his portrayal of a lemony Piper Cub poised on an emerald-green field. William S. Phillips, often referred to as the Rembrandt of aviation artists, is a master of the genre, sometimes employing a baroque style that resonates with breathtaking skyscapes, as in his canvas of Spitfires on the prowl. Mike Machat, who has soared in sailplanes over crisp desert vistas, is in love with the airliners of his youth so that his depictions of them, like the Pan Am 707, are as sleek, idealized objects cutting a vivid profile in a pristine sky. Jack Fellows churns out an almost preternatural volume of aviation paintings with an eye acutely focused on the intricacies of planes in flight, whether trainers lolling along or fighters locked in mortal combat. Craig Kodera was a high-time air force and airline pilot whose perspectives on the flight deck get translated into creations that reflect both technical detail and artistic sensibility. Russell Smith is fascinated by early aircraft and their historical settings, usually showing biplanes with a refined Impressionistic flair, like the venerable JN-4 Jenny maneuvering over an airfield nestled in a soft-hued landscape that beckons the trainer home. Stan Stokes produces an enormous output that reflects a profound versatility, meaning he is as equally adept at portraying a commercial transport cruising over a spectacular landmark as he is revealing the extreme gyrations of dogfighting pursuit planes against the backdrop of a battle-scarred sky. Ronald Wong likes the modern platforms and he is uncannily proficient at recreating them with amazing detail, down to the minutia that virtually no one but subject-matter experts, aerospace engineers, or passionate enthusiasts would even notice. Keith Ferris, the acknowledged dean of aviation artists, grew up on a fabled air corps training base where the thrill of daily mass formations instilled an undying devotion to depicting military aircraft in accurate and heart-stopping renderings of action aloft, as evinced in the canvas of the duel between a propeller-driven Mustang and a jet-powered Messerschmitt. We thank these gifted painters for their contributions, which add an incalculable dimension to our book. Their unmatched artistry will surely be savored for years to come.

We extend heartfelt thanks for the insightful and stirring textual contributions that set the tone for our book. These essays come from three distinguished individuals whose names are esteemed within aviation circles. Each has made a mark in the field in his own way.

William Lloyd Stearman is the son of the legendary Lloyd Stearman, an aeronautical pioneer who entered into partnership with Clyde Cessna and Walter Beech in the 1920s. A short time later, as the three industry trailblazers set off on their own, the Stearman Aircraft Company made an enduring impression on an air-minded public with its beautiful Golden Age biplanes. Then, as Lockheed Aircraft Corporation emerged from a corporate reorganization in the depths of the Depression, Lloyd was hired as the company's president.

Being the son of an early industry leader, Bill Stearman came of age in a household where aviation permeated every aspect of daily life. After service in the US Navy and the Central Intelligence Agency, he chose a career in the US Foreign Service and eventually joined the staff of the National Security Council in which capacity he was a regular guest in the Oval Office where he advised presidents. In meetings with George H. W.

Bush, conversations often turned to the military biplane trainer that Bill's father had spawned and in which the president had learned to fly as an aspiring naval aviator during World War II. In his preface, Bill offers a singular perspective of the aviation industry's formative years and, as a combat veteran of World War II and the Vietnam War, highly personal insights into military aircraft of later years.

As an aircraft designer, Burt Rutan is unequaled. In the 1960s, his career started at Edwards Air Force Base where he was a flight test engineer. It was an ideal launch pad for a life devoted to aeronautical innovation.

Burt established his reputation among do-it-yourself pilots who relished the hands-on challenge of assembling the designer's futuristic-looking planes that employed innovations like unconventional configurations, canard surfaces, and high-tech materials. The resulting aircraft were reliable and efficient; they have often been referred to as "those Rutans." His ultimate "homebuilt" design was the grassroots-supported *Voyager* which was the first aircraft to fly around the world without stopping or refueling. As the founder of Scaled Composites, a highly creative and nimble prototyping shop in the Mojave Desert, he received many assignments to do the impossible. His accomplishments include the billionaire-backed *SpaceShipOne*, which was the first privately developed and privately operated manned vehicle to penetrate space. Burt offers a foreword loaded with nuggets from a lifetime of prolific aircraft design.

Norman R. Augustine is one of the elder statesmen of the aerospace industry. Armed with an honors degree from Princeton, he entered the industry as a research engineer at Douglas Aircraft Company in the 1950s. In the ensuing four decades, he rose steadily at various aerospace and defense organizations with a few detours into government service, which included a stint as undersecretary of the Army. He was appointed chief executive of Martin Marietta, and after that company merged with Lockheed to form Lockheed Martin Corporation, the world's largest defense contractor, Norm was eventually elevated to the top job.

Owing to his demonstrated expertise, deep intellect, and insatiable curiosity, even in retirement Norm has been sought out by other corporations, academic institutions, and government agencies. Notably, he chaired the 2009 panel charged with reviewing options for the future of US manned spaceflight. Another endeavor among his many retirement activities was a return to his alma mater to impart the wisdom gained in a fruitful career and inspire the coming generation of engineers. Norm's introduction is a lively discussion on the industry he knows so well, sharpened by his keen incisiveness and leavened by his trademark wit.

We would be remiss if we did not express our gratitude for the assistance of Jeffrey P. Rhodes of Lockheed Martin and John Helzer of the Unicover Corporation. We thank Burt Rutan for taking additional time out of his busy schedule to suggest changes to our chapter on his *SpaceShipOne* that enhanced the chapter's accuracy. The publications department of the Experimental Aircraft Association kindly granted permission to reprint portions of two articles. Our editor, Gene Brissie, saw the potential for this book when others didn't and he helped to deftly shepherd it to fruition. His able assistants, Stephanie Scott and Lynn Zelem, added editorial polish. Special thanks go to our agent, Grace Freedson, for her unflagging perseverance and timely encouragement.

Most of all we recognize the unsung contributions of our spouses, Terri and Mary. Without their patience and sustenance the book would have remained a figment of our imagination, a promising idea rather than a finished product to be shared with others. Our spouses are loving partners and more; they are the wind beneath our wings. Because of their faith in us, we can soar.

AUTHORS' NOTE

When asked to devise a list of the most influential aircraft, the choices of a knowledgeable enthusiast will almost without exception contrast with the picks of another. This phenomenon, the virtual certainty of differences in opinion as to which aircraft constitute the most influential or the most famous or the best to fly, illustrates the diversity of viewpoints. No omniscient source or magical formula exists to generate consistent computer-like answers.

The question is simply one for which there is no right or wrong; the inquiry falls into a domain where absolutes give way to subjectivism. In the absence of hard truth, personal belief reigns. Ultimately, this exercise proves to be eminently human, causing no two lists to be exactly alike.

Precisely because we are human, we have deep affection for certain aircraft we have flown—the Stratojet and Stratofortress for Walt and the Cub and Stearman for Philip. Not surprisingly, then, these planes occupy places on our list. Simply stated, our point is that the selection process hinges more on individual preferences than scientific criteria. This is not to say that quantifiable information hasn't gone into our basket of considerations.

Speed records, market share, kill/loss tallies, and other measures count in arriving at choices for inclusion. Mixing tangible metrics with revealing anecdotes and actual experience, it is all but obligatory that aircraft like the DC-3, P-51, and Spitfire have a place on our list. Others have made the cut because they were the first to cross a threshold.

Where would aviation be if not for the Wright *Flyer*, the *Spirit of St. Louis*, and the Bell X-1? These trailblazing platforms did not just break barriers; they altered perceptions of commerce, war, science, and technology. Their influence at the hands of brave pilots did even more by inspiring people to dream that civilization could overcome the seemingly impossible.

Admittedly, there are more than twenty-five aircraft that qualify as highly influential, and, if we had one more slot, we would likely have inserted the popular Lockheed SR-71 Blackbird into it. Also, readers may wonder why we did not include at least one drone. As in-cockpit pilots, we explain this omission with a simple acknowledgment of our partiality to manned aircraft. Additionally, we feel that drones, as still relatively new platforms in the everyday world of flight, will make for more compelling entries on future lists.

Our purpose is not to promote our list over others, for no one has a list that is better or worse than anyone else's list. We seek to describe the subject aircraft with enough specificity so that, in turn, their impact—dare we say their influence—is revealed. In other words, through concentrating on the particular, we hope to achieve the universal. What we learn from the design, production, and operation of one type may enlighten us about many types.

It has been our good fortune to meet and at times develop a friendship with certain of the aviation pioneers whose intellect, imagination, courage, and persistence gave birth to or animated the twenty-five phenomenal aircraft covered in the pages that follow. We share some of the personal interaction we have had with these mostly larger-than-life personalities—designers and aviators, geniuses and showmen, warriors and explorers. In doing so, we strive to make the human side come across as an integral component behind the machines we showcase.

Also, our flying lives, when combined, stretch more than ninety years. In that time we have flown, or flown in, nearly half the planes covered in the pages that follow. We invite you to come along for what we hope will be a memorable and enjoyable ride!

PREFACE

William Lloyd Stearman, PhD
Former Staff Member, National Security Council

What a delight to read the "biographies" of twenty-five of the greatest aircraft ever built. All aviation buffs would favor some planes not listed, but you have to draw the line somewhere and the authors have done a masterful job of doing just that.

I believe that a larger list would have included the F4U Corsair, a great World War II fighter which I witnessed performing incredible feats of close air support. Of the listed planes in that war, I saw the Zero, the P-38, and the SBD Dauntless in action. The great planes of the Vietnam War (my second war) were certainly the A-4 and the F-4. In World War I you had the SPAD and the Sopwith Camel.

I grew up in aviation and can hardly believe the advances since those early days. Just think of the newly formed Travel Air Company in 1925. You had Walter Beech, Clyde Cessna, and Lloyd Stearman (my father) in partnership with each other. Some days all three could be seen in the shop together, building with their own hands a new design by my father. They were aided by a few former auto mechanics. Just contrast this with the huge aircraft companies of today.

My father is best known for his World War II-era primary trainer, the prototype of which he designed and which was manufactured by a company he had founded in 1926. I was happy to see three Lockheeds on the list. My father was, in fact, the principal founder of the Lockheed Aircraft Corporation in 1932. This company was formed for the express purpose of manufacturing an all-metal passenger plane, which my father had designed and which became the Electra 10. I saw my father begin this design in our living room and in 1934 I flew it after it became airborne.

I saw much of the trials and tribulations that went into making airplanes and can only have the highest respect for all those involved in the design and manufacture of the great airplanes covered in this incredible book which I wholeheartedly recommend to aviation enthusiasts and others.

FOREWORD

Burt Rutan
Founder, Scaled Composites

While many books have been written about various lists of history's "best" or "fastest" or "ugliest" airplanes, this book is very different. It combines the more important definition of "most influential" with an excellent, detailed, behind-the-scenes history of the personal stories of their designers and pilots. The words "most influential" indicate criteria that demand a real historic proof for an airplane to qualify for the list. This book beautifully provides that required detailed proof.

I occasionally get requests to write forewords or reviews of new books, which I usually decline, since my focus has been on developing airplanes and test reports, not writing about them for public exposure. Instead, I usually play the role of fact-checker or critic, not the writer of original copy. But I really do need to get in the habit of writing, because for the five years since I retired, I have been struggling with just how to structure my own autobiography and how to bring clarity to a fun career in aerospace development. So this exercise has been beneficial for me.

I said "of course" to this request, upon learning that the authors are my favorite aerospace historian, Walter Boyne, along with Philip Handleman, a prolific writer of dozens of wonderful aviation books that have enriched all of us and inspired our youth to pursue aviation as a career.

I certainly need to comment on the selection of the twenty-five most influential aircraft because there had to be extensive debate over which ones would make the cut. I also guess that there was debate on the number twenty-five, beyond just the rough size of the book. I will state my viewpoints on only the listed airplanes that I am familiar with. I will also candidly state where I disagree with the selection. I am not known to be shy, so I will risk not being asked for an opinion again.

Wright *Flyer*

I made my opinion of the Wright brothers clear when I accepted the Wright Memorial Trophy from the National Aeronautic Association in December 2015. While I applaud their impressive creativity and building/testing skills as they moved from basic gliders to the 1903 *Flyer*, using a homemade wind tunnel and beautifully designed, hand-carved propellers, I am not their fan knowing what they did after their historic fourth flight on December 17, 1903. Unlike Glenn Curtiss and many others around the world who aggressively and successfully worked to improve and promote powered flight, the brothers tested in secret, focused on working with lawyers and threatened to sue anyone marketing any airplane that had to bank to be able to turn. Had they instead continued their previous research and prototyping methods, they would have contributed much more. Also, due partially to the lawsuit with Glenn Curtiss and the continued support the Smithsonian Institution had for the Langley Aerodrome, the first long-term display of the *Flyer* was not in America. It was at the British Museum in London, starting in 1928. It was not on permanent display at the Smithsonian until 1948. Neither of the brothers lived to see the Smithsonian's display of their *Flyer*.

Curtiss aircraft, not Wright aircraft, contributed to the World War I effort. The Wright brothers never won the Collier Trophy for an airplane design. Glenn Curtiss (also Kelly Johnson and I) won two Colliers for airplane designs.

Historians continue to refer only to the 1903 *Flyer*'s first flight at Kitty Hawk, North Carolina. According to their diary, the first flight of 120 feet was an uncontrolled divergence to a crash, as was the second and third. Only after the fourth flight of some 852 feet did they feel mildly confident to claim that they had achieved controlled, sustained powered flight, in spite of the fact that it ended in a sudden dive into the ground causing major damage to the front of the airplane—another crash, not a landing.

I believe the Wrights' greatest accomplishment was in 1908 when Wilbur flew their Wright Model A in Paris, proving to the European doubters that they did indeed have an airplane far superior to any other at the time. The Wrights then became world celebrities overnight. Compared to the phenomenal worldwide progress in aviation in the five years following 1908, not much happened in the five years following 1903. In the big picture, those two hundred Model A flights in Europe were far more influential than the four flights at Kitty Hawk in 1903.

Spirit of St. Louis

A read of any Charles Lindbergh biography takes you through a wonderful adventure of a young man with unlimited courage, enjoying to the fullest all that airplanes could offer in the 1920s. His legacy was not made only by his New York to Paris flight in 1927, but by what he did after his historic flight. Along with his young wife, Anne Morrow, they flew many exploratory flights that soon opened new routes for airline travel, and he worked as a technical advisor to several airline companies. International airline transportation flourished in the late 1920s and Lindbergh was instrumental to its growth.

I was raised in a Seventh-day Adventist family, and was prohibited from seeing movies or enjoying sports on the Sabbath. The first movie I ever saw was the James Stewart film *Spirit of St. Louis*, released when I was fourteen years old. The church school I attended decided that no harm would be done to the children by bringing a large projector to the school and showing the film to us kids. I was thrilled and it was years before I saw another film. I was hooked. Charles Lindbergh became my hero. I was inspired by how a handful of focused workers in San Diego could, along with Lindbergh himself, build something as complex as an ocean-crossing airplane in only two months. That single film screening in 1957 probably had a lot to do with why I later became a successful aircraft developer.

After college, my aviation accomplishments allowed me to meet many aeronautical design heroes—Wernher von Braun, Jack Northrop, Kelly Johnson, Ed Heinemann, and Bill Lear. However, it was clear that I would never meet Charles Lindbergh since he had become an environmentalist recluse after the mid-1960s, refraining from all interfaces with the media and the aeronautics industry. Then, something wonderful happened in September 1969 at the Beverly Hilton Hotel. The event was the annual Society of Experimental Test Pilots symposium banquet, which I attended. Lindbergh had agreed to address the event if no media were notified and no advance information about him was released. Neil Armstrong, just out of quarantine from his moon landing, Bob Hoover, and Charles Lindbergh all dined together in a darker corner of the room, then each of them addressed a very surprised audience. I am sure it's the only time in 1969 that Neil Armstrong got upstaged by someone else.

Lindbergh told stories of his early years teaching himself to fly. I will never forget one of his anecdotes, about flying a Jenny or some similar airplane in the 1920s. "I entered the spin at twenty-five hundred-feet altitude [gasps were heard from the audience, primarily jet fighter test pilots]. It would not come out of the spin. At six hundred-feet altitude I unstrapped and pulled the parachute ripcord [louder gasps from the audience]. I can assure you that in 1925, twenty-five hundred feet was a lot higher than it is today. However . . . six hundred feet is EXACTLY the same altitude as it is today!" That evening Lindbergh remained for hours to chat with the world's flight test people, including me. My father, who was eleven when Lindbergh flew to Paris, also got to chat with Lindbergh that evening! Thirty years later I became good friends with the Lindbergh family, being awarded the Lindbergh Foundation Medal, the Lindbergh Eagle, the Lindbergh Foundation Award, and the American Society of Mechanical Engineers' Spirit of St. Louis Medal. Grandson Erik Lindbergh built a metal model rocket for my trophy case.

X-15

The X-15 is an excellent choice here, since that program was clearly the most influential of all the research X-planes of the 1950s and 60s. Those three X-15 research aircraft racked up 199 test flights, many of which expanded the envelope of human flight. My tenure at Edwards Air Force Base included the last sixty-four of the X-15 flights and I always went over to Test Ops to watch the crude live video coverage of the high-risk tests. I remember helping to install the sign over Pete Knight's desk in 1966 just after he flew the record Mach 6.7 flight—"Lickety-Split Pete—Fastest Man Alive." As a young engineer, just a year out of college, I wondered how future X-planes at Edwards would perform. I would not have guessed that fifty years later, of runway-landable aircraft, only the Space Shuttle would fly faster.

The X-15 was a true manned space rocket launch system. Until *Space-ShipOne* in 2004 it was the only vehicle to be hand-flown to space. Joe Walker flew two consecutive flights to above one hundred kilometers altitude in the summer of 1963, making it the third out of seven different manned space launch systems that America operated in the 1960s. For *SpaceShipOne*'s third space flight, I asked my test pilot, Brian Binnie, to run the rocket motor longer than needed, in order to beat Joe Walker's altitude record. Brian did, and I seemed to be the only one around who thought it was super cool that our little spaceship had flown two miles higher than any X-15.

The only fatal accident in the X-15 program, an atmospheric entry control problem, was to have a lasting effect on my work thirty years later. I had been haunted by how Mike Adams lost his life due to an inability to align the ship for entry. The Space Shuttle had the same requirement—the need to accurately align pitch and yaw attitudes during entry into the atmosphere. Those risks forced me to design only parachute landing capsules in the mid-1990s when I became obsessed with developing a light suborbital spacecraft. But being an aircraft designer, not a capsule designer, I set an unusual goal: a glider that landed on a runway that would self-align (no pilot or autopilot needed) for the supersonic atmospheric entry. The solution was the "Care-Free-Reentry," feathered configuration of *SpaceShipOne*, also used later for *SpaceShipTwo*. The event that encouraged me to achieve this goal was Mike Adams's X-15 accident in 1967.

Ford Tri-Motor

My father, Pop Rutan, was twelve years old in 1928 when his father drove him from their farm to a small California airport to see the arrival and departure of a Ford Tri-Motor. It seemed huge to him and made the most wonderful noise as it approached and pulled up close to the airport fence. Pop's father, noting the cars in the parking lot, told his son that only real rich people got to fly in airliners. They watched the Ford depart until it became a speck in the distance. Pop was thrilled, but concluded that he would probably never be able to fly in an airliner. Forty years later, Pop and Mom occasionally flew in jetliners for free, using the family coupons from my sister, who worked as a stewardess for American

Airlines. In those days anyone flying with family coupons in first class was required to be dressed in coat and tie even though the stewardesses sported miniskirts!

The Ford is another excellent choice for the list. In America this was the most successful airliner during the first few years of scheduled passenger service. In 1927 its safety statistic of one fatal crash per five thousand flights, while dangerous, was safe enough so that the growth of the industry was not severely limited by fear. Within a few years the risk improved to one in thirty-three thousand. The improvement was not due to major changes in the aircraft. They just added seat belts to the wicker seats and stopped flying in the worst weather.

Douglas DC-3

This is another most influential aircraft, indeed. My flying career involved the "Gooney Bird" on two occasions.

In 1970 while on a tour to brief every air force F-4 pilot in the world about spin recovery, one of my short flights was in a C-47, the military version of the DC-3. My test pilot, Gerry Gentry, and I were sitting on the bare floor of the cabin without seat belts. We made a very tight turn right after liftoff from Da Nang, Vietnam. They told us it was to stay away from reported gunfire from the surrounding jungle. Being a civilian, I guess this was the only time I was ever close to gunfire.

In 1973 my boss bought a DC-3 with a cargo door in order to ferry his three BD-5J aerobatic team aircraft around the air-show circuit. We dropped off the Experimental Aircraft Association president, Paul Poberezny, at Milwaukee and headed out over Lake Michigan after midnight, bound for the Reading, Pennsylvania, air show. Settling in for a long flight I took a look out to the right before rolling over to sleep. There, in the hole opened by the extended cowl flaps on the right engine was a fire, in the accessory section. I ran to the cockpit and hollered, "Fire in the right engine!" then returned to watch the fire before the pilots could say, "Huh?" They pulled the fire extinguisher handle, shut off the fuel, feathered the engine and we returned to the Milwaukee airport. Our crew had very limited experience in the DC-3 so I found a pay phone and called Paul. He said, "Oh, it's probably a leak in a fuel pump line. It's close to the hot exhaust." Paul then came back to the airport, fixed the leak and then proceeded to hand-prop the DC-3! There was nothing wrong with the starter; it was just Paul showing off to us youngsters who had bet that hand-propping an airliner was impossible.

Learjet

I agree that a business jet deserves to be on this list, and the Lear 23 is the best choice. If one looks at how Bill Lear developed and certified his first Learjet in the early 1960s, you see a story of a never-give-up business-man fighting to make his dream happen against the odds. He had a tiny company, compared to the established general aviation firms. If he had taken the same route to certification that Beechcraft and Cessna followed with their new airplanes, he would have gone bankrupt long before get-ting certification.

In 1975 while Lear was planning the development of the Lear Fan, a beautiful all-composite, high efficiency, twin engine turboprop pusher, he flew a Learjet to Mojave, thinking a visit with the new Rutan Aircraft Factory might give him useful information about all-composite aircraft structures. It was not a good time to visit. Minutes before Lear's arrival, my only full-time employee, George Mead, landed our little fiberglass VariEze short of the runway, damaging the nose and the landing gear. George was not hurt, but it was a clumsy way for me to meet the legend while I was picking up the pieces from the dirt. Bill did not find anything useful that day for his program to develop an all-carbon fiber Lear Fan. However, I will never forget the three hours I spent with him in my shop, each telling the other about our careers and how smart we were.

His program for the Lear Fan was even more grueling than the Learjet. It never was certified, partially due to his difficulty in convincing the FAA that it was a redundant twin in spite of its single gearbox and propeller.

In 1978 Bill Lear died of leukemia at the age of seventy-five, not knowing if the Lear Fan would be a success. On his deathbed he whis-pered to his wife, Moya, "Finish it, Mommy. You've got to finish it." Moya took the reins of the company and struggled for about five years trying her best to fulfill his wish.

Concorde

I suppose the Anglo-French Concorde belongs on the list, being the only ride the public could take at supersonic speeds. It flew about fifty thousand commercial flights during its twenty-seven-year run. Concorde is the classic example of how technology does not improve without the pressures of competition in the marketplace. Its last passenger flight, in 2003, had the same speed, efficiency, community noise level, etc., as its first passenger flight in 1976. If it had had competitors, the financial pressures of fighting for market share would have resulted in great improvements during its life cycle. If that had happened, a lot more than the super wealthy would have flown, and maybe today all of us would be enjoying that three-and-a-half-hour flight from New York to London.

Boeing B-47 and 707

The beautiful B-47 (first flight date 1947) has always been a favorite of mine. Its aerodynamic efficiency was unmatched for decades. I think the main reason it deserves to be on the "most influential" list is what Boeing later did with its wing and pylon-mounted engine configuration. In the early 1950s while Boeing's airline designers were still trying to evolve improvements in the Model 367 (straight wing, piston engine C-97 configuration), the British DH 106 Comet jetliner was unveiled. Boeing's designers, operating in secrecy, mated the B-47 wing/engine to a fuselage that would carry 140 passengers and designated it the Model 367-80. Its model name was changed to 707 only after it was revealed to the public in the mid-1950s. Today, the prototype is still called the Dash 80.

Piper Cub

I think no one would argue with the Piper Cub being included in this list. My best story about the Cub is from 1969 when I learned that my F-4 program test pilot, Gerry Gentry, had never flown a taildragger. Major Gentry was arguably the "Chuck Yeager of the 1960s." As an air force test pilot, he flew nearly all the new high-performance fighters as well as the NASA lifting-body research aircraft, the forerunners of the Space Shuttle. I coerced him out to the deserted Mojave airport and gave him the controls for a Piper Cub crosswind landing. I was all smiles, of course, when I had to grab back the controls to prevent a ground loop.

In the 1950s, the Cub had a very similar competitor, the Aeronca 7AC Champ. When I was a fifteen-year-old student in high school, I took a series of flying lessons in the Champ: dual instruction totaling five hours and forty-five minutes, all at Alta, California, a small crop-duster field. The day I turned sixteen, in 1959, I was legally able to solo. My instructor, Johnny Banks (the country/western DJ at the local radio station), to my surprise got out of the Champ and said, "Rutan, go ahead and fly three patterns by yourself." My lasting memory of the day was that now my flying would cost only $4.50 per hour, not having to pay the DJ his $2.50 per hour. It gets better—my high school buddy Gilbert Hutchison had also recently soloed a Cub at a different airport. We soon were flying together illegally—because neither of us was licensed to carry passengers—by sneaking over to Sequoia field, an abandoned World War II training field. By sharing the airplane, we were paying $2.25 per hour to fly. It was a long time before I told my parents about that cheating.

WHAT IS MISSING FROM THE LIST?

SR-71 Blackbird

I have to admit that I am biased about this, but I believe that the SR-71 was history's most technically significant and most beautiful aircraft. It had been unveiled only the year before, when I started my first post-college job in 1965 at Edwards Air Force Base. While I was not assigned to its test program, it was exciting to watch them outside my window as a power cart with multiple V-8 auto engines went through the gears while mechanically turning the big J-58 engines up to their light-off rpm. The SRs are more than 107 feet long, so they appeared slow, graceful, and mesmerizing when I saw them on landing approach during my daily commute to and from Edwards.

The A12/YF12/SR-71 family of airplanes was initially designed only twelve years after the introduction of the P-80, our first operational jet. The Blackbirds were operational for thirty-four years and none were shot down. Their titanium structures and stealthy shape were enormous break-throughs at the time, and to this day no operational military aircraft has ever had better performance.

Any Successful Airplane from 1908 through 1914

None of the most influential airplanes on this book's list come from the most important six years of aircraft development—1908 through 1914. In 1908, when Wilbur flew his Wright Model A in Paris, less than twenty people had flown an airplane, and many of those had not flown a controlled turn. In less than six years, hundreds of new airplane types were flying in thirty-nine countries, and factories in Europe were producing more than five hundred airplanes a year. Tens of thousands of airplane designs were tried—"Hey, if some bicycle shop guys can do it then I can do it too." Almost all of these failed, but the few who succeeded had defined the basic design criteria for almost all the airplanes that followed. The airplane was created by natural selection: The few that had partial success were tweaked until they could fly better. Those that could not fly went extinct. Few fledgling pilots had access to any type of flight training, so if their new design was intact after its first flight, by definition it had good flying qualities!

In 2003 *Aviation Week* asked me to define the most important people in the first hundred years of aerospace. I selected nine people*, and realized later that they all had been young children during that extreme expansion of airplane development in that six-year time period. The kids, observing huge progress by smart and courageous heroes, were later unafraid as adults to take big risks to achieve the impossible.

Which early airplane should be on a "most influential" list? You could pick almost any successful airplane that appears on this list of fifteen hundred individual types built from 1908 to 1914: https://en.wikipedia.org/wiki/List_of_aircraft_(pre-1914).

* Wernher von Braun, Kelly Johnson, Charles Lindbergh, Jack Northrop, Ed Heinemann, Howard Hughes, Sergei Korolev, Alexander Lippisch, and Bill Lear.

INTRODUCTION

Norman R. Augustine
Retired Chairman and Chief Executive Officer, Lockheed Martin Corporation

For centuries humans have dreamed of flying. Walter Boyne and Philip Handleman have drawn upon their deep familiarity with aviation and their remarkable writing abilities to tell the fascinating story of the machines that made those dreams become a reality. But one simply cannot read this intriguing tale of *The 25 Most Influential Aircraft of All Time* without offering one's own candidates for the list, or even narrowing the question to a more personal one: "What were the most influential airplanes in the reader's own life?"

Based on the aircraft in which I have flown (as a passenger since aeronautical engineers, such as I, know better than to pilot the machines they design!), the top three aircraft have to be the C-47, the F-16, and the Citation, only one of which, incidentally, appears in the authors' "Top 25" . . . but I'll get to that later! The reasons, in reverse order, for these flying machines appearing on my own list were, first, that I survived a midnight crash in a snowstorm at liftoff in a Citation (not the aircraft's or the pilot's fault, rather a piece of ice frozen on the runway that drove the nose-gear into the cockpit as the aircraft rotated into flight). Next, I was performing aerobatics in the back seat (emphasis) of an F-16 fighter the morning after I had fallen into an old aviation joke when I innocently asked Lockheed Martin's chief test pilot what I should eat the morning of the flight. His answer: "Bananas." Apparently this is not because of the potassium content but because, in his words, "They taste about the same coming up as going down."

Then there was my very first flight. It took place during World War II when I was a Cub Scout. We boarded an Army Air Corps C-47, fondly known to those who flew it as the "Gooney Bird"—presumably having something to do with its struggles to get aloft. On that occasion we circled the city of Denver for twenty minutes as we sat on canvas benches staring wide-eyed at each other (the windows were small, few, and behind our backs anyway). We each had been issued a parachute, but no explanation of how to use it. No legal releases were required and no parental permission was needed . . . it was simply up, up and away! And mighty impressive, too.

As the years passed, I flew (in) other aircraft spanning from a Waco biplane and a glider to the Mach 2 Concorde.

There was, of course, that incident when I was sitting in the copilot's seat "steering" a ski-equipped C-130 four-engine turboprop (also not on the authors' "Top 25" list!) on the way to the South Pole. The *real* pilot was entertaining me with the story of a C-130 that had encountered serious damage at the Pole and had been abandoned there to begin sinking into the nine thousand-foot-thick ice before it was dug out and repaired seventeen years later. When I asked the pilot whatever became of that aircraft, he casually replied, "You're flying it."

Part of the pleasure of reading this book is deciding which aircraft *you* believe should, or should not, be on the "Top 25" list. This of course becomes a matter of one's definition of "impactful." I once asked Kelly Johnson, leader of Lockheed's famous Skunk Works that built, among other things, the U-2 and the Mach 3-plus SR-71, which airplane that he had worked on he considered to be the most important. To my surprise, his answer was: "the crop duster." He went on to explain the role the crop duster had in feeding the world's people and improving lives.

Being a bit facetious, the hands-down winner for most "impactful," by at least one definition, would be the B-58 bomber: twenty-six of the 116 that were built *crashed*.

There is also the debate about whether aircraft that swing their wings wildly around in a circular fashion should be candidates for the list. The authors apparently decided not. And what about the potentially significant Osprey that acts as *both* a helicopter and a fixed-wing aircraft? How does it fit into the grand scheme of things? Or the pure-jet vertical takeoff and landing Harrier? Writing this book must have been as difficult as it was fun.

None of the products produced by the firm founded by my predecessor as CEO, thrice-removed Glenn Martin, made the list. But Mr. Martin, as he was known, can claim a great deal of credit for impactfulness in the field of heraldry: Employees of his fledgling aviation firm included Don Douglas, James McDonnell, Chance Vought, Lawrence Bell, and "Dutch" Kindelberger, among others. At one point he was a partner of Orville Wright. Oh, yes, he also taught Bill Boeing to fly.

Behind the stories of the twenty-five remarkable aircraft described in this remarkable book is the story of the technological advancements that made them possible—and how quickly they all came about. I once calculated that if the Space Shuttle's huge external fuel tank were placed on its side, the Wright Brothers' famous flight could have taken place entirely inside it!

In the field of aircraft structures we have advanced from airframes made of wood and cloth to airframes made of carbon fibers. The only electrical equipment on early aircraft was a magneto and a set of spark plugs. Today, even with the ability to place over a billion vacuum-tube equivalents on a single chip the size of one's thumbnail, over 10 percent of a combat aircraft's empty weight (and, not incidentally, one-third of its cost) is consumed by electronics. For navigation, the old-fashioned compass has given way to satellite-based GPS; and piston engines have been replaced by turbojets or even rockets.

The immense wind tunnels used to design earlier aircraft, some requiring the nighttime power of the TVA to function, have now largely been replaced by high-speed computers with millions of lines of software. The laborious six-axis mill, so prevalent in aircraft factories of the past, is being replaced by 3-D printers, and NASA recently "beamed-up" a wrench to the space station using radio waves to transmit software that guided a 3-D printer aboard the station. In the case of military ordnance, the change has spanned a pilot carrying a pistol in a biplane to bombs that can be guided through a particular window of a building or onto a moving vehicle. And in the most daring and controversial step of all, pilots are being replaced by robots in many military aircraft. One asks, "Could that ever happen in commercial aviation?" Before saying "no," it is useful to recall that only a decade ago the notion of autonomous vehicles cruising the nation's highways was the stuff of science fiction; today it is approaching faster than most people are prepared to realize.

Arguably the driving factor in the evolution of aeronautics over the years is what today is referred to as the aerospace industry. With its modest beginnings in bicycle and carriage shops it quickly morphed into such industrial giants as Airbus, Boeing, and Lockheed Martin. Indeed, the US aeronautics industry built a hundred thousand aircraft in a single year during World War II; it placed humans on the moon and returned them safely; and, together with the informatics industry, brought us globalization. Bill Gates has referred to aviation as the internet of the twentieth century.

But the denizens of the aerospace industry have also seen their share of turmoil. When I once asked Jimmy Doolittle what the greatest hazard faced by early aviators was, without hesitation he answered, "Starvation!" More recently, the end of the Cold War saw 40 percent of the employees in the industry lose their jobs and three-fourths of the companies simply disappear, all during a five-year period. It was perhaps the most abrupt transition any industry has ever endured.

What might the "Top 25" list look like some fifty years from now? One thing for sure, the "Top 25" list will need to have at least fifty members if it is to do justice to aviation progress over the years. Candidates will, no doubt, include the first practicable supersonic commercial transport, the first economic hypersonic aircraft, the first thousand-person transport, the first air/spacecraft to enable large-scale orbital tourism, the first aircraft to help launch humans on their way to Mars, and more . . . much more.

But there are threats out there to the realization of such dreams. The first of these is, in the case of military aviation, the growing cost of aircraft. Exactly fifty years ago, in my book *Augustine's Laws*, I reluctantly predicted that in the year 2054, a single tactical aircraft would cost the United States an entire year's defense budget. According to *The Economist* magazine's recent update of my extrapolation, my prediction of that singular event is right on track.

The second, possibly even more significant, threat is the impact of burgeoning conservatism forced on the aerospace industry—risk adversity, if you will. I of course do not argue for taking frivolous, ill-considered chances; rather, I believe that the foundation of technological progress is creativity, imagination, and genius—each of which calls for stretching the envelope to its very limits.

With that as introduction, let me wish the readers a truly informative and interesting experience. (Although I still wonder how the C-5A, MiG-15, F-4, B-36, C-130 and, most egregious of all, the SR-71, didn't make the "Top 25" list. But that sort of controversy is part of what makes this book such a fascinating read.) The authors have taken aviation writing to a new height!

Section 1

On the Edge:
Pioneering Platforms

CHAPTER 1

Birth of a Revolution: The Wright Brothers and Their World-Changing *Flyer*

Many millions of words have been written about the Wright *Flyer* and its incredible contribution to modern civilization. Now a beautifully restored work of art in the National Air and Space Museum, the 1903 Wright *Flyer* debuted as a relatively inexpensive, if highly ingenious, working aircraft. Orville and Wilbur were meticulous craftsmen who leaped in four short years from prosaic bicycle builders to future earth shakers. In their product, everything, including aesthetics, was sacrificed for one thing: success in flight. Their workmanlike assembly of essential factors into the Wright *Flyer* provided exactly that—the success that had eluded all of their predecessors.

If you thumb rapidly through the photographs of many of the aircraft efforts of the time, some of which were genuine rivals for the honor and glory of being the first to fly, you will find many beautifully detailed examples. The Langley Aerodrome was an amazing combination of handsome structure and formidable support equipment. Otto Lilienthal's gliders were delicate beauties, with the curves of each component lovingly executed. Other pioneers sought beauty with flight, as did Jean-Marie Le Bris with his Albatros II in 1868, or Victor Tatin, just eleven years later. In contrast, some of the innovators seemed to ignore aesthetics, preferring brute strength as the means by which to fling themselves into the air. Sir Hiram Maxim was one of these as he sought to combine sheer power, an excessive number of wings, and a track from which to beat the air into submission. In France, Clement Ader roughly mimicked the shape of birds, but in a heavy craft that needed not one but two steam engines for power.

The Wrights moved rapidly to success with their experiments that were stimulated by their observation of birds, from which they concluded that they needed, and could achieve, roll control. In their systematic fashion, they flight tested this by warping the trailing edges of their kites, using multiple control lines. From this they advanced in 1900 to gliders, with their first piloted version being a wing-warping biplane with canard surfaces. They followed the same format the following year with a larger aircraft that possessed decidedly troubling control problems that puzzled them. Always preferring data to intuition, this led to their building a wind tunnel to test airfoils and wing shapes. As a direct result, they introduced longer narrow wings, with a thinner airfoil in 1902. These subtle but crucial steps showed exactly how their deep involvement in research paid dividends.

Economy and availability called for the use of giant Sitka spruce wood, and the locally available size of this material dictated that the wings would be forty feet in span. They chose to use a relatively slight 1:20 camber (the relationship of the width of the wing to its height). Ideally they would have found an existing commercial internal combustion engine with a usable power-to-weight ratio. This proved to be impossible and they were forced to rely on the local—but highly talented—Charles Taylor to design and build the engine they needed.

Taylor has never received the attention he deserved, a fact reflected in his life and finances; born in a log cabin, he died at the age of eighty-seven in relative poverty. Taylor was almost a stepfather to the Wrights in the way he managed their bicycle business as they became ever more focused on the problem of flight. But he did far more, as he would provide the means by which an otherwise unavailable internal combustion engine would become available to them.

In a very innovative move, Taylor used a cast aluminum crankcase to reduce weight in the four-cylinder horizontal inline engine configuration that he chose. The four-inch bore and stroke cast-iron cylinders were cooled by water circulating through the jacket formed by the crankcase. It was masterful simplicity, designed to operate briefly for the single purpose of keeping the airframe in the air for a few fleeting but historically important moments. The Wrights' habit of combining diligent research with the creation of testable hardware was a great factor in their eventual success, and it was a process that suited Taylor's methods exactly. Many of the Wrights' predecessors tended to move too swiftly. They would do enough research to inflame their desires to fly, build an inadequately thought-out design, crash, and give up. Not so Wilbur and Orville. With them it was cut and try, survive, learn, then cut and try again.

The simplicity of the engine was matched by the crude but effective power transmission they selected from their long history of work with bicycles. The engine operated a sprocket chain drive that powered the twin propellers. A simple loop in the chain drive permitted the propellers to spin in opposite directions, obviating torque, and making control much easier as a result. As discussed in greater depth later, the design of the propellers was as challenging as the design of the wings, and the Wrights were perhaps more innovative in this than in any other part of the aircraft.

The Wrights were much more aware of the importance of drag than many of their would-be competitors, and designed the controls so that the pilot could fly the airplane lying flat on the lower wing. A cradle fitted to his hips operated the wires that warped the wings and turned the rudder. Perhaps the most dangerous element of the Wrights' design was their use of a too-responsive canard surface for pitch control—a mistake that many made because it seemed so natural to have the pitch control out in front of the aircraft. A huge advance came with the introduction of a fixed vertical rudder which was subsequently modified so that it could move in concert with the wing warping. This combination provided three-axis control and became their patented solution to manned flight. The term "patented" was most liberally interpreted by their followers and imitators around the world.

The Wrights' efforts succeeded in great part because they created designs that featured a positive means of control about all three axes of flight. The latter objective, oddly enough, was often ignored by pioneers, some of whom felt that their intuition combined with the judicial use of shifting their weight would be sufficient. As curious as it seems now, the Wrights were among the very few pioneers who understood that even if they were fortunate enough to build a flyable aircraft, they, themselves, would have to learn to fly for their invention to be of any use. And perhaps more important than anything else, they recognized that they would have to learn to control the aircraft. Their series of gliders, which were quite beautiful in their simplicity and proportions, brought them safely through four years of experiment to the remarkable *Flyer* of 1903.

A number of prosaic elements helped dictate the Wright *Flyer's* ultimate shape. One was expense. The Wrights were not wealthy, and although they used relatively inexpensive materials, cost was an important factor. Even if they had imputed value to a machine the size of Maxim's, they would not even have considered building it—it would have been far too expensive. Transport was another factor. There was neither a runway nor proper winds in their Dayton backyard, so they knew they had to take their craft to a distant spot such as Kitty Hawk to properly test it.

There were of course other important engineering reasons for the configuration of the Wright *Flyer*. A biplane layout was inherently much stronger than a monoplane of the same wing area. It also provided shorter distances for the control systems to operate.

The Wrights could not avoid some problems. As mentioned, they included a canard surface—destined to be both sought-after and troublesome for the next century of flight—and they positioned the engine in a good spot for weight and balance, but where its location was lethal in the event of a crash.

They knew from the start that their aircraft would require an internal combustion engine for flight, and that none was available that would meet their needs for "high" power and light weight. Their early computations (which included the mysteries inherent in their own propeller design) indicated that a minimum of 8-horsepower was required. Balancing considerations of power and weight led to the selection—for the first time—of the aluminum engine block. As noted, while the Wrights prioritized practicality over aesthetics, it might well be said that the Wright *Flyer* itself is pleasing to the eye; however, the same is not true of its power plant and its accessories.

A closer look at the power system makes it obvious that things could easily have gone wrong for the Wrights at many points. They made clear choices of utility over aesthetics because they knew exactly what they were seeking to do: achieve controlled, sustained, piloted flight, not for any great distances, nor for a great speed. To do so they elected for simplicity and weight savings time and again.

As director of the National Air and Space Museum, I made a decision that the aircraft would be restored on the floor of the museum, where the public could watch the project. This was protested hotly, first, by the workers, for whom of course it made a change in workplace and interfered with some carpools, and, second, by the Smithsonian security office. The latter felt that having the necessary tools, liquids, and other such things at the museum would present a hazard. It took a great deal of persuasion to convince everyone that educational and entertainment value to the public made taking the projected risks worthwhile. In the event, the restoration was carried off with no difficulties whatever, and the visiting museum goers were delighted to see the work in progress.

Part of the public's pleasure came from a much closer involvement with the aircraft. As an example, the Wrights' 12-horsepower engine (four more horsepower than they thought they needed) had always been mostly overlooked, hidden away, so to speak, in the aircraft itself. As the aircraft was restored, the public became much more interested and informed about the powerplant. Many onlookers were surprised to find that it did not use a throttle—it ran full out from start to cutoff. There was no fuel pump or carburetor. Gasoline flowed by gravity from a small, strut-mounted tank, mixing with air as it passed into the intake manifold and thence to the cylinders. Not much has been written about the probable fire hazard of such an arrangement, but it must have been considerable. A camshaft controlled the ignition, with a magneto providing current while the engine ran. To get it started, four dry-cell batteries and a coil supplied the initial spark.

It can be said that the Wrights' greatest leap of genius might be found in their design of the two propellers, for which there was no antecedent. Ships used propellers, of course, but their size and the speeds at which they operated made them irrelevant for aircraft design. It is entirely fitting that the genius of the Wrights allowed them to see that the propeller was "simply" a turning wing, and to use a pair of them for power.

The simplest possible arrangement would have been to use a single propeller driven directly by the engine's crankshaft, and positioned either before or after the wing. This layout was seized upon by many of the Wrights' followers, most particularly Glenn Curtiss.

However, the Wrights chose to use two large chain-driven propellers to absorb the power from their engine, and to avoid the torque that a single propeller would have induced. One chain was twisted to allow one of the propellers to rotate in the opposite direction from its mate. The two propellers, turning at a relatively low speed in opposite directions, were far more efficient and did not offer as challenging an effort in handling, mounting, and other problems of a single large unit.

Somewhat surprisingly, the Wrights also equipped their *Flyer* with three instruments. These included a revolution counter for the engine, a Richard anemometer to measure the speed and a stopwatch. In their typical farsighted fashion, they created a lever that cut all the instruments off at once when the flight was over. These were not exactly suitable for night-instrument flight, but certainly provide insight into their engineering style.

The control system for the successful 1903 *Flyer* was of course derived from previous practice—a duplicate of that found in their functional 1902 glider. The ability of the Wrights to take the best from their previous work and unhesitatingly jettison that which was not contributing was important. They were not wedded to their own concepts in a way that many inventors in their field were, and this facilitated their fascinating passage from kite constructors to world-changing inventors.

The careful choice of Kitty Hawk, North Carolina, was a typical Wright decision, based on facts, but not without danger, as would too soon be seen. The winds and the general layout of the land fit their needs, but they had to accept the facts that the very benefits they were seeking—fairly constant winds of fairly constant speeds—could be upset in an instant, given the powerful nature of the climate. Aware that they would need some form of assisted takeoff, the use of a "junction railroad" system of rails and wood permitted them swiftly to create a track most advantageous for takeoff given the existing wind. As with the rest of their project, costs were kept to a minimum.

The Wrights' reaction to the primitive life comforts of Kitty Hawk was as usual—they made the best of the situation, always keeping a careful eye on the dollar. One wonders what must have been going through their minds, given that while the winds of Kitty Hawk were essential to their success, too much of them could spell disaster.

The comparative ease with which the main components of the Wright *Flyer* could be built, transported to a relatively remote location, and then successfully assembled was quite remarkable. It may have been the effect of the Wrights' need for economy, but whatever the cause, it was a positive factor.

The Wrights began their 1903 season at Kitty Hawk very well equipped, bringing the successful 1902 glider along to refresh their flying abilities and the new, powered 1903 version. By December 14th, they, not without some trepidation, were ready for powered flight. They called on the local government lifesaving station for help. (The lifesaving station organization was transformed into the Coast Guard by 1915.) The men there had watched the Wrights with a range of emotion that ran from amusement to awe, and they were delighted to have the opportunity to help. With their assistance, the Wrights moved the *Flyer* and the vital launching rail to an incline in the beach.

Much more conscious of the very real danger than of any potential prestige factor, they flipped a coin as to who should be the first to try. Wilbur won the toss, but while the *Flyer* left the inclined launch rail, he overcontrolled, stalled the airplane, and landed three seconds later, with only minor damage. They decided that it did not count as a true flight, and set about repairing the minor damage.

Three days later, the repairs were complete and the wind was just right, so that they did not need an inclined launch rail. Orville launched himself into history with a twelve-second flight, covering roughly 120 feet. The brothers made two flights each that day. Three of the flights were short (120, 175, and 200 feet) but verifiable flights nonetheless. Wilbur made the last and most impressive attempt, covering no less than 852 feet in fifty-nine seconds. Neither man had attempted to make a turn, content to be airborne in a straight line for as long as possible. Each flight had caused some damage on landing, the last one breaking the front elevator supports. Excited by their success, they envisaged a four-mile flight to astound the little Kitty Hawk village. It was probably fortunate that a gust of wind tumbled the aircraft end over end, severely damaging it, and ruling out any celebratory flights.

No one, perhaps not even the two brothers themselves, seemed to grasp the monumental importance of their success at Kitty Hawk. Initially, the Wrights were disposed to destroy the 1903 *Flyer*—it took up space, and they had a replacement already built. Then they stored the damaged remains for nine years, during which time the delicate wood and fabric structure was submerged in floodwaters. Some of their lack of care of this incredibly important artifact probably stemmed from the stubborn resistance of the Smithsonian Institution to recognize its place in history and exhibit the aircraft. After Wilbur died of typhoid fever in 1912 (the disease was a widespread menace in those years), Orville repaired the *Flyer* for exhibit in 1916 at the Massachusetts Institute of Technology, as the Smithsonian clung to its delusion that Samuel Pierpont Langley should be honored for designing the first aircraft "capable of flight."

As a ploy to get the Smithsonian to react properly and exhibit the *Flyer*, Orville offered the historic aircraft to the Science Museum in London. The Smithsonian did not react as he wished, and the *Flyer* went on display in London in 1928.

In 1942 the Smithsonian finally agreed to exhibit the *Flyer* under the stringent conditions that Orville Wright demanded, but it was not until 1948 that the historic plane finally went on exhibit in the old Smithsonian Arts and Industries Building. In 1976 it was moved to a position of prominence in the newly built National Air and Space Museum, where it was restored in situ in 1985.

Given that there is no historic evidence of mankind's use of either the spark or the wheel, it is especially fortunate that the Wright *Flyer* was able to evade the many accidental and deliberate attempts to destroy it. The extraordinary little biplane endured windstorms, crashes, floods, bureaucratic indifference, scientific shortsightedness, and many other hazards, and now, beautifully restored, is able to continue contributing both knowledge and inspiration to an admiring public.

CHAPTER 2

The Big Leap: Charles Lindbergh
and the *Spirit of St. Louis*

One of the many perks of working in an air and space museum is the opportunity it provides to meet many of the greats, and families of the greats, in the industry. This is often done on a very personal basis, because it usually stems from a request from the visitor, or the family, for a little special attention. In regard to the fabled silver Ryan NYP *Spirit of St. Louis*, it was my great pleasure to be able to provide, at different times, that custom service to both T. Claude Ryan and to members of Charles Lindbergh's family.

While the exact date (as so much) has slipped from my memory, I remember a call coming up from the National Air and Space Museum's visitors' desk inquiring if I was available to see a Mr. T. Claude Ryan, who had asked for a tour of the Museum by the director. I agreed immediately, never having expected to have the pleasure of meeting him.

Ryan proved to be an impressive personality, slightly reserved but friendly, and inclined to tell me about the museum's aircraft rather than to hear what I had to say. Curiously enough, while he inspected the *Spirit of St. Louis* at some length, he was more interested in the Space Hall. Two things attracted his attention. The first was the large, cylindrical Skylab Orbital Workshop, which he entered and studied quite intently. The second was the smaller air-to-air missiles, which was natural enough, given the Ryan firm's pioneering in the area. Ryan's reactions to the various exhibits were interesting, but not as full of fun as those of the Lindbergh family.

Charles Lindbergh's daughter Reeve brought members of the family to the museum, and I was pleased—although a bit worried—to bring out a maintenance hoist platform, which allowed them to go up, two at a time, to inspect the cockpit of the NYP through its open door. It was well worth the look, for it emphasized the lack of forward visibility Lindbergh had built into the aircraft. Also retained were the penciled fuel markings he had made on the instrument panel, a very human, almost eerie, touch.

As museum director, I had made a decision earlier not to restore the aircraft any more than necessary. In practice this meant redoing the fabric filets which disintegrated when the aircraft was disassembled for movement. As a result, the aircraft had an appealing patina of age that emphasized how long ago the May 20th and 21st, 1927, flight had been, and consequently how important it was.

In the case of the *Spirit of St. Louis*, as with far too many museum aircraft, there was insufficient emphasis placed on the importance of the engine, the 225-horsepower Wright radial which did so much to advance aviation. There is no curatorial explanation for this. It results from the fact that the museum's funds are limited, and the public is more interested in airframes than engines.

This is particularly true in the case of the famous Ryan aircraft. It arrived at a time when the liquid-cooled engines that had been used so extensively in World War I and beyond had quite simply outlived their usefulness. The drag and weight of the liquid cooling increased as engines and their horsepower grew larger. In time, improvements would be made in coolants and cooling systems to permit liquid-cooled engines (as in the Avro Lancaster or North American P-51) to be once again fully competitive.

But it was the genius of a now almost-forgotten man, Charles Lanier Lawrance, who set the stage for Lindbergh's success. Lawrance created the Lawrance J-1 air-cooled engine which was subsequently developed into the fantastic series of Wright Whirlwind radial engines. The US Navy urged the Wright Aeronautical company to purchase Lawrance's small firm in 1923 to ensure an adequate production capability. A further serendipitous event was the departure of Wright's president, Frederick B. Rentschler, to found Pratt & Whitney, thus providing the country with two sources of marvelous radial engines for the coming of World War II.

It is easy to forget the prevalence and the shortcomings of the liquid-cooled aircraft engines of the time. Curtiss OX-5s were widely used despite their cranky nature and high-maintenance demands. The Army Air Corps was still firmly attached to the World War I Liberty engine for most of its needs, reserving the later Curtiss liquid-cooled engines for its fighters. The navy launched its shipboard naval operations on October 27, 1922, from the deck of the USS *Langley*, converted to be an aircraft carrier from the USS *Jupiter*, a collier. Lt. Virgil C. "Squash" Griffin flew the Vought VE-7, which was powered by a Wright-Hispano E-3 liquid-cooled engine of 180-horsepower. It was almost immediately discovered that liquid-cooled engines were not desirable for carrier operations, particularly during cold weather.

Thus, matters of circumstance, practical operations, and expense made the arrival of air-cooled radial engines of extraordinary importance. The Wright Model J-5 engine was a giant step forward, not only in layout but in its use of modern innovations. These included extreme care in selecting the right cooling considerations, aided by the use of aluminum cylinder heads and sodium-cooled exhaust valves all molded into a clean, low-drag design. Weighing slightly less than five hundred pounds, the J-5 produced 200-horsepower and used fuel sparingly. Ultimately the engine's power was increased, and it was priced affordably.

The young but very experienced airmail pilot Charles Lindbergh was motivated, in part, by the famous $25,000 Orteig Prize. Established in 1919 by hotel owner Raymond Orteig, it was to be awarded to the first pilot to fly from Paris to New York, or New York to Paris. Only Allied pilots could compete—no Germans allowed!

Lindbergh was only twenty-four, but his reputation in St. Louis was so firm that he was able to obtain financial backing for his goal, for which there were many competitors. The Orteig prize inspired seven major efforts, along with many spurious announcements of intent to participate. The first and perhaps most glamorous attempt was made in 1926 by the inimitable Rene Fonck, the leading Allied ace in what was then called "the Great War" with seventy-five victories. Fonck teamed with the great Russian expatriate Igor Sikorsky to build an extremely attractive tri-motor aircraft. Sadly, testing was rushed and insufficient as was so often the case at the time. Fonck overloaded the aircraft and was forced to improvise with a crude supplementary landing gear system.

This lash-up, so incompatible with the rest of the design, failed, and the airplane crashed in flames. Fonck and his copilot survived but two other crew members were killed. Ironically, the two extra crew members were not really necessary (if Lindbergh could fly alone, Fonck did not need a crew of four) and may have been the crucial amount of extra weight that caused the disaster.

This left three groups of the most famous, most competent aviators in the United States preparing for the New York / Paris flight. All were adequately financed, and were using aircraft that seemed most suitable for the task. They worked concurrently, racing to be first, and inevitably suffered the consequences of hurrying. Sadly, six brave pioneers of ocean flight would die in the hectic process.

Two navy pilots elected to modify a standard Keystone LB-5 bomber of the day with an additional central engine and a large cabin. Lieutenant Commander Noel Guy Davis and Lieutenant Stanton Hall Wooster substituted three Wright radials for the usual two heavy Liberty engines with their complex cooling systems. They named the aircraft the *American Legion*, for its sponsor. Feeling the competitive pressure, they rushed the test program and, sadly and unnecessarily, crashed on April 26, 1927; both pilots, seated in the cockpit, plunged to the ground.

A wiser and more cautious American hero, Richard E. Byrd, the famous polar explorer, was also in the game. Financially backed by Rodman Wanamaker, a department store magnate, Byrd instinctively went with what many people considered the best—and the most expensive— aircraft then available, a tri-motor Fokker. He named it the *America* and that made it seem the best choice, for at the time, three engines meant more safety to the public. The truth was otherwise, of course, for three engines meant three times as much chance of failure, and none of the tri-motors had really adequate twin-engine performance should one of the three engines fail. Byrd selected two well-known aviators as crew members, Floyd Bennett and George Noville.

A third set of capable if less well-known flyers, Clarence Chamberlain and Bert Acosta, chose a single-engine Bellanca monoplane named the *Columbia* for their mount. Acosta was strictly a fair-weather flyer with no skill in the primitive instrument flying techniques of the time. Financial backing was provided by a difficult source, the contentious Charles Levine, whose wealth often exceeded his judgment.

In the spring of 1927, time was precious and the various teams pressed forward to make the attempt. Chamberlain and Acosta systematically tested their Bellanca, going to the extra effort of setting an endurance record to be sure they could fly the distance. Unfortunately, their team was rife with arguments with its backer, Levine, and others. Acosta left the team, and his replacement, Lloyd Bertaud, became another who sued Levine in a contract dispute.

As was his custom, Admiral Byrd made extensive preparations, including improving the runway at Roosevelt Field and building a ramp for the *America* to roll down on takeoff. This was theoretically—but erroneously—intended to reach takeoff speed more quickly. An accident occurred during an April 8th test flight which turned the *America* over on its back. Bennett was injured and had to withdraw.

There were rivals across the Atlantic as well. The often-wounded war ace, Charles Nungesser, and Francis Coli prepared a handsome Levasseur aircraft for an east-west crossing. Named the *L'Oiseau Blanc* (*White Bird*), the Levasseur was equipped with elaborate safety measures that included tanks intended to assist the aircraft floating after a forced landing and landing gear that could be dropped to reduce drag. The pressure of time was felt on both sides of the ocean. On May 8, 1927, Nungesser and Coli set off from Paris in *L'Oiseau Blanc* to attempt the east-west crossing, a more difficult proposition given the prevailing winds. They were last seen off the coast of Ireland, but never arrived in North America. No trace of them was ever found, creating one of aviation's great mysteries that periodically generates a new search for the truth.

Of all the groups only Lindbergh planned to fly solo. The young airmail pilot had been impressed by the Ryan series of monoplanes and thought that the Ryan M-2 could be modified for the attempt. A visit to the San Diego plant and discussions with chief designer Donald A. Hall quickly revealed that a redesign was not feasible and a completely new aircraft was required. Lindbergh's bottom line for the new Ryan aircraft was a takeoff capability with four hundred gallons of fuel, all placed in front of the pilot. He specified the use of a Wright J-5C engine. The total price was $10,580, about equal to the cost of twenty-four Model Ts of the time, and the aircraft was to be delivered in just sixty days.

The work was entrusted to the Ryan Company, which had been founded as an airline in 1925 by Ryan and the too-often forgotten B. F. "Frank" Mahoney. Ryan remained with the company after Mahoney bought out his interest in 1926. Mahoney hired Donald Hall as designer and Hawley Bowlus (of later glider fame) as the factory manager. Although only twenty-nine, Hall was widely experienced, having worked with a number of major aviation firms including Curtiss, Douglas, Elias, and L.W. F. Lindbergh worked closely with Hall on the design.

The aircraft itself was a straightforward development of previous Ryan designs, which began with the M-1 in the fall of 1925. This airplane was vested with state of-the-art simplicity—steel tubes, wood, and fabric shaped into the conventional lines of a strut-braced, high-wing monoplane. For his purpose, however, Lindbergh knew that huge changes had to be made. These must have concerned the original designers, for the changes immediately violated many of their previous decisions on such vital elements as the center of gravity, visibility, wingspan, and gross weight.

Lindbergh was deeply involved in the construction process of "his" Ryan and would carefully test the new aircraft. Close consideration of both weight and balance and safety led him to have the big fuel tank installed ahead of the pilot's position. This greatly impaired forward visibility, but he knew there would be little traffic en route, and a curved landing pattern was often flown into the big open fields then available. Such an approach was no real challenge to a man who'd flown the mail in rebuilt de Havilland DH-4s.

The pilot, young in years but long in experience, tested the new Ryan extensively, checking its fuel consumption carefully. He was pleased, rather than annoyed, to find that his plane did not "fly itself" but required a steady hand on the controls. The reason, of course, was he knew that it was a trip of thirty-plus hours, and he did not want to fall asleep at the controls. (Many years later, when the multitalented Elbert "Buck" Hilbert and Verne Jobst created a replica of the *Spirit of St. Louis*, they were gracious enough to give me a chance to fly it. I was amazed at the required throw and pressure the controls required.)

Personal contact was always key with the charismatic Lindbergh—it enabled him to know the product and also to inspire his project leaders with his drive. Arriving in San Diego on February 23, 1927, he used the standard Ryan monoplanes as the basic planform and worked closely with Hall, Bowlus, and other Ryan employees to get what he wanted in terms of wing area, weight reduction, and even more important, weight distribution. The *Spirit of St. Louis* would be designed and built at the promised combination of at-cost price ($10,580) and breakneck speed (sixty days).

Its modern Wright Whirlwind was placed farther forward than usual on a typical Ryan fuselage, with the large fuel tank ahead of the pilot's controls, which were farther aft than usual. It was topped by a forty-six-foot-wingspan wing, ten feet more than the standard Ryan. The design might be called the acme of streamlining in the premodern period, with as much attention paid to reducing drag as possible. Its stout spars and rugged fixed landing gear had streamlined filets to smooth out the attachment points. Most important, its fuel tanks could carry 425 gallons of fuel. At a minimum of six pounds per gallon, this converted to 2,550 pounds of fuel.

Pleased that his customized plane was delivered within budget and on schedule, Lindbergh was gracious (not always his strong suit in later life) in his 1927 book, *We*. There he fully acknowledged the achievement of the builders, paying tribute to them with a photograph captioned "The Men Who Made the Plane." He identified Mahoney, Bowlus, Hall, and sales manager A. J. Edwards standing with him in front of the NYP.

Lindbergh made personal and aviation history when he took off on May 20, 1927, to make the thirty-six hundred-mile flight from Roosevelt Field, Long Island, to Le Bourget Field, northwest of Paris. He landed amidst some hundred thousand cheering Frenchmen, and neither he nor aviation was ever the same again.

The details of the wildly successful thirty-three-hour, thirty-minute flight from New York to Paris were recounted by Lindbergh often, first in his quickly written and published book *We*, in which he attributed a full partnership in his success to his faithful Ryan, and in many later sources. The combination of his winning personality—at once boyish, modest, confident, and inspiring—and the brilliance of the flight made him an unprecedented international star. He channeled his fame for the flight into immediate service to aviation, touring the United States and much of the Western Hemisphere, advocating the creation of airports, intercity air travel, and flight in general.

Lindbergh was backed in his post-flight tours by Harry Guggenheim and the Daniel Guggenheim Fund. He flew the *Spirit of St. Louis* on a three-month tour that saw the famous duo touch down in forty-eight states while visiting eighty-two cities, where he gave hundreds of speeches and rode in dozens of parades. He was the living personification of aviation, arriving on the scene exactly when the public and the economy were ready for it. He set a nonstop record flight from Washington to Mexico City prior to extensive flights in Central America. In 1928 the famous silver Ryan was flown from St. Louis to Washington, D.C., for presentation to the Smithsonian Institution, where it may still be seen.

CHAPTER 3

Pierce the Sound Barrier: The Bell X-1 and the Brotherhood of Test Pilots

The best time to enter the expansive domain of Edwards Air Force Base is at the crack of dawn, as shafts of the first light define the eastern horizon along the jagged ridgeline of the distant mountains. The radiance sparkles and races westward across the scrub of the great Mojave to illuminate the baked surfaces of the continent's largest naturally occurring dry lakebeds. Sagebrush and Joshua trees punctuate the outer reaches of the sight picture, standing eerily silent and motionless in the stillness, impervious to passersby.

From the roadway at the property's outer perimeter where a billboard welcomes you to the Air Force Flight Test Center, it is a long but evocative drive to the main gate. There, heavily armed security guards scrutinize visitors in keeping with their charge to use lethal force if necessary to protect the crown jewels of the country's military aerospace program. For pilots and for dreamers in general, arriving at this special place, touching its hallowed ground, always has the feel of coming home.

At first the roadway ranges as straight as a runway, taking advantage of the desert floor's level contour. Midway into the drive, on your right, the car's tires nearly brush against the edge of Rosamond Dry Lake, the first of the two adjacent sandy-colored flatlands that were destined to go from desolate railroad corridors marked by a watering station in the late nineteenth century to the fountainhead of the Golden Age of Flight Test and the hub of the modern world's most advanced flight testing installation. After a sharp jog in the road, the twice-as-large Rogers Dry Lake hugs your ride until you near the laboratories, workshops, hangars, offices, classrooms, and assorted infrastructure that have mushroomed on the vast reservation since 1933 when Lieutenant Colonel Henry H. "Hap" Arnold (later to become chief of the air corps and the commanding general of the army air force) first started using the lakebeds as auxiliary sites for his March Field squadrons.

The morning chill soon fades as the stalwart sun rises. The base habitually stirs to life early to take advantage of the calm before the day's persistent surface heating causes the air to roil and throw wicked currents into the way of the test pilots. Soon a variety of exotic shapes, some manned and others not, launch into the sky, sustaining the tradition of pushing the edge of the proverbial envelope in pursuance of the center's longstanding mission expressed in its motto, *ad inexplorata*, "toward the unexplored."

Little could the first settlers, Clifford and Effie Corum, have imagined when they arrived on the edge of what was then known as Rodriguez Dry Lake in 1910 that one day their tiny homesteading outpost would become the nerve center of aeronautical experimentation. But it was inevitable. The remote location and its sweltering temperatures discouraged an influx from metropolitan Los Angeles about eighty miles to the southwest while, at the same time, the enormous dry lakebeds offered the perfect landing site just as the climate promised blue skies almost without interruption year-round.

It was not long before the Corums' settlement took on the appearance of a fledgling community with the establishment of a general store and the construction of a church. Effie petitioned the post office to name the site "Corum," but the request was rejected because another town in California was similarly named. The petition was then amended to suggest the name "Muroc," the family name spelled backward.

Muroc was accepted and remained the official name of the locale for nearly four decades. In step, the desert air base adopted the name. However, in 1947, the air force became an independent service and doubledowned on the custom of naming bases in memory of heroic airmen, preferring native sons where possible.

Captain Glen W. Edwards, an air force test pilot from Lincoln, California, died when his hard-to-control Northrop YB-49 flying wing broke up in flight and crashed at the base on June 5, 1948. A year and a half following this tragic loss, the base was named for him. Ever since, the Edwards name has been synonymous with flight test.

For the first couple decades of its use as a military airfield, the secluded location was enlivened by the existence of the Rancho Oro Verde Inn Dude Ranch, a combination bar, restaurant, dance hall, motel, riding stable, and airstrip set up on the base's periphery by highly accomplished air racing and movie stunt pilot Florence Lowe "Pancho" Barnes. Eventually known as Pancho's Happy Bottom Riding Club, the ranch became inextricably linked to the test pilot folklore of the immediate post–World War II period. At Muroc, service members and civilian contractors worked in extremely austere conditions and under tremendous stress, so to get some relief they would party at Pancho's.

Amid the music blaring from the juke box and the aroma of freshly served steak and fries, off-duty base personnel and aviation company employees conversed casually on their projects, making headway that might not come so easily through formal channels. New wing shapes and fuselage configurations were scribbled on the backside of many a napkin. At other times, the pilots and engineers sat back in the air-conditioned rooms to enjoy their meals and let the worries of the workday evaporate in the after-hours heat. In any case, guests invariably felt the larger-than-life presence of the proprietor.

The pioneering female aviator, who had competed in air races with her peers of the 1920s and 1930s and who had organized the movie stunt pilots into an association to address unsafe industry practices, maintained relationships with aviation notables and spoke with great authority on the subject of flying. Base personnel respected Pancho and listened to what she had to offer. Despite a prim upbringing in affluent San Marino, California, she aspired to be "one of the guys" and could "out cuss any mule skinner" as one of the ranch's patrons later recalled.

Pancho had favorites among her flying-oriented clientele. If anyone dared to speak ill of those she venerated, the offender would get an earful as Pancho passionately upheld her friends. None more fiercely than a young fighter ace and up-and-coming test pilot with an impish smile who spoke in a disarming West Virginia drawl—Charles E. "Chuck" Yeager.

During the war, as new fighters like the P-38 and P-51 expanded the speed envelope, designers came upon the nagging phenomenon of compressibility—the buildup of air molecules on aircraft surfaces as the speed of sound was approached. This implacable "wall" loomed as a giant problem for the aeronautical world. Without a solution the wartime development of the jet would be relegated to a speed range far below its potential. Overcoming the hurdle presented by compressibility and finally breaking through the so-called "sound barrier" became a top priority, requiring the expertise of the finest minds and the skills of talented test pilots.

As early as 1939 an engineer at Wright Field in Dayton, Ohio, by the name of Ezra Kotcher proposed a research aircraft to explore the transonic speed regime, the sector through which a vehicle transitions from subsonic to supersonic flight. It was only after pilots flying the new high-powered piston fighters had encountered the deathly consequences of compressibility that the army air force revisited the Kotcher proposal. In 1944 the idea of a hybrid transonic aircraft gained momentum, and Kotcher found a willing contractor in Bell Aircraft.

A debate arose over whether the experimental platform should be powered by one of the emergent turbojet engines or the more radical option of a rocket engine. Kotcher favored the rocket engine, and Bell agreed. It was mutually perceived as offering the better chance of achieving the desired performance.

Another advocate for the test platform was John Stack, an engineer with the National Advisory Committee for Aeronautics (NACA, the civilian government agency that was eventually reconstituted as the National Aeronautics and Space Administration or NASA), who was a fervent believer in such research vehicles. Accordingly, as the project unfolded, it had the interest of the army air force and NACA, as well as Bell. With the government and industry team in place, configuration studies ensued. Three planes would be built for the test program.

Perhaps most telling was the decision to use a fuselage shape that matched the shape of a .50-caliber bullet. Given the lack of a supersonic data base, it was a logical progression to the adoption of a shape that was known to have been successfully propelled through the air at supersonic speed. Aircraft-grade aluminum alloy was deemed sufficient for construction of the fuselage. The cockpit canopy would be blended with the bullet-like form to preserve the fuselage's design integrity.

Wing thickness was another critical design consideration. Experience with compressibility suggested that a thin wing would perform best. A compromise was struck with the first and the third planes getting a wing with a width-to-chord ratio of 8 percent while the second plane got a slightly thicker wing with a 10 percent width-to-chord ratio.

The thinner wings were harder to construct, but they offered the more conducive configuration for slicing through the transonic region, which was the army air force's chief objective. The 10 percent wing, on the other hand, was optimized for NACA, which sought to accumulate a storehouse of transonic flight data through a methodical research program. The wings were mounted at the fuselage midpoint to minimize drag.

The rocket engine was developed by the small entrepreneurial outfit Reaction Motors Inc., founded in 1941 by four rocket propulsion enthusiasts, with headquarters located north of Newark, New Jersey. The design was a relatively simple four-chamber engine that produced 1,475 pounds of thrust in each chamber for a total of 5,900 pounds of thrust. Each chamber had its own exhaust tube, which together formed a diamond-like shape as seen from the rear in the plane's tapered tail cone. The engine was designated 6000C-4 by the company and XLR-11 (Experimental Liquid Rocket-11) by the army.

Fuel was an alcohol/water mix with liquid oxygen as the oxidizer. Because of problems developing a turbo-pump, the designers were forced to fall back on a pressurized fuel system. This meant thick steel spheres holding inert nitrogen would be required.

The additional weight and volume brought on by the pressurized-fuel system, with its concomitant reduction in available fuel, limited the powered flight time to no more than a little over four minutes. In turn, this necessitated air launches rather than conventional takeoffs on the ground. This was a case study in how an obligatory option like the air launches involved tradeoffs—the benefit of a longer powered flight at altitude in return for the hazard inherent in coupling a plane loaded with volatile liquids to a mothership.

Various design factors contributed to the penetration of the sound barrier, but arguably none more so than the tail configuration. NACA and Bell realized that the supersonic research vehicle needed an all-moving or "flying" tail. The design involved a nitrogen-powered motor driving a jackscrew linked to the stabilizer. The pilot's inputs could change the pitch trim in minor increments, which is what it would take to finesse the rocketplane through the sound barrier. The stabilizer's overall deflection range was five degrees up and ten degrees down.

The stabilizer was positioned as far above the wing as possible. This was so the stabilizer would not be adversely affected by the wing's wake. Also the stabilizer had to be proportionally thinner than the wing to preclude contemporaneous adverse aerodynamic impacts on the wing and tail in the event that the dreaded phenomenon of compressibility raised its ugly head.

While the designers felt that the controls did not need power-boost because of the diminutive nature of the platform, they installed an "H"-shaped control yoke to give the pilot more control authority. To simplify the pilot-systems interface, various controls were placed on the wheel, including those for the engine and stabilizer. However, forward visibility was limited because of the severe sweepback of the cockpit canopy. This blending was viewed as another necessary tradeoff to preserve the overall bullet-like configuration.

Glide tests commenced in late January 1946 at an old bomber base at Pinecastle, Florida, situated in the center of the state, which offered decent weather in winter and a partially secluded location. Bell assigned its most experienced jet pilot as the senior test pilot on the project. Jack Woolams had accumulated lots of hours in the company's P-59 fighter, America's first jet aircraft. A Boeing B-29 Superfortress, the largest bomber then available, was highly modified to carry the test vehicle on a bomb shackle and drop it at altitude.

Originally designated XS-1 (for Experimental Supersonic-1), the "S" was removed early in the flight test phase. Redesignated the X-1, Bell's rocketplane was the first in an impressive and still-growing line of more than fifty research platforms by a host of contractors that have carried an "X" in their designations. Built in limited quantities expressly for advancing the state of the art with a presumed economic benefit at a point in the undefined future, these aerospace research vehicles known as X-planes have made many of the breakthroughs that have helped to preserve America's aerospace preeminence since World War II.

The X-1's tests in Florida confirmed the rocketplane's maneuverability, stall characteristics, compatibility with the mothership, and efficacy of the release protocol. In August, as Woolams was wringing out a World War II-era P-39 piston-powered fighter in preparation for the upcoming National Air Races, the former combat aircraft smashed up, mortally injuring Woolams. The vacancy on the supersonic project was filled by Chalmers "Slick" Goodlin, a young test pilot at Bell. Also, around that time, NACA's John Stack was reassigned and replaced with engineer / test pilot Richard H. "Dick" Frost.

During the Pinecastle tests, the Florida base proved to be less than ideal. On landings, Woolams had struggled to align the unpowered X-1 with the sole runway. In addition, concerns mounted about possible prying eyes. A different location was needed to finish the tests, preferably an airfield that offered a more accommodating set of touchdown options for test pilots trying to land unpowered craft and that ensured a greater buffer from the outside world.

The logical place was Muroc Army Airfield. In fact Bell's P-59 had been tested at the desert air base starting in 1942. In September 1946, a NACA team headed by new X-1 project engineer Walter C. Williams arrived at Muroc.

Major changes occurred in the flight test program in the early summer of 1947. The army air force blanched at the cost increases sought by Bell in the lead-up to the expected supersonic flight. Moreover, as the prospect of a successful supersonic flight seemed within reach, officials overseeing the project at Air Materiel Command in Dayton thought it made more sense to let the service, rather than the contractor, have the opportunity to be first to break the sound barrier.

At the time, Goodlin had begun to bargain for a substantial bonus from Bell Aircraft on the premise that he would be taking exceptional risk as the first pilot to attempt supersonic flight. The cost for any such pay hike would have to be footed by the military. The entreaty was frowned upon by all parties, especially the service's test pilots who were expected to do the same kind of flying for less compensation than the standard pay of the contractor's pilots, let alone any bonus of the type requested by Goodlin. In June Goodlin ended up resigning.

Apart from the Goodlin matter, NACA and the army air force had differences in how the program should proceed and the matter came to a head at the end of June. As a civilian agency with academic leanings and a commitment to advancing the aeronautical knowledge base, NACA wanted to go slowly. By contrast, the army air force's primary interest was in maintaining its qualitative edge by leaping way ahead of adversaries through the mastering of supersonic flight as soon as possible.

In the end the military got its way and moved swiftly to achieve its objective using the first of the three test platforms. Much of the responsibility for the program fell on the shoulders of Colonel Albert Boyd, a strict disciplinarian and visionary who headed Air Materiel Command's Flight Test Division. He demanded a lot from those serving under him and comprehended the great strides possible through well-managed flight test programs. As for NACA, it went forward at its own pace using the second X-1, which had the thicker wing.

Boyd picked twenty-four-year-old Chuck Yeager as the program's lead test pilot. The fact that he was a World War II ace, with the attendant flying prowess, was part of the decision. But even more important was Yeager's mechanical aptitude.

Yeager did not have a college degree, yet he had been an air corps mechanic before becoming a pilot in the Flying Sergeants program. Also as a child in West Virginia, his mechanical inclination was nurtured by his father who worked as an independent gas drilling contractor. Yeager later said that helping run his father's equipment in the gas fields of West Virginia did much to acquaint him with the mechanical systems in the rocketplane that propelled him to immortality as the first person to reach Mach 1.

Yeager has always acknowledged that the historic flight was a team effort. His uniformed colleagues included Captain Jack L. "Jackie" Ridley, who was a rare breed in those days, having earned both military wings and a college engineering degree. Sadly, an aircraft accident ended his life well ahead of his time, but not before he had made an enormous contribution to the advancement of aeronautics as the foremost flight test engineer at Edwards, where he helped to bridge the divide between the flying and engineering communities. Yeager's backup pilot was Lieutenant Robert R. A. "Bob" Hoover, a fellow World War II fighter pilot. In time Hoover parlayed his love of flying and extensive cockpit experience into a fruitful career as perhaps the world's most ubiquitous air show performer.

Members of the ground crew were the unsung heroes, and Yeager recognized their value. After all, not that many years earlier he was an enlisted maintainer himself. Yeager's X-1 was crewed by Jack Russell, Garth Dill, and Merle Woods. Fittingly, their names were stenciled below Yeager's in block white letters aft of the cockpit.

The military men now running the program wasted little time. Yeager made three unpowered flights and eight or nine powered flights (depending on how records are counted) in which he nibbled ever so gradually towards the prize of supersonic flight. These were partly orientation flights and partly envelope expansion flights. With each new experience aloft in the rocketplane he gained greater confidence. He liked the X-1's maneuverability and is reported to have engaged in mock dogfights with his friend Bob Hoover, who served as a chase plane pilot.

In keeping with the military custom, Yeager was permitted to name the X-1 he would be flying (the first of the three X-1s). The words "Glamorous Glennis" were painted in red with white fringe on the nose of the burnt-orange rocketplane in honor of his wartime sweetheart, Glennis Dickhouse, who he had married in the closing months of the war. Personalization of research platforms did not last long as the practice seemed inappropriate for the type of flying.

When the big day arrived, Chuck Yeager was in physical discomfort. A couple days earlier, he had gone to dinner with Glennis at Pancho's, followed by an hour-long horseback ride. In the evening's fading light, he did not see that the corral gate had been closed behind him. Galloping ahead of Glennis, his horse slammed into the gate and threw him for a nasty tumble that cracked a couple of his ribs.

The injury was painful, but Yeager refused to give up his chance to be the first to go supersonic. Though Glennis had reservations about assisting her husband with the flight, she drove him into town where a civilian physician taped up the wound. This kept news of the mishap from reaching Yeager's superiors. The care gave Yeager some relief, but his range of motion remained limited. His buddy Ridley improvised a means by which Yeager could close and lock the rocketplane's hatch from inside the cockpit with a ten-inch piece of a broomstick.

On the fateful morning of October 14, 1947, not quite a month after the air force had become an independent service, the hobbling but determined young fighter ace was poised to race the bullet-shaped X-1 into "uncharted territory," proving humans could travel faster than once believed possible and opening up the stymied field of high-speed flight to new vistas. When the B-29 mothership was established at its cruise altitude, Yeager climbed excruciatingly down a ladder "one rung at a time" into the bomber's frigid cold belly and then into the cockpit of the rocket-plane. As he had practiced doing with Ridley, he successfully manipulated the hatch using the sawed-off broomstick.

Major Robert Cardenas, the B-29 pilot, followed the agreed flight profile and put the Superfortress into a dive, dropping the X-1 at twenty thousand feet. Yeager immediately pitched down to keep the X-1 from stalling, then he ignited the XLR-11's four chambers in rapid succession. The lithe craft began to climb rapidly. At Mach .88, buffet was encoun-tered, requiring Yeager to input a two-degree stabilizer correction. The stabilizer actuation device had been improved for faster responsiveness, which vastly improved the X-1's performance in transonic flight.

Two rocket engine chambers were shut down on the way to forty thousand feet. Nevertheless, the ascending test vehicle kept accelerat-ing. The elevator was no longer effective, but the stabilizer performed as anticipated.

Leveling occurred at forty-two thousand feet, Yeager reignited a third chamber and the X-1 lunged ahead at a progressively faster speed—past Mach .93. Then, as Yeager put it, "The faster I got, the smoother the ride." The needle in the Mach meter spun up to 1.02. It suddenly stopped and just as suddenly shot to 1.06 (approximately 660 miles per hour), the momen-tary hesitation showing the effect of the shock wave on the airspeed sensor. Yeager claimed that the Mach meter "tipped right off the scale."

Yeager expertly steered the X-1 to pierce the imposing sound barrier! Personally amazed at how seamlessly the rocketplane had passed through the final stages of the historic speed run, he later commented, "And it was as smooth as a baby's bottom." NACA personnel tracking the flight in a radar trailer down below said that they had heard drumfire over the desert as if a distant storm had emitted a rumble of thunder. It was the first sonic boom from a craft with a human on board.

In the lead-up to the accomplishment, Pancho had let the word out among her clientele that the first military test pilot to go supersonic would enjoy a complimentary dinner at her place. On the eventful day, when Yeager and chase pilot Bob Hoover, who trailed in a P-80 Shooting Star, made their final turn back to Rogers Dry Lake they had Pancho's offer uppermost in mind. Once the lakebed was within gliding distance and the two compatriots felt they had the mission in the bag, Hoover radioed Yeager in a jubilant voice: "Hey, pard, you'll get a free steak at Pancho's tonight!"

Indeed, that night at the homes of the participants and a little later at Pancho's (after Yeager's ribcage pain began to subside), the X-1 teammates were effusive over the breakthrough they had achieved, not knowing or appreciating in the immediate aftermath the degree to which the air force brass aimed to keep the news of the supersonic flight under wraps for national security reasons. What had happened was common knowledge to people who worked on base and lived in the surrounding communities. Concerned with the potential ramifications, the air force clamped down with a secrecy order three days following the flight.

Regardless, information about the flight leaked to the media. On December 22nd, just two months after the flight, industry publication *Aviation Week* broke the story. Articles appeared the same day in both the *Los Angeles Examiner* and the *New York Times*.

The Defense Department was not happy with this widespread exposure. Yet there was nothing officials could do to roll back the story. Grudgingly, on June 15, 1948, the air force officially announced the simple facts about Yeager's supersonic flight and others that had followed in the ensuing eight months.

The first two X-1s were flown a total of 150 times by a variety of Bell Aircraft, Air Force, and NACA pilots. Eventually, new speed (Mach 1.45) and altitude (66,846 feet) records were reached. The third X-1 completed only one glide test before it exploded on the ground, severely injuring its test pilot.

Last flight in the series was of the second X-1. It occurred July 31, 1951, helmed by NACA test pilot Scott Crossfield, whose name would become, like Yeager's, intertwined with the early X-planes. So-called second-generation versions of the X-1 that included the X-1A and the X-1B exceeded the speeds of their progenitor.

The ultimate derivation of the type was the sheer white X-1E, which incorporated ultra-thin airfoil sections and a perfected low-pressure turbo-pump. It had twenty-six flights from 1955 through 1958. The string of bullet-shaped X-1 variants ushered in the era of the X-planes, which enduringly altered the realm of flight. Like the first X-1, which is on display as a prized artifact in the Milestones of Flight gallery at the Smithsonian's National Air and Space Museum, the X-1E stands on display in front of the NASA facility at Edwards Air Force Base. Not by coincidence, that facility is named in memory of famed astronaut and lunar explorer Neil Armstrong—one of the NACA X-plane pilots with four flights logged in the X-1B.

The ever-faster and higher-flying X-planes expanded the margins of the envelope all the way to the edge of space by the 1960s. This indeed had been a new Golden Age, a time when fascinating shapes vivified the Mojave's crystalline sky. The flurry of extraordinary aerial feats made the world take note.

It seemed that there was no limit to the possibilities for the test pilots who skippered the exotic rocketplanes. The aerospace pioneers personified by Chuck Yeager who braved the oppressive heat in baggy flight suits at the desert air base went from supersonic to hypersonic within a few short decades. In doing so, they laid the foundation for future flights to heights that in earlier times had been the stuff of dreams.

•••

During one memorable open house at Edwards long after the first supersonic flight, Chuck Yeager made a dramatic takeoff in an F-15 fighter, shooting virtually straight up on the afterburner thrust of its twin jet engines, more rocket-like than the X-1 rocketplane itself. High above the base, a muffled double-clap reverberated across the desert floor in a repeat of what it must have been like on that momentous fall day back in 1947 when the sound barrier was pierced for the first time. Some of the many onlookers applauded and cheered, but others did not see the point since the honoree was well out of earshot.

Once the fighter touched down in a picture-perfect landing, it taxied the length of the flight line. People began to wave to the helmeted airman under the bubble canopy, communicating in the one way they knew to express their adulation over the din of the jet. In flash mob style, the waving broke out along the entire line. Chuck Yeager, who had been greeted on the lakebed following his maiden supersonic flight by crew chief Jack Russell in a Jeep along with a handful of other coworkers, now waved back to thousands of admirers.

He could hardly catch his breath extricating himself from the F-15 before television crews swarmed him for comment, shoving microphones at him as cameras rolled. The celebrated test pilot delivered a statement with head cocked for emphasis. His words incorporated a deep-seated rationale for his ascents into the unknown: "I do it for the country. When the country calls, I will be there."

He took his leave and strode confidently, knowingly across the capacious concrete apron one more time. The receding sun, now low in the western sky, cast a long shadow to one side of the prominent figure as a pickup truck adorned in familiar air force blue prepared to whisk him to what one imagined to be a gathering of eagles, a conclave of the brotherhood, a modern Pancho's place, to revel in the day's flights with an exchange of exhilarating episodes aloft, accentuated by plentiful hand gesticulations as is the proclivity of flyers. Briefly, before the sky turned dark, a warm glow blanketed the apron and the many impressive aircraft parked upon it. The air stood still once more, and in the moment, you could feel empowered to believe that even the stars that would shine brightly soon enough over this patch of the vast desert are really not so far away.

CHAPTER 4

Going Hypersonic: Higher and Faster in the North American X-15

Albert Scott Crossfield was a standout among the post–World War II test pilots. On November 20, 1953, he gained distinction as the first person to exceed Mach 2 at the controls of the Douglas D-558-II Skyrocket. Five and a half years later, he became the first of twelve pilots to fly the X-15, arguably the most successful X-plane ever built.

In the motion picture version of *The Right Stuff*, Tom Wolfe's instant classic about the X-plane pilots and the early astronauts, Crossfield was shown in period newsreels as a stouthearted explorer opening the skies over the dry lakebeds of Edwards Air Force Base. It was flattering coverage of his aerial accomplishments, but when asked about the caricatured Hollywood depiction of the flight test milieu, he had a pat answer that invariably surprised and usually delighted the questioners. Deadpan, he would earnestly say: "I didn't see the movie; I saw the play."

The sardonic humor was vintage Crossfield. However, his drollery caused some to consider him distant and aloof, a stuffed shirt in a flight suit. He carried himself like one of the air base's civilian eggheads, not like a backslapping, happy-go-lucky, hell-bent-for-leather military pilot-turned-test pilot. Despite the knock for haughtiness, those who got to know him came to appreciate his candor. Friends called him Scotty.

As he rose to fame with his record-setting flights, he did not seem to mind how the general public perceived him, though he did covet the respect of his fellow test pilots. When Chuck Yeager, the lord of the brotherhood, used his memoir to come down on Scotty's purported cold demeanor, Scotty was stung but refused to lash out and instead deflected the blunt commentary by joking that his celebrated colleague was "a great novelist." In his later years, Scotty went out of his way to defend Yeager on the occasions that the outspoken ace sparked public controversy.

Despite careers that overlapped at Edwards during the heyday of the X-planes, Scotty was in important ways the antithesis of Yeager. For one thing, Scotty never saw combat. As a US Navy pilot during World War II, he spent most of his flying hours as a stateside instructor; his Pacific duty late in the war flying the Corsair was devoid of battle.

Another difference was that while Yeager had a high school diploma, Scotty could claim two aeronautical engineering degrees from the University of Washington. This highly educated test pilot epitomized the new face of the breed. Indeed, Scotty's type of credentialing has become a prerequisite for those seeking to fill today's test pilot slots whether in government, industry, or the military.

In June 1950, the year after he completed his studies, Scotty was hired by the National Advisory Committee for Aeronautics (NACA was the forerunner of the National Aeronautics and Space Administration, NASA). Scotty's time at NACA was marked by a hundred rocketplane flights, more than any other pilot. He reveled in going to Pancho Barnes's ranch near the desert base for drinks to celebrate the setting of new speed records. He considered it a "milestone on man's inexorable journey toward the stars."

In his view the X-15 offered the next great leap in aeronautics research. He wanted to be in on the project from the ground floor, to not only fly the alluring X-plane, whose general configuration would be formulated by late 1955, but also to use his training as an engineer to help shape the overall build/test program. He sought NACA's permission for a leave to work on the X-15 at the contractor's plant. His request was denied, so he left NACA to join North American Aviation.

With his impeccable engineering education and impressive flying experience as a NACA test pilot, Scotty was considered a "catch" by the giant aircraft manufacturer when it snagged him from NACA in 1955. The company had plans for the new rocketplane that at least notionally would leave others in the dust. Scotty would assist the platform's incubation and serve as the program's lead engineering test pilot. For lack of a more descriptive job classification, his title at the company was design specialist; it did not do justice to his broad portfolio on the rocketplane program, yet he came to terms with it.

Regardless of the title, for a still-young pilot-engineer midway through the Golden Age of Flight Test and at the doorstep of aviation's second half-century this was a dream job—working at what was reputed to be the industry's premier airframer, a corporate Goliath that could boast it had built more airplanes than any other company in the world. North American Aviation had received a Department of Defense contract for more than $40 million for the X-15 and the engine builder, Reaction Motors, was to be paid over $10 million, which, when combined, Scotty realized roughly approximated the entire annual budget of his former employer, NACA.

His first day on the job, Scotty reported to Building 20, the cafeteria building amid the company's crowded campus-style facilities adjoining Los Angeles International Airport in Inglewood. Because of space limitations, a small closed-off and guarded suite of offices was set aside in a loft (or "garret" as Scotty referred to it) above the North American cafeteria for the elite team that would shepherd the X-15 through construction to flight. From where he sat, as North American's lead test pilot on the program who would be the first to fly the promising new rocketplane, this was the place to be, the center of the emerging X-plane universe with the hottest ship on the boards.

In the secure area atop the company cafeteria, Scotty's boss, the rumpled but razor-sharp Charles H. Feltz, handed him a sheaf of papers that contained nearly two dozen renderings of the X-15, commenting, "Maybe you can give us some idea what this darned thing is all about." The two men, both engineers, talked for a good while about the project's hurdles, replete with corresponding opportunities. Afterwards, Scotty returned to his desk, "lost in wondrous thought."

•••

When Scotty left NACA, the fastest flight in a manned research aircraft was Chuck Yeager's December 12, 1953, speed run up to Mach 2.44 in the X-1A variant of the famous X-1. That flight narrowly averted disaster, for the Bell rocketplane had to be wrestled back to the ground after tumbling out of control. By the mid-1950s, Bell's next-in-line research aircraft, the pointy-nosed, swept-wing X-2, was poised to push the edge of the speed envelope to new levels, though the speed demon proved to be problematic from the start and fell behind in its flight test schedule.

On September 27, 1956, the X-2 hit Mach 3.196, the first manned flight to exceed three times the speed of sound, an unofficial new record. However, the achievement was fraught with tragedy, for moments later the rocketplane encountered the then little understood phenomenon of inertia coupling and started to roll violently. The X-2 slammed into the desert and the pilot, Air Force Captain Milburn Apt, was killed. For the time being, prospects for manned high-Mach flights, let alone flights into the hypersonic range, were deferred; future hopes hung on the X-15, which in light of the enormous complexities encompassed by the program would be under development for a few more years before taking to the skies.

The groundwork for achieving hypersonic flight, generally regarded as involving speeds in excess of Mach 5, was laid in the several years following World War II. In 1947 NACA engineer John V. Becker devised a game-changing Mach 7 wind tunnel at the Langley Research Laboratory (later called a Research Center) in Virginia. Despite having a small cross-section, the wind tunnel represented an enabling technology that was crucial to configuring the X-15. Separately, the US Army had begun testing rockets at White Sands, New Mexico, using modified German V-2s as boosters. Before the decade of the 1940s ended, hypersonic flight, albeit unmanned, had been achieved when a powered second stage, the WAC Corporal, shot into space at more than 5,000 miles per hour and fell back into the atmosphere at nearly the same speed.

By the early 1950s researchers were theorizing that if a controllable hypersonic rocket could be made to accommodate a pilot, manned hypersonic flight would be possible as manned supersonic flight had proven to be when Chuck Yeager rocketed into aeronautical history in the Bell X-1 on October 14, 1947. It was an invigorating time. The storehouse of aeronautical knowledge was growing profoundly, hastening the demystification of longstanding riddles. Development of the means to fly an order of magnitude faster than existing manned air vehicles appeared to be within reach.

Not surprisingly, advocacy for a hypersonic research aircraft came from Bell Aircraft. In 1950 the company, which was already a leader in purpose-built experimental aircraft, had hired former German major general Walter Dornberger, a long-time colleague of Germany's leading rocket scientist, Wernher von Braun. The two men, along with others in the German rocket program, had surrendered to American troops as Germany neared defeat. Dornberger wound up in a British prison for two years before being transferred to the United States as part of Operation Paperclip, a controversial government project to utilize the talents of the German rocket scientists in the coming Cold War that would include a burgeoning missile competition with the Soviet Union.

With a background as an artillery officer dating to World War I, Dornberger earned an engineering degree from the Berlin Institute of Technology in 1931. During World War II, he was the Third Reich's senior uniformed officer on the V-2 rocket program, in which capacity he oversaw the manufacturing complex at Peenemunde, where slave labor was utilized under deplorable conditions. While his morality was dubious to say the least, he shared von Braun's passion for the emerging technology.

As an engineering consultant for Bell, Dornberger prepared a preliminary proposal calling for the development of a hypersonic rocketplane that could fly to the edge of space. The proposal was influenced by the concepts of Dr. Eugen Sanger, an Austrian rocket pioneer who, as a competitor of Dornberger and von Braun during the war, had tried to bring a hypersonic bomber to fruition for the Luftwaffe. More theorist than practical experimenter, Sanger's ideas regarding propulsion systems and structures, considered radical and infeasible in the 1940s, helped shape hypersonic and lifting body designs for the next few decades, notably the X-15, the US Air Force's ill-fated Dyna-Soar spacecraft, and the Space Shuttle.

The seed for the development of the X-15 can be traced to January 8, 1952, when one of Bell's cofounders, Robert J. Woods, sent a letter to the

NACA Committee on Aerodynamics asking that a special study group be formed to consider the technical issues presented by endo- and exo-atmospheric hypersonic flight. Attached to his letter was the Dornberger proposal. A couple NACA studies were dutifully prepared.

Importantly, on October 5, 1954, the Committee on Aerodynamics met at the NACA facility at Edwards Air Force Base and gave its stamp of approval to the manned hypersonic research aircraft. Committee members included the facility manager Walter Williams and NACA test pilot Scott Crossfield. The vote would have been unanimous except that the Lockheed representative to the committee refused to go along.

Surprisingly, this lone dissenter was Clarence L. "Kelly" Johnson, the hard-charging and prolific design genius who had founded the Lockheed Skunk Works. Johnson described his opposition in an opinion attached to the majority report. Rather than rejecting the idea outright, Johnson recommended an unmanned platform to focus on the two critical areas in the still-new science of hypersonics—structural temperatures and control/stability.

A year before, the Air Force Scientific Advisory Board's Aircraft Panel, headed by Aeronautics Professor Clark B. Millikan of the California Institute of Technology, concluded that "the time was ripe" to consider an advanced manned research aircraft. The air force signaled its interest and shortly after the NACA Committee on Aerodynamics voted to proceed, the air force and NACA entered into a memorandum of understanding (which included the navy in a minor role). The military would fund the project for three airframes, with the air force responsible for design and construction while NACA would handle the flight test program. At the end of 1954, twelve contractors were invited to bid on what would shortly become Air Force Project 1226, with the platform's designation being X-15.

Bids were received by May 5, 1955. Only a little more than ninety days later, on August 12th, North American's proposal was selected. There was a touchy period during which it looked like the contract would go instead to Douglas, the second choice bidder. However, on September 30th the potentially deal-killing delivery timeline issue was resolved and on December 6th North American received the contract. Six months passed before construction was authorized and another three years elapsed before the first flight.

Leading the contractor team was Harrison A. "Stormy" Storms, Jr., chief engineer of North American's Los Angeles Division. He had studied under the legendary Caltech aerodynamicist Theodore von Karman, and upon graduating in 1940 he joined the company just as it was to embark on the development of the P-51 Mustang. During the war, he rose through the corporate ranks, gaining invaluable experience. It came in handy on the X-15 program, which was arguably one of the most demanding design projects undertaken by the aviation industry up to that time.

Storms's purview included the whole roster of projects in the company's Los Angeles Division. Daily responsibility for the X-15's design effort was vested in Feltz, the project engineer. Scotty liked working with both men. He said Storms was "a man of wonderful imagination, technical depth, and courage . . . with a love affair with the X-15." Scotty's praise for Feltz was equally commendatory, saying that Feltz "was very much a source of the X-15 success story."

The design goal was ambitious. Performance objectives were an altitude of 250,000 feet and a speed of 6,600 feet per second. The X-15 was to be *the* platform to explore hypersonic flight. The vehicle itself was the experiment with the appurtenant subsystems, propulsion technologies, advanced materials, unique structures, and endo- and exo-atmospheric control techniques. As it turned out, the X-15 did this and more. Once proving itself early in the flight test program, the rocketplane *per se* receded as the test focus and the platform became the carrier of other experiments.

The biggest hurdle faced by the designers sprung from the fact that a platform's aerodynamic heating rises by the square of the Mach number. This simple mathematical postulate inferred that any vehicle flying in the hypersonic regime would encounter extraordinary surface temperatures. Accordingly, the structure's design driver was reduction of aerodynamic heating as opposed to reduction of wave drag, as in the case of supersonic platforms like the early Bell X-planes and the emerging fleet of jet fighters where streamlining and sleekness of form were stressed.

NACA research in the early 1950s suggested that blunt leading edges create shock waves in front of a hypersonic platform that have the salutary effect of deflecting the higher air temperatures. This explains the X-15's relatively chunky frontal cross-section with a rounded-type nose (later modifications incorporated an instrumented ball known as the Q-Ball which measured dynamic pressure, angle-of-attack, and sideslip) and blunt-wing leading edges (despite thin wings). The same blunt style of structural shaping can be seen in the now-retired Space Shuttle which began its glides back to Earth from orbit at Mach 25.

For the rocketplane's skin, North American chose to go with Inconel-X, a high-temperature alloy made mostly of nickel and lesser parts chromium, columbium, and iron. The alloy had demonstrated its ability to withstand temperatures of 1,200 degrees Fahrenheit, which were expected at speeds up to and including Mach 7. Internal structures were made of high-strength aluminum and titanium alloys.

The fuselage center section, accommodating the fuel and oxidizer tanks, was of pure monocoque, or shell-like, construction. Tunnels, sometimes called chines, ran lengthwise along the outer starboard and port sides. These bulbous fairings not only accommodated internal plumbing and electrical needs, but served to enhance aerodynamic lift, supplementing the wings' contribution by more than half.

The laminar-flow wings were thin with a 5 percent thickness-to-chord ratio. Also, they were short, spanning barely over twenty-two feet. A twenty-five-degree sweep defined their trapezoidal shape.

Instead of ailerons, roll control was achieved through the differential operation of the all-moving horizontal stabilators, or so-called "slabs." These control surfaces were mounted at a fifteen-degree downward angle, known as anhedral, and they could be used not only differentially for roll control, but symmetrically for pitch control. Outboard sections of the vertical tails (both dorsal and ventral) were all-moving for yaw control. At altitudes above two hundred thousand feet, where the air is too thin for control surface effectiveness, small peroxide-powered reaction jets in the nose and wingtips provided attitude control.

Because of the wide speed and altitude profile of the X-15, the cockpit was equipped with three hand-operated controllers. The first was a conventional centered-mounted control stick for low-speed atmospheric flight. The second was linked to the first through hydraulic boost actuators and mounted on the right side, making it a side-stick controller sensitive to wrist movements. The third was what the company called the "space attitude control" which used the thrust from the reaction jets to steer while outside the atmosphere. It should be noted that the last of the three X-15s was equipped with a Minneapolis Honeywell MH-96 adaptive flight control system that automatically sensed external conditions and provided stability augmentation with blending of aerodynamic and ballistic controls.

Aviation historian Jay Miller has pointed out in his magisterial history of the X-planes that Scotty argued against the temptation to install an escape capsule and instead to adopt an ejection seat. The ejection seat ended up saving time, money, weight, and precious space. The seat was rocket propelled and could operate within a speed range of 90 knots to Mach 4 and at altitudes up to 120,000 feet.

X-15 pilots wore custom-fitted full-pressure suits made by the David Clark Company, an innovative developer of pilot paraphernalia having morphed from its roots as a manufacturer of girdles and bras. Scotty helped guide the suit's development. In the process, he got to know Dr. Clark, the firm's chain-smoking majordomo, who had invented special knitting machines to produce sturdier-than-normal women's garments. The full-pressure suit evolved from the early MC-2 model to the more comfortable A/P22s-2 model. Astronauts wore later iterations of this "space suit."

Reaction Motors Inc. was tapped to supply a new rocket engine for the X-15. However, delays in development caused the North American team to opt for a temporary solution. The first two airframes were outfitted with a twin-pack of RMI's tried and tested XLR11 rocket engine, which precluded further delay in the flight test program.

The XLR11 had been used in successful research aircraft, including the Bell X-1 and the Douglas Skyrocket, so it was a logical substitute until the new engine could be readied. Two XLR11 engines were mounted, one on top of the other, in a cradle. Each had four thrust chambers with a dedicated nozzle. Fuel was water/alcohol with liquid oxygen as the oxidizer.

Each chamber was capable of a boosted two thousand pounds of thrust for a total per engine of eight thousand pounds of thrust. Because there were two engines, the combined thrust amounted to sixteen thousand pounds. This was far less than the design called for, but was still sufficient to enable speeds up to about Mach 3.

After the first thirty flights, the new RMI XLR99 was installed. This highly complex engine with a single thrust chamber and nozzle represented a major advance. It could produce 57,850 pounds of thrust at a hundred thousand feet, a vast improvement over the earlier engine type. Importantly, the XLR99 could be throttled. Fuel was anhydrous ammonia and, as with the XLR11, the larger engine used liquid oxygen as the oxidizer.

Operationally, engine ignition occurred shortly after the X-15 was dropped from its NB-52 mothership. Typically, the fuel burn lasted until the propellants were exhausted, a duration of generally between eighty and ninety seconds. The remainder of the eight-to-ten-minute flight was unpowered.

In their history of the X-15, aerospace industry veterans Dennis R. Jenkins and Tony R. Landis make the point that the success of the X-15 would not have been possible without the often overlooked role played by the radar tracking stations constructed expressly to facilitate the ultra-fast and exceptionally high-flying research platform. Of course, the main facility was at Edwards Air Force Base. Other stations were established in Nevada, at Beatty and Ely. These underlay the X-15's general flight profile that stretched from Edwards on a northeast line to Wendover, Utah, near the Bonneville Salt Flats and back again to Edwards.

The flight testing was almost certainly made safer because of the extensive time the pilots spent in simulators. Typically, each eight- to ten-minute flight was preceded by fifteen to twenty hours in the simulators. In-flight malfunctions occurred and the pilots were prepared because their simulator training included exactly those contingencies. However, the simulators lacked the capacity to replicate landings. Preparation for landing the X-15 came via flights in Lockheed F-104 Starfighters, the Mach 2 interceptors that had high landing-approach speeds that mirrored the landing profile of the rocketplane.

To approximate the sensations expected upon reentry from the edge of space, when precise steering would be critical to make it back to the designated landing site of Rogers Dry Lake, the navy made one of its major contributions to the program. After World War II, the service had developed the country's most advanced centrifuge in Johnsville, Pennsylvania. It was a two-axis device with a pilot-carrying gondola fitted on an arm fifty feet long that could be swung at a rate of 250 feet per second to produce accelerations with a force of up to forty g's.

During the centrifuge runs, researchers cranked up acceleration to nine or ten g's, the tolerance limit for most people, which caused Scotty to black out. It was part of the job and, while griping about it in test-pilot style, Scotty took it in stride. With a touch of sarcasm, he later wrote, "I spent many hours whirling around in that crazy machine."

On October 15, 1958, the first of the three X-15s was ready to fly and rolled out of the North American factory in a highly publicized ceremony that drew Vice President Richard M. Nixon as the keynote speaker. The Soviets had launched Sputnik into orbit approximately a year earlier, kicking off the space race and turning public attention on America's answer to the challenge. Five and a half months after the X-15 rollout, the seven original astronauts in the Mercury program were announced and they quickly became the prime symbol of the nation's determination to gain the lead. But until then, an anxious population's hopes rode with the X-15's pilots personified by Scott Crossfield.

America was in a mad dash to catch up. Only two weeks before the X-15 rollout, the Eisenhower administration created the National Aeronautics and Space Administration using the National Advisory Committee for Aeronautics as the foundation. Basically, NASA became the modern incarnation of the old NACA. In the spirit of the moment, North American erected a neon sign above its Inglewood factory doors that proclaimed, "HOME OF THE X-15."

At the rollout, Nixon prematurely but confidently praised the X-15 as having "recaptured the US lead in space." In a classic photo op, the vice president was positioned at the nose of the X-15 with various program participants, including Scotty.

Nixon turned to Scotty and said, "You certainly have a dangerous job." With his bantering repartee in full swing, Scotty unhesitatingly replied, "My job is not nearly so risky as yours, sir." Three years after the contract was signed, the X-15 was about to be trucked to Edwards Air Force Base where Scotty would finally get to fly it.

Unlike in the case of the early X-planes, which were carried under their mothership's fuselage, enabling the test pilot to climb into the research vehicle shortly before the drop, the X-15 was carried under the mothership's right wing. This meant that the pilot had to ride in the rocketplane from takeoff. Another difference was that before the drop occurred, liquid oxygen was fed into the X-15's oxidizer tank from a supply in the mothership. This was to compensate for the boiling off of some of the X-15's liquid oxygen in the pre-drop phase.

Two of the early-production B-52 Stratofortresses in the Strategic Air Command fleet were handed over to Edwards Air Force Base to expressly serve the X-15's mothership needs with the designations NB-52A and NB-52B, respectively. The first of these had serial number 52-0003 and the second 52-0008. For this reason they were informally nicknamed "Balls Three" and "Balls Eight."

After four failed attempts to perform a glide flight because of a host of mechanical difficulties, Scotty got his chance on June 8, 1959, in the first of the three X-15s. Usually Scotty was the archetype of the diligent and disciplined test pilot, but he had a bold streak, and with the release into free flight having been in the works for years he was not able to resist the fighter jock impulse upon separation from Balls Three. He executed the equivalent of an aileron roll. It was as if the lead test pilot needed to get the unscripted maneuver out of his system during the rocketplane's baptism.

The X-15 performed more or less as anticipated until on final approach. Scotty's control inputs led to exaggerated pitching up and down of the rocketplane's nose. The wild oscillations were potentially life threatening. Scotty, though alarmed, kept his cool and through deft handling brought the bucking ship back to Rogers Dry Lake for a safe landing.

The first powered flight did not come easily. Various hindrances led to aborts before the second of the three X-15s would be ready. On

September 17, 1959, the rocketplane was dropped by its mothership. Like with the initial unpowered flight, Scotty ceremoniously rolled his ship at the launch, later noting that it rotated "very clean" because of the control authority afforded by the tail-mounted surfaces.

He roared up to more than fifty thousand feet and reached a speed in excess of Mach 2. Not bad for the maiden powered flight. However, upon landing a fire broke out which could have been ruinous if firefighters had not jumped into action immediately to extinguish the flames. The rocketplane was grounded for three weeks until repairs returned it to flight status.

In successive flights, progress was made. However, the advances were not without incident. An in-flight engine fire prompted an emergency landing at excessive weight, causing the nose wheel to collapse and the fuselage to break in two. Amazingly, Scotty escaped with nary a scratch.

In a surprising irony, Scotty's closest brush with death during his time on the X-15 program came not in-flight but during a ground test. On June 8, 1960, he sat in the cockpit of the third X-15 for a static test of the new XLR99 engine. He first got an indication that something had gone wrong when a valve-malfunction light illuminated.

Suddenly an explosion erupted that blew the rocketplane's forward section, including the cockpit with Scotty in it, a distance of about thirty feet. Film of the mishap shows a fireball engulfing the whole assembly before fire crews could douse the flames. Once again, the gods smiled on Scotty for he exited without serious injury. The problem had been the combination of a faulty relief valve and gas regulator that caused over-pressurization of the fuel tank.

As repairs were made to the damaged airframe, the second X-15 got one of the new XLR99 engines. Like a gritty equestrian thrown from a rambunctious stallion and determined to ride again, Scotty piloted the newly outfitted rocketplane in November, becoming the first person to fly with the newer, more powerful engine. For a change, the flight went without a hitch.

The next month, Scotty flew the X-15 for the last time. Completion of his fourteenth flight represented the end of the prime contractor's demonstration flights. (Scotty's expertise was subsequently applied to the Hound Dog cruise missile and later to the Apollo manned lunar program.) NASA and air force test pilots had begun flying the X-15 in March and April of 1960, respectively, overlapping Scotty's flights. Starting with Neil Armstrong's flight on December 9th, the flight test program would be conducted exclusively by military and government pilots.

As hoped, the rocketplane program was generating valuable data across multiple disciplines—thermodynamics, hypersonic stability and control, structural loading, and biomedicine. The National Aeronautic Association took note and selected the X-15's constituent organizations as recipients of the Robert J. Collier Trophy, America's most prestigious annual aerospace award. On July 18, 1962, the trophy was presented by President John F. Kennedy on the South Lawn of the White House to the first four X-15 pilots from the participating organizations—Scott Crossfield of North American, Joseph Walker of NASA, Robert White of the air force, and Forrest Peterson of the navy.

The X-15 attained its highest altitude on August 22, 1963. Joseph Walker got off to a good start. He let his engine run until the propellants were depleted at an altitude of 176,000 feet and a speed of Mach 5.58. From there he coasted on the momentum upwards in a ballistic trajectory to 354,200 feet before arcing over. At sixty-seven miles above earth's surface he was in space by any definition.

The decision was made to substantially modify an X-15 damaged in a November 1962 flight so that it could carry mockups of advanced ramjet engines attached to the ventral fin. When the reworking was complete, the airframe's designation had changed to X-15A-2. Among other modifications, two large external tanks (oxidizer in the left and fuel in the right) were carried, adding sixty seconds to the engine run time.

Also the X-15A-2 was coated in an ablator, a material devised to provide enhanced heat protection. This material was pink, but it was covered with an off-white seal to prevent wear and to prevent adverse reactions along the surface if excess liquid oxygen were to come into contact with the potentially explosive ablator. The modified rocketplane with the sparkling silver and bright orange external tanks was an eye-catcher and a photographer's dream.

On October 3, 1967, Air Force Captain William "Pete" Knight flew the X-15A-2 to the all-time speed record for a manned, powered air vehicle. Once released from Balls Eight, he lit the engine and established a climb at a twelve-degree angle of attack which led to a pitch angle of thirty-five degrees. At 72,300 feet and Mach 2.4, he followed the flight plan and pushed over, jettisoning the two external tanks. Freed of the extra weight and drag, the rocketplane continued to accelerate until reaching the blistering speed of 6,600 feet per second or Mach 6.7.

Tragedy struck on November 15, 1967, shortly after Air Force Major Michael J. Adams launched on his seventh X-15 flight in the third airframe. On his way to 266,000 feet, it is believed that an electrical disturbance originated in equipage related to an onboard experiment and this caused the dampers in the MH-96 adaptive flight control system to trip out. Sensing the lack of control authority, Adams began using the dedicated thruster control on the left side of the cockpit.

Adams was not able to overcome the oscillating motion induced by the flight control system. At sixty-two thousand feet, the rocketplane was hopelessly up against its load limits and began to break apart. The airframe was wrecked beyond reuse. Adams's death was the only one in the X-15's multiyear flight test program.

Only seven X-15 flights followed. Funding dried up at the end of 1968. The program closed inauspiciously with the final attempt at a two hundredth flight being scrubbed when snow started to fall on the baked surface of Rogers Dry Lake five days before Christmas.

•••

The X-15 program's contract period covered thirteen years and in that time a little more than a day's worth of flying occurred in the exotic rocketplanes. Costs rose over time as the program continued to grapple with unseen challenges. As the program matured, each X-15 flight was costing nearly $600,000. Yet the program made enormous contributions to aerospace progress. As Scotty so aptly put it, "In terms of weight, each [X-15] would be worth three times as much as solid gold."

Scotty spent a good deal of his time late in life encouraging young engineers, pilots, and others venturing into the aerospace world. On April

6, 2006, the morning after he addressed a group of newly minted officers at Maxwell Air Force Base near Montgomery, Alabama, he climbed into his 1960 Cessna 210A single-engine aircraft for the flight home to Manassas, Virginia.

While over Georgia, he got caught in a ghastly thunderstorm. The forces of nature shredded his plane to pieces, causing it to disappear from air traffic control's radar. During the subsequent search, a door from the plane was found a mile from the bulk of the wreckage where it appeared the body of the plane had plummeted straight down through a thicket of trees.

It was a strange turn of events for someone who had fearlessly withstood the hazards endemic in rocketing to record speeds at lofty altitudes in exotic research planes. Scotty had cheated death so many times. The eighty-four-year-old had reportedly philosophized with a friend, in the way old people sometimes do, about death the day before his final flight, saying he did not want to expire in bed or the bathtub, but to go in the air. Then he and his friend just laughed it off as not a fitting end to an otherwise good airplane.

When Scotty's ashes were interred that August at Arlington National Cemetery, the hundreds of mourners included his fellow X-15 test pilot Neil Armstrong. Visible in the distance across the Potomac from the majestic overlook of the resting place of America's heroes sits the marble-and-glass-walled National Air and Space Museum where Scotty's famous planes, the Mach-busting Skyrocket and the first X-15, are suspended from the ceiling, examples of a lasting legacy. Before the haunting notes of "Taps" were played, and before a naval officer in dress uniform presented the flag of a grateful nation to Scotty's son Paul, the funeral's serenity was pierced by the kind of ear-splitting sound that had animated Scotty's excitement for flying machines.

A four-ship formation of US Navy F/A-18 Hornets swooped low over the funeral, a final farewell from airmen to one of their own. Perhaps the formation's pilots knew that the supersonic strike fighters in which they flew were made possible in some measure because of the fallen flyer they were honoring. Once the jets were directly overhead, one of the pilots evinced the symbolism of the "missing man" as he, in the time-honored tradition, vacated his position within the formation and pulled up—straight up, like a rocket!

•••

Recently interest has intensified in air-breathing hypersonic concepts. Instead of engine runs lasting a matter of seconds or at most a minute or two as necessitated by the rocket's finite supply of oxidizer, air-breathing hypersonic planes will be able to sustain powered flight for much longer duration. In theory, such planes offer a multitude of possibilities. Applications include unmanned and manned military platforms, executive transports, priority cargo carriers, and commercial airliners.

NASA made strides with its X-43 Hyper-X program and the air force likewise crossed important thresholds with its X-51 Waverider. A number of programs are underway around the globe using wedge-shaped structures and supersonic combustion ramjet (SCRAM) engines. Researchers are on the cusp of making air-breathing hypersonic flight an everyday reality.

When that time comes, the teams responsible for the breakthroughs will owe a debt of gratitude to the dreamers behind the X-15. For the time being, the X-15 holds the records for the fastest and highest flying ever done by humans in winged, powered platforms. Those records date back to the 1960s and, as Scotty might have said, records are made to be broken.

CHAPTER 5

Space Tourism: From Dream to First Steps with *SpaceShipOne*

Perhaps the most disconcerting thing in coming to know the young group of ardent, enthusiastic geniuses—and "geniuses" is not too strong a word—who compose the group engaged in the creation of *SpaceShipOne* is the refreshing normality of their personalities. Although they are participating in one of the most advanced experiments in modern civil aeronautics, breaking rules of flight as they create new ones, adapting their business and company makeup as they go, they all remain friendly, approachable human beings, as willing to talk to you about the weather as they are their amazing reaches into the future. The standard, of course, is set by Burt and Dick Rutan, whose influence on this group—and on aviation in general—is powerful.

Any Hollywood film would populate their company with mad scientists, dictator bosses, megalomaniac engineers and the like, with Britney Spears playing a key role as scientist / test pilot. Instead, you find a well-rounded group of friendly people willing to overlook your lack of engineering depth and pleased to explain in layman terms the importance of their mission, and just how groundbreaking it is.

SpaceShipOne made the first privately funded human space flight on June 21, 2004. Known as Flight 15P, it was piloted by Mike Melvill, who became the first licensed US commercial astronaut.

The radical-appearing spacecraft was created by Burt Rutan's Scaled Composites for Mojave Aerospace Ventures, an aptly named joint venture that linked Rutan's Tier One program in a dynamic pairing with

Microsoft's cofounder, Paul Allen. Not surprisingly, their development, done entirely (and proudly) without government funding, won the Ansari X Prize of $10 million on October 4, 2004.

The three-and-a-half-year program was covert for the first two years, with only insiders aware that it was in progress until the flight-ready spacecraft was unveiled in April 2003. The FAA, as the pertinent regulatory agency, was briefed a week prior to the unveiling while NASA found out about the program the same time as the public.

The very name of the project, *SpaceShipOne*, is important for it portrays at once the firm's acknowledgment that this was an initial attempt, and a promise that it would not be the last. The vehicle *SpaceShipOne* itself was intended for suborbital flight. It was powered by a hybrid rocket motor after being air launched from an equally advanced mothership. In the past, atmospheric reentry has been achieved by the use of heavy heat shield, much of which burns away in the process.

The *SpaceShipOne* design had a unique atmospheric reentry system that allowed the rear half of the wing and the twin tail booms to "feather." In this system, the twin tail booms and the rear half of the wing fold upward along a wing-long hinge line. This induces sufficient drag to keep the spacecraft stable and heat tolerant during the critical reentry phase and then becomes available for a normal glide to landing at the designated airstrip. It is a totally revolutionary development in aerodynamics, incorporated in the follow-on vehicle, *SpaceShipTwo*, and certain to see application in other craft in the future.

SpaceShipOne was a typical out-of-the-box example of Burt Rutan's thinking. It was able to make the very first manned private space flight because the extremely advanced design goals were fulfilled. These included creating a radical airframe with a maximum gross weight of seventy-nine hundred pounds. Of this, an incredible six thousand pounds was made up of the loaded rocket motor.

After *SpaceShipOne* was awarded the much sought-after Ansari X Prize, it was retired from experimental flight and ultimately transferred to its current position in the Boeing Milestones of Flight Hall of the National Air and Space Museum.

SpaceShipOne required enormous backing for its success, and this was provided by the aforementioned Mojave Aerospace Ventures. This was hardly a pickup organization of amateur enthusiasts, backed as it was by the sizable commitment from Microsoft cofounder and aviation patron, Paul Allen, and by Rutan's company, Scaled Composites. These are two men of vastly different personalities, but with deep similarities in their grasp of advanced ideas that have a genuine possibility for success and thus worth the work and the financing. They have, to my knowledge, not yet decided, and may never decide, that an effort should be made to place humans on Mars. But if they do decide to do it, you can count on a good chance of their striving being a success. It is just their style—don't attempt the truly impossible, but make the "impossible" possible to occur.

SpaceShipOne's cigar-shaped fuselage has the crew cabin in front, followed by the oxidizer tank, fuel casing, and a hybrid rocket that has no throttle and cannot be steered. The aerodynamic control surfaces are controlled manually. The sixteen-foot, five-inch-long wings have a chord of almost ten feet. They are distinguished by huge vertical tail booms, each with a horizontal stabilizer and landing gear.

The flight path of *SpaceShipOne* required an elaborate control system for flight within and without the atmosphere. The atmospheric control surfaces had to operate at both supersonic (during boost flight) and subsonic (during gliding) speeds. Control by typical aviation-style stick and pedals was achieved in subsonic flight by cable and rod linkage to elevons and rudder, while supersonic flight used electrically controlled horizontal stabilizers for pitch and roll plus separate electrically controlled rudders for yaw. Interestingly, the first manned supersonic air vehicle, the Bell X-1, had a similar system for pitch control—rod linkages for elevator and electric stabilizer. Outside the atmosphere, *SpaceShipOne* used twelve thrusters, mounted in three sets for reaction control. Fuselage thrusters controlled pitch and yaw, while wingtip thrusters governed roll.

SpaceShipOne's wings were placed in a high-drag "feathered" state by being pneumatically tilted forwards, making for what is referred to internally as a "carefree reentry." As the leading edge of the wings experienced the greatest heating, they were coated with ablative thermal protection material. Landings were made on the two widely separated main wheels and, curiously enough for a space vehicle, a nose skid.

The designers made thoughtful efforts to have the cabin fairly comfortable, given the mission requirements. There were places for three people, with the pilot sitting forward, and two others aft. The cabin area was designed against failure so that the pilot and crew would not require pressure suits or even oxygen masks. The System Navigation Unit (SNU) formed the backbone of the avionics systems. It worked with the Flight Director Display (FDD) to comprise the Flight Navigation Unit. The SNU had a GPS-based inertial navigation system, which down-linked telemetry data to mission control by radio. The FDD had different display modes for each of the different phases of flight: boost, coast, reentry, and gliding.

Well aware of their own place in aviation history, the group elected to have *SpaceShipOne* achieve supersonic flight on December 17, 2003—a hundred years after the Wright brothers' success at Kitty Hawk. The first official space flight, piloted by Mike Melvill, was from what would become the first commercial spaceport, the Mojave Air and Space Port.

The air-launched *SpaceShipOne* needed a mothership, which itself was an extraordinary groundbreaking design that received worldwide attention. Officially named Scaled Composites Model 318, it was popularly known as *White Knight*, and was designed to avoid the expense and complexity of Cape Canaveral-style rocket launches. Instead, it was a highly functional and successful aircraft that took off and landed horizontally and could reach some fifty thousand feet in altitude carrying *SpaceShipOne* in a parasite aircraft configuration. (The history of parasite aircraft is a dim one historically and internationally. The Soviet Union attempted it with massive aircraft, while the US Navy assigned Zeppelins to do so. Neither system worked well, nor did a more sophisticated postwar McDonnell XF-85 Goblin, intended to protect intruding Convair B-36s.)

In many ways *White Knight* was an extremely satisfying method of launch. It didn't require the blast and bravado of a rocket tearing away from Cape Canaveral, nor did it impose dangerous flight loads on *SpaceShipOne* at any point. Two reliable, relatively low-thrust (thirty-five hundred pounds static thrust each) General Electric J-85-GE-5 engines did the trick.

Typically for this project, *White Knight* replicated the interior, avionics, flight control system, environmental control system, electrical system, etc., of *SpaceShipOne*. In fact it incorporated every system of its smaller sibling except the rocket motor. For example, servos for stabilizer trim on the spacecraft were identical to the trim servos on *White Knight*.

The *SpaceShipOne* components that unlocked and moved the reentry wing were used to retract the landing gear of *White Knight*. Thus nearly every working part of the spacecraft had the benefit of testing at the frigid fifty thousand-foot maximum altitude accessed by *White Knight* before *SpaceShipOne* even flew. This meant that the mothership became a near-perfect test vehicle and a stand-in if needed for comparison.

Flying *White Knight* granted experience for *SpaceShipOne*, as well as providing a link to potential problems, spares and so on. A *White Knight* pilot was qualified to be a *SpaceShipOne* pilot, and vice versa. The transition was made easier by *White Knight's* trim system which could replicate *SpaceShipOne* characteristics. Great leaps forward in construction can be found in the eighty-two-foot-span wings built in a thin "W" shape, dual tail plane, and four-wheel undercarriage.

White Knight would take off with *SpaceShipOne* attached and climb to the desired altitude. If an emergency had occurred, the pair could land still connected together.

A "typical" *SpaceShipOne* flight was a well-programmed adventure. *White Knight* had *SpaceShipOne* attached, almost in marsupial fashion, then took off in an event-filled one-hour climb to about fifty thousand feet. If the check system protocol revealed no problems, *SpaceShipOne* was released.

The initial portion of the flight was an unpowered glide, and the pilot could elect, if he wished, to continue that unpowered glide back to the airfield. But if all systems were go, *SpaceShipOne's* rocket engine was ignited and a startling sixty-five-degree climb initiated.

Acceleration quickly built to four g's and a speed of Mach 3.3 was achieved. When the power shut off, the craft continued to climb in a ballistic profile to well over three hundred thousand feet. There the gutsy pilot placed the innovative wings into their high-drag mode, and a high-speed dive began.

On the return trip, the craft reached speeds comparable to those it attained in the climb. It encountered a violent deceleration upon reentry into the atmosphere, sustaining about five g's in the process. As it returned to lower altitudes (ten to fourteen miles high), it reconfigured back into a "low-drag glider," and glided down to a landing after about twenty minutes. Not surprisingly, *White Knight* took longer to descend, and usually gave *SpaceShipOne* precedence on landing.

Rocket engines have advanced a long way since the days of the Messerschmitt Me 163, and this innovative leader used a hybrid rocket engine with a solid rubber fuel and a liquid nitrous oxide oxidizer. In a minute and twenty-seven seconds it generated seventeen thousand pounds of thrust. The rocket could not be throttled but it could be stopped after being lit. After its 2004 upgrade, the engine was capable of twenty thousand pounds of thrust for one minute and forty-five seconds.

Burt Rutan patented his design of the engine configuration, which used the oxidizer tank as the primary structural component of the spacecraft's fuselage. In line with Scaled Composite's usual far-ranging design, the engine used a great deal of composite materials. For those of us oldtimers who devoutly believe that engines mean tons of red-hot first-rate steel construction, it is always surprising to find composite materials chosen for *SpaceShipOne*'s engine.

SpaceShipOne is a relatively tiny vehicle, given its demanding mission. Only twenty-eight feet long, with a sixteen-foot, five-inch wingspan and weighing only 2,640 pounds (empty), it nonetheless provided room for extensive scientific experimentation. The hybrid rocket carried it to an amazing Mach 3.09 in only eighty-seven seconds. The craft had a glide range of about forty miles.

The demanding terms of the Ansari X Prize specified that the craft must reach a hundred kilometers in height twice within a two-week period, carrying the equivalent of a three-person crew. *SpaceShipOne* became the first privately funded, reusable manned spacecraft to exceed Mach 2 and Mach 3, and also the first to exceed a hundred kilometers in altitude.

The FAA registered *SpaceShipOne* as N328KF, with the 328 standing for 328 kilofeet, approximately the hundred-kilometer mark designated officially as the "edge of space." The first test flight occurred on May 20, 2003, in the unmanned mode. As noted, the first powered flight took place on December 17, 2003.

Contrary to the usual reports maligning government bureaucrats, the US Office of Commercial Space Transportation issued the first license for suborbital rocket flights to Scaled Composites on April 1, 2004. A little more than two months later, the long-standing Mojave Airport, home to unusual vehicles of all kinds, was given an additional name: Spaceport.

On October 4, 2004, this remarkable combination of vehicles, pilots, support crew, and backers witnessed an extraordinary flight. Michael Melvill and Max Stinemetze were pilots in *White Knight*, while Brian Binnie flew *SpaceShipOne*. After having made the first flight of the two required X-prize flights on September 29th, their goal was to make the second, ballasted for a crew of three with the goal of reaching or exceeding 328,000 feet. (An additional incentive was to attempt to break the longstanding X-15 record of 354,000 feet.)

White Knight, with its "baggage," *SpaceShipOne*, took off at 6:49 a.m. Launch altitude was set as 47,100 feet. At 7:40 a.m., *SpaceShipOne* was released, with Binnie firing the rocket immediately. An eighty-three-second rocket burn pushed *SpaceShipOne* to a speed of 2,186 miles per hour (Mach 3.09) and lifted it to 213,000 feet; the impetus carried it on to 367,500 feet. At its peak altitude, Binnie used the unique feathering system to prepare for the descent, in the meantime experiencing weightlessness for almost four minutes. During the descent, the maximum speed approached Mach 3.25, and Binnie experienced deceleration forces up to 5.4 g's. Binnie then reconfigured *SpaceshipOne* as a glider at about fifty thousand feet, and from that point on had what could only be considered an anticlimactic flight to landing.

In this relatively short time, *SpaceShipOne* broke the X-15 altitude record by more than thirteen thousand feet, won the Ansari X Prize, and landed normally, with no maintenance write-ups! The *SpaceShipOne* team took well-earned pride in the fact that their success had been achieved in a thirteen-month, seventeen-flight test program.

SpaceShipOne's success as a proof-of-concept platform was nothing short of remarkable. But airline mogul Richard Branson's long-held vision of a thriving space tourism business has been delayed for years. Commercializing breakthrough technologies has proven to be an intimidating task, with rising costs, fickle public interest, safety concerns, and human tragedy in the ground and flight test programs.

Whether sufficient numbers of tourists will flock to buy tickets at a few hundred thousand dollars apiece for a brief arc into space to sustain a fledgling industry remains anybody's guess. Yet, the yearning to travel to other domains, even if momentarily, is an enduring impulse in people. Sir Richard's space transport business, Virgin Galactic, will be there to cater to the willing and able passengers once the follow-on platforms are finally ready.

Like all great adventures, space tourism started out as a dream. In the face of myriad challenges, the dreamers continue to await the regularly scheduled flights for paying passengers into the realm that until *SpaceShipOne* used to be the exclusive preserve of government-funded explorers. If and when that day arrives, it will be in large measure because of the strides of the Mojave geniuses led by the now-retired but still-inventive Burt Rutan.

Section 2

Airways: Commercial Platforms

CHAPTER 6

The Tin Goose: Henry Ford's Tri-Motor

The name Henry Ford is synonymous with automobiles. Yet the genius of modern mass production had wide-ranging interests, as evidenced by the eclectic collection at his Dearborn, Michigan, museum which would ultimately house giant locomotives and resurrect Thomas Edison's laboratory and the Wright brothers' bicycle shop in the adjoining Greenfield Village. In the age of Lindbergh, how could anyone of Henry Ford's voracious curiosity, vast resources, business sense, and vast ambition not look to the skies?

Henry and his son, Edsel, were intrigued by the possibilities of aviation. It was a flirtation not unlike the much later obsession of dot-com billionaires with the prospects of commercializing the uncharted void of space through the development of new transportation technologies. The enterprising Fords saw the chance to establish a foothold in an embryonic industry that with each breakthrough increasingly captivated the public's imagination and thereby do for flying what they had done for motoring; after all, the airplane lent itself to assembly-line construction much like the automobile.

In the immediate post–World War I era, there were few airports dotting the American landscape. Aerial navigation and communication facilities were sparse with no reliable nationwide weather service. Moreover, even if an adequate infrastructure existed, there was no practical passenger-carrying aircraft to use it. With a safe and economical commercial platform, large numbers of people might begin to try out airlines as an alternative to traditional modes of long-distance transportation.

In 1921 the beginning of transcontinental air mail service offered the hope that a viable airline industry might be on the way. But air mail flying proved to be hazardous and failed to outperform the rails in delivery times. When airways were established using equidistantly spaced revolving beacons of 7.5 million candlepower to enable nighttime air mail carriage in 1925, efficiencies improved and the emergence of a viable airline industry seemed only a matter of time.

The year before, William Bushnell Stout, an entrepreneur with a knack for mechanical things and a vision for commercial aviation, met with William Benson Mayo, a top executive at Ford. Stout, who had a talent for explaining complex engineering concepts in easy-to-understand terms, laid out a two-pronged vision for developing Detroit as a center of aviation. In Stout's mind, success depended on the establishment of a new airport and the adoption of a promising new material in aircraft construction.

Mayo was attentive and advised Stout to put his idea for an airport in a letter to Henry Ford. The letter went out in early 1924 suggesting the creation of a civil airport on the Ford property in Dearborn, just west of Detroit. It would fill a gaping void within the larger community which had no airport except for Selfridge Field, an army flying facility located well northeast of the city. Ford sat down for a meeting with the proposer and in April 1924 the towering figure in American industry committed to build "the finest landing field in the world."

Stout's association with Ford can be traced to his background which included stints as a technical writer for the McClure syndicate and the *Chicago Tribune*. His prominence had brought him into contact with engineers and executives at major companies. In 1917 he joined the Packard Motor Car Company and spent time in Washington where he assisted the government's oversight of the wartime Liberty engine contract. He conceived an innovative monoplane called the Batwing cabin plane or Vampire Bat, a flying wing made of wood and powered by a 150-horsepower Hispano-Suiza engine. However, government interest waned when the war ended.

In 1922 he started his own company, the Stout Metal Airplane Company. Importantly, he realized the inherent disadvantages of wood and the potential for a composite metal sheet known as duralumin, an alloy pioneered in Germany that consisted mainly of aluminum and lesser amounts of other minerals and compounds. The hybrid metal offered high strength and relatively low weight, an ideal combination for aircraft construction.

The Stout plant, located on Beaubien Street near Ford's original assembly building in Detroit, produced the first all-metal aircraft in the United States. In the same year that Stout had formed his company, the ST All-Metal Torpedo Plane rolled out to satisfy terms of a US Navy contract. The twin-engine aircraft sported a massive wing, an unusual split tail, and a streetcar-style nose.

The navy prototype was a radical departure in shape, size, and material. Initial flight tests at Selfridge Field were on track. However, when flight test duties shifted from the company's Eddie Stinson to a navy pilot, fortunes reversed. The navy pilot narrowly averted death or serious injury when the plane went out of control and fell to the ground, causing a total loss. The navy dropped the project, leaving the newly formed Stout company in a precarious financial position.

Feeling let down by the military, Stout turned his attention to commercial aviation and sought investment capital from the city's leading industrialists. Ultimately, he persuaded 128 businessmen to buy shares in his company. Most prominent among them were Henry Ford and his son, Edsel.

The first commercial endeavor was called the Air Sedan. Featuring all-metal construction with a thick-cambered and cantilevered high-wing that had a dramatically tapered chord outboard to the wingtips, the transport had room for only four seats. It was clearly underpowered with a single 90-horsepower Curtiss OX-5 engine.

Rather than being discouraged when Stout came to him with the request for additional funds, Henry Ford is reported to have said, "Son, you don't need more money, you need more airplane." It was a recognition that the Air Sedan was just too small to be commercially viable. Stout had already conceived a follow-on configuration.

Designated the 2-AT (for Air Transport), the new plane had a payload capacity of a thousand pounds, which meant it could carry that much weight as cargo or eight passengers. Corrugated duralumin was the choice for the outer skin. A thick wing with a span of sixty-six feet was mated to the top of a boxy fuselage. Power came from a World War I-era 420-horsepower Liberty engine.

Among Stout's friends and investors was prominent boat builder Garfield "Gar" Wood. In the summer of 1923, Wood's Liberty-powered speedboat competed in a highly publicized race on the Detroit River. Subsequently, the racer was renamed *Miss Detroit VII*, keeping a naming tradition alive that emphasized pride of place.

Inspired by the speedboat's name, Stout called his new plane *Maiden Detroit*. It was a fitting choice for the first in his line of truly commercial aircraft. The name was also a play on words because in spoken form it sounded like "made in Detroit."

Events started to unfold quickly. On November 16, 1924, the Fords opened their airport in Dearborn featuring a couple intersecting grass runways laid out from their twelve thousand-acre property. It was a fabulous aeronautical waypoint that in the next half-dozen years would be refined with paved runways and fine accommodations for passengers and flight crews. Amenities included an Albert Kahn-designed hotel, a suitable restaurant, and a limousine service. As would be expected, the first aircraft to operate from the airport was *Maiden Detroit*, which had flown out of Selfridge Field during its initial flight tests.

The airport's formal dedication occurred on January 15, 1925, amid much fanfare. A dozen glistening Curtiss Hawk biplane fighters from Selfridge's First Pursuit Group commanded by Major Carl "Tooey" Spaatz (later to become the first chief of staff of the US Air Force) dazzled thousands of spectators who turned out for the occasion. The Fords were betting on Stout and his metal airplane. That bet was hedged by their support for a new duralumin dirigible being promoted by Ralph Upson's Aircraft Development Corporation as a possible alternative to fixed-wing commercial air transports. Accordingly, the airport was outfitted with a one-of-a-kind airship mooring mast that reached more than two hundred feet high and that boasted an elevator for passenger comfort.

Just weeks ahead of the airport's official opening, the US Post Office purchased the *Maiden Detroit* for $25,000. The government's vote of confidence served as vindication of Stout's belief in all-metal aircraft construction and of Ford's support for the project. Additionally, it portended future possibilities. In February 1925 Congress passed the Kelly Air Mail Act which spurred commercial aviation by turning air mail flights over to private contractors with the sweetener of subsidies.

The next month Stout's new factory at the Ford Airport rolled out its first product, an improved 2-AT named, appropriately enough, *Maiden Dearborn*. Its wings were emblazoned with big block letters that spelled "FORD" and its fuselage was decorated with the company name in the highly stylized script the world has long recognized as the central element of the Ford logo. Befitting the metal transport's grandeur, the plane and those of the same type that followed were generically designated Stout Air Pullmans, a reference to the luxurious railroad cars of the Gilded Age.

On April 13, 1925, regularly scheduled flights of these planes were inaugurated between Dearborn and Chicago, ferrying auto parts and other freight for Ford Motor Company. Under the banner of Ford Air Transport Service, America's foray into scheduled commercial aviation had begun. Newspapers nationwide trumpeted the accomplishment in top-of-the-fold headlines.

Henry Ford insisted on punctuality and he closely monitored his air service's real-time performance. According to one account, Edsel wanted to meet up with one of the planes before it took off for Chicago, but due to circumstances beyond his control he got to the Dearborn terminal twenty minutes after the scheduled departure. When the young Ford showed up, he discovered that the transport had already left. His father, ever the stickler, reminded him: "This is an airport, not a yacht."

Despite his noted tartness, the elder Ford several times went out of his way to publicly credit his son with the idea of expanding the company's aviation footprint by buying Stout's company, which happened on July 31, 1925. Referring in part to Edsel, the patriarch said, "There is a wonderful future in aviation, but it belongs to another generation." At the same time, he was quoted on his hopeful vision for flight: "I feel about aviation as I did about autos thirty years ago. It is now or never to get hold of commercial aviation and make it go."

When the airplane company changed hands, William Mayo, the Ford engineer, was placed in charge of Ford's new aviation division. Stout became a consultant to the division while his employees transferred to the Ford payroll. Further change was in the offing.

In early September George Prudden, Stout's chief engineer who had retained that title at Ford Aviation after the change in ownership, was summarily fired for allowing himself to be photographed for a front-page story in a local newspaper. Henry Ford did not like his employees usurping, even unwittingly, the publicity that he felt was his family's prerogative. Ford promptly replaced Prudden with Harold Hicks, a young talent within the company. Hicks would be assisted by Tom Towle.

None of this happened in a vacuum. As commercial aviation took shape, a field of intensely competitive players was developing aircraft to meet the needs of hoped-for demand. As a new plane manufacturer, Ford adopted promotion techniques to its aviation venture that had worked in the automotive industry.

Early in the twentieth century, when cars were still a novelty, Charles Glidden of Boston had started a series of long-distance driving trips over the open roads to convince the public of the automobile's practicality. The Fords and other like-minded businessmen trying their hand at aviation embraced the idea for their newly chosen endeavor. In the fall of 1925, sixteen aircraft from manufacturers like Curtiss, Martin, Waco, Swallow, Fokker, Junkers, and, of course, Ford gathered at the Ford Airport in Dearborn for a one-week "tour" of Midwest cities. The tour covered nineteen hundred miles to prove that aviation had progressed from its infancy to the point where flights were nothing to fear. The event was considered a success and became an annual project.

At first, the event was called the Edsel B. Ford Reliability Tour for the Development of Commercial Aviation, and participation was rewarded with an engraved plaque on an elaborate trophy underwritten by Edsel Ford. For future tours, a point system was developed to score planes and pilots, making the tour not just a promotional affair but also an efficiency contest. Over time, the event evolved as the National Air Tour. The exercise continued through 1931 and did much to acquaint the public with aviation and to advance safety and reliability.

Meanwhile, the still-new Stout factory on the airport grounds burned down for undetermined reasons on a Sunday in January 1926. Sensing that the company's airplane venture had been stagnating as it sought to leap to the next plateau, Henry Ford spoke of the destruction in welcoming terms. Addressing Stout, who was distraught over the loss of the factory, he proclaimed: "It is the best thing that ever happened to you."

The Stout-Prudden tri-motored civil transport, which was to be the next platform in the line's evolution, had gone up in smoke. Designated the 3-AT, it was a disappointment in its early trials. The aircraft had been conceived as little more than a scaled-up Air Pullman. The big plane even looked clunky and anachronistic. It had become clear that Stout and his team, for all their insight, innovation, and acumen through the mid-1920s, had suddenly atrophied. If Ford's investment into the rapidly advancing field of aviation was going to have any chance of success, it needed to be revitalized.

Moving forward, Ford charged his new design team with the development of a better plane. They kept the proven aspects of the 3-AT, including the all-metal construction, the high-wing monoplane configuration, and a three-engine arrangement. The redundancy of multiple engines would assuage public fears of an engine stoppage in flight. Engendering public confidence was considered as important as achieving economical operation.

For this new tri-motored airliner, Henry Ford wanted an indigenous engine. His company built thousands of automotive engines, so he reasoned it should be able to develop a competitive engine for aeronautical applications. However, efforts to do so fell short and the company opted for off-the-shelf Curtiss-Wright J-4 Whirlwind engines and later went with improved J-5 engines. Later still, Ford chose Pratt & Whitney's Wasp and Hornet engines. These were all highly reliable air-cooled radial engines that provided years of service.

Henry Ford had taken a personal interest in the new tri-motored plane and proved once again how quickly he could mobilize the diverse facets of industry to prototype a new and complex machine for market introduction. In a mere four months the groundbreaking aircraft went from design to flight.

Known as the 4-AT or simply the Ford Tri-Motor, the new plane took to the sky for the first time on June 11, 1926. The hefty transport with the corrugated metal surfaces turned heads and heralded the age of practical airline travel. At a cost of up to $50,000, this airliner was not cheap, but a variety of airlines felt such a modern design was worth it.

In the airliner's heyday, people called it the "Tin Goose." The nickname derived from the all-metal construction and the plane's waddle-like motion when taxiing, which struck some observers as reminiscent of fowl shuffling along on the ground. Not coincidentally, before Ford's move into aviation, the company's ubiquitous Model T had acquired the sobriquet "Tin Lizzie."

For his part, Edsel saw the rugged plane's potential as an expeditionary platform with a huge publicity benefit to be derived from such use. He had been introduced to Lieutenant Commander Richard Byrd in the early 1920s and, in 1926, decided to help underwrite the naval officer's daring attempt to become the first to fly over the North Pole. Of course, the idea was to do it in a Ford Tri-Motor. But the factory fire precluded that from happening.

Instead, Byrd down-selected one of Anthony Fokker's fabric-covered tri-motored transports. In deference to Edsel's considerable financial backing, the aircraft was named the *Josephine Ford* after Edsel's three-year-old daughter. A controversy has simmered over the years as to whether Byrd's navigation succeeded in steering the plane over the North Pole, but it is undeniable that the exploratory flight grabbed the public's attention, making it seem that no corner of the planet was beyond the reach of air explorers.

Byrd's next self-chosen challenge was to do the same thing on the other end of the globe. With even more support from Edsel, a specially equipped Ford Tri-Motor was provided for the bold mission. The aircraft was named the *Floyd Bennett* in memory of the pilot of the Arctic adventure, who Byrd revered and who had tragically lost his life trying to save others in 1928.

In November 1929, Byrd overflew the South Pole with pilot Bernt Balchen at the controls. It was a triumph that, combined with the earlier Arctic journey, catapulted the expedition organizer into the ranks of the world's greatest explorers. Unfortunately, the aircraft had to be abandoned on the frigid ice floes of Antarctica following the historic flight. In 1935 Byrd returned to fetch the stranded flying machine.

Byrd found the marooned Tri-Motor in generally good condition, perhaps because it was encased in a protective layer of snow and ice. Upon its delivery back to the United States, the *Floyd Bennett* was restored to like-new condition. It rests now in the Henry Ford Museum in Dearborn, not far from where it was manufactured.

Another prominent aviator had a memorable flight in a Tri-Motor a few years earlier. On August 11, 1927, fresh from his celebrated solo transatlantic flight in May, Charles Lindbergh came to Dearborn in the *Spirit of St. Louis*. Henry and Edsel Ford invited him to fly one of their newly built Tri-Motors. Still wearing his leather flying helmet, with goggles pushed up to his forehead, the famous pilot consented.

Lindbergh then helped the family patriarch board the airliner bearing the Ford logo. Other passengers included the company's chief engineer, William B. Mayo; the Tri-Motor's godfather, William B. Stout; commander of nearby Selfridge Field, Major Thomas Lanphier; and several newspaper journalists. Assisting Lindbergh at the controls was the company's chief pilot, Harry Brooks.

The celebrity-laden Tri-Motor leveled off at three thousand feet and spent an hour passing over landmarks of note—Detroit, the urban oasis of Belle Isle, and the sprawling industrial complex built by Henry Ford on the banks of the River Rouge. At one point, Lindbergh got up, left the flying to Brooks, and joined the distinguished passengers seated in the cabin. Ford queried Lindbergh about the plane's altitude and seemed genuinely happy to be aloft for only the second time in his life. (Lindbergh had earlier treated Ford to a short hop in the cramped cabin of the *Spirit of St. Louis*.)

When the Tri-Motor landed and rolled to a stop, Ford was heard to say: "I wouldn't mind taking a spin every day. It's like going on a picnic." Despite the high praise, the businessman who did so much to advance aviation never flew again.

An improved version of the Tri-Motor was introduced in July 1928. The 5-AT was more powerful, faster, and bigger than its predecessor. This model was popular among commercial operators and ended up outselling the 4-AT by forty-one units. Indeed, in 1929, the first full year of 5-AT production, Ford sold more Tri-Motors than in any other year.

The output generated by the 5-AT's three engines jumped to 1,300-horsepower. Cruise speed increased to 112 miles per hour and top speed to 135 miles per hour. The new airliner was three and a half feet longer and weighed a thousand pounds more with a payload capacity almost double the prior model. Passenger seating capacity went from twelve to fourteen.

The price for these improvements was steep. Buyers had to pay $65,000, a third more than the prior model. Pratt & Whitney, the engine supplier, bought the first one.

Other purchasers quick to snap up units of the new airliner included Robertson Aircraft, Cia Mexicana de Avacion, Pan American Airways, Maddux Air Lines, and Stout Air Services (the fledgling airline started by the originator of the family of metal planes). Notably, Transcontinental Air Transport, recently started by Wall Streeter Clement M. Keys (who had previously established the shuttle carrier National Air Transport), became the largest purchaser of 5-ATs. The idea was to offer the first transcontinental airline service, albeit with night transportation provided by train. Two days by air and two nights by rail would get the passenger from one coast to the other.

To give credibility to the promotion, Keys hired Charles Lindbergh as the face of the airline. Lindbergh threw himself into the job and helped set up the routing and assured adequate weather and navigational resources. The Pennsylvania Central and Santa Fe Companies were brought into the mix to provide the night-time rail service.

The newly organized airline bought ten 5-ATs in what was the largest airliner purchase up to that time. TAT soon merged with Maddux and then with Western Air Express to form Transcontinental & Western Air, which evolved into industry giant Trans World Airlines or TWA. In its early years, the company was nicknamed the "Lindbergh Line" for the foundational role played by the famed aviator.

Just as Ford was nearing its commercial aviation zenith, tragedy struck. Henry Ford's dream of making flight accessible to the common man, as he had done for ground transportation by putting a Model T in thousands of home garages, came to a crushing halt. On February 25, 1928, Ford test pilot Harry Brooks was at the controls of this dream plane, the Ford Flivver, and careened into the Atlantic Ocean off the Florida coast about two hundred miles north of Miami, in an attempt to set a light-plane distance record from the Ford Airport in Dearborn.

The Flivver was a light single-engine, open-cockpit monoplane. Though economical, easy to maintain, maneuverable, and appealing for its clean lines that represented a break from the then common biplane configuration, it is questionable that it ever would have become the plane of the masses. After the fatal accident, in which the wreckage was recovered without Brooks's remains being found, Henry Ford is said to have lost much of his enthusiasm for his company's fling into aviation. Brooks was the son of one of Ford's close friends and Ford looked on the twenty-five-year-old pilot as if he were his own son.

Some who knew Ford said that he was ready to pull the plug on his aviation activities in any case for the competition was heating up, but others suggested that the sudden loss of Brooks constituted the deciding factor. No more Flivvers were built. Despite a brief rekindling of the plane-for-the-masses concept in the mid-1930s, Ford's pursuit of commercial aviation, whether airliners or personal planes, was about to wane.

The next aircraft being readied in the Ford line of commercial transports was the largest ever. The 14-AT was an attempt to scale up the 5-AT's payload and performance. Designed to carry thirty-two passengers in a level of comfort unimaginable up to that point in time, this metal plane measured over eighty feet long and had a wingspan in excess of a hundred feet. Somehow three Hispano-Suiza liquid-cooled engines, including one mounted clumsily in a protruding nacelle high above the wing's center section, were to lift the massive airliner off the ground.

Looking like a gigantic praying mantis, the awkward prototype could hardly replicate the insect's agility. In fact, after one failed attempt to get airborne, the 14-AT was grounded. The latest Ford model was obsolete at its inception, similar to the 3-AT, which had been too tied to past concepts to be viable in the face of competitors' forthcoming aircraft. During the early 1930s Lockheed, Boeing, and Douglas ushered in sleek new designs that advanced the state of the art.

If this were not enough, German aircraft designer Dr. Hugo Junkers had taken umbrage over what he perceived as Stout's and Ford's encroachment on his innovations involving the use of metal construction and the cantilevered wing. Junkers had succeeded in getting some European courts to side with him. However, his claims failed to recognize that the Americans had arrived independently at their aeronautical solutions.

Ford had incurred losses of $10.3 million from the start of its aviation investments in 1926 through 1932. Tri-Motor sales had dried up to virtually nothing by then. The Great Depression was underway, disposable income for airline tickets had become scarce, and the main business of selling cars required more of the executives' attention. Pan American Airways took delivery of the last Tri-Motor in July 1933.

From 1926 to 1933, a total of 199 Ford Tri-Motors were built. Though the number was relatively small, these planes were the first airliners to be mass produced. Henry Ford had based civil air transport manufacture on his famous automobile production techniques, which emphasized organizing resources and labor into repeatable operations in the assembly process to achieve consistency with each unit. The Tri-Motor actually shared several parts with the company's automobiles, including the Johnson bar brake lever, the door handle, and ashtrays.

The all-metal airliner represented a step up in existing manufacturing methods and commercial passenger service. The fact that it came from the same industrial empire that put the country on wheels only helped to solidify public acceptance. Although the entry into the emerging world of flight was not financially rewarding for the auto magnate, Henry Ford's fixation on exactitude and fetish for safety added immeasurably to the reputation of commercial aviation.

During and following World War II, many airports opened to handle burgeoning aircraft production and expanded air traffic. These new airports included Ford's sprawling Willow Run Airport in Ypsilanti, Michigan, which was initially devoted to the manufacture of desperately needed warplanes, notably the B-24 Liberator, which Ford built under license during the war. But the Ford Airport in Dearborn had become aviation's stepchild. In 1946 the airship mooring mast, which had been used only twice, was removed from the airport's grounds, eliminating a landmark that had symbolized the Ford commitment to aviation. The next year, Ford transferred its flight operations to a larger commercial airport in the area, which ended the historic airport's flight operations altogether.

In 2003, upon the company's centennial celebration, several antique planes received clearance to land on the Ford property in Dearborn to celebrate Ford's contributions to aviation. The aircraft touched down on the automotive test tracks where the runways once dominated the landscape. For the occasion, three restored Tri-Motors returned to their origination point.

•••

The dream of barnstorming the country in a Ford Tri-Motor, which first materialized during the Golden Age of Flight and returned at other times in fits and starts, refuses to die. The airliner made out of corrugated duralumin, its three round engines clattering over public squares and church steeples, rousing townsfolk to look skyward and gather at local airfields to experience old-time flying, has become the centerpiece of a glorious contagion. No longer spearheaded by individual entrepreneurs trying to make a business of it, now a well-funded nonprofit group oversees an operation that marshals more than forty eager volunteers for the task every flying season.

Starting each spring, the highly motivated volunteers with the Experimental Aircraft Association set out in the organization's Tri-Motor from the organization's base in Oshkosh, Wisconsin. Their mission is to share this piece of living aviation history throughout Midwest communities and beyond, selling rides to adults for seventy-five dollars and to children for fifty dollars. Flights last ten to twelve minutes, but may resonate for a lifetime.

The EAA's Tri-Motor was the 146th to roll off the Dearborn production line. First flight occurred on August 21, 1929. Soon after it went into revenue service for Pitcairn Aviation's passenger division, Eastern Air Transport, in whose colors the plane has been decorated.

Before the airliner ended up in the caring hands of EAA volunteers, it made the rounds, touching virtually every facet of aviation in a manifestation of its amazing versatility. It saw service with Compania Nacional Cubana de Aviacion Curtiss in Cuba and later with the Dominican Republic's air force. By the 1950s, it was back in the United States serving commercial interests as an agricultural applicator. At that time, its 300-horsepower Wright radials were swapped out for 450-horsepower Pratt & Whitney R-985 Wasp Juniors.

From spraying crops in Arizona it went on to fight forest fires in Idaho, where on one mission the airplane is reported to have saved several firefighters otherwise doomed by an enveloping flash fire. Further modifications enabled its use as a platform for smoke jumpers, the firefighters who parachute into the vicinity of raging wildfires to snuff them out. There was one last stint as an aerial sprayer, servicing farms out of Ottawa, Kansas.

In the mid-1960s, the airplane entered a new phase. It was featured in the 1965 Jerry Lewis comedy *The Family Jewels*. Afterwards, pilots Dale Glenn and Chuck LeMaster used it to barnstorm, selling rides as others had done with different Tri-Motors in years past. Regrettably, on June 16, 1973, the adventure came to a sudden end at a fly-in at a small Wisconsin airport not far from EAA's home base. A violent thunderstorm's tornadic winds tore the airplane from its tie-down moorings and flipped the metal airliner on its back, breaking it in two. It was considered a total loss and would have been scrapped at a junkyard except for the affection for old aircraft of Paul Poberezny, the EAA's founder, who happened to be in attendance.

Ownership was transferred to the EAA a month after the accident. The restoration to flying status took more than twelve years. Since flying again in 1985, the airplane has introduced thousands of people to Golden Age flying. In the 2003 reenactment of barnstorming in the days of the Ford Reliability Tours, this Tri-Motor was one of the restored models that landed on Ford property in Dearborn. Five years later, the airplane's silver wings made it back onto the silver screen with a role in the Johnny Depp movie *Public Enemies*.

One of only a handful still flying, this Tri-Motor is maintained in immaculate condition. During its extended off-season in 2015/2016, it underwent a complete makeover to the point that one of the volunteers who keeps it flying declared, without exaggeration, "We have the finest Tri-Motor ever." As the antique set out on its yearly barnstorming tour in May, another volunteer predicted, "It's going to outlast all of us!"

CHAPTER 7

A Superb Combination of Beauty and Performance: The Immortal DC-3

Well, I have a couple thousand hours in the Douglas C-47 transport, the air force version of the DC-3 airliner. And they credit me with 140 combat hours in it, most memorable by being at Da Nang in Vietnam during a rocket attack. I recall dropping rabies medicine to a ship at sea—a sailor's monkey bit him, and he threw it overboard, then realized he didn't know if it had rabies or not. It's memorable to be in a C-47 in weather, with rainwater running in behind the windshield and down your arms and legs; or in icing, where you can look out and see a couple of inches of ice building up, then having the deicers inflate and break off the chunks, which the props sling into the fuselage like machine guns.

Perhaps the scariest thing is being a C-47 instructor pilot, working with ex-B-52 bomber pilots who have never flown a taildragger, have no experience with handling piston-engine throttles, etc. I've had a couple of them come close to killing me on takeoff and perhaps half a dozen on landing. They shove the throttle around, wrestle with the controls. No idea whatever about making a smooth wheel- or three-point landing. You want to be very careful stalling the C-47—don't do anything fancy such as having wheels or flaps down if you attempt a full stall.

I remember coming back to Dayton in terrible weather—ice, snow, thunderstorms, etc.—with a smart aleck as a copilot. He wasn't checked out in the airplane and I was an instructor pilot. He bitched and moaned the whole time. We got back to Wright Field (still landing there in those days) and I took the C-47 down, bucking and kicking in the weather, and made one of those incredible landings when you cannot tell when the tail wheel and the mains touch down; it was like velvet. The passengers broke into spontaneous applause, and the smart-aleck copilot said: "Well, clutch player, eh?"

Absolute confidence—that's what you had in the C-47. It was going to get you there and safely. But it wasn't an airplane you could be careless with or ignore—it could bite. Long after we're past the age of flying, they will still be debating airplanes, and the DC-3 / C-47 will always be in the running for the title of "the best."

•••

When Donald W. Douglas looked back over his prodigious career as one of the early giants in the aviation industry, he acknowledged that his endeavor to build airplanes was a business, hastening to add: "But it was more than that. It was an adventure." In 1920, with his wife's savings of $2,000 and his own savings of $1,000, he left his secure job as the chief engineer at Glenn L. Martin's company in Cleveland, Ohio, and set out to start his own in Southern California where the weather would be more conducive.

It was a bold move for a twenty-eight-year-old with a wife and two children to support. No financial institution would back the budding aviation entrepreneur, for in the post–World War I environment, manufacturers were reeling from the government's cutback in airplane orders. Through a friend who had worked in public relations at Martin and who had become a sports editor at the *Los Angeles Times*, Douglas found the necessary financing to launch his company.

David R. Davis, a millionaire who wanted an airplane that could be the first to fly nonstop across America, put up the money. The investment was for the one-off design only. And, there was another catch: The resulting entity was the Davis-Douglas Aircraft Company. Regardless of the limitations, the infusion of cash got Douglas started.

Five of Douglas's former colleagues at Martin were lured to join the new company. When they arrived as a group on their first day at their new employer, it looked like someone had either sorely misled them or played a practical joke on them because the given address on Pico Boulevard in

Los Angeles was a barbershop. After milling around, they discovered a rear entrance with the new company's name on a sign. The company that would eventually produce tens of thousands of transports and warplanes got its start in an obscure rented space behind that barbershop.

Douglas knew from childhood that aviation would figure in his future. The bug bit when his parents took him to the Smithsonian Institution, which displayed engines of Samuel Langley's ill-fated flying machine. Sharing an almost equal affection for the sea as the sky, Douglas entered the US Naval Academy. With a paucity of aviation-related courses, he decided to resign as a midshipman and try the Massachusetts Institute of Technology instead.

He came under the tutelage of Jerome C. Hunsaker, a pioneering academician and naval reservist who had graduated first in his class at the Naval Academy and subsequently received graduate degrees from MIT. Hunsaker established MIT's aeronautical engineering curriculum and developed the first modern wind tunnel in the United States. The relationship between these two men would, in time, bear dividends for both.

In the meantime, Douglas was busy designing the aircraft for the transcontinental flight. Called the Cloudster, it was a plump biplane accommodating the heavy fuel load for the planned aerial odyssey. On June 27, 1921, the aircraft managed to get airborne on its west-to-east track. Upon reaching El Paso, Texas, the 400-horsepower Liberty engine gave out. An emergency landing was safely executed, but the honor of being first to span the nation without stopping went to army aviators flying a Fokker monoplane.

With the race lost, Davis had no reason to retain his interest in the company. He sold out and his name was removed from the corporate marquis. Even though the Cloudster was not successful in its highly specialized objective, the navy took a liking to a torpedo design Douglas had based on the one-of-a-kind airplane. The navy placed orders for it, and as hoped, Donald Douglas's aviation gamble was finally making its mark.

Needing more production space, Douglas relocated to a voluminous abandoned movie studio on Wilshire Boulevard in Santa Monica in 1922.

A pasture out back substituted as the company's airfield. Almost from the beginning, this improvised airfield proved inadequate and the company's new planes were trucked for testing several blocks south to Clover Field (later Santa Monica Municipal Airport). In 1928 the company went public and used a portion of the proceeds to establish its headquarters at the airport.

Within a decade of its founding, the Douglas Aircraft Company had built a solid reputation. The design talent at the drafting tables and the vision of the founder meant that the company was poised for its biggest success ever. Yet, by the early 1930s, the patriarch recognized the need to diversify his company's product lines; the Depression raged and military budgets would be subject to drawdowns.

The Ford Tri-Motor was on the way out and intimations of the next-generation of all-metal, multiengine passenger planes floated about the industry, with Boeing set to deliver its new ten-seat twin-engine Model 247 to United Air Lines. Not wanting to be left behind, Transcontinental & Western Air (later to become Trans World Airlines or TWA) circulated a letter with specifications for an even higher-performing airliner. Dated August 2, 1932, and signed by Jack Frye, the airline's vice president of operations, the letter went to a half dozen manufacturers, including Douglas, seeking their proposals.

In retrospect, Douglas described the letter as "the birth certificate of the modern airliner." He convened his senior staff to ponder the question of whether to respond substantively. He weighed the mostly positive input and decided to submit a proposal for what became the first in the Douglas Commercial ("DC") family of airliners.

Point man on the design was Arthur E. Raymond, a young engineer who had had a circuitous journey to his position at Douglas Aircraft. In 1921 Raymond graduated with honors from Harvard and then earned a master's degree in aeronautical engineering at MIT. One day in 1925 he wandered into the converted movie studio in Santa Monica looking for work. Douglas was his company of choice, in large part because the year before, its hefty biplanes, called the Douglas World Cruisers, had been the first aircraft to circumnavigate the globe in a highly publicized six-month army expedition that originated at Clover Field.

Raymond persisted day after day until the company offered him a manual laborer's job on the shop floor. It was not exactly what he was looking for, but it would be a start at the company he had his heart set on. For the superbly credentialed aeronautical engineer, anything in aviation would be preferable to working at the Raymond Hotel, his wealthy father's property in Pasadena.

Coincidentally, within a few weeks Douglas sent a letter to his old professor at MIT, Jerome Hunsaker, asking if he knew someone able to fill an open aerodynamics engineering slot. A telegram soon arrived advising that an ideal candidate, named Arthur Raymond, was already at the company. Without knowing it until then, Douglas already had the man he was looking for.

In short order, Raymond went from the shop floor to the engineering offices, the fastest promotion up the ladder before or since. Ten years later, after James H. "Dutch" Kindelberger vacated the top engineering post to head up North American Aviation, Raymond would become the company's chief engineer as it ventured boldly into the civil aviation marketplace. Of his time developing the DC-3, Raymond wrote: "It was a lot of fun to work for Douglas in those days. The DC-3 was virtually unchallenged, for we had such a head start that nobody else could catch up. We knew each other and our customers intimately. We were not overburdened by organization. But best of all, we were proud of our boss and felt that he was proud of us."

According to Donald Douglas's biographer, Wilbur H. Morrison, one reason for the success of the company was the founder's "uncompromising standards." In what today would qualify as a corporate mission statement, the company's founder laid out his guiding principles via advertising copy distributed in 1921: "Those who know most of superfine quality and workmanship find the cost of quality a small item when measured in terms of satisfactory performance. Quality is the basic feature of all successful aircraft."

In discussing the founder's commitment to quality workmanship, Morrison pointed out that "no one who ever worked for him was allowed to forget it." It was not lost on company employees that their boss's last name was embossed on the data plates bolted to every plane that rolled off the assembly lines. There was a person behind the name, and through the force of his demanding personality he lent a special meaning to it.

Another reason for the rise of the company amid intense competition and challenging economic times could be traced to the founder's refusal to let aloofness seep into his relationships with employees. Staying connected to the activities on the shop floor, maintaining the respect of machinists and welders by listening to them, being open to the ideas that might percolate from the hands-on assemblers remained an unwavering constant through his tenure. About the early days when it was still possible for the founder to know his employees by name, Morrison wrote: "The atmosphere at the Douglas plant was so informal that, if one had a problem, he just went up to Douglas and told him about it."

This culture of inviting employees to speak up and share their thoughts animated staff discussions on the design prompted by Jack Frye's letter. The new airplane, to be designated the DC-1, would be an all-aluminum alloy twin-engine configuration with a standup passenger cabin and retractable landing gear. The wing would draw on the taper in some of Jack Northrop's recent cantilevered designs and the center section would be an integral part of the fuselage with outboard sections bolted on.

Raymond spent considerable time in the airline's offices in both New York and Kansas City clarifying technical matters. The biggest question mark was the feasibility of single-engine flight at every segment of the airline's cross-country route, especially at the highest elevation in New Mexico known for its summertime temperatures that could exceed 90 degrees Fahrenheit. The airline had incorporated single-engine operation into its specifications for safety's sake.

Tension ran high in long-distance phone conversations between Donald Douglas and Arthur Raymond as the latter attempted to assure the airline that the new design could satisfy the single-engine requirement over the mountainous American Southwest. But could it really, Douglas wanted to know over the phone. Raymond, who had been meeting in New York with Frye and Charles Lindbergh, the newly hired high-profile consultant to the airline, is reported to have confided, "I sure did some fast slide ruling." In the end, Raymond expressed "90 percent" certainty to his boss, who considered that level of confidence from his fellow engineer to be bankable.

During construction of the DC-1, decisions were made to install the new Wright Cyclone air-cooled engines with new three-bladed Hamilton-Standard variable-pitch propellers. The aircraft had a sound-proofed and heated cabin. It was ready for its maiden flight on June 22, 1933, less than a year from contract signing.

In keeping with the founder's regard for his employees and bolstering of their morale, Douglas called for the flight test to occur at the lunch hour when the hundreds of plant workers could come out and watch their handiwork rise from the Clover Field runway. According to Morrison, before the flight Douglas conferred with his chief test pilot, Carl Cover. When asked if the plane was ready, a smiling Cover said: "She's born to fly, and belongs up there with the angels." When the DC-1 lifted off, Douglas had to turn away from Raymond to hide his tears.

The euphoria quickly turned to alarm. Every time the new Douglas airliner tried to climb, its engines quit. But when it pointed down, the engines came back to life. Cover skillfully returned the airplane to the airport and subsequent inspection revealed that the carburetors had been installed backwards. The problem was fixed and the DC-1 continued its flight test program, which discovered the need for more tail surface area.

The DC-1, which was delivered to TWA in December 1933, raised the bar for commercial air transportation. But it was obvious to both the manufacturer and the airline that this airplane, great as it was, could be made even better. A lengthened fuselage would add seats and that would mean more passenger revenue.

No more DC-1s were built. Instead, work began on the enlarged airliner, the DC-2. It would have fourteen seats (two more than the DC-1), an automated landing gear system, power brakes, and improved instrumentation, including an autopilot. Initially TWA committed to twenty-five DC-2s. The first was delivered on May 14, 1934.

Two and a half months later, TWA entered DC-2s in its transcontinental service with one it had labeled the *Sky Chief*. It left the East Coast in the late afternoon and arrived on the West Coast the next morning with three stops along the way. New long-distance speed records were set.

The DC-2 was deemed the greatest aviation achievement of the year, and Donald Douglas received the annual Robert J. Collier Trophy on behalf of his company's workforce at a White House ceremony in 1935. That year, another airline executive contacted Douglas for an even bigger passenger plane. Cyrus R. Smith, the president of American Airlines, wanted to quickly update his fleet, which consisted of obsolescent Ford Tri-Motors and Curtiss Condors.

Smith believed that he had to outdo his competitors, TWA and United. They had recently converted to the Douglas DC-2 and the Boeing 247, respectively, so in Smith's view, American would need to offer its passengers something not yet available to the other airlines. His idea was to offer sleeping berths in greater comfort and quantity than was possible in American's Condors.

American's engineering vice president, William Littlewood, had overseen preliminary design work for an enhanced DC-2 to accommodate the berths. Arthur Raymond was brought into the discussions and explored the idea's viability. Things were brought to a head when Smith called Donald Douglas to advocate for the new airliner. Douglas was reluctant because the DC-2, which at the time was halfway through its production run, commanded so much of the company's attention, and a new design with its associated tooling would be expensive.

Another factor in the eyes of the Old Man, as some now referred to the company's founder, was the implausibility of sleeper planes. Berths did not make sense to him because, in his view, they would not be popular with passengers nor be as economical as seats. Nevertheless, Smith persisted in his phone call which lasted a few hours and resulted in a long-distance tab of more than $300.

Despite his reservations, Douglas consented to proceed with the DST (Douglas Sleeper Transport). In the end, only seven DSTs were delivered. Douglas's intuition was right: Replacing the fourteen double-wide seats that converted into sleeping berths with a seats-only configuration that accommodated twenty-one passengers proved more practical. Through this unpremeditated process, the legendary DC-3 was born. The aircraft dominated prewar commercial air traffic and became indispensable as a military transport during World War II.

Using the DC-2 as the basis for the DST, the new plane was slightly more than thirty inches longer and twenty-six inches wider. It was ready for its first airborne trek on December 17, 1935, the thirty-second anniversary of the Wright brothers' famous first flight. To the eternal disappointment of aviation historians, no photograph appears to have been taken to memorialize the occasion. The Santa Monica plant was humming right along and the new plane was seen then as an extrapolation of the existing string of airliners.

The press was not called out to the airport nor did the company's executives bother to stop work and observe the takeoff. Even the flight crew, led by Carl Cover, considered the initial test hop to be nothing special. The people hatching this soon-to-be-dominant transport were simply too close to the trees to see the forest. The DST rose from Clover Field at 3:00 p.m. and returned after an hour and a half of uneventful flying, indicative of the quiet excellence that would characterize countless flights of the workhorse in the years to come.

Nine months later, on September 18, 1936, the DST initiated the upgraded American Airlines Skysleeper service. Although, as mentioned, the DST was soon superseded by the DC-3, in either configuration the airliner upped cruise speed to 200 miles per hour, which when combined with the aircraft's range, made transcontinental flight possible with just two stops. The miracle of the evolved Douglas design was that it could carry a third more payload than any other competing airliner for half the operating cost.

The DC-3 became the first profitable passenger-carrying airliner, not reliant on mail contracts to pay its way. Among domestic carriers, the next to buy the DC-3 after launch customer American Airlines were Eastern and United in 1937, followed by TWA and Western in 1938. Many others, including Braniff, Northwest, Pennsylvania Central, and Delta, added the type to their fleets in the years before America's entry into World War II.

Within three years of its introduction, the DC-3 accounted for 95 percent of all commercial air traffic in the United States. From commencement of service to the Japanese attack on Pearl Harbor, the DC-3 increased domestic revenue passenger miles more than fivefold. Of the 322 aircraft operated by the country's airlines in December 1941, 260 were DC-3s.

At the prewar peak, thirty foreign airlines operated the DC-3. On the eve of war, the plane's scheduled flights represented 90 percent of international air traffic. Interestingly, the first foreign airline to buy the DC-3 was KLM, the Dutch company that had entered the DC-2 in the London-to-Melbourne Air Race.

The Army Air Corps had a keen interest in the Douglas series of transports. Such a groundbreaking airliner obviously had tremendous utility as a troop transport and cargo plane. The trouble was sluggish funding in the prewar years, given the country's isolationist temperament.

During DC-2 production, the air corps bought small numbers of the type and modified them with the designations C-33 and C-39. The first DC-3 variant for the air corps was delivered in 1939. It was decked out in classic prewar markings which included wings decorated with blue roundels containing a white star marked by a solid red circle in the middle and the rudder emblazoned in an alternating red-and-white candy stripe pattern.

Designated the C-41A and configured for command transport, this model was initially assigned for the use of Secretary of War Henry Stimson. The aircraft had 1,200-horsepower fourteen-cylinder Pratt & Whitney Twin Wasp R-1830 engines, an upgrade from the DC-3's 1,000-horsepower nine-cylinder Wright Cyclone SGR-1820 engines. Other modifications included military instruments and communications equipment.

Orders picked up in 1940 and again in 1941 as the likelihood of war escalated. The army issued contracts for the C-47 and C-47A, which had a two-panel cargo door on the port side of the fuselage and a reinforced floor. Wingspan was lengthened by six inches and an astrodome was installed behind the flight deck for purposes of enabling navigation to exotic locations. The army named its new transport the Skytrain, but more often it was called the Gooney Bird.

The aircraft typically had a crew consisting of pilot, copilot, and radio operator. Payload could be up to six thousand pounds of cargo or twenty-eight fully equipped paratroopers arrayed in folding canvas seats on both sides of the cabin. It was also possible to outfit the transport as a flying ambulance with fourteen stretchers and positions for three medical attendants.

Over half the total military variants were the C-47As. These were built at new Douglas plants in Long Beach and Oklahoma City. Erected expressly to cope with the dramatically increased wartime demand, Donald Douglas had to plead his case for the Long Beach location since the authorities wanted new plants to be away from the West Coast out of fear of attack. Douglas argued that the skilled labor and myriad aviation parts suppliers in Southern California made it only logical to open a new plant in the area. The aircraft designation generally included the suffix "DL" or "DK," denoting the production venue as the Long Beach plant or the Oklahoma City plant, respectively.

The C-47B was tweaked for high-altitude operations, most notably for over-the-Hump missions in the China-Burma-India theater. These transports were equipped with engines that incorporated two-stage blowers. Unfortunately, the engine modification was not successful and the blowers were removed. This caused the aircraft to be redesignated the C-47D.

A number of the D models lived on and saw continued military service into the 1960s, first as navigational systems testing aircraft and then as gunships. The gunship model gained notoriety during the Vietnam War. Designated AC-47D (with the "A" for Attack) and nicknamed *Puff the Magic Dragon*, the type was generally outfitted with three 7.62-mm Miniguns on the port side. The idea was to lay down sustained fire on enemy positions that would otherwise escape unscathed by ordnance dropped in a strike fighter's traditional bomb run.

The basic C-47 was considered a good platform for the gunship mission because of its altitude and speed envelope. Over time, the workhorse turned warhorse proved vulnerable to ground fire. However, the concept was proven and the US Air Force has continued to deploy evolved gunships with extraordinarily sophisticated sensor systems and armaments in a fleet of highly modified C-130s, which like the C-47s, were initially designed as transports.

Another variant was the C-53 Skytrooper, which was made to haul up to twenty-eight people in fixed metal seats and to tow a troop- or weapons-carrying glider by means of a towing cleat cutout in the tail section. The last DC-3 derivative to be built for the army air force was the

C-117A, a staff transport that utilized a civilian-style seating arrangement to accommodate twenty-one passengers. It is important to note that the US Navy and Marine Corps operated over five hundred DC-3 derivatives under the designation R4D in a variety of rolls including personnel/staff transport, polar operations, radar countermeasures, air-sea warfare training, and navigation training.

Before production could be ramped up to meet the military's needs, the army impressed into service about a third of the domestic civilian fleet of DC-3s. These were generally leased from the airlines, but not in all cases. Each of these civilian airliners was given a distinct army designation from C-48 to C-68, based on the Douglas specification number, adding immensely to the "alphabet soup" of the DC-3s or their derivatives used by the military.

The British Royal Air Force, Royal Canadian Air Force, and Royal Australian Air Force operated DC-3 derivatives during World War II. These Commonwealth air forces uniformly referred to the aircraft as the "Dakota." The name was drawn from the acronym formed by the first letters of Douglas Aircraft Company Transport Aircraft (DACoTA). In abbreviated usage, the aircraft was called the "Dak."

Soviet manufacturing rights were obtained before the war. During the war, production, which had begun in Moscow, continued in Tashkent. The original Soviet designation of PS-84 was changed to Lisunov Li-2. It is not clear how many of these models were built, but estimates range from two thousand to nearly five thousand.

In an extreme case of unintended consequences, manufacturing rights were also bequeathed before the war to Japan. Showa Hikoki Kogyo assembled 416 for the Japanese navy. These aircraft were designated the L2D. Nakajima Hikoki built another seventy-one. The total of 487 DC-3 derivatives served as "the standard wartime transport aircraft of the Japanese Navy." Allies knew the type by its code name, *Tabby*. Regrettably, the extensive use of the type in the Pacific theater caused misidentification among the Allies with sometimes fatal consequences.

Altogether, Douglas Aircraft built 10,654 civilian DC-3s and their military variants. Aftermarket modifications have included luxury interiors for corporate conversions and turboprop upgrades to increase the plane's freight capacity. A number have been beautifully restored in World War II markings and elicit outpourings of emotion by aged veterans who flew them fresh out of the factory.

The talented and close-knit Douglas engineers who conceived the DC-3 had no way of knowing back in the midst of the Depression that their creation in modified form would become the ubiquitous Allied transport of the war. The aircraft served in all theaters, providing timely delivery of men and materiel. Arguably, its finest hour came on June 6, 1944, when the Allies staged their daring cross-channel invasion to liberate continental Europe.

More than a thousand C-47s and related variants are reported to have participated in D-Day operations, dropping paratroopers and towing troop-laden gliders into the field of battle. The transports were painted in the blanket scheme ordered by General Dwight Eisenhower, the Supreme Allied Commander. Whether a fighter or bomber or transport, all friendly aircraft had to have alternating black-and-white stripes applied to wings and fuselage as a means of identification in skies that would be overflowing with more aircraft than at any one time in the course of history.

After the war Eisenhower posited that the majority of senior officers under his command considered the militarized version of the DC-3 to be one of four pieces of equipment most important to winning the war in Africa and Europe. The others were said to be the bulldozer, the Jeep, and the two-and-a-half-ton truck. Eisenhower went on to note: "Curiously, none of these is designed for combat."

In 1948 the Communist blockade of West Berlin prompted Operation Vittles, the aerial resupply of the city's Western zones in what became known as the Berlin Airlift. The first transports to fly missions were C-47s. The valiant effort to provide the affected Berliners with necessities for daily survival had to be augmented by the C-47's big brother, the four-engine Douglas C-54. With a cargo capacity of three-and-a-half tons, the C-47 simply lacked the ability to do the job by itself; newer and larger transports were required to step up the pace of the humanitarian program. But the C-47's contribution helped and eventually the Soviets relented in what was a victory for the West in the emergent Cold War.

The DC-3 won't die. The airplane has found dozens of uses to retain its viability. Of the roughly four hundred still being flown worldwide, some carry skydivers, others fly tourists to remote parts of the African outback, a few still deliver freight, while yet more are flyable museum pieces dropping in at air shows to spread the type's rich history.

The DC-3 has outlasted most of the airliners and cargo planes that entered service after it started plying routes for American Airlines in 1936. That longevity speaks volumes about the plane's efficiency and durability, qualities that have been hard to match in the many years since the trend-setting airliner launched. Rarely is an airplane at once a utilitarian and aesthetic success, but Donald Douglas and his colleagues managed to pull it off with this fine-tuned machine.

The people flying the DC-3 in any of its multitudinous iterations know that their ship's most salient quality, the feature that explains its adoration, is its propensity to pull through. Like the affirming personality of Donald Douglas, who said, "We can do it," when asked if the aircraft industry could meet the president's ambitious prewar call for fifty thousand planes a year, the product emitted from the factory radiated the can-do spirit. I don't think it is going too far to say that the great industrialist's attitude, his inclination and conviction, were minted into the stressed aluminum skin of the airplane bearing his name.

This artistry and passion that went into the DC-3 are inseparably woven into the airplane's character, its disposition, its mettle. We who have manhandled its yokes, stomped on its toe brakes, and advanced its throttles in good weather and bad, above mountain peaks and the open plains, on life-or-death missions and on daily milk runs, under fire and in gentle winds, know of its over-performing, exceeding expectations, putting out ever so much more than what the specifications state. This is the immortal DC-3, my mistress of the sky, and I love her.

CHAPTER 8

Propliner Extraordinaire: Triple-Finned Connie

During 1938 Lockheed set out to design a game-changing airliner. The impetus was the latest project of the insuperable Douglas Aircraft Company—a forty-two-seat airliner that could potentially control the market for years to come. The many lessons learned and certain key contacts established since Lockheed's forays into the civil market with the Model 10 were to eventually coalesce to bring the long-delayed success.

The new Lockheed design was conceived as a departure from the usual twin-engine airliner. Going by the working title Excalibur, or simply Model 44, it was to represent a leap beyond anything the company had produced. Ambitions would grow, following meetings with prospective airline customers.

Howard Hughes, who only a year before had flown around the world in a twin-engine Lockheed Super Electra and who had recently taken a controlling stake in Transcontinental & Western Air (later renamed Trans World Airlines), and airline president Jack Frye met with senior Lockheed team members in Burbank in June 1939. Hughes and Frye laid out a set of specifications that went beyond those of the Excalibur. At a later meeting at Hughes's palatial home on Muirfield Road in the stately Hancock Park neighborhood of Los Angeles, a Lockheed delegation that included company president Robert Gross, chief engineer Hall Hibbard, and chief research engineer Clarence L. "Kelly" Johnson upped the ante even more with a proposal that focused on the use of huge Wright radial engines then under development for the gargantuan B-29 Superfortress.

Johnson said that TWA's desired airliner "would carry more people farther and faster than ever before, and economically enough to broaden the acceptance of flying as an alternative to train, ship and automobile." The Model 44 Excalibur became the Model 49 Excalibur A. Lockheed plunged into the project, but owing to technical issues and wartime priorities that caused no less than seventeen stops to the program, the aircraft's major production did not occur until after the war. The prolonged gestation period provided extra time to iron out the formidable undertaking's many engineering challenges.

The company's pioneering work on a pressurized cabin really paid off, for it was becoming increasingly obvious that modern airliners would be pressurized to enable flight at higher altitudes where inclement weather might be avoided. Similarly, work on the P-38 fighter translated into advantages on the airliner project. For example, the airliner's wing was essentially a scaled-up P-38 wing, incorporating Fowler flaps. Other features borrowed from the fighter included hydraulically boosted flight controls and tricycle landing gear.

To understand the order of magnitude of change brought by this new airliner over its predecessors, the Constellation—as the plane was named—had more horizontal tail area than the entire wing area of the early Electra designs. The Connie's unusual triple-finned tail was necessitated by the TWA requirement that the plane fit within the airline's existing hangars. Vertical tail surface area was thus spread out laterally rather than carried upward as would have been the case if a single- or even double-fin configuration had been used. Oval-shaped surfaces were adopted as a way to convey Lockheed's heritage going back to the tail surface motif of the Model 14. This identified the plane's lineage, but dated it at the same time.

To the casual observer, the most striking feature of the four-engine propliner, which measured an impressive ninety-five feet in length, was its dolphin-like appearance. Instead of being a simple cylinder with tapering at either end, the airliner's side view revealed a gentle down-up-down-up profile from nose to tail, what some commentators loosely describe as an "S" shape laid lengthwise. This was said to be designer Ward Beman's way to match the fuselage shape to the airflow crossing over it for the most efficiency in flight.

The lowered nose was an effort to reduce the length of the nose gear to maintain its structural integrity. The empennage was swept up to keep the horizontal tail surfaces out of the slipstream. Another benefit of the raised tail section was the reduced chance of inadvertent scraping of the bottoms of the two outboard fins during takeoffs and landings.

Form and function merged in a happy union for what became the Model 049. The aircraft was a rare instance where engineering brilliance rendered a utilitarian object of picturesque quality. Its name, the Constellation, was a less than subtle embrace of the Lockheed penchant for product names drawn from the stars.

The forty-four-seat or twenty-sleeping-berth Connie was powered by a choice of either Wright Double Cyclones (R-3350 series) or Pratt & Whitney Twin Wasps (R-2800 series), both twin-rowed radial engines in the 2,000-horsepower class. Advertised maximum speed was a snappy 360 miles per hour at twenty thousand feet, a performance that eclipsed the DC-3, the airlines' mainstay, and even some fighters. Using a pressure differential of approximately four pounds per square inch, the cabin altitude could be maintained at an equivalent of eight thousand feet.

The new airliner represented a leap in technology that promised to profoundly change perceptions of air travel. The stature of the plane's manufacturer began to rise commensurately in the eyes of the industry. Lockheed's top engineer, Hall Hibbard, was quoted as saying, "Up to that time we were sort of small-time guys, but when we got to the Constellation we had to be big-time guys. . . . We had to be right and we had to be good."

Orders came in from TWA and Pan Am. Each committed to forty of the new aircraft, a promising start to the order book. However, World War II interrupted deliveries; production was diverted to wartime needs. The army air force acquired the first of TWA's order under the designation C-69. Maiden flight occurred on January 9, 1943, with Boeing's highly regarded Edward T. "Eddie" Allen on loan as lead test pilot. Next to him was Lockheed's Milo Burcham. The fifty-minute flight originated at Burbank and went smoothly all the way through landing at Muroc Army Airfield, a remote bombing range and proving grounds north of metropolitan Los Angeles that eventually would become home to the Air Force Flight Test Center and renamed Edwards Air Force Base.

The next year, as testing progressed, Hughes decided to show off the plane that he had fostered. Before he could fly it, a standard checkout by company pilots was necessary. Seasoned test pilot Milo Burcham, flight engineer Dick Stanton, and the ubiquitous Kelly Johnson took Hughes up for his indoctrination in the Constellation.

Only a few thousand feet above the foothills surrounding Burbank after takeoff, Hughes asked for a stall to be demonstrated. Burcham deployed flaps and gear, added a little power, and eased the plane up until it stalled. The new airliner had been designed to be forgiving, so it recovered mannerly. Hughes, who had not yet turned into the notorious eccentric as later captured in a variety of sordid Hollywood depictions, was beginning to show signs of losing his grip.

He insisted on performing a stall himself. With flaps still fully extended, Hughes added full takeoff power and yanked all the way back on the control yoke to the stop. Like a bronco released into the corral, the Connie was soon pointed discomfortingly high and the airspeed indicator bled down literally to zero. The only airflow over the airplane's surfaces came from the prop-wash. Suddenly turned into a lame mule, the big airliner lurched forward, causing Johnson to float to the ceiling.

Johnson, who at that point must have felt much as the designer of the *Titanic* when the ostensibly invincible ship struck the iceberg, shouted out: "Up flaps! Up flaps!" Now pitched in a steep dive with forces building on the flaps and tail, Johnson feared a catastrophic structural failure with not only the potential of an ignominious end to the company's long struggle to bring a state-of-the-art airliner to market but the loss of several lives, including his. Burcham saved the plane by retracting the flaps and pulling it out of its descent.

No one wanted to offend Hughes, who held tremendous leverage over Lockheed through his control of TWA's purse strings. Under the circumstances, the flight continued north over then largely unpopulated desert terrain to Palmdale, where Hughes was to practice takeoffs and landings. Hughes's performance worsened; he veered closer to the control tower upon alighting from the runway with each successive go-round in the landing pattern.

Finally, Johnson had had enough. He ordered Burcham: "Milo, take this thing home." There were awkward stares and silence, but Johnson was firm; he repeated his instruction and Burcham headed back to Burbank. Lockheed executives were angry and alarmed because they thought this insult to Hughes's flying prowess, no matter how justified, would result in the cancellation of the TWA order for Connies.

However, by the next weekend Hughes was back in the cockpit for his checkout. This time the Lockheed flight crew received a special bonus to go up with Hughes. The company's chief flight test engineer, Rudy Thoren, took Johnson's place since Johnson opted never to fly with Hughes again. To everyone's relief, Hughes was in a more reasonable frame of mind and the checkout was satisfactorily completed.

On April 19, 1944, Hughes and a professional crew that included Jack Frye took off from Burbank and landed at Washington National Airport six hours, fifty-seven minutes, and fifty-one seconds later to set a new transcontinental speed record with an average speed of 331 miles per hour. Adding to the flight's noteworthiness was that on the return Hughes stopped at Wright Field in Dayton to pick up Orville Wright, the first person to ever successfully pilot a powered airplane.

Orville's flight aboard the Connie would be the last of his life. It is believed he operated the airliner's controls for a short time. Reportedly, he remarked how far the science of aeronautics had come since his first flight a mere forty-one years earlier. He is said to have pointed out that the Connie's wingspan exceeded the 120-foot length of his 1903 flight by three feet.

Commercial deliveries of the Model 049 began the year the war ended, with both TWA and Pan Am initiating their new Constellations on international routes in February 1946. TWA put the Constellation into transcontinental service the next month, beating flight time of the much slower American and United DC-4s by at least a couple hours. Douglas would begin delivering its pressurized DC-6 late in the year in the reverse role of catch-up.

Of course the military was well aware of the Connie's attributes. In February 1948 a small batch of the postwar Model 749 was ordered for cargo and personnel transport. Most of these were converted to the

VC-121A configuration for VIP use. Specific airframes were assigned to Generals Douglas MacArthur and Dwight Eisenhower. Each put his personal stamp on his transport—MacArthur's was called the *Bataan* (after the disastrous 1942 battle on the Bataan Peninsula, which was avenged by the retaking of the Philippines later in the war) and Eisenhower's went by the name *Columbine* (after the Colorado Blue Columbine, the official flower of the adopted home state of Ike's wife, Mamie).

As president, Eisenhower used a VIP version of the Constellation named *Columbine II*. A later version, designated VC-121E, was dubbed *Columbine III*. It is worth noting that in the early days of presidential aircraft the tail numbers were used for identification purposes by flight crews and air traffic controllers. On a 1953 flight, Ike's first presidential Constellation was transiting New York airspace when ground controllers confused its tail number 8610 with Eastern Airlines flight 8610. The potentially catastrophic mix-up caused the president's pilot, Lieutenant Colonel William G. Draper, to suggest a distinctive call-sign for whatever plane carries the president. Ever since, the call-sign has been "Air Force One."

The first Constellation configured expressly for the civil market of the postwar period was the Model 649. Gross weight increased and other improvements included better soundproofing and air-conditioning. New Wright engines were installed with an increase to 2,500-horsepower. In a break for maintenance crews, the engine cowlings were redesigned for easier access.

The Model 749 was developed for international routes and carried more fuel in outer wing sections. Gross weight was increased to 102,000 pounds with the strengthening of the landing gear. Again TWA was the largest buyer with a smattering going to a couple other US carriers and various foreign airlines.

In one of the more intriguing stories involving the aircraft, a supporter of Israel bought three surplus army air force C-69s in the lead-up to the Jewish state's formal establishment in 1948. Using a Panama corporation as a front for his surreptitious activities, the Connies carried weaponry needed during the War of Independence. Later the planes were refurbished and joined the El Al fleet in scheduled passenger service.

The never-ending competition with Douglas heated up as more and more airlines saw value in the DC-6, especially the DC-6B variant. In response to the market threat, Lockheed produced the Model 1049 Super Constellation. The fuselage was lengthened eighteen feet and five inches. Seating expanded dramatically to accommodate ninety-two passengers, who could enjoy better views through larger rectangular windows. Gross weight grew to 120,000 pounds, but the available engines did not put out the desired power.

With Lockheed's introduction of the Model 1049C, the Super Connie had the engines required to make the aircraft competitive. This model was the first commercial airliner certificated with the newly developed Wright 872TC-18DA-1 Turbo-Compound engines, which employed three turbines to convert the heat from exhaust gases into additional power. Gross weight increased yet again to 133,000 pounds. Cruising speed was a respectable 330 miles per hour.

First flight occurred in February 1953, three months before the DC-7, which had the same engines. On October 19, 1953, TWA initiated the industry's first scheduled nonstop transcontinental service. This much-ballyhooed Ambassador service operated only on the eastbound flights from Los Angeles to New York Idlewild because the prevailing winds allowed an elapsed flight time of just under eight hours, a must to avoid a crew change otherwise mandated by federal regulations. Westbound routes included a stop in Chicago.

Successive models of the Super Connie kept emanating from the factory, reaching their commercial zenith in 1955 with the Model 1049G, the most successful of the line known affectionately as the Super G. The aircraft benefited from 3,400-horsepower Wright Turbo-Cyclone engines, a gross weight of 137,500 pounds, and the option of six hundred-gallon wingtip fuel tanks for longer range. The Super G was competitive with the DC-7B, which entered service the same year. Not surprisingly, TWA purchased the largest quantity of the new Lockheed model.

For all the intense effort and considerable investment to make a mark in the airline business with the Constellation, it has been said that Lockheed would have lost money on the program had it not been for sales of specialized versions of the versatile aircraft to the military. Indeed, during the life of the program, the company sold 346 Connies to the US Navy and US Air Force. These aircraft served as transports, reconnaissance planes, electronic warfare platforms, and in many other roles, including mappers of the planet's magnetic field.

The air force's EC-121 Warning Stars were fitted with vertical dorsal and horizontal ventral radomes for height detection and search, respectively. These aircraft saw extensive use during the Vietnam War, often orbiting outside enemy engagement envelopes as part of Big Eye and then College Eye task forces, providing real-time command and control data streams to the aircraft engaged in combat operations. The Warning Stars presaged modern Airborne Early Warning (AEW) aircraft like Boeing's E-3 Sentry, known as AWACS (for Airborne Warning and Control System).

The quintessential Connie came in the final chapter of the long-running tit for tat propliner competition between Lockheed and Douglas. As was often the case, the new Lockheed model was spurred on by a fresh Douglas variant, in this case the Pan Am-inspired DC-7C known as the Seven Seas. Introduced in 1956, the Seven Seas' wingspan was stretched ten feet which made possible nonstop airline flights across the North Atlantic in either direction.

Lockheed's answer was an entirely new straight-taper, high-aspect ratio wing with a massive 150-foot span mated to the Super Constellation's fuselage. The stunning aircraft that resulted was the Model 1649 Starliner. The last iteration of the Connie was arguably the most aesthetically appealing. It also promised what in any traditional evaluation would have been excellent payback to commercial users. Simply put, it was the ultimate in propeller airliners.

The problem bedeviling the new airliner was that its entry into service on June 1, 1957, came only sixteen months before the Boeing 707 jetliner revolutionized air travel. Illustrated TWA print advertisements from the period show the majestic Connie's wings dominating the page with references to the aircraft being "the largest and most luxurious airliner ever built." In a strained, or some might say desperate, effort to minimize the perception gap between props and jets, those ads referred to the newest Constellation as the "Jetstream."

Jet orders were already outstripping Starliner orders by three to one. A trifling forty-four Starliners were ever sold, TWA taking the largest share with lesser quantities to Air France and Lufthansa. A spectacular airliner had arrived on the scene, the most capable in a distinguished line, only to be usurped by designs that featured the new standard in propulsive technology.

Based strictly on sales, it could be said that the Constellation was inferior to its propeller competition from Douglas. In fact, some observers have gone so far as to call the Connie a marketplace failure. These assessments, taken without context, are far too harsh.

The Lockheed airliner offered high speed, decent reliability, and credible operating economics. Unlike the other offerings in its day, the Connie broke dramatically from convention; the plane's design was an audacious reach for the next level, an exercise in expanding the limits of what was possible. The adoption of emergent technologies and the challenges of forming materials to the unusual shape presented risk that might have been economically cataclysmic elsewhere.

By creating something so unorthodox, people took notice. This gangling leviathan of the sky stood imposingly on the ramp, its gear legs longer than most to allow ground clearance for the especially large diameter propellers. Rather than leaning back on an old-fashioned tail wheel, the new vessel rested perfectly parallel to the surface as if ready at any moment to fire up and sail aloft on its vast outstretched wings. The humpback contour encasing a circular cross-section combined with the traditionalist cleanly curved wingtips and the Electra-era rounded tail fins—all three of them—to elevate the public's air travel expectations.

The Connie's triumph was in its passenger appeal. By being so big and sensational, it offered the idea that ordinary travelers could experience the extraordinary in their long-distance flights. As something so extensively engineered and pleasing to the eye, the Connie instilled a sense that it had to be world class.

Lockheed's ingenious airliner, massive and powerful yet stylish and graceful, projected glamour and excellence during the postwar boom in transcontinental and transatlantic air travel, which contributed to the collective wanderlust. TWA maintained the Constellation on certain of its heavily trafficked routes well into the 1960s, not retiring the propeller-driven plane until it became undisguisedly anachronistic. For passengers in love with flight, the Connie had no equal.

CHAPTER 9

Betting a Company on a New Design: Boeing Builds a Jetliner

To understand the predicament faced by Boeing in the lead-up to its fateful decision to proceed with a jet airliner, it is important to recall that in the immediate aftermath of World War II military contracts were being slashed precipitously. Airframe manufacturers like Boeing were forced to lay off tens of thousands of workers as once-thriving plants shut down completely. Just exactly where the future aviation mother lode was to be found presented the industry's postwar executives with their most pressing question.

The decision of Boeing president William M. "Bill" Allen in the early 1950s to forge ahead with the jet transport by investing $16 million, or a quarter of the company's net worth, is often hailed as a bold move, very much in keeping with the plane maker's tradition of betting the farm on an educated hunch. Yet there was method to his madness, for as with prior Boeing projects, there was a hedging of the bet. If the proposed jet didn't work out as an airliner, then perhaps the military would see its merits or vice versa, or in the best of both worlds, the airlines and the military would embrace it.

This was the company's tack as far back as the mid-1930s with the Models 299/300, one military, the Flying Fortress, and the other civil, the Stratoliner. In the postwar era, Boeing's first new commercial entrant was the Model 377 Stratocruiser, a bulbous four-engine, propeller-driven airliner that looked like a holdover from the past rather than a leap into the next generation. But the point was that it had a military sister ship, the Model 367 Stratofreighter which was designated the C-97 by the air force.

The C-97 was derived from the wartime B-29 heavy bomber. And this new military transport shared the versatility of the airplane from which it evolved; a tanker version was built with the designation KC-97. In pursuing a jet transport, Boeing was essentially advancing the existing template. The military counterpart of a jet for the airlines might find a welcome home in the air force.

The development of the jet transport could be seen as having stemmed in part from a kind of domino effect related to Boeing's recent introduction of the B-47 and the B-52. Once one mission segment like long-range bombing converted to jets, it would be followed by the aerial refueling segment converting too. The new jet bombers would need new jet tankers to be effectively refueled in flight, as the propeller-driven KC-97 had trouble keeping up. If Boeing made its new jetliner available as a military tanker/transport, surely the air force would have to accord it a careful look-see.

In its jet sales pitch to US and European airlines, as early as 1950, Boeing was uniformly rebuffed. It was a bit of a surprise since de Havilland, seeking to corner what it perceived as a vibrant market for jetliners, had already flown its stunning Comet prototype in 1949. Most airline executives were not moved; these new-fangled aircraft employing the propulsion technology associated with modern military platforms would cost as much as $4 million apiece and their turbojet engines were notorious gas guzzlers.

Nevertheless, Bill Allen saw the future even if the airline industry doyens didn't. John E. Steiner, an MIT graduate and chief aerodynamicist on the 707's development, said that Boeing had the "conviction that 'jet was right.'" Rolled out on May 15, 1954, the Boeing prototype was a head-turner decked out in a reddish chocolate-brown and canary-yellow paint combination on top with a gleaming silver underside.

The ceremony was held at the company's Renton, Washington, factory outside Seattle during the four o'clock shift change so workers could see it. William Boeing, though no longer active in the company he founded, was there with his wife. As he clasped a bouquet of roses, Mrs. Boeing, draped in a fur shawl, christened the aircraft. With a swift swing of a bottle of champagne across an abutment placed on the nose right where the brown and silver colors merged, she declared: "I christen thee 'The Airplane of Tomorrow.'" Indeed, the production version was destined to shrink the world in half (demarcated by travel time).

The object of Mrs. Boeing's affection was a low-wing configuration with four ten-thousand-pound thrust Pratt & Whitney JT3 turbojet engines mounted underneath the wing on individual struts. The wing was swept a dramatic thirty-five degrees and incorporated both high-speed and low-speed ailerons as well as an advanced flap and spoiler system. The designers knew that certain components like thrust reversers and noise suppressors would be necessary, but the prototype would not tackle everything at once.

According to Steiner, the company knew at this point that the privately funded jet would be called the 707. The two preceding classification tiers of 500 and 600 "were reserved for 'pilotless aircraft,' missiles, and non-aircraft products" and the lower numbered tiers were already used up, which left the 700 series as the default choice for the jetliner. While 700 would have been the logical number to use, the company's marketing department thought 707 had a "better ring." However, for security reasons the company assigned the prototype the model designation 367-80. The 367 was the KC-97's model number and the -80 reflected that the prototype's design was the eightieth version to be developed under the model number. Boeing staff referred to the garishly decorated prototype as simply the "Dash 80."

Maiden flight occurred on July 15, 1954, which was the thirty-eighth anniversary of Boeing's founding. As big an event as it was, the show-stopping flight came a little over a year later. On August 7, 1955, the quarter-million people attending the Gold Cup hydroplane race on Lake Washington, which culminated Seattle's annual Seafair Week, had no way of knowing the thrilling spectacle that awaited them.

By prearrangement, the Boeing flight test team would perform a fly-over in the Dash 80, right behind the navy's Blue Angels air demonstration squadron as they exited the racecourse airspace at the conclusion of their always electrifying performance. The Boeing prototype's flight was to be a way to boost hometown pride and show off the cutting-edge plane to special visitors. In town for their yearly conventions were a couple of aviation-related professional associations whose members would be watching. Additionally, Boeing hosted a number of airline executives at the festivities.

On cue that sunny Sunday afternoon, following the Blue Angels, the Dash 80 began its pass by whisking towards the lake at a mere two hundred feet while its airspeed indicator was clocking a torrid 490 miles per hour. At the controls in the left seat was the company's chief test pilot on the project, a man who everybody called Tex and who Boeing's insurer insisted be the only authorized pilot-in-command of the plane that had a fortune riding on it. To understand Alvin M. "Tex" Johnston and what he was up to you had to know his flying background.

To begin with, Johnston was not from Texas. He grew up around Emporia, Kansas, and acquired the nickname when he started his first test pilot job flying P-39 Airacobra fighters for Bell Aircraft in Niagara Falls, near Buffalo, in western New York. He arrived at the flight line office one chilly morning in January 1943, hung his Stetson on the wall, and polished his cowboy boots, which caused a company mechanic to call him Tex. From that point until he died fifty-five years later, he went by Tex.

In 1925 when Tex was eleven years old, a barnstormer landed in a pasture near his home and the passion for flight was born. Licensed as a pilot and mechanic while still in his teens, he joined Inman's Flying Circus, which paid him five cents per ticket sold plus instruction in a Ford Tri-Motor en route to air shows. With enough money saved up, he bought a rare Command-Aire biplane and, fulfilling a dream, he barnstormed on his own over the prairies, selling rides at each stop as he had done as an apprentice with the traveling air show.

It was a charmed life, but by 1934 the harsh realities of the Depression adversely affected Tex's ability to continue barnstorming. In what he called the "last hurrah," he teamed up with wing-walker Page Winchester for a final show circuit through Oklahoma and Texas. Looking ahead, he realized his interest was in "the development of aircraft" and that meant going back to school for a technical education.

With savings he had from his barnstorming and money from a band he performed in, he enrolled in Kansas State, taking mathematics, drafting, shop, and foundry. Before he could finish, war clouds dimmed the horizon. He joined the Civilian Pilot Training Program as an instructor and then went to the Army Air Corps Ferry Command shuttling multi-engine aircraft. But, a year into the war, he felt that he was stagnating in the ferrying job; he craved being at the forefront of innovation, getting his hands on the latest planes and being the first to fly them.

To his delight, Bell Aircraft accepted his application for a test pilot slot. Timing was good because, during and immediately after World War II, Bell was one of the prolific aeronautical innovators. While Tex was at the company, his logbook filled with exotic entries.

Flying the Bell XP-59A, America's first jet aircraft, meant spending time at Muroc Army Airfield in Southern California's Mojave Desert. Tex made the most of the assignment. Shortly after arriving at the base, he noticed a ranch near the dry lakebed during flights in the new jet and decided to drive over in a Jeep on the weekend to check it out.

He walked in through the screen door and introduced himself with a hearty "Howdy" to the "short, scraggly-haired woman" tending the bar. It was the inimitable Pancho Barnes, the famed aviatrix who had settled down as the proprietor of the riding club just off base that had become the watering hole of choice for the cadre of test pilots. Tex had a lot to prove to this patron saint of the test pilots, for her contacts within aviation circles were boundless and she countenanced no foolery or fakery.

If you saw Tex outfitted in his usual regalia of cowboy boots, Stetson, bolo tie, and metal belt buckle, it was easy to picture him as a stand-in for stereotypical cowboys of the silver screen like Tom Mix and Gene Autry. In fact given his aerial exploits yet to come, which included flight testing the B-47 and B-52, and his rising reputation as the ultimate cowboy-pilot, Tex would be parodied in the 1964 film satire *Dr. Strangelove*. The actor Slim Pickens plays a yahoo of a bomber pilot who rides a nuclear bomb down to the target as if bucking a bronco at a rodeo.

Tex asked to ride one of Pancho's horses for rent and was pointed in the direction of the stable. With Pancho peering out at him, he cleverly saddled up a pesky bay mare so as not to be kicked. He mounted the unfamiliar animal without incident, as if he had done it a thousand times, and then he rode that mare at a gallop across the steaming desert like a master equestrian.

Back to the club in time for lunch, Tex ordered a beer. Pancho nodded and winked. "Comin' up, Pardner," she said. When Pancho set the glass full of foaming brew on the counter, she added, "It's on the house."

It was Pancho's extempore stamp of approval, the Bell test pilot's entrance into the clique of aviators presided over by Mojave's grand dame of flight, an informal fellowship which in short order would further expand to include the likes of Chuck Yeager and Scott Crossfield. Not inconsequently, a few years later both Tex and Yeager would fly the X-1, the Bell rocketplane that smashed through the sound barrier for the first time. The friendship between Tex and Pancho that began that afternoon under the blazing desert sun lasted a lifetime.

In 1946 the National Air Races were scheduled to resume at Cleveland, Ohio, after a wartime interruption. Tex did some figuring based on all the time he had accumulated flying the P-39 and concluded that his company's unusual fighter, if modified appropriately, could speed ahead of all other propeller-driven fighters of World War II expected to be competing for the coveted Thompson Trophy in the main pylon race. It was to be a field jammed with as much air racing talent as Cleveland had ever seen—Lockheed's Tony LeVier, North American's George Welch, racing entrepreneur Steve Wittman, engine designer Art Chester, Navy fighter ace Cook Cleland, and veteran racer Earl Ortman to name a few of the contestants.

Tex, not one to hold back his feelings, gave his ground crew pep talks spiced with colorful language during preparations. "If anyone screws up, I'm going to be the roughest S.O.B. you've ever seen." Yet, he was a taskmaster with a heart of gold. "Okay, boys, you're half of this team." He told them that if they gave him a "perfect airplane," he'd return the favor by giving them the trophy.

Fourteen fighters from the recent war, each tweaked for speed, were arrayed line abreast on the field for the horserace start. The flagman brought his flag down in a flourish and the racers were off. Sure enough, Tex pulled ahead of the pack in his souped-up all-yellow Airacobra. He stuck close to the pylons, reefing his fighter over on a wingtip and inducing at least four g's at each turn for the entire ten-lap race. It had to have been exhausting, but he later wrote: "It was beautiful."

He came sizzling over the finish line, wings level in a slight downward pitch to maximize speed—crossing at a fevered 430 miles per hour, only fifty feet off the deck. Not only did his first-place finish against supposedly faster fighters surprise participants and fans, he set a new closed-course speed record with an average speed around the pylons of 373.908 miles per hour. But Tex was not done yet.

Emboldened by his clean sweep as the underdog, he kept the throttle hot and took a victory lap. Replicating speed and altitude of his previous rounding of the course, on the final stretch, in front of the overflowing grandstands, he yanked his fighter up a dramatic sixty degrees for a perfectly coordinated slow roll—a victory roll to cap off the victory lap! Among the first to come forth from the sea of spectators to congratulate Tex was three-time Thompson Trophy winner and prior speed record-holder Roscoe Turner.

This was the Tex Johnston with his hands on the control yoke of the Dash 80 screaming in over Lake Washington nine years later. He let his copilot know on the run-in, "I'm going to roll this bird." Warned that he might be fired for such a stunt, he answered his concerned copilot while continuing to gain momentum. Referring to the hundreds of thousands of people at the Gold Cup event, he said: "We're going to get their attention and make this plane famous."

His airplane at the moment could just as well have been the P-39 racer at Cleveland or the Command-Aire biplane at shows in the Southwest or one of the aircraft of Inman's Flying Circus at any of dozens of Midwestern towns, for Tex was of that ilk within the flying fraternity, the rugged stick-and-rudder men learned in the art of their trade from hardscrabble barnstorming, who believed that you could roll any plane. Now Tex was again in his element: at the controls of a ship, fast and low. That it was on a day when he had the largest audience in his career and that all eyes would be turned skyward to get a glimpse of the hometown company's latest creation was gravy on the potluck.

Like a maestro conducting his well-rehearsed orchestra, he elevated the nose and hauled the yoke all the way over to the stop, holding it there while relieving back pressure so as not to overstress the structure. The massive wing, all 127 feet and ten inches in span, arced over and the more than fifty-ton jet was on its back halfway through the maneuver as onlookers below stared in disbelief. Tex deftly completed the roll, careful not to let g-forces build up to jeopardize the priceless aircraft.

Continuing in a straight line, he whipped the Dash 80 around for another pass from the opposite direction. In front of the stunned crowd, which was still coming to grips with the totally unexpected sight of such a huge plane rotating around in a classic barrel roll moments before, Tex went and did it all over again! By one account, Tex was "letting out whoops of joy" as he flipped the big plane upside down and then back to right-side up for the second time.

Boeing's Bill Allen was on a boat watching from the lake. One of his guests was Larry Bell, founder of Bell Aircraft, who took pills for a heart condition. According to observers, when Tex finished his second roll, Allen turned to Bell with a request: "Larry, give me one of those pills. I need it more than you." Laughing, Bell, who had employed Tex as a test pilot, replied: "Bill, you don't know Tex very well. He just sold your airplane."

Allen was not amused and the next morning Tex was called on the carpet. If there had been a hiccup and the Dash 80 had gone down, the company would have followed it into oblivion. Tex was prepared to defend his aerobatics. When Allen asked him what he thought he was doing when he rolled the prototype that represented the company's future commercial prospects, Tex simply said: "Selling the airplane."

Much has been written about how Allen remained upset over the incident, but thirty-six years later Tex revealed in his memoir that the friction between them dissipated on the night of the very same day that he had to explain his Gold Cup antics to the boss. Allen invited him to dinner at his home. Allen's other guest was Eddie Rickenbacker, America's top-scoring ace of World War I and, at the time, the head of Eastern Airlines. According to Tex's account, Rickenbacker was in a playful mood and greeted him by tugging the ubiquitous Stetson "down over my ears." Rickenbacker then exclaimed: "You slow rollin' S.O.B. Why didn't you let me know? I would have been ridin' the jump seat."

Tex summed up their meeting: "It was a terrific evening, just the three of us, talking about the airline conversion to jets." At a time when many airline executives had risen from flying careers in often inadequate platforms and knew from personal experience what it meant to roll an airplane, the wild display of the Dash 80 appeared to engender confidence in the new jet among the handful of airline decision makers who mattered. Though Eastern initially gave its nod to the competing DC-8, Rickenbacker's reaction to the Dash 80's aerobatic escapade suggested that the airlines would not be turned off and might come flocking to Boeing for the production version of its uncommonly displayed prototype.

Anxious to operate jet tankers, the air force went ahead and ordered the Boeing jet configured for air refueling well before the hubbub surrounding the Gold Cup demonstration. It was done as an interim measure just weeks after the prototype's first flight. As contract work proceeded, the provisional program became the program of record under the Model 717 designation.

The tanker's width had to be enlarged by a whole foot beyond the prototype's width, at the behest of the air force. Landing gear was reinforced to support heavier loads and a forward cargo door was installed on the port side. Most importantly, a telescopic flying boom was added to the underside of the aft fuselage. An operator would manipulate the boom in the prone position looking out a window referred to as "the balcony" while communicating by radio with the receiving pilot.

In the postwar period, Boeing initially experimented with the British drogue-and-probe refueling system whereby a basket on a hose is suspended behind the tanker and the receiving aircraft directs a probe into the basket to initiate the refueling. While this system has its merits, it simply did not allow for a rapid enough transfer of fuel for the bigger multiengine bomber types that devoured fuel at a much faster rate than fighters. Accordingly, Boeing developed its own system based on the boom-and-receptacle configuration that became the default refueling system on the tanker, designated the KC-135 and officially nicknamed the Stratotanker.

In their long service life, Stratotankers have undergone a series of upgrades. The most recent models, the KC-135R and the KC-135T, were fitted with the F-108-CF-100 engines, the military version of the CFM56-2B-1 civilian engines made by a partnership of General Electric of the United States and SNECMA of France. These engines greatly improved fuel efficiency while at the same time noticeably lowering the noise footprint compared to the older engines they replaced. A further upgrade to the KC-135 fleet occurred in the 1999 to 2002 period which brought the instrument panel truly into the twenty-first century with the installation of so-called glass cockpits that included color weather radar screen, a GPS navigation system, a ground proximity warning system, and a traffic alert and collision avoidance system. The avionics modernization eliminated the need for the navigator in most missions.

For many bomber pilots like me, the KC-135's aerial refueling system was important not so much for what it provided us as for what it saved us from. Because it enabled aerial refueling at altitudes compatible with our B-47s and B-52s, we no longer had to descend to take on fuel. Also the similar speeds and configurations of the tanker and the receiver aircraft made close formation flight much easier. The wakes of the refueler and bomber types were similar, as were the control responses.

Nevertheless, in-flight refueling remained a demanding and dangerous procedure. One aircraft at perhaps 250,000 pounds or more had to fly within contact distance of another aircraft of the same size and speed. When aerial refueling was first attempted to extend range or endurance using primitive improvised systems, it became a news sensation, with coverage in newspapers, newsreels, and on radio. Today, despite the inherent hazards, the act of transferring large amounts of fuel from one aircraft to another during flight is a routine operation taken for granted largely because of the professionalism exhibited consistently by KC-135 crews stretching back more than a generation to the present day.

No doubt some other aircraft might have filled the role played by the many variations of the Stratotanker, but as things worked out the aircraft proved to have what it takes to dominate the air refueling scene (with the KC-10 Extender, a refueling variant of the Douglas DC-10 jetliner, picking up some of the slack). And, as if to prove that sometimes history repeats itself, on February 24, 2011, the air force selected its next generation tanker, the KC-46A Pegasus, a design based on the highly regarded Boeing 767 jetliner. The new air refueler is expected to become operational in early 2018 after a highly contentious and protracted procurement and development process.

It is possible, based on the new aircraft's unhurried production rate, that replacement of the last of the aged Stratotankers may not be completed until 2040. If so, the legacy tanker will have been in continuous service for eighty-three years. The last of the 732 KC-135s was delivered on January 12, 1965, which means the youngest of the fleet will be celebrating its seventy-fifth anniversary at the time of its presumed retirement.

At the time the 707 was introduced, the air force was on its pathway to jet tankers, but it had an equally important need for jet transports. Ultimately, it chose to pursue a purpose-built cargo plane, the Lockheed C-141 Starlifter. As a design starting from scratch, it would not reach the inventory until the mid-1960s, which meant a platform would have to serve as a stopgap.

The logical choice was a version of the already contracted tanker, the KC-135. Under the circumstances, the air force bought forty-five of these planes, designated C-135 and officially dubbed Stratolifter. With deliveries underway in 1961, the refueling tanks and boom equipment were removed at the same time modifications to enhance the cargo mission, such as reinforced flooring, were adopted.

The first tranche of fifteen C-135As were powered by Pratt & Whitney J57-59W turbojets and could carry loads of forty-five tons a distance of twenty-seven hundred miles. The cargo hold was large enough to accommodate moderately sized equipment. Depending on seating configuration, as many as 160 passengers could be carried.

The second tranche consisted of thirty C-135Bs, which had higher-thrust Pratt & Whitney TF-33-5 turbofans. These cargo planes were soon eclipsed when the Lockheed Starlifter entered service. Nevertheless, the Boeing planes possessed a certain utility which the air force recognized, converting many for use in such missions as VIP transport, training, and electronic reconnaissance.

The conversions to specialized missions reflected the type's fundamental strengths that included jet speeds, high service ceiling, decent range, operational reliability, and a spacious cabin able to carry large crews and bulky electronic hardware while giving the appearance of a noncombat platform. These aircraft and a limited number of similar design built soon after in the 1960s proved their worth, as a high percentage have continued to soldier on, usually with engine upgrades. Their exotic nicknames like Rivet Joint, Cobra Eye, and Combat Sent speak to the variety of missions they serve, mainly within the category of intelligence-surveillance-reconnaissance (ISR).

Boeing wanted to build the military and civil versions of its four-engine jet transport/tanker on a joint assembly line, but this proved infeasible when it became necessary to expand the dimensions of the airliner fuselage from the tanker baseline to accommodate a six-seat-across configuration to be competitive with the Douglas DC-8. Besides the new competition, there was another concern that, at least temporarily, hindered orders.

The Comet, which entered commercial service with British Overseas Airways Corporation (BOAC) in May 1952, was soon plagued by a series of accidents. The first pointed to a design flaw in the wing that caused a loss of lift at high angles of attack such as when taking off. It was correctable through a quick wing modification.

However, during the investigation a couple Comets on scheduled flights went down for unknown reasons, killing all aboard. The problem was eventually traced to metal fatigue caused by the repeated pressurizations that occurred in the normal course of high-altitude flights. In turn, that fatigue led to catastrophic structural failures.

It was a major setback for de Havilland, and despite offering a totally revamped Comet with improved performance under a new model number, the aircraft failed to gain market traction and the company never recovered. The early checkered track record of jet airliners gave pause to airlines. There was concern that passengers might avoid the new form of commercial air transport for fear of some inborn defect peculiar to aircraft housing the still-new propulsive technology.

Against this backdrop, Boeing had to persuade airlines to not only have faith in jets generally but to go with its jet rather than the offering of Douglas Aircraft, the long dominant player in the airliner business (or, for that matter, the 1956 Soviet entrant, the Tupolev Tu-104, which bore an uncanny resemblance to the Comet in general layout). Boeing could say that its platform had already flown; whereas the Douglas design, with more wing area, more powerful engines, and greater range, was so far just a promise based on blueprints. Making headway hinged on winning over Juan Trippe, founder of Pan American.

The airline was willing to buy twenty 707s, but only because the Boeing jet would be ready sooner than the Douglas DC-8. Troublingly for Boeing, Pan Am had ordered twenty-five DC-8s because the airline considered the Douglas product to be superior based on the performance projections. Boeing's Steiner reminisced that "we decided we had to meet the competition or face failure."

The desperate attempt by Boeing engineers to salvage the airliner project revolved around frantic meetings and expedited redesign at the Ritz Tower Hotel in New York in the fall of 1955. Steiner later wrote: "We laid out a new wing and made aerodynamic estimates in the hotel room." It was as if the company's design staff was reliving the scenario that unfolded seven years earlier in connection with the effort to secure the B-52 bomber contract from the air force. Back then, the make-or-break changes in aircraft configuration were arrived at over a weekend spent in a suite at the Van Cleve Hotel in Dayton. The Boeing team hoped to be as lucky this time.

The hotel drama replay did pay off, for as Steiner put it, "In the end Pan Am standardized on Boeing 707s." The first 707 airliner was rolled out on October 28, 1957, and entered service in Pan Am livery about a year later with the designation 707-121 and the customized FAA registration N707PA. Pan Am's North Atlantic service with the Boeing jet was initiated on October 26, 1958.

Powered by four 13,500-pound thrust Pratt & Whitney JT3C-6 turbojets, the civilian equivalent of the military J57, the aircraft could cruise at 600 miles per hour. Service ceiling was an impressive forty-one thousand feet and published range was three thousand miles. As had been promised, en route times were cut virtually in half.

Standard configuration was for 181 passenger seats. Placement of more than a hundred windows meant that airlines could reconfigure the seating and still allow for desirable views out the cabin. List price was $5.5 million, although airlines typically negotiated better deals based on volume purchases.

The new load factors made possible by jetliners and the convenience offered by jet speeds were no longer idle speculation but increasingly part of the daily reality. Any remaining doubts about the commercial jet transport were quickly erased and orders grew, especially for the 707, which was first in the US and which stayed on top in large part through the company's dogged determination to hold the initiative. Another part of the answer was Boeing's introduction of follow-on models to cover market niches.

The second variant was the Model 720, really a downsized 707. It served airlines operating shorter routes like the popular New York to Chicago route. A maximum of 167 passengers could be seated.

Next came the 707-320, which the company promoted as the "Intercontinental" because of the vastly extended range. With a range of forty-two hundred miles, the aircraft could fly more than a third farther than the original production model. More powerful Pratt & Whitney JT4A turbojets were installed, producing 15,800 pounds of thrust each. Passenger capacity was upped to 189.

A major improvement in this model occurred when Boeing upgraded the engine to the Pratt & Whitney JT3D turbofan. Not only did the new engine boost thrust to eighteen thousand pounds, but fuel efficiency was improved. The ducted bypass technology was a huge advancement that helped to solidify the jet as the preferred type for most trunk line carriers. In addition, some of these planes were built as "combi" aircraft, meaning they could be converted from passenger to cargo or cargo to passenger configurations or any combination of the two. As a result of the engine upgrade and the cabin versatility, the 707-320B and C models racked up the best sales of all 707 models.

The Intercontinental was so successful that variants were even sold to BOAC, the operator of the ill-fated Comet. As an inducement, Boeing installed the Rolls-Royce Conway Mk. 508 turbofan engines on a special model. Thirty were delivered.

Production of the 707 continued through 1978. A total of 725 were built for commercial airlines. Interestingly, the only four-engine passenger plane Boeing continued to produce was the 747 jumbo jet. Advances in engine technology meant that most jetliners could fly safely, even over oceans, and generate sufficient thrust to carry heavy loads with just two engines. The fuel and maintenance savings made such configurations the way to go.

In hindsight, an obvious factor contributing to the success of the 707 was the ability of Boeing management to jump on changing circumstances and adapt accordingly. Also, there was a profound interest in servicing potential purchasers by accommodating individualized needs. For example, Australia's Qantas Airways got an especially long-range model for overwater routes and US-based Braniff International Airways got a higher-thrust model for the high elevations of its destination airports in South America. These small production runs in and of themselves did not do much for Boeing's bottom line, but they helped build customer loyalty, which was an important step in the company's move to build market share.

The 707 had wide-ranging military applications distinct from the Model 717 airplanes used mostly as air force tankers. In March 1977 Boeing delivered the first E-3A Sentry aircraft to the air force. Perhaps the most recognizable of the 707 military variants because of its large top-mounted spinning radome, the type is known generically as AWACS (Airborne Warning and Control System). These aircraft, which use their sophisticated electronics to monitor air activity, have had their electronic suites updated over the years, resulting in their being redesignated E-3B and later still E-3C. From the early 1980s through the early 1990s, E-3s were delivered to NATO, Saudi Arabia, Britain, and France.

An electronic cousin of the E-3 is the E-8 J-STARS (Joint-Surveillance Target Attack Radar System) which uses a radar antenna mounted in an underslung canoe-shaped radome to monitor ground movements on the battlefield. Program aircraft have been converted from preexisting airframes. Interestingly, the two preproduction models were used operationally during Operation Desert Storm in early 1991.

The navy took delivery of the E-6A Mercury beginning in August 1989 to fulfill the communications relay mission linking military commanders with ballistic missile submarines. In October 1998, the first upgrade to the E-6B standard became operational, enabling the type to be used as airborne strategic command posts with the ability to launch the air force's land-based ICBMs. These last-of-the-line 707s use a couple very low frequency trailing wire antennas and are often referred to by their acronym TACAMO (Take Charge and Move Out).

The most famous of the 707s, either civilian or military, were those operated as Air Force One. The first was delivered October 9, 1962, in the definitive two-tone blue-and-white paint scheme with the words "United States of America" stretched across the upper fuselage on both sides. An American flag was emblazoned on the fin and rudder and the presidential seal appeared just aft of and below the forward door.

All subsequent presidential aircraft came decorated in the same scheme, which had been developed by famed designer Raymond Loewy in consultation with First Lady Jacqueline Kennedy. In addition to an executive interior that could accommodate up to fifty passengers, the aircraft was equipped with a sophisticated communications system allowing secure telephone calls. Based on the 707-320B, to which Boeing assigned the distinct model number 707-353, it carried air force designation VC-137C and serial number 62-6000. It was often referred to in shorthand as "SAM 6000" with the acronym standing for Special Air Mission.

This is the aircraft that flew President John F. Kennedy to Dallas, Texas, in November 1963 and transported his body back to Washington after the assassination. For everyone old enough to remember the tragic event, this Air Force One featured prominently during the hours that the nation worked its way through the trauma. The stately aircraft projected a sense of stability in those trying times.

Perhaps it is overly nostalgic to say so, but I think there was still a romance about new aircraft when this first American jetliner was introduced and adopted as the official air transport for the leader of our country. This feeling was shared by Hugh Sidey, my late friend who served as *Time* magazine's White House correspondent at the time. He eloquently expressed his emotions in a foreword to one of my books, which I excerpt here:

There is a story I carry in my heart about an Air Force plane that bore no weapons, yet it strode the globe as a great symbol of liberty and hope and may have done as much in that cause as any other plane in the Air Force arsenal. Air Force One, then a Boeing 707, landed one rainy night in Paris carrying President Kennedy and his wife, Jacqueline. . . . The plane had been reconfigured and painted in the cool and elegant blues that have become so familiar on television today. The sun broke through the threatening clouds and limned this small drama. . . . The message from that plane just then in that distant place was one of beauty and grace inseparable from strength. That same jet flew in a heartbreaking but proud tribute over Arlington Cemetery when John Kennedy was buried, a last salute and an enduring promise that the Air Force would hold the heavens for this nation. A promise kept.

CHAPTER 10

Bill Lear Takes Private Flying
to a New Level: The Learjet

The name Lear is to business jets what apple is to apple pie. Saying Lear-jet is like saying Kleenex even if the business aircraft on the ramp, like the tissue paper on the counter, is a different brand. Inevitably, when the executive transport spawned by maverick inventor William P. Lear is mentioned, the image of a luxurious, fighter-like private plane, a sports car of the sky, assuredly comes to mind.

Love of the flying life grabbed ten-year-old Bill Lear in the summer of 1912 when he saw Lincoln Beachey, the era's quintessential exhibition pilot, perform above the grounds of an open stadium in rural Iowa. Seven years later, by then a high school dropout in Chicago, he observed mail planes landing at the city's Grant Park airfield. He wrangled a ride in one of the rickety aircraft and despite its flipping over on landing, he knew that he belonged to this milieu of rugged individualists operating unconventional machinery and seizing adventure with every heartbeat.

His imperious mother forbade his airport activities, but the boy was stubborn and rebellious. The character traits that showed themselves in his early years would resurface time and again through adulthood. Disregarding the parental edict, Bill paid a pilot at another area airport to give him a ride. Aviation was definitely in the youngster's future, but getting away from home had become his priority.

Imagining fame and fortune in the movies, the naïve adolescent set out for the film industry in Southern California without his mother knowing his plans. He made it halfway—to Colorado—before running out of funds. Too embarrassed to alert his mother of his whereabouts, he joined the navy, which in the ultimate irony sent him back to Chicago for training as a radio technician.

Within six months, the navy cut back on its personnel roster, and Bill, by then a radio instructor, decided to leave the service. He worked briefly as a Western Union teletype operator, but entrepreneurial pursuits befitted his taste. Before long he was running a start-up to capitalize on the radio fad that had spread across the country like wildfire in the early 1920s. Known as Quincy Radio Laboratories, the company sold radio sets from its shop in Quincy, Illinois.

Flying was still the fledgling businessman's burning interest, and when he could he ventured to the local airport for flights. Alas, in 1924 he tired of his radio company and sold his interest. He quickly spent the proceeds, which threw him into financial chaos given that he had married the year before and his wife was pregnant. Shifting direction and risking everything on a whim was to be the enterprising young man's pattern for the rest of his life. Meantime, the struggling couple moved in with Bill's widowed grandmother in Tulsa, Oklahoma.

Bill ran the radio station owned by the church that his grandmother attended. Combined with other radio work, he was able to buy a do-it-yourself airplane kit. He built the airplane, but it never flew. The failure symbolized the troubling turn his life was taking just then.

Soon he was broke again, divorced, in trouble with the law, and married again. Following a circuitous route, he ended up back in Chicago in 1926. His first real success came a couple years later when he invented a radio coil for the AM frequency band that was only half the size of the standard industry coil. Not only was the Lear coil more efficiently sized, it resulted in higher-quality audio.

Zenith Radio Corporation bought the coil in large quantities. However, because Bill was making the products in the garage of his mother's Chicago house, the limited space became an issue as the big orders required more work room. Bill found the necessary space in a warehouse that was partially occupied by the Galvin Manufacturing Company, a maker of radio parts.

The market crash of 1929 practically ruined the Galvin firm, whose owner, Paul Galvin, had already been through two bankruptcies. Bill suggested to his stablemate that he consider using the Lear coil in a line of car radios. At first, Galvin was hesitant, but there were a number of manufacturers around the country starting to bring such products to market.

Thinking it over, Galvin gave the go-ahead early the next year and demanded that a working model be installed in his Studebaker in time for the Radio Manufacturers Association convention in Atlantic City, New Jersey, during the Memorial Day weekend. Bill and a small team of trusted assistants devised a car radio that excelled in reception quality and yet could be purchased at a very competitive price. The product was a smashing success at the convention.

On the drive back to Chicago in the Studebaker, Galvin and Lear ruminated over what to call their device. They mutually hit upon a combination of the words "motor," which derived from the placement in an automobile, and "ola," which was a play on the RCA Victrola name. Thus was born the Motorola Corporation!

Bill was on a tear. He developed devices to improve radio reception and listening convenience, which he sold for big bucks. His success gave him the wherewithal to buy a Fleet biplane. But he needed to learn how to fly.

He paid an airline pilot to teach him, and they flew the biplane to the East Coast. During this flight, Bill realized that aerial navigation was still in its infancy. On their journey, he and his instructor had largely navigated by following railroad tracks. A later flight in a Monocoupe, a peppy enclosed-cockpit monoplane suited more for businessmen than barnstormers, had to be scrubbed due to fog and low ceilings. These early flying experiences convinced Bill of the need for better navigational equipment.

The key in Bill's mind was an electronic device that could hone in on ground-based radio stations and give pilots a course to or from the station. In short order, he developed an automatic direction finder, also known as a radio compass. The system entailed an externally mounted loop antenna and a gauge with a needle that the pilot would strive to keep centered to remain on course to the signal emanating from the broadcast station. As Bill realized, he and his new company, Lear Avia, were not alone in the scramble for modern air navigation systems.

Through the 1930s Bill constantly improved his ADF, transforming the big ring-shaped antenna into two smaller coil loops that fit in a teardrop-shaped protective shell the size of a watermelon. He had moved his company to New York and in the lead-up to World War II he moved again to the Dayton, Ohio, area where he was close to the air corps' Wright Field, a center of military aviation research, development, and procurement. Not surprisingly, his entrepreneurial ways did not mesh with the entrenched bureaucracy and he fumed that his larger competitors continued to win contracts of much greater magnitude.

Bill Lear had unquestioned talent as an "ideas man," but he was mercurial, firing people as fast as he hired them. He also lacked focus beyond the invention stage. Once he developed a solution, he went on to another problem. A further drawback in doing business with him was that he lacked quality control when his designs went into mass production. For as good as his original inventions might be, his wandering mind did not dovetail with the manufacturing regimen expected of an institutional customer like the War Department.

Nevertheless, the diverse Lear enterprises enjoyed a modicum of success during the war. The sheer volume of the government's materiel needs opened opportunities for a go-getter like Bill. By war's end, Lear components could be found in most US combat planes.

To his acquaintances and business associates, it was remarkable that Bill could focus on such a wide-ranging assortment of work because he ran his personal life on the ragged edge with free-flowing alcohol and nonstop womanizing. By 1940, at thirty-eight years of age, Bill had been thrice married and divorced. Family members attributed his philandering and otherwise boorish behavior to the strained maternal relationship, insecurity stemming from self-doubt, and a desperate yearning for affirmation.

As recounted by his biographer, Richard Rashke, the inventor's hedonistic lifestyle was evinced in a half-sarcastic comment to his secretary one day. In connection with the company's prewar expansion to a larger building in rural Piqua, twenty-five miles north of Dayton's city center,

Bill's secretary pointed out: "There are twenty-six churches and only two bars in Piqua." Her boss answered: "Well, we'll correct that."

After the war, Bill moved again. This time he settled in Grand Rapids, Michigan. His main company, now known as Lear Incorporated, was an umbrella organization that included a potpourri of businesses with a concentration on producing electronic devices of various kinds.

Bill made a big push into the home-radio market, leaning on the reputation of Grand Rapids as a center of quality furniture construction to produce handsome cabinetry for his consumer line. He continued to pursue his civilian aircraft radio business, firmly convinced that underserved private pilots should have the means to communicate as did airline and military pilots. Also, a natural outgrowth of his government contracts for ADF equipment was an attempt to penetrate the civilian side of the ADF market.

Meanwhile, private flying in the latter 1940s did not enjoy the sustained growth as some had forecasted, and Lear was in dire straits again. As he had done before and would do again, Bill drilled down into the well of his fertile imagination which swirled with fresh ideas and, like a magician pulling a rabbit out of a hat, he introduced a winner among his hoard of so-so devices to save the day. The masterstroke was an advanced autopilot that used an innovative triple servo to minimize weight. The air force committed to buy the autopilot in large quantities for its expanding fleet of jet planes. With the buildup sparked by the Korean War and the intensifying Cold War, Lear benefited from a steady income stream throughout the next decade.

The Lear F-5 autopilot was augmented by another of Bill's innovations, the vertical gyro indicator which, when coupled to the autopilot, permitted "blind" landings. The air force finally had reliable instruments to enable operations in inclement weather. For the achievement, the team involved in the development was awarded the Robert J. Collier Trophy, one of the highest aviation honors. All team members agreed that Bill should be the one to accept the trophy from President Harry Truman at the White House ceremony.

From the despair of impending insolvency, Bill had a way of rising to the triumph of technological and commercial success. As one of the army air force procurement officers who had overseen Lear contracts during World War II and who went to work for the company said of him: "Bill didn't have all the limitations of an education. He didn't know what couldn't be done." Interestingly enough, around the time that the Collier was awarded, the University of Michigan conferred an honorary engineering degree on Bill , the first of a half-dozen honorary doctorates for the high school dropout.

However, as happened when he went from trough to peak, Bill felt a void—that he needed a new challenge. He decided it was time to turn to his first love of flying, notwithstanding that his first talent had always been electronics. He had reveled in flying to business appointments around the country in aircraft like cabin Wacos and Beechcraft Staggerwings, well-appointed and comfortable enclosed-cockpit biplanes for the pilot-businessman. During the early 1950s, he jaunted around in a World War II-era Lockheed Lodestar, an Art Deco low-wing twin-engine transport, and perceived a profit potential in refurbishing and reselling the few hundred copies that could be bought on the open market.

Suddenly, he was off on this new tangent. To facilitate the new venture, he created the Aircraft Engineering Division within his company. A uniquely talented team was assembled to help guide the remaking of the Lodestar under the name Learstar.

Bill brought in Benny Howard of air racing fame; Benny's assistant, Gordon Israel; Ed Swearingen, who would later design his own twin-engine commuter airliner and executive aircraft; and as test pilot, Clyde Pangborn, a grandee from aviation's pioneer days. The operation set up in a movie company's hangar at the Santa Monica Airport in Southern California.

The Learstars were extravagant updates of a venerable type. In the refurbishment process, each of the old twin Lockheeds was, of course, outfitted with a full complement of Lear avionics. Bill priced them accordingly and big-name companies as well as wealthy individuals bought several dozen of the reconditioned ships.

It was the start of a niche within the aviation industry—opulent personal transports for the well-heeled. The owners would more often than not be flown by hired flight crew as opposed to piloting the gussied-up aircraft themselves. But the revamped planes were so expensive and the concept of chauffeured aerial limousines so new that the market was not as robust as Bill had thought. Moreover, competition heated up in the limited marketplace when Dee Howard (no relation to Benny Howard) hired away Gordon Israel and started sprucing up other aircraft in the twin Lockheed series for resale as corporate transports.

By 1959 it was time for Bill to move on yet again. He turned over the daily operation of Lear Incorporated to a trusted lieutenant and looked to build an executive aircraft from the ground up. He was off to Switzerland to make it happen.

In formulating the design of his scratch-built executive aircraft, Bill took an interest in a highly unconventional configuration being researched by Dr. August Raspet at Mississippi State University. The Raspet project was funded by the US Army with an eye towards perfecting a plane with a short takeoff and vertical landing capability. Called the MARVEL (for Mississippi Aerophysics Research Vehicle with Extended Latitude), the experimental six-seat platform would be built entirely of fiberglass, making it the first all-composite aircraft.

Another innovation was the use of a single turboprop engine to drive a ducted propeller located in the tail. A wraparound-glass cockpit afforded excellent visibility for observation purposes while the high wing used a camber-changing system instead of standard surfaces for in-flight control. The aircraft's configuration resembled the anatomy of a fiendish-looking insect, hardly the design one would associate with an executive transport.

Before he could even ferret out his grand scheme for a world-beating private jet in the shadow of the Swiss Alps, he had to contend with the board of directors of Lear Incorporated, which looked dimly on the business aircraft project. It is not that the company's directors thought the plane would fail, but rather they didn't see the synergy—the company was an electronics supplier to airframers. Those plane makers would take umbrage if Lear Incorporated became a direct competitor of theirs. Additionally, the board felt that Bill had a way of underestimating development costs for big projects, which the proposed jet would definitely be.

In the early 1960s Lear Incorporated was an attractive merger candidate. Though Bill did not want to sell the 27 percent of the company's stock that he and his family controlled, he could see the handwriting on the wall. The only way he could hope to have the funds necessary to plow into his latest passionate endeavor was to take the money, just over $12 million, and run. By agreement, the merger with the equally sized electronics manufacturer Siegler Corporation would result in the combined company being called Lear Siegler. Also, under the agreed terms, Bill would be able to call his new company the Lear Jet Corporation.

Back in Switzerland, Bill's new infusion of cash did not help straighten things out at his Swiss American Aviation Corporation. Trying to coordinate the multitude of departments required to get a brand-new design from the drawing board to the plant floor and then into the air was complicated enough under the best of circumstances. In a foreign land where language and culture intervened and where partnerships with firms in surrounding nations required smooth coordination, the situation became untenable. Bill chose to move to Wichita, Kansas, known as "the air capital of the world" for its history of producing more general aviation aircraft than anywhere else.

Bill knew that his finite budget did not permit the risks that would come with a bold departure from the state of the art. With seating for up to seven passengers, the Lear Jet, as he had immodestly dubbed his executive aircraft, would take existing design theory and make the most of it. A couple features that stood out were the T-tail (for enhanced stability and fatigue reduction) and the wingtip fuel tanks (for extended range). Both of these gave the plane a distinctly speedy, almost fighter-like look. Power came from two 2,850-pound thrust General Electric CJ610 engines mounted on either side of the tail.

At work, Bill showed no mellowing even as he turned sixty years of age. He stormed through the hangar like an emperor confronting his lowly subjects. His employees detested the slights and recoiled at his insistence that every detail be approved by him personally. But even if grudgingly, they knew the man was a genius and eccentricity came with the territory. The feeling that something important was occurring on the shop floor lent an air of excitement that resonated through the voluminous building, which in turn kept spirits high.

Bill excelled at the avionics installation; it was, after all, his forte. The instrumentation and the way it was laid out were second to none. As a longtime pilot of propeller planes designed with the business flyer in mind, Bill applied his hands-on knowledge to ensure comfortable seating in his design for the pilot and copilot. He labored to find and fabricate a durable Plexiglas windscreen that could be wrapped around the flight deck to provide an expansive 270-degree field of vision.

He believed that part of the answer to success was keeping the weight down. His goal was to bring the jet in at less than 12,500 pounds, for that would make it fast and, at the same time, qualify for certification under less onerous FAA standards. At one point, Bill hollered that he would sell his grandmother to save a pound. Company engineers and shop foremen knew what the boss was trying to do, so they started referring tongue in cheek to each optional pound in the design as a "grandmother."

The biggest nail-biter in the process of this high-stakes adventure was Bill's decision to proceed without the customary step of a flying prototype. Some said that Bill simply felt he did not have sufficient funds for a standard development program, but others speculated that Bill's ego and his desire to get his product to market before competitors were the reasons for the unconventional move. The first jet to roll out of the Lear hangar would have to be right in all respects because it would be a production model.

Bill considered his most serious competition to be the Jet Commander under development by Ted Smith's Aero Design and Engineering Company in Bethany, Oklahoma. Smith was a former Douglas Aircraft engineer who in his subsequent career as a budding aviation entrepreneur had introduced the well-regarded Aero Commander piston twin and later the Aerostar, the world's fastest production piston-twin. Smith's jet prototype had its first flight five days before construction had even begun on the Lear Jet. Bill knew he was playing catch-up in a race to establish market dominance in his chosen niche.

Other companies had already begun selling corporate jets, but these he did not consider direct competitors. Lockheed's four-engine Jetstar and North American's roomy Saberliner were for a more upscale end of the market and priced accordingly. French manufacturer Dassault was on the verge of coming out with the Mystere 20, a finely sculpted jet with a stand-up cabin. Bill's sights were not set on serving the elite, but aimed at the larger market obsessed with efficiency and affordability. When he was asked about the stand-up cabin he famously barked: "If you want to take a walk, go to Central Park." On other occasions, he was heard to exclaim, "Hell, you don't stand up in your Cadillac, do you?"

The Lear Jet proceeded apace. From first metal-bending in early February 1963 to rollout seven and a half months later, the team Bill had organized and led in his taskmaster fashion beat the odds and quieted the doubters. Three weeks after the rollout, on October 7th, the plane was ready for its maiden flight.

The event was delayed until near sunset because of last-minute repairs to the nose wheel's swiveling mechanism. It was a metaphor for the whole project—one hurdle after another, but none insurmountable because of the obsession driving the project's architect and the innate talents of his unlikely admixture of coworkers. Virtually the entire factory workforce stood parallel to the runway, backing up the boss, who sat in a truck preparing to monitor the flight and communicate with its pilots via a portable radio.

While the event would not excuse Bill's many failings, project participants could for a moment join with the originator to relish their contributions and take pride in a job well done. Lear Jet Model 23, sporting FAA registration number N801L on its prominent fin, taxied into position. The svelte ship, with a sign reading "Experimental" visible in the cabin window and the name "Lear Jet" painted tastefully on the side of the nose under the wraparound windscreen, lifted gracefully on a gentle climb into the Wichita sky.

The engineers and draftsmen, welders and machinists, along with colleagues from the multitude of disciplines required to build an aircraft from the bare bones of an idea, looked up at the object of their devotion. The emotional undercurrents streaming through the throng of employees were strong and many broke out in tears. They and their irascible, cantankerous, overbearing boss had accomplished what many said couldn't be done. The Lear Jet was flying!

The immediate future was punctuated by the many bureaucratic and regulatory obstacles of aircraft certification. On June 4, 1964, the first Lear Jet, which had conducted dozens of uneventful test flights, took off on what was to be another routine part of the certification effort. However, shortly after becoming airborne the plane plunked into a cornfield.

The crew climbed out uninjured, but leaking fuel came in contact with hot engine parts and the ship that had set sail to the delight of so many only eight months earlier burst into flames. Within minutes it was no more. The incident could have easily brought the struggling company to its knees; Bill had just barely enough funds to get this far.

Yet when things seemed bleakest Bill always managed to recover and then go on to thrive. This time the answer came in the form of insurance money. Incongruous though it was, the infusion of desperately needed funds from the crash kept the company afloat through the certification process.

To allay concerns of potential buyers and to debunk unfounded rumors, Bill flew his one and only other Model 23 to a big air show then underway in Pennsylvania. The plane had been pre-purchased as a personal favor by Bill's friend, Justin Dart of the Rexall Drug chain. At the air show, Bill explained that the loss of the first plane was attributable to a simple pilot error—forgetting to retract wing-mounted spoilers after takeoff—rather than some inherent design flaw. His spirited defense won the day. The next month, on July 31st, the Lear Jet's type certificate was delivered personally by FAA administrator Najeeb E. Halaby. The Jet Commander's certification did not come through until four months later.

The company obtained deposits of $10,000 for each of the fifty-two Lear Jets already ordered, but had spent the aggregate. Without a penny to spare, Bill wasted no time ramping up production. In a mere two and a half months from certification, the company delivered the third Model 23 fresh off the new production line.

The Lear Jet represented a quantum leap beyond the Learstar. For one thing, the jet's cabin was pressurized. The system worked off of engine bleed air. At cruise altitude, the maximum pressure differential of 9.4 pounds per square inch provided an eight thousand-foot cabin.

Service ceiling was forty-five thousand feet, which was unthinkable for the converted twin-prop Lodestars. Flying above the weather became a regular part of the sales pitch for Lear Jet marketers. Maximum speed was a sizzling 561 miles per hour. The published performance specifications combined with the new aircraft's streamlined shape prompted people to say: "The Lear Jet looks like it's going nearly 600 miles an hour sitting on the ground."

In addition to offering impressive altitude and speed, the Model 23 was built "like a tank." Multiple spars formed the core of wing and tail surface structures so that a failure of any one would not be catastrophic. Flight controls were simple, employing standard mechanical linkages.

The Model 23 would not be known as affording great motility inside. Occupants had to hunch over to move through the cramped cabin. With a range of 1,830 miles, you could be precluded from standing and stretching for a while. It was a design choice: Size was sacrificed for performance and economy.

Also there was no partition separating the flight deck from the passenger cabin, which was not a problem for do-it-yourself owners. For non-pilot owners, the open space was accepted and even savored as an element of the traveling adventure. Bill decided not to include a lavatory, rationalizing that if a passenger needed to relieve himself onboard it meant that the plane wasn't going fast enough. Subsequent thinking on the topic changed, especially as improved models had greater endurance and range.

Within short order, the aircraft set a new transcontinental speed record and a time-to-climb record up to forty thousand feet. The Model 23 was the darling of jetsetters. By the end of 1965, the first full production year, Lear had sold more than eighty, establishing itself as the market leader. The general aviation industry's so-called Big Three—Cessna, Beech, and Piper—had sat on the sidelines theorizing that Bill Lear's romance with private jets was a passing fancy. By the late 1960s, Cessna reversed itself and entered the jet market in a major way, ultimately developing the most complete "family" of business jets from entry level to ultrasophisticated.

The Model 23 and all subsequent models have been alluring to pilots. The brand's airplanes enjoy a rightful mystique because their appearance and performance make them the closest a pilot will get to a jet fighter without joining the military. Those who have flown a Lear say it is the

Ferrari of business aircraft, a plane you like to fly hands-on and, when executives aren't aboard, to maneuver with a touch of flair.

Yet, in its early days, the Lear Jet had a scary side. It was precisely the hot performance that made the plane a handful for pilots not used to flying jets. Accidents occurred that raised the specter of pilot error, especially on landing because of the type's fast approach speeds. A combination of thorough pilot training, wing modifications, and systems upgrades brought safety improvements.

A month after the first production aircraft's delivery, on November 30, 1964, Lear Jet Corporation went public. Facing a working capital crunch, the windfall came in the nick of time, and, with a 60 percent ownership share, Bill returned to the ranks of the wealthy. Many company employees benefited as well since during the lean times Bill paid them partly in stock.

Unlike other private jets already on the market or those to come, this one had a person's name on it; the Lear Jet was a brand with a recognizable, indeed, a very colorful figure behind it. In a way, owning one was like owning a Hermes belt or a Chanel purse. The Lear Jet became a buzzword for a certain lifestyle.

Bill was riding high. He rubbed elbows with celebrities like singer Frank Sinatra, comedian Danny Kaye, television personality Art Linkletter, and Chinese political activist Madame Chiang Kai-shek. The company continued on a roll, expanding manufacturing floor area to four hundred thousand square feet as sales reached a total of 120 jets by June 1966.

Not content to simply manage the executive aircraft business, Bill delved into other fields. He developed the eight-track stereo cassette player, expanded into avionics, and bought a small helicopter manufacturer. To reflect the broad range of loosely connected ventures, in September the company changed its name to Lear Jet Industries Inc.

Timing could hardly have been worse. A recession struck that year and as is often the case under such conditions the private plane market got walloped as if the sour economy had gone into a depression. As the saying goes, when a cold hits the nation's economy, the general aviation industry catches pneumonia. This is because in tough economic times, individuals and corporations tend to shed their aircraft as a cost-cutting measure.

Lear's aircraft sales dried up. As unsold jets occupied space on the ramp in Wichita, Bill's rags-to-riches story was suddenly turning again to rags. His choices came down to selling his interest or going bankrupt.

On April 10, 1967, after a laborious negotiation, Bill sold his controlling stake in the company to the Gates Rubber Company of Denver. The rubber company's head, Charles C. Gates, was not only a pilot but an aviation enthusiast who had previously purchased a chain of fixed-based operators, the outfits that service, repair, and fuel aircraft at airports. On the advice of Harry B. Combs, who had built the chain, Gates implemented a new marketing plan that helped to turn around the lagging sales performance.

Bill's influence at the company waned and he eventually had a falling out with Gates. In April 1969, Bill severed his ties completely from the organization he had created. On December 2, 1969, a reorganization resulted in the company being renamed Gates Learjet Corporation. The iconic aircraft was officially known from that point as the Gates Learjet, but most people kept referring to it in the familiar short-form of Learjet. Sticklers noticed that on paper the name was no longer two separate words but a joined pair: the words "Lear" and "jet" combined into "Learjet," incorporating the lower-case "j".

Bill sought to make his new fortune in Reno, Nevada and set up a bevy of new companies. One endeavor sought to develop steam engines for the automotive market as a way to rectify the problem of toxic emissions from internal combustion engines. Another project envisioned a mixed-use real estate development of approximately twenty-five hundred acres around the Reno-Stead Airport. The venture closest to his life's experience entailed the design of another corporate jet.

Bill's new aircraft concept, called the Learstar 600, was to incorporate a supercritical wing to provide extremely long range while also enabling slow landing speed. Power would be supplied by high-bypass fanjets that promised the dual advantages of plentiful thrust and improved fuel efficiency. Of course, he wanted to finish developing it himself with production to follow in his own plant.

His finances, which were running low again, simply would not allow it. In 1976 Bill entered into a licensing agreement with Canadair Limited of Montreal. In addition to an initial option of $375,000, terms called for the Canadian company to pay a royalty on every Learstar 600 it sold. However, Bill's relationship with Canadair soon deteriorated amid its changes to his design that included a widening of the cabin cross-section. The aircraft was renamed the Challenger 600, which further alienated Bill from the project.

Bill then focused on what he called the Lear Fan. It was the outgrowth of his fascination with the experimental MARVEL from years before. The fuselage resembled the classic Learjet shape, but like the MARVEL, it would be built of composite material. Turboshaft engines would power a single pusher-propeller in an inverted Y-shaped tail. Two flyable proof-of-concept demonstrators were built. The aviation press played up the design, and followers of the high school dropout who had spent his professional life proving the naysayers wrong believed that Bill Lear might be able to pull off another success against overwhelming challenges.

But time ran out. Bill died on May 14, 1978. His fourth wife, Moya, had been an uncommonly forgiving and warmhearted soulmate since marrying the insufferable industrialist in 1942. Loyal to the end and beyond, she strove in widowhood to bring her late husband's revolutionary executive transport concept to fruition. Despite her gallant attempt, which parroted Bill's indomitable spirit, technical problems with the complex gear shaft plagued the aircraft, and in 1985 the Lear Fan project went bankrupt.

More than a half century after their introduction, Learjets traverse extensive swaths of airspace around the globe every day, a vivid testament to the success of the planes and their outsized progenitor. If Bill were still alive, he would probably be more than a little surprised and perhaps even miffed to see his old company's shifting tides of ownership. In May 1990, Learjet was sold to Bombardier Inc., the large Canadian transportation equipment manufacturer.

Four years earlier, Bombardier purchased Canadair, the company that had acquired an option on Bill Lear's design for the Learstar 600. It turned into the Challenger series of business jets with "walk-around cabins." What a reaction that would have sparked from the design's creator!

In fairness, Bombardier has been a faithful steward of the Lear brand. It has followed industry practice and created a "family" of business aircraft. Learjets are marketed as light business jets; Challengers are advertised as medium business jets; and the company's top-of-the-line series, the aircraft branded under the Global imprint, are touted as large business jets.

Although the parent company canceled the development of its most ambitious Learjet model, the Learjet 85, it markets the latest incarnation of the brand, the Learjet 75. This model boasts an impressive cruise altitude of fifty-one thousand feet. Also, it offers a "stand-up cabin."

Bill Lear was a complex human being—stubborn, visionary, pragmatic. It is easy to imagine him castigating those who tinkered with his "baby." But what a thrill he would get knowing that his invention, modified though it has been, continues to soar in the open sky, spreading the excitement of flight.

CHAPTER 11

Cordial Intent:
The Anglo-French Concorde

Even years after its retirement, the name Concorde continues to conjure up thoughts of refinement, taste, and splendor—all, oddly, virtues associated with the mainline commercial air travel of at least a generation earlier when impeccably attired passengers could retreat to an onboard lounge and be served by a white-gloved steward. The Anglo-French airliner's pointy nose, slender fuselage, and gracefully curved delta wings exuded equal measures of speed and class. Its twenty-seven years of passenger revenue service represented a valiant, if evanescent, attempt to hold onto a vestige of the era in which getting to one's destination was savored as much as being there.

The Concorde was fascinating in the way that the airlines, British Airways and Air France, did everything so well to match the image one would expect, from the point you entered the airport until you were installed in the airplane. Terrific waiting area, champagne supplied liberally. The inside of the airplane was smaller than I had expected—no lounge, but the flight was comfortable, even soothing, and, like at the terminal, supplied with good champagne—Moet as I recall. During taxi-out and taxi-in, the aircraft was given precedence over other ground traffic, as it moved very swiftly to and from takeoff and landing spots.

Of course, it was all by design. The carriers knew that most of the ticketholders were splurging on a once-in-a-lifetime adventure, much as couples make the Atlantic crossing on oceangoing luxury liners. Only here the whole voyage was but a flash by comparison—the passage across the proverbial pond being compacted into a few hours. It was so fast and joyous, like a fairytale in which you were pampered every minute and where all participants, passengers and flight attendants alike, interacted good naturedly.

What made these dreamlike flights possible was the behind-the-scenes attention to detail, the extraordinary lengths taken by technical and flight personnel to ensure zero-defect operations. Supersonic airliners were a breed apart and the two carriers that fielded their small fleets were cognizant of the need for strict adherence to their playbooks. It was precisely this insistence on exactitude that afforded the Concorde its sterling safety record.

Like the laws of physics, the Concorde regimen imposed by the two airlines operating it was inviolable. No one in the operational or maintenance chains was immune from the harsh application of the unbending rules. Even a high-time captain nearing retirement could be summarily suspended for the smallest infraction of the supersonic jet's flight procedures.

In hindsight it is easy to say how logical all this was—the puritanical mindset coupled with the bon vivant's objet d'art. But when the Concorde took shape in the late 1950s and early 1960s it was a break from the existing conventions, a shape dramatically different from the standard jetliner's cigar-like fuselage with podded engines slung under a modestly swept low-wing. The new jet's design parameters enabled a huge jump in performance yet with serviceability possible at existing hub airports.

The Concorde routinely flew at the rarefied altitude of sixty thousand feet or roughly four miles higher than ordinary jetliners while speeding at just over Mach 2, which was more than double the top speed of other air transports. Inside the cabin, up to a hundred passengers could relax in shirtsleeved comfort, dining on caviar and chips. This technological sensation was at the same time a visual showstopper certain to turn the heads of even the most jaded air travelers. At least equally remarkable was that the airplane resulted from an international collaboration that presaged similar industry partnerships.

•••

The development of the Concorde grew out of a formal study undertaken by Morien B. Morgan of Britain's Royal Aircraft Establishment at the behest of the research organization's director, Sir Arnold Hall. In 1954 Morgan reported that it would be technically feasible to develop a Mach 2 airliner for transoceanic flights, but the existing state of the art would limit such an aircraft to only fifteen passengers, rendering such a project uneconomical. Morgan's findings were predicated on a proposed supersonic Avro bomber, later cancelled.

But the advances of the postwar years kept coming with the advent of enabling technologies. Two years after Morgan's study, the Fairey Delta FD 2, a delta-winged research platform employing an afterburning Rolls-Royce Avon RA5 turbojet, set a new speed record of Mach 1.7. The Fairey aircraft's configuration was especially sleek with no horizontal tail surfaces and proved to be a game changer.

Encouraged by this breakthrough, the Supersonic Transport Aircraft Committee was formed in November 1956. Chaired by Morgan, the committee was composed of twenty-eight individuals from Britain's airframe manufacturers, engine makers, major airlines, research institutions, and government. The country's renowned aviation corporations still competed as freestanding entities and, in hindsight, this time could probably be considered the apex in the arc of their fiscal trajectory.

During the years that the committee convened, English Electric made strides in the development of its P.1 design, which had been initiated in the late 1940s. In 1958 a later version of the swept-wing twin-jet became Britain's first aircraft to reach Mach 2. Named the Lightning, it entered Royal Air Force operational service in 1960. Importantly for the British, their routine Mach 2 flights represented the crossing of a major threshold.

On March 9, 1959, the committee submitted its report, which concluded that Britain should proceed with the development of two supersonic airliners, a large one for New York-to-London flights at Mach 2 cruise speed and a smaller one for regional flights at Mach 1.2 cruise speed. Fearing other countries were perhaps poised to usurp the competitive position of Britain's aviation industry, the authors of the report urged that the development project proceed without delay. Perhaps letting enthusiasm for the technology impair judgment on cost, the committee's estimates of developmental expenditures were overly optimistic as were its perceptions of operational economics.

The British government's deliberations were occurring in a rapidly changing environment. While de Havilland was first to reach the civil jet market with its Comet 1, catastrophic structural failures of some of these airliners due to pressurization-related metal fatigue caused the company to nosedive and never recover. Another eminent name within Britain's aviation industry, Vickers, introduced its impressive VC-10 in 1962. Alas, this was too late to catch up to the popular and already in-service Boeing 707, which had become the darling of major airlines around the world.

Given the grim picture of British airliner prospects, the government felt the need to boost the flagging industry by supporting the development of a supersonic transport (SST). Yet, going alone would be precarious, so the decision was made to proceed with a partner. The logical choice was France.

Unlike Britain, whose aviation industry advanced enormously during World War II, France's had declined. However, France had moved swiftly after the war to get its once-thriving aviation industry back to its former grandeur. In the 1950s France reclaimed its proud aviation heritage by developing a number of highly successful and uncommonly attractive supersonic research and fighter aircraft, including the SNCASO Trident, Nord Griffon, SNCASE Durandal, and Dassault Mirage, all of which cultivated a pathway to the SST.

At the Paris Air Show in June 1961, French airframer Sud Aviation (later to become Aerospatiale and ultimately Airbus) raised eyebrows with the display of an SST mockup. The brainchild of Lucien Servanty and called the Super Caravellle, the configuration was optimized to carry seventy passengers a distance of two thousand miles. Interestingly, it bore a stunning resemblance in general profile to the BAC 223, the SST concept developed by Bristol Aircraft (which was absorbed into the British Aircraft Corporation in late 1961). The BAC 223, which evolved from the Bristol Types 188 and 198, differed from Sud Aviation's mockup in that the British design was physically larger with a notional transatlantic capability.

The British government prodded George Edwards, chairman of BAC, to explore an SST partnership with his French counterpart, Georges Hereil of Sud Aviation. Talks remained deadlocked due to the question of the supersonic jet's size and range. Edwards wanted an airliner based on the BAC 223 whereas Hereil was stubbornly fixated on his company's Super Caravelle.

The impasse was broken by the ascendency of General Charles de Gaulle in 1962. France's new president replaced Hereil at Sud Aviation with Andre Puget, a member of the Free French squadrons that had operated from British airfields during World War II. A good working rapport between the French and British was finally established.

On November 29, 1962, the two countries entered into an agreement to build the SST. Britain and France would be equal partners, with responsibility for the airframe split between the two countries on a 40/60 basis, respectively, with the reverse ratio for the engines. This framework fostered a review process that assured a technically sound aircraft, but it also invited a cumbrous bureaucracy that would prolong the project past the time a single prime contractor would have needed to produce the airliner.

Brian Trubshaw, the British Aircraft Corporation's chief test pilot at the time, tartly remarked later on: "The complexity of Concorde was only matched by that of the organization behind it." The bilateral relationship had its ups and downs. In 1967, supposedly because of escalating costs, Puget was removed. His replacement was Maurice Papon, a former prefect of police in Paris and a political ally of President de Gaulle.

The political operative was replaced the following year, but came to international attention in the 1980s when newly released evidence revealed that during the war, as a member of the Vichy regime he had collaborated with the Nazis in the deportation to death camps of Jewish men, women, and children from the Bordeaux region. Papon's successor at Sud Aviation was Henri Ziegler, another member of Free French air units in the war and a former Air France executive who had previously enjoyed cordial relations with BAC. The turnover on the French side continued, but by Ziegler's departure the Concorde was on its way.

On the British side, the threats to completion came at the political level. The Labor Party superseded the Tories in 1964 with the intent to cancel the government's participation in the project. President de Gaulle lashed out in dramatic fashion and the Labor government backed down, noting that the 1962 partnership agreement contained no escape clause. In 1970, when the Conservative faction regained power in Britain, there was a brief flirtation with a freeze on funding, but calmer heads prevailed and this move was scrubbed.

Just how easily the partnership's charged atmosphere could erupt into dissension was illustrated in the controversy over the spelling of the aircraft's name. The name "Concord"—connoting unity, harmony, and friendship—had been suggested by the eighteen-year-old son of BAC's director of sales. The name was officially embraced by President de Gaulle in a speech several weeks after the signing of the partnership agreement. He expressly mentioned the name and hailed the "new *entente cordiale*."

As time passed, the French spelled this new name with an "e" at the end while the British continued to leave out the dangling vowel. The contrasting spellings continued for five years. Finally, in 1967, a senior British official stepped up to correct this lack of conformity by accepting the French form with the "e" at the end, diplomatically implying that the "e" stood for "excellence, *entente*, and Europe."

The project was co-headquartered at Filton and Toulouse. Construction of the two prototype Concordes 001 and 002 began in April 1965. These were not long-range SSTs as there was still hope for a supersonic regional airliner. Even the two preproduction Concordes, 01 and 02, that followed the prototypes lacked long-range. Only the production models, serial numbers 201 to 216, had transatlantic range, though the first two did not enter commercial service. By the time production started, project participants realized that the regional version's inherent economics, combined with an overland sonic boom, made it infeasible. The long-legged (transatlantic) version was the only viable option.

Right off the bat, Concorde's engineers had to confront the challenge of heat buildup on the surfaces of supersonic aircraft. Although it is very cold at the higher altitudes, the friction produced by an aircraft moving through the air at Mach 2 causes its nose and leading edges to heat up beyond the boiling point for water. This necessitated the use of a heat-resistant aluminum alloy for the outer skin of the fuselage and wings.

Another major challenge was the slim margin afforded by the super-sonic jet's payload-to-gross-weight ratio. At only 5.5 percent, much attention was focused on minimizing drag. This was the era of the slide rule; sophisticated computers with software allowing visualization were still off in the future. Accordingly, hundreds of test models were studied in wind tunnels and a couple research aircraft were developed to refine aerodynamic concepts.

The solution was a delta wing because of its speed potential. And it would have to be a slender delta wing, keeping in mind that at super-sonic speeds the wing's drag increases by the square of its thickness. Of course, because the Concorde's flight profile would include takeoff, climb, descent, and landing, it would have to fly at low speeds too.

The various static and dynamic tests showed that at high angles of attack a sharply swept wing can provide a 25 percent increase in lift because of the vortices that form on the wing's upper surface. Taking this into account, the Concorde was given a double-delta wing with the forward section dramatically swept and the aft section flared outward at much less of a sweep angle. The wing's aft section greatly expanded wing area which improved aerodynamic efficiency at the lower speeds. Also the rounded wingtips offered enhanced stability in certain flight attitudes.

Known as an ogival wing, it was sometimes referred to as the High Gothic because it resembled the ogee or double curve popular in medi-eval architecture. Test aircraft were indispensable in arriving at this shape. The Handley Page HP 115 began flying in 1961 to investigate low-speed handling characteristics of the slender delta wing. In 1965 a modified Fairey Delta FD 2, known as the BAC 221, began to explore flight per-formance at both ends of the speed envelope. In addition, French fighter and business jet manufacturer Dassault provided flight-test data on its then new delta-winged Mirage IV.

One of the most innovative aspects of the Concorde design was the invention to cope with the phenomenon by which an aircraft in super-sonic flight tends to nose down. Counteracting this by upward deflection of tail surfaces would work, but doing so would add considerably to drag and thus significantly reduce range. The answer was a fuel transfer system that would adjust the Concorde's center of gravity within a pre-calculated envelope by pumping the fuel to appropriate tanks as required based on the mode of flight. This was a fine methodology, but there are almost always tradeoffs. The fuel transfer system entailed complex plumbing with commensurate weight and internal volume penalties.

The Concorde had a nose-high attitude which required a "drooping" nose to provide forward visibility to the pilots during taxi, takeoff, and landing. The "droop" angle was five degrees at takeoff and twelve and a half degrees on approach to landing through touchdown. During en route cruise, the nose was raised, along with a visor to protect against the intense heat at supersonic speed. The original metal visor was replaced by a transparent Triplex visor.

Bristol Siddeley Engines (which was acquired by Rolls-Royce in 1966) and SNECMA (Societe Nationale d'Etude et de Construction de Moteurs d'Aviation) collaborated on the Concorde's engine development. The only realistic candidates for the Concorde were derivatives of engines for military aircraft as no civil aircraft until the Concorde had a supersonic capability. The basis for the engine collaboration was the Bristol Olympus, which had been fathered by the brilliant Sir Stanley Hooker.

Early versions of the engine were employed in the Avro Vulcan bomber and a later version in the BAC's stillborn TSR-2 strike/reconnaissance aircraft. The ultimate evolution was the Olympus 593 afterburning turbojet. Four such engines powered the Concorde.

The engines were paired in under-wing nacelles outboard of the main landing gear. In addition to the engines themselves, each nacelle incorporated air intakes and exhaust nozzles. Internal engine parts were made of titanium and a nickel-based alloy to withstand high temperatures.

Slowing down intake airflow as required for supersonic flight was accomplished through the use of intake ramps. By partially closing, the ramps would produce a shockwave at the intake lip. This system operated automatically with sensors providing essential inputs. One of the jobs of the flight engineer, who sat sideways behind the captain and first officer, was to monitor the workings of the sophisticated air intake control units and the position of the ramps.

The original plan to use a conventional nozzle was scrapped by the second preproduction aircraft. The Thrust Reverser Aft (TRA) was added as a weight and noise reducer. Each engine was rated at 38,050 pounds of thrust with afterburner.

First flight of the Concorde occurred March 2, 1969. Lead test pilot was Sud Aviation's Andre Turcat who had been on the project dating back to the days of the Super Caravelle concept. He and his five crewmates lifted off runway 33 at Toulouse and for the next forty-two minutes proceeded to check out handling and systems. The aircraft reached an altitude of ten thousand feet and a speed of 250 knots.

For all the technological genius that went into the making of the Concorde, the simple elegance of its arrow-like profile made it look like it belonged in the sky. Brian Trubshaw, who as Turcat's British opposite would fly the British prototype for the first time the following month, remarked, upon seeing the airliner finally take to the sky: "The beauty of Concorde in flight captured the whole of the aviation world and was a thrilling sight." After that maiden flight, Turcat declared: "She flies! And she flies well."

The aesthetically pleasing and technologically advanced Concorde sparked heaps of controversy as it inched its way to commercial service on January 21, 1976. Some critics echoed the longstanding claim that the project should be cancelled on economic grounds since profits were, in their view, unlikely to ever materialize. But the British and French governments had simply invested too much to pull the plug on the eve of airline operations.

Environmental activists rallied against the new airliner, alleging it would pollute the atmosphere, destroy the ozone layer, and disrupt any semblance of peace and quiet for a large segment of the world's population because of the sonic boom. Yet the handful of supersonic airliners would emit such infinitesimal quantities of nitric oxide as to be immeasurable. Responses of a scientific nature should have allayed the fears of the protesters, but their agenda seemed intent on shutting the Concorde down in any case.

The problem of the sonic boom would be solved by restricting supersonic operations to overwater flights. Regarding localized noise at takeoff, a particular concern of some vocal New York–area residents, Concorde's operators, British Airways and Air France, agreed to fly noise abatement patterns at John F. Kennedy International Airport. As scheduled service began to the United States, first Washington, D.C., on May 24, 1976, and then New York on November 22, 1977, the environmental clamor dissipated much as the sound of a departing Concorde.

In response to the 1962 Anglo-French announcement of a partnership to build an SST, the administration of President Kennedy committed to the development of an American supersonic airliner. This happened in the context of America playing catch-up with the Soviets in space. The perception that America might also be falling behind Europe in aeronautics was unacceptable.

The stated intent of Pan American World Airways to buy six of the new European jets sent shivers down the spines of US policymakers and stiffened the resolve to move ahead on a homegrown SST. The FAA would oversee a design competition. Boeing and Lockheed entered submissions. Both designs resembled the Concorde; however, the Boeing layout was much larger and involved a variable-geometry or "swing" wing.

At the end of 1966, Boeing won the competition with its B2707-200 that presumed to fly three times as many passengers as the Concorde and outrun it by 400 miles per hour. The project was to be funded 90 percent by the US government, with the remainder of the cost assumed by the contractor. This formula would change to a 75/25 split in the event of cost overruns.

Once Boeing got started on development, it had to scale back its ambitions. The swing-wing turned out to be impractical and was dropped, while horizontal tail surfaces were added. Also the cabin had to be downsized, reducing the passenger count. Other technical problems were being encountered much as occurred with the Concorde.

Perhaps more importantly for the American SST's future, by the late 1960s / early 1970s the public's mood (and therefore the level of political support) was shifting in a less favorable direction. The country had caught up and surpassed the Soviet Union in the space race as measured by the yardstick of a successful manned lunar mission. One-upping the Soviets was becoming redundant. A stalled war and domestic strife contributed further to a growing consensus that the country needed to reorder its priorities.

The environmental movement emerged as a force to be reckoned with. At the same time, fiscal hawks found an opportune whipping post in the costly aircraft. The groups joined in common cause. Even fair-minded observers questioned whether any supersonic airliner could be economically viable once in service, given the expected high operating costs and the limited clientele for what would have to be extravagantly priced tickets. In May 1971 Congress cut off funds, forcing Boeing to bring the project to a screeching halt.

The Soviet Union's SST, looking much like the Concorde and jocularly referred to as the Concordski, proceeded apace. Indeed, it flew two months before the Concorde's first flight. Developed by the Tupolev design bureau, the Tu-144 required many modifications including wing shape, engine placement, and the addition of retractable canards.

At the 1973 Paris Air Show, the Tu-144 suffered a fatal crash during a display performance. No cause was officially determined, but speculation centered on possible last-minute tweaks for the flying display's maneuvers. In any case, the aircraft went into service with Aeroflot in late 1975 as a mail and freight hauler between Moscow and Alma-Ata, the capital of Kazakhstan. The distance of eighteen hundred miles suggested that the aircraft lacked the range for transatlantic flights.

In 1977 Aeroflot inaugurated Tu-144 passenger service on the same overland supersonic route, but canceled it the next year because of another crash. The plane was then withdrawn from all flight operations including the non-passenger service. Commentators reflected on the incongruity of a professedly Communist country having produced and operated the type of jetliner normally equated with Western decadence and hedonism. In an odd twist, during a period of thawed US/Russian relations following the collapse of the Soviet Union, NASA wanted to conduct studies on a possible new, larger supersonic airliner and paid for access to a couple of Tu-144s that Russia maintained in airworthy condition.

The beginning of the end for the Concorde came on July 25, 2000. Air France Flight 4590 was on its takeoff roll at Charles de Gaulle Airport outside of Paris when a piece of debris severed a tire. A chunk of the tire's rubber pitched up and ruptured a fuel tank in the port wing. Even before the aircraft lifted off, signs of an engine fire in the number two engine were evident.

The flight crew would not have had enough remaining runway to abort the takeoff, so the aircraft, though trailing a plume of flame, rose into the sky. A valiant attempt was made to land, either at De Gaulle or Le Bourget, but the loss of an engine and then a second one limited speed and altitude to perilous levels. Meanwhile, the fire was spreading and its heat began to melt portions of the wing.

Trying to correct for the asymmetric thrust caused by the loss of power on the airliner's port side, the flight crew throttled back the two starboard engines. This further reduced airspeed, which caused the heavily loaded Concorde, straining to maintain lift, to enter a stall. The plane dipped dramatically to one side and smashed into a hotel at Gonesse.

The accident was the first fatal flight of the supersonic aircraft. Until then, the Concorde was considered one of the safest airliners in history. All 113 people on board and another four on the ground were killed. Amateur video of the tragedy horrified audiences around the world. The crippled plane, its occupants helpless to extinguish the raging fire, gave the appearance of a wounded animal doomed to the most awful fate.

The aircraft in both British and French fleets were grounded pending an investigation. Some improvements were instituted including puncture-resistant tires. On November 7, 2001, the two airlines resumed service. Timing was not good, for only two months earlier, on September 11th, coordinated terrorist attacks had taken down four conventional airliners in the United States.

The Concorde was always a dicey economic proposition. For Air France, flying the supersonic jet was a mostly unprofitable affair. British Airways, which enjoyed better occupancy rates on supersonic flights, reportedly turned a profit on the plane's operations. In the aftermath of the horrific accident and the 9/11 attacks, occupancy was running below 50 percent capacity. The airlines faced up to this unsustainable reality and announced the Concorde's retirement on April 10, 2003.

The last Air France flight occurred on May 31, 2003. It was a flight from New York to Paris. British Airways followed suit on October 24,

2003, with a flight from New York to London. The end of service was an emotional experience for the thousands of people at the airlines and the contractors who had invested so much of their lives—indeed, their dreams—into this special plane.

The final flights to the capitals of the countries that had created this technological wonder represented the ultimate homecomings, a source of pride for what had been achieved against the refrain of doubters who questioned whether the project would ever get off the ground. As part of the official farewell, Her Majesty Queen Elizabeth II instructed that the lights of Windsor Castle should brighten the sky for one of the last flyovers, a high honor and a symbolic salute. When British Airways' concluding Concorde flight touched down at London's Heathrow Airport, it was directed to an isolated section of the tarmac where fire crews scurried out and shot high-pressure streams of water into the air to form an arch above the stately plane, at once a celebration and a wake, as if shedding a giant's bittersweet tears variously of joy and sadness.

The Concorde was the most recognizable aircraft in the world with its distinctive, highly streamlined shape, a brand unto itself. Gracing the sky, its figure had represented the heights to which humans could soar. The project's struggles and triumphs were Shakespearian in scope. So, at the end of the run, as the surviving members of the creative teams that had brought the concept into being and the line personnel who had made it work bid their splendid machine adieu, it was a reminder, in the words of the great bard himself, "parting is such sweet sorrow."

In routinely bringing the miracle of supersonic flight to business travelers and tourists alike, the Concorde was about the aviation future. In its thrilling early days, it was not unreasonable or unusual to think that within a generation airliners would be flying faster, higher, and farther at more accessible prices. After all, the parallel achievements in manned space exploration prompted many to speculate then that it was only a matter of time before the founding of a lunar colony and the setting of footsteps on Mars.

Yet, in the many years since 1969 when the Concorde thundered aloft on its maiden flight and astronauts touched the face of a new world for the first time, the opposite happened. After these thrilling air and space programs played out, society reverted to subsonic-only air travel and workaday space missions no more distant than familiar, low earth orbit. We can only hope that this hiatus is but a breather, for when a people do not employ available technologies in the pursuit of daily life and peaceful commerce, let alone advance those technologies to the next plateau, it is a sign of intellectual stagnancy and spiritual destitution, a civilizational atrophy that is to be dreaded.

Happily, from time to time during this extended interlude, murmurs of a bold new age have sounded through the din of our common existence. President Ronald Reagan, trying to rekindle the excitement that animated the manned lunar adventure, called for a hypersonic transport, what he termed the Orient Express, to regularly carry passengers halfway around the world in a flight of only ninety minutes. More recently, an array of entrepreneurs has stepped forward to promote space tourism in specially designed craft. We still await completion of the platforms and techniques that will transform these long-simmering dreams into reality.

On the plus side, the march of progress over the last half century has rendered enabling technologies that, if harvested by the right aggregator, could yield the wanted advance in commercially viable supersonic flight. As an example, the primary aircraft structures of certain jetliners are now made of carbon-fiber composites. These modern materials are stronger and lighter than the metals that formed the body of the Concorde. In theory this means that a next-generation SST could be bigger, seating more passengers to generate proportionally more revenue and holding more fuel to extend range.

Another step forward has been the quantum leap in computing power. Some of the developmental work of the past which required physical models or prototypes does not necessarily have to happen today. Digital simulations in many instances can provide the vital data. With reliance on computer modeling, time and money can be saved by obviating the need for old-style testing.

If Asian economies continue to flourish, international business will increasingly shift to the nexus of the Pacific Rim. This would give aircraft and engine manufacturers additional incentive to develop transpacific airliners with supersonic capability. Or it could be that before scheduled air carriers return to the supersonic fold, operators of smaller and less costly business jets will make the initial move to bring supersonic jets back into the civil fleet. Of course, the makers of executive aircraft would have to have the technical know-how in hand and see payback opportunities before gearing up to supply this ultra high-end niche market.

A potentially game-changing development would be the introduction of designs that produce low-intensity sonic booms. Research suggests that improvement in the acoustic footprint of supersonic aircraft can be achieved. Further investigations hope to demonstrate that specially configured jets with exaggeratedly long "Pinocchio" noses can create a shaped sonic boom signature that reduces the disruptive clap to a distant "thump," a level that might be tolerable for people who underlie prospective overland routes. If such a breakthrough occurs, it could open the way for the lifting of the Congressionally imposed ban on supersonic overflights of the US mainland.

Various museums around the world showcase examples of the Concorde. This is as it should be, for the trailblazing SST broke new ground and opened new vistas. For its full value to be appreciated, it should be seen not only as a charmed relic steeped in an invigorating history but as a shiny steppingstone to an even more illustrious tomorrow.

Section 3

Sky Warriors: Military Platforms

CHAPTER 12

A Reputed Scourge: The Flying Dutchman and the First Fighter

He came to be known as the "Flying Dutchman." On April 6, 1890, Anthony Herman Gerard Fokker was born in Java, the Dutch East Indies. An idyllic early life on his father's coffee plantation encompassed his mimicking barefooted native boys who scaled trees with simian dexterity and even picked up nails with their toes. Indeed, Tony's "feet didn't know the feel of a shoe" until he was six years old.

Concerned that their son, Tony, and older daughter, Katharina, would not receive an adequate education in the tropical settlement eight thousand miles from home, parents Herman and Anna decided to return to Holland and enroll their children in school. In 1894, twenty years after arriving in the tropics to make his fortune, Herman moved his family to Haarlem, fourteen miles west of Amsterdam. Like other retired Dutch plantation owners in Haarlem, Herman planned to live out the remainder of his years enjoying his riches.

But the cramped backyard did not please Tony, who was used to the expansive grounds of the plantation estate. Nor did he care for school, where he found his studies to be "a boring routine, monotonous in the extreme." Instead, he retreated to the third-floor attic in the house where he set up a workshop that he considered "infinitely superior to a classroom" for learning what mattered to him.

Projects included toy trains, for which Tony fabricated miniature electric, gas, and steam engines. He built a canoe, fitted a sail to it, and played hooky by taking it for sojourns in the nearby Spaarne River on school days. At school he invented a clandestine relay system to appear knowledgeable during stand-up quizzes and a peephole arrangement to answer questions on written exams. The precocious student eventually showed the teachers how his schemes worked, since, as he put it, "they were too dumb to find out for themselves."

The pupil harbored contempt for his teachers and vice versa. Tony, who liked only math, the natural sciences, and drafting, was held back two years behind his classmates. In late 1908, during his second to last year, already aged eighteen, Tony dropped out of high school.

Before his departure, the school's *enfant terrible* made the acquaintance of another mischievous son of a privileged family in the janitor's room of the school, where they had been exiled for their misbehavior. Tony became friends with his derelict classmate and the two spent their post-school days on larks driving the Peugeot that belonged to the classmate's family. Importantly for Tony's future in the world of complex aviation machinery, he came to know the "automobile inside and out" so that he "could repair the motor and anything else which went wrong."

From Wilbur Wright's grand European exhibitions that started in LeMans, France, on August 8, 1908, to Louis Bleriot's first crossing of the English Channel on July 25, 1909, and the early experiments of Henri Farman at that time, Tony was fascinated by the new science of flight. He believed that all of the aircraft flown by these pioneers suffered from inadequate lateral stability and that their turning capability was stunted. He immersed himself in the study of aeronautics in his attic workshop and conjured up a competing design that strove to provide better stability and maneuverability, attributes that would resurface as major design goals when he began his aircraft manufacturing business in earnest.

Tony's parents did not at first encourage his interest in flying. To them flying was inherently dangerous and a "passing fad." In March 1910 what anyone thought about the ostentatious plans of the would-be plane-builder made little difference because Tony, having left school, was drafted into the Dutch military.

A free spirit and an independent thinker who abhorred authority, Tony and the army didn't get along well together. He shunned his assignment to an artillery regiment and, while on leave, sustained an ankle injury.

During his recuperation in a military hospital, the scheming young man bribed an orderly to obtain a medical discharge from his service obligation. No sooner had Tony been conscripted than he finagled his way out of uniform to pursue his dream of flight.

Tony still had to contend with his father, who insisted that the answer to the fetish with aviation was to go into a formal engineering program. This way his capricious son could make himself "fit for something important in the world." The *Technikum* in the German town of Bingen offered coursework that blended the theoretical with the practical. It seemed like it might be a good combination for Tony, who preferred hands-on experimentation to book-learning and classroom lectures.

Once in Bingen, Tony got word of a trade school in nearby Zalbach that was about to open an aeronautics department. Almost immediately, he changed his plans, persuading his father to accept the transfer, with scant mention of the aviation component. The flying program proved to be short on resources and its doors were closed.

When all seemed to be going against Tony, he showed that he had been endowed "with a spirit which strengthens miraculously in adversity." Using a quasi aviation metaphor to describe his determination, he later wrote that at this nadir in his life he "dusted off the seat of my pants, swallowed my tears, and decided to build a plane of my own." To fund his latest venture, he recovered his deposit for classes not attended at the *Technikum*, somehow persuaded his father to advance additional money, and attracted the investment of retired Oberleutnant Franz von Daum, a fellow student at the defunct aviation school.

Inspired by nature's example, Tony loosely patterned the design for his first plane after birds, theorizing that since birds do not have ailerons or rudders, an aerodynamically efficient plane ought to not have them either. But the young entrepreneur woke to the realization that "No one can build as wonderful a machine as a bird." Reflecting on the difficulties in matching nature's perfection, he wrote: "We succeed only by duplicating her result rather than her methods."

To help build his design, Tony chose a small German aircraft construction company near the ill-fated flying school. The company was producing an aircraft modeled on Igo Etrich's dovelike Taube. Tony's ideas paralleled characteristics of the Taube—an externally braced monoplane with ample wing area and, as seen from above, a feather-like empennage fanned out at the tail. The Fokker plane, known informally as the Spider because of its "web" of many bracing wires, was equipped with a 50-horsepower Argus engine.

Completed in October 1910, the Spider was moved to a larger field in Baden-Baden for flight testing. The then-vacant Zeppelin hangar was used to house the plane. Shortly before Christmas, Tony gingerly lifted his creation into the air for a series of runs in straight lines only, each a distance of about a hundred feet at minimal altitude. "It was pure elation," as the enterprising aerial experimenter taught himself to fly.

Tony's excitement was not enough to stave off the effects of riding in the open air amid frigid temperatures. He came down with pneumonia. While recuperating at home in Haarlem, Tony's business partner tried to replicate his feat.

The flight ended badly, but the plane was repairable. Sometime later, after the repairs were made, von Daum insisted on trying again. Against his better judgment, Tony consented.

It was another debacle. Von Daum, "more bewildered than hurt," crawled out of the wreckage declaring that he was "through with flying." Tony bought out the retired officer with funds advanced by his father. The experience foreshadowed the young inventor's future problematic partner relations. Tony liked being his own boss, but often needed capital infusions from outside sources which invariably came with strings attached.

On May 16, 1911, Tony earned a pilot's license. It was a notable accomplishment, especially since he remained essentially self-taught. To celebrate Queen Wilhelmina's birthday on August 31st, Tony flew his third plane, an improved Spider, over his hometown of Haarlem where his performance elicited "the first and biggest ovation" of his life. About his fifteen-minute flight and the outpouring of local citizens the next day, Tony said: "It remains the high point of my life."

Later in the year, Tony moved to Johannisthal, a center of aviation activity on the southeast fringe of Berlin. On February 22, 1912, he registered his business under the Fokker name, the formal start of his plane-building career. In his drive to make his company one of the world's best-known aviation brands, he encountered extreme opposites: sometimes, underhanded industry rivals and, at other times, the warm camaraderie of like-minded flyers.

Soon after arriving at Johannisthal, Tony's plane was sabotaged. An unknown party, presumed to be a competitor on the airfield, surreptitiously contaminated its fuel tank with sugar, which fouled the engine and prevented flight on a busy weekend with lots of rides to sell. Rather than be discouraged, the incident made Tony more determined than ever to outbuild and outfly the other designers and pilots on the grounds.

There were happy times too. Tony fondly reminisced about the cordial spot at the airport where members of the flying community could relax—"in the gay, sportive little café run by Papa Senftleben." According to Tony, it was "where wine, women and song were permanently on the menu." From the description, the café's conviviality among airport patrons bore a similarity to Pancho Barnes's Happy Bottom Riding Club near Edwards Air Force Base in California at a later period in time.

Tony's popularity resulted in a drink at the café being named after him. Kaffee Fokker was notably differentiated from other drinks named after airport personalities. Absent alcohol, it was "a tall beaker of warm milk with an inch of coffee." The blandness of the beverage reflected the man's devotion to getting his aircraft right by laboring long hours in his grease-stained coveralls. The portion of coffee may have connoted Tony's untiring energy as much if not more than his father's former link to the coffee plantation in Java.

Tony continued to struggle, weathering one financial crisis after another as flight instruction sustained his company when aircraft sales did not. Prospects of a Russian deal fell through and a planned sale in the Dutch East Indies did not materialize. He was back to begging his father and uncles for more funds to keep his business alive. In July 1913 fortunes of the beleaguered company suddenly began to improve when the German military placed the first of successive orders for aircraft derived from the Spider design.

The infusion of cash was followed by German officers requesting that Tony move his company to Schwerin, a town well north of Berlin. Officials wanted to expand the country's aviation industry and there just wasn't enough room at Johannisthal's airport for Fokker and the other more mature aircraft builders. As an inducement, Schwerin would construct an airport.

Tony agreed to the move, but as quickly as the military's orders for Fokker planes had come, they dried up. Tony realized that his basic design, the Spider, even with upgrades, was an aircraft of fading interest. Desperate for a quick leap ahead, he bought a damaged Morane-Saulnier Type H monoplane at a substantially discounted price in Paris, with the express purpose of reverse engineering it as the next model in his company's product offerings.

The French plane had a lighter engine than anything produced by German manufacturers. Also the purchased plane was known to have superior maneuverability. The insipid practice of copying one's competitor was not Tony's normal way of doing business, but when in a bind he did what he thought he had to in order to survive. For his part, Tony claimed that while his version "resembled" the Morane in "general appearance," "from a detailed engineering standpoint it was radically different."

Indeed, not content to simply replicate the French design, Tony worked with a newly hired designer to improve it. The fuselage's wooden frame was replaced by a welded tubular structure that was both sturdier and lighter. This metal structure was covered in fabric as were the shoulder-mounted wood-frame wings.

The Fokker team kept the 80-horsepower Gnome rotary engine, which would be made under license in Germany. Although the resulting Fokker M.5 (the "M" stood for *Militar* or military) incorporated a crude control system reliant on wing-warping, it was remarkably agile for the time and could cruise at 80 miles per hour. The new plane featured materials that would be standard on some single-seat fighters throughout the coming war.

In the spring of 1914, Tony showed off the partial copycat plane in aerial performances, to the delight of German officialdom. As the French had already demonstrated, the still-exotic maneuver of the loop was possible in such a plane. Tony threw himself into the stunt that he called "looping the loop," thrilling crowds at German airports.

His show at Johannisthal led to his being "hailed as the most daring pilot in Germany." Tony's timing was fortuitous for World War I would erupt in a matter of months, requiring large numbers of training and combat aircraft. For the first time since entering the aviation business, Tony appeared to be on the verge of financial success.

As a matter of fact, Fokker's order book began to fill. Tony wished to buy out his partners, including his father and other family members. This was done within a few months after war broke out in August 1914.

With war under way, German authorities voiced concern over Tony's nationality. It was peculiar to them that a Dutchman should be building warplanes on German soil in the middle of a deadly conflict. Tony gave in to the duress; he quickly applied for German citizenship, which was almost as quickly granted.

The first couple months of World War I offered much opportunity for aircraft to be used as reconnaissance platforms. In general, the Fokker M series fit this niche well. One highly regarded pilot reflected the consensus when he described the light and maneuverable Fokker reconnaissance plane as his "best Christmas treat." Yet Tony's shift to mass production led to quality control issues. Also his engine supplier, Oberursel Motoren Werke (which built a clone of the Gnome engine) suffered in this regard as well, prompting some pilots to complain about the engine's lack of reliability.

By early October 1914, when a French plane shot down a German plane, flying machines became more than a means for passive observation. Suddenly this still-new military instrument became a deadly weapon. Air forces and the airframe manufacturers that supplied them began to adjust.

The year before the outbreak of war, Raymond Saulnier of the successful French manufacturer Morane-Saulnier had experimented with a forward-firing machine gun synchronizer to see if bullets could be shot through the propeller arc of pursuit planes, permitting pilots to hit enemy aircraft directly in line with them. The tests met with mixed results. The synchronizer's timing was not able to fully account for the lack of uniformity in the firing of hand-packed bullets, which caused the out-of-step bullets to strike the back side of the propeller. Saulnier's solution was to install metal deflector plates over the affected sections of the propeller.

At first, little interest was shown in such a system, but when war engulfed Europe the attitude of French officials changed. In December

1914 France's acclaimed prewar exhibition and racing pilot Roland Garros worked with his mechanic, Jules Hue, to refine the Saulnier system. After extensive tests with a Hotchkiss machine gun, the answer to preserving propeller functionality was to use more effective steel wedge deflector plates.

Although far from perfect with up to 10 percent of rounds ricocheting off the deflector plates, the system was considered worthy of deployment. On April 1, 1915, a month after France's first dedicated fighter squadron had been established, Garros took the revised gun synchronizer into combat near Dunkirk. Flying a Morane-Saulnier Type L parasol design, he is said to have shot down three German planes in the next fifteen days.

What happened next has been recounted differently, but the effect was the same. By one version, Garros's LeRhone rotary engine malfunctioned, and by another version, his plane was disabled by ground fire. In either case, Garros made a forced landing behind enemy lines near Ingelmunster in West Flanders on April 19th. Upon extricating himself from the Morane-Saulnier, he attempted to set it on fire to destroy what he could of the plane and its unique forward-firing gun system.

German troops soon arrived on the scene to capture Garros and salvage his still mostly intact plane and gun synchronizer. Referring to the downed French aviator and the confiscation of his forward-firing system, Tony wrote: "Then his secret was out."

There are conflicting versions of events from that point. By one account, the German military turned the system over to a small group of experts who failed to replicate the interrupter mechanism and then called on Tony. In Tony's account there is no mention of others having been consulted, only that German officials summoned him to Berlin where the plane and its gun system had been sent for analysis. Tony admitted that he had never held or fired a machine gun before, but he claimed that with his mechanical savvy he quickly grasped the workings of the French system and crafted a solution to ensure that the gun fired only when there was an opening between propeller blade revolutions.

Some historians contend that Tony was not really the one to make this breakthrough. Instead, his staff at Schwerin are said to have come up with the answer to an effective synchronizer. For his part, Tony stated that he reduced the problem to basic technical considerations starting with his understanding that the two-bladed propeller of his plane revolved twelve hundred times per minute (which meant the blades passed a given point twenty-four hundred times per minute). Also the Parabellum machine gun he had been given for the developmental effort fired approximately six hundred times per minute.

In fabricating a preliminary device, Tony "attached a small knob to the propeller which struck a cam as it revolved. This cam was hooked up with the hammer of the machine gun, which automatically loaded itself." Having reached a baseline, he took the fabrication a step further the next day. "To the cam was fastened a simple knee lever, which operated a rod, held back by a spring. In order that the pilot could control the shooting, a piece of the rod which struck the hammer was hinged to hit or miss as the operator desired." The final touch was to increase the firing rate to prevent rounds from striking the propeller.

The new system with the Parabellum machine gun was fitted to a Fokker M.5K (the "K" stood for *Kurz* or short-span wing) and took the designation M.5K/MG. For trials, the modified plane was towed the 220 miles from Schwerin to Doeberitz by Tony in his Peugeot touring car. Both static ground test firings and airborne firings proved the system worked. The whole process from start to finish took about one week.

The consensus among the still-skeptical staff officers was that the uniquely equipped plane needed to demonstrate its efficacy in combat before it could be accepted. Against his protests, Tony was pressed into service at the rank of *Leutnant* and sent in uniform with his plane to the air base at Douai. Before going on patrol, he demonstrated the system to German Crown Prince Wilhelm, commander of the German Fifth Army near Verdun.

Tony put on an aerobatic display and then performed a series of dives, sending bursts of bullets into a nearby stream which sent up "a chain of geysers." The crown prince was duly impressed and remarked: "He seems to be a real flying Dutchman." Plaudits came as well from Max Immel-mann, a future ace and originator of a reversal maneuver that became a lasting staple in the repertoire of fighter pilots who wrote in a letter home: "Fokker amazed us with his ability."

After several unsuccessful attempts to make contact with French or British aircraft from his patrols out of Douai, Tony finally spotted a two-seat pusher-style Farman observation plane a few thousand feet below his six thousand-foot cruising altitude. His chance to conclusively prove the synchronizer mated to his monoplane by shooting down a French aircraft had arrived and he instinctively "dived rapidly toward it."

Yet the closer he got to the sitting duck, the more pensive he became. He could see the French flyers staring at him as he approached. It turned out that he did not have the fortitude for combat or at least this kind of cold-blooded assassination.

Tony later wrote: "It was too much like 'cold meat' to suit me. I had no stomach for the whole business, nor any wish to kill Frenchmen for Germans. Let them do their own killing!" He returned to Douai empty-handed and declared his refusal to go back on patrol, which caused some consternation. The next day, the task of proving the device fell to Leutnant Oswald Boelcke, destined to become Germany's first ace and, arguably, the best frontline air commander of the war. On his third flight in the Fokker, Boelcke scored a kill. Instantly, the German military leadership became believers and ordered more of the combination Fokker mono-plane and synchronized forward-firing gun.

By some people's reckoning, it was the birth of the true fighter, a passably maneuverable aircraft equipped with an effective weapon system. The ability to shoot through the propeller arc meant that it was no longer necessary to lug a gunner along in a separate cockpit or to mount guns on the upper wing of a biplane. Now the pilot could aim at and shoot his quarry in the direct sightline from his seat in the cockpit. In fact Fokker soon installed a headrest in its newly configured pursuit plane so that the pilot could be assured of the correct alignment.

From a tactical perspective, fighter pilots henceforth could channel their energies into acquiring optimal firing positions. Once thus situated, scoring hits against the adversary would be a comparatively simple matter of letting loose with bursts straight ahead. The military designation for the production variant of the armed Fokker was E.I (the "E" stood for *Eindecker* or monoplane).

As talented pursuit pilots like Boelcke and Immelmann went into combat with the new type, they began to rack up victories against Allied aircraft. For several months that followed, the armed Fokker gave pilots in the German Flying Corps a qualitative advantage over their British and French nemeses. The lopsided outcomes in aerial engagements from the summer of 1915 into early 1916 gave rise to the so-called "Fokker Scourge" which allegedly made Allied airmen "Fokker Fodder."

For a time, morale fluctuated proportionate to the good or bad on either side among airmen at the front and their countrymen back home. However, despite the period's sensationalized reporting on the effect of Fokker's cutting-edge fighter, the truth was that the Fokker production line was limited in the volume it could generate. Only twenty-one planes a month rolled out through December 1915, with peak production of thirty-six aircraft being reached in August 1916. There simply were not enough armed Fokker monoplanes to substantially dent the overwhelming numbers of Allied aircraft.

More importantly, the Allies hastened their efforts to get competing synchronizer systems fielded and they introduced better-performing pursuit planes like the Nieuport 11. Despite updated Fokker monoplanes, including the E.II, E.III, and E.IV—some of which were equipped with improved synchronizer systems that were driven directly by the engine and could be adapted to different guns like the Spandau—the plane once dreaded by its opponents was fast becoming outclassed. Be that as it may, the E-series had made clear that in air combat, as in warfare generally, technological superiority (and perhaps its mere perception) can hold sway.

Competition from German industry heated up as well. Manufacturers like Albatros and Halberstadt gave Fokker a run for its money with designs that were more maneuverable than the little monoplane. Even worse for Tony, both he and his company were sued for patent infringement by Franz Schneider who had invented a gun synchronizer just before the war. While Tony vigorously defended his position with a team of lawyers, near the end of the war an appellate court upheld the lower court ruling in favor of Schneider's claim. Tony, who is said to have genuinely believed he had developed the gun synchronizer independently, refused to pay. The litigation dragged on for years after the war, until finally it was dropped when the plaintiff's resources ran out.

On the heels of his E-series, Tony entered a dry period in which his designs fell short of expectations. His rebirth as a successful designer was attributable to his Dr.I (the "Dr" stood for *Dreidecker* or triplane), which was ironically inspired by a captured Sopwith Triplane. The extra wing surface area offered enhanced maneuverability, which was considered of greater value to the dogfighting pursuit pilot than raw speed. After wing defects were corrected, the new Fokker entered service in December 1917. Germany's highest-scoring ace, Manfred von Richthofen, menaced the skies in his flamboyant all-red Dr.I, leaving an enduring imprint as the "Red Baron."

Fokker's finest wartime design was the D.VII (the "D" stood for *Doppeldecker* or biplane), which went into service in spring 1918. Impatient to get large numbers into flying units, the government proposed that it be built under license by large German manufacturers, which reflected both the limited capacity of the Fokker operation in Schwerin and the ongoing issue of the facility's dubious quality. At the front, the D.VII was a match for Allied pursuit planes like the SPAD XIII.

After the war, at twenty-eight years of age, Tony reestablished his business in Holland where he regained his Dutch citizenship. His name had emerged as a recognizable brand and his ambitions extended to America where he organized a separate company in the 1920s to mirror the production of his Dutch-built tri-motor transports. The planes filled a niche in the commercial airline market.

From the mid-1920s to 1930, Fokker tri-motors attained a mystique as pioneering platforms. They were used by Robert Byrd for his expedition to the North Pole and his flight across the Atlantic Ocean. Amelia Earhart became the first woman on a transatlantic flight, hopping a ride as a passenger in the Fokker tri-motor named the *Friendship*. Charles Kingsford-Smith circumnavigated the world in the *Southern Cross*, a sister ship to the one used on Byrd's polar flight.

On March 31, 1931, the reputation of the prominent aircraft suffered a debilitating blow. The limitations of the Fokker tri-motor's wooden wing construction became painfully apparent. An F-10A tri-motor operated by

Transcontinental & Western Air (the precursor of Trans World Airlines or TWA) crashed in Kansas, killing all aboard. Among the passengers was venerated University of Notre Dame football coach Knute Rockne.

Americans were horrified. The investigation showed that the cause was material fatigue combined with poorly glued wooden wing structures that had flexed in more than three hundred hours of turbulent flying. In the aftermath, most US-operated models of the Fokker were grounded. Fokker businesses in the United States, by then beset with a managerial myopia that ran deeper than a design/construction deficiency, never really recovered.

Nearly two years prior to the devastating accident, in May 1929, amid rising stock prices and frenzied aviation industry consolidations, a controlling interest in Fokker had been sold to General Motors. The dominant automaker thought it prudent to buy into the largest direct competitor to Ford's all-metal tri-motor. GM, which would soon enough rue the day it invested in Fokker, operated its new acquisition under the name General Aviation Manufacturing Corporation.

After four years of mostly losses, GM's aircraft unit was merged into North American Aviation where it was downsized into a production division. Tony had kept the rights to the Fokker name, but his design and build activity in the United States had shriveled up to a mere shadow of its former self. Tony's 1931 autobiography, which had gone to press before the Rockne crash, ended on an optimistic note with the boast that airlines flying his tri-motors were "adding to their admirable safety and operation records." In the book's closing sentence, he wrote of his "pioneer work becoming the nucleus of a world-wide enterprise" through his affiliation with GM. Little did he know when penning those words that it was just a matter of time before GM would unload its investment in his aviation business.

From his trips to the United States starting after World War I, Tony believed the future of the aviation industry was in America with its open skies overlaying its vast territory and with its pervasive free enterprise mindset. He became a permanent resident and eventually a citizen. When his company's fortunes soured, he set out as a sales representative for US companies like Douglas and Lockheed that recognized the value of the Fokker connections in European aviation markets.

In 1939 Tony died in New York of complications from a sinus-related surgery. He was only forty-nine years old. His ties to the Dutch company bearing his name had by then unraveled. Subsequently, with the onset of World War II and the invasion of Holland in May 1940, the company's projects were halted on orders of the Nazi occupiers.

In a strange twist, the Fokker plant was forced to produce parts for the German tri-motor transport, the Junkers Ju 52. After the war, the company resumed independent operations under the Fokker name. After all, Anthony Fokker had been Holland's most illustrious aviation personality, a source of national pride.

•••

Anthony Fokker had to have been pleased with the praise lavished on him by a universally recognized authority. The laudatory introduction to the aircraft designer's 1931 autobiography was written by his former enemy, the American ace of aces, Edward V. Rickenbacker. Referencing his time with the 94th Pursuit Squadron, the combat veteran wrote that his "admiration for Tony Fokker" began with the first Fokker D.VII he had encountered "many thousand feet above the Western Front during the dramatic days of 1918."

Rickenbacker was effusive in his remarks about Fokker, writing that his admiration continued "through constant clashes with [Fokker's] amazing combat planes in the hands of daring German pilots. One understands the superiority of Fokker's fighters when it is realized that the Germans, with approximately one-third of our equipment and pilots on the western Front, competed with us with deadly results." As an aviation executive involved in the marketing of Fokker aircraft in the United States starting in the late 1920s, Rickenbacker noted the irony that it had become his "duty to send Fokkers into the air, instead of bringing them down."

In candor, Rickenbacker acknowledged his initial reservations about meeting Fokker four short years after the war and almost turned away the visiting industrialist. But Rickenbacker was curious to meet "this aeronautical genius" who had produced the planes that challenged him at the front more than any other. Rickenbacker admitted: "Curiosity won."

In fact, Rickenbacker hosted Fokker at the 1922 Indianapolis automobile race, sharing his living quarters, arranging for the necessary credentials, and serving as personal guide. For three days, the two men ate all their meals together and enjoyed "many hours of pleasant conversation." The former adversaries not only broke the ice but hit it off. Rickenbacker offered his unreserved endorsement of Fokker's book as "an inspiration to the youth of the world" and to all people in "need of a stimulus to help them face the many trials of the age."

Rickenbacker lamented that Fokker had rendered his services to the Germans during the war. He used his introduction to chide the Allies for not bringing the Dutchman into their fold. This was convenient hindsight, however, for in 1914 Fokker was a young, unproven tinkerer overshadowed by more established plane makers. When Germany was first with an order for his monoplanes, Fokker accepted it and went to work in the service of his new patron.

In the end, the bond among these men of the air transcended questions of politics and nationality. Like other machines wielded by humans, planes could be devoted to good or ill, most often with those building and flying them having little, if any, say in the matter. Both Fokker and Rickenbacker recognized this simple truth, spurring Rickenbacker to end his introduction to the Fokker book with the observation that his friend had provided a "genuine service to mankind."

CHAPTER 13

Pacific Menace: The Mitsubishi Zero

Japan's greatest fighter during World War II, the Mitsubishi Zero, continues to be an object of fascination for aviation and military historians. Twenty-five years after the war, the plane's chief designer, Jiro Horikoshi, suggested that the reason why the "legend of the Zero" survives is because he and his team "were trying to surpass the rest of the world's technology, not just catch up to it." For emphasis, he added: "That was the goal of the Zero I designed."

As Horikoshi acknowledged, the incentive for the design came from the Imperial Japanese Navy's new fighter requirements of 1937. The requirements "were severe and at first appeared to be impossible." He boldly stated that in developing the Zero he and his colleagues "strove to make the impossible possible."

Thirty-four years before he received the fighter design assignment that would define his professional life, he was born in Gunma Prefecture, northwest of Tokyo. It was 1903, and the coincidence of that being the year of the Wright brothers' first successful powered flight is something that Horikoshi did not shy away from telling people. World War I unfolded as he came of age, and like youths in other countries he scoured magazines that reported on daring airmen in dramatic dogfights.

He later wrote that the air combat stories "excited my young blood." The names of the famous French, British, and German pursuit planes stuck with him and he "would often dream of flying in a small airplane" of his own construction. His pathway to a career in aviation was clinched when his brother introduced him to an aeronautical engineering faculty member at the University of Tokyo, Japan's premier institution of higher education.

Coursework in the aeronautical sciences was not rigidly structured at the university during the early and mid-1920s, given the newness of the curriculum. Also the enrollment was minimal and the student-instructor ratio was two to one, resulting in a collegial atmosphere that engendered the free exchange of ideas. The highlight for the aeronautical engineering students was a day at a naval air base where they were treated to a ride in a two-seat open-cockpit Avro trainer.

Horikoshi had no briefing, so when his pilot performed a series of aerobatic maneuvers that included a hammerhead, loop, and spin, he was taken by surprise and suffered spatial disorientation. The lingering dizziness wore off only after he had set foot back on the ground. Despite the ill effects, he appreciated the experience. The wild ride impressed him with the need to make fighter aircraft easily maneuverable because the combat pilot would be intently focused on mission objectives and subject to the physical strain of inevitable g-forces.

Upon graduation, he joined Mitsubishi Heavy Industries' Nagoya aircraft manufacturing plant. With trepidation he entered the design room to take his place at one of about fifty desks with drawing boards. His was near a window to provide natural illumination for his sketching.

Working next to him and the other college-trained design engineers were engineering aides. Elsewhere in the room were draftsmen who generated intricate drawings. In the adjacent room young women made tracings of the drawings. Horikoshi described his workspace as "full of action" yet as having "quite a carefree atmosphere."

The young engineer immersed himself in his work, later saying that he had "exhausted" himself in the design of his famous fighter. Yet he never forgot the admonition of his professors, "Don't forget to keep studying." Accordingly, after a full day at his drawing board and in conferences with company colleagues, he returned home to read the latest aviation journals from the United States, Britain, and Germany.

In looking to the West with an open mind and a thirst for modern engineering information, Horikoshi's adventure in discovery reflected the operative mentality of Japan's leadership which aimed to lift the country out of the lingering effects of its long hibernation in feudalism. Not until the latter nineteenth century did Japan begin to remove its veil and cease being a closed society cut off from the outer world. Because of the country's past, Horikoshi had a steep hill to climb; competing in aeronautics internationally entailed more than creating an exemplary design—you needed a reliable supply chain, skilled workforce, and precision machining tolerances, which were hard to come by in his native country, given that it was still playing catch-up.

In the late 1920s and early 1930s, Japan's navy knew that its aviation technology was behind the industrialized nations. One of the projects to turn the situation around fell into Horikoshi's lap. In 1932 Mitsubishi picked him to lead the development of the Prototype 7 fighter, which the navy hoped would narrow the technological gap between its aircraft and those of the great powers.

Horikoshi speculated that he was chosen to lead the project despite only five years on the job because his bosses felt his relative inexperience left him open to emerging concepts. Indeed, they had sponsored trips for him to several of the countries acknowledged as in the forefront of the aeronautical sciences. The travel allowed Horikoshi to interact with his counterparts in Europe and America, giving him insight into the latest design theory, preferred materials, and engine developments.

Thus when it came time to choose the configuration for the Prototype 7, he abandoned the biplane and parasol traditions. Instead, he opted for a monoplane configuration. The fuselage was metal and of semi-monocoque construction. He wanted the wings to be metal as well, but this was not to be because of manufacturing limitations that required the use of wood and fabric.

The rotund little fighter with massive fairings on the fixed main landing gear bore a passing resemblance to the Boeing P-26 Peashooter, but it proved to be impractical; the two test articles crashed during evaluation flights. Paradoxically, the Japanese navy ended up selecting a biplane to fill its requirement. Though Horikoshi's desire to design the first carrier-based monoplane had been dashed, the exercise taught him valuable lessons. Also, he retained the confidence of both his employer and military procurement officials.

His next project was the navy's Prototype 9, a metal low-wing mono-plane like his last fighter. Hirokoshi emphasized weight reduction to achieve speed and maneuverability. A 550-horsepower Nakajima Koto-buki Type 5 engine was used rather than more powerful engines then available, because holding weight in check was the priority.

Retractable landing gear was considered but rejected because fixed gear ensconced in streamlined fairings actually involved less of a weight penalty. In keeping with the convention of emergent fighter design the-ory, this aircraft had an enclosed cockpit. A greenhouse-style canopy was adopted, which gave the lone pilot excellent all-around visibility.

As hoped, the Prototype 9 proved faster than any other fighter tested in extensive comparison fly-offs in the fall of 1935. Horikoshi's design bested the other fighters by a margin of as much as 60 miles per hour. Except for the fixed landing gear, the new fighter had the appearance of a trimmed-down Seversky P-35, an American prewar fighter inspired by air power advocate Alexander de Seversky and designed by Alexander Kartveli. A year after the fly-off, the Prototype 9 was delivered to the Japanese military, which designated it the Type 96.

Both the navy and army operated it with impressive real-world results. Horikoshi got the news of air combat victories in the Second Sino-Japanese War, like every other private citizen in Japan. On Septem-ber 19, 1937, two years after the speed and maneuverability competition that validated the fighter, he picked up the morning newspaper, which reported that twelve Type 96 fighters had downed three times as many Chinese fighters in only fifteen minutes over the Chinese city of Nanking.

Horikoshi was not one to rest on his laurels. Moreover, he knew that air warfare, and for that matter war in general, required technological advancement to stay a step ahead of one's enemies. With this in mind, he looked forward to his greatest design challenge so far—the Prototype 12. The number was derived from the year of the project's origination, 1937 (or 2597 on the Japanese calendar), which represented the twelfth year of the reign of the then-serving Japanese emperor.

The first order of business was selecting the engine. The process, like that for the Type 96, was influenced most by weight considerations. Hor-ikoshi opted to use the 780-horsepower Mitsubishi Zuisei Type 13, a less powerful engine than the other leading candidate. Calculations showed that the more powerful engine, due to its additional weight, would require upscaling major airframe components and that in the end the extra power would not pay for itself.

The fuselage would be streamlined with clean lines punctuated by a bubble-type canopy for 360-degree visibility. Fuel tanks would be fitted between the engine and the cockpit as well as in the wings. The wing's leading and trailing edges would have roughly equal taper with modest dihedral and rounded tips. To achieve the desired performance, landing gear would have to be retractable. A 20-mm cannon would be installed outboard of the wheel well in each wing and a couple of 7.7-mm machine guns fitted in the nose.

So perceptively did Horikoshi grasp the challenge that his preliminary three-view sketch, seeking to improve on the Type 96, came remarkably close to the Prototype 12's final design. He showed his trusted coworkers the drawings and assigned detail work for major components to them based on their specialties. As before, weight control was paramount and Horikoshi went to great lengths, including adoption of a new zinc aluminum alloy as opposed to the then common copper aluminum alloy.

During an intense ten-month period, more than three thousand drawings were generated to arrive at the design of the Prototype 12. Horikoshi reviewed each of these, often sending them back with detailed instructions scribbled in the margins. He had become a stickler for keeping weight as low as possible and aerodynamics as clean as possible.

Following an aerodynamic trick employed on the Type 96's wing, Horikoshi decided to use the same feature on the Prototype 12's wing. It was a barely discernible two-and-a-half- degree washout angle, or downward twist, on the outermost section of the leading edge. Incorporating this curvature delayed wingtip stall to provide for continued roll authority in high angle-of-attack maneuvering. The result would be a vital edge in the arena of tight-turning air combat.

As the first Prototype 12 was being readied for transport to the airfield for its flight test, Horikoshi was overcome with emotion. The slender aircraft could have been mistaken for a racer and, in Horikoshi's eyes, "looked as though it wanted to leap into the sky." On March 23, 1939, it was disassembled and hauled the twenty-nine miles over rough roads by two ox-drawn carts to Kagamigahara airfield.

First flight occurred when weather cooperated on April 1st. The pilot was Katsuzo Shima, a former naval aviator known for his excellent stick-and-rudder skills as well as his daring if brusque personality. He regularly tested combat planes for Japan's Naval Aeronautical Establishment.

Horikoshi "breathlessly" watched as the Prototype 12, "which was born to be in the sky, came into its element." As planned, the aircraft rose thirty feet and tracked over the runway for fifteen hundred feet before touching down and rolling to a stop. This "jump" flight was just to get a feel for the controls. Shima climbed down from the cockpit where he was surrounded by all interested parties, none more so than the designer himself. All was pronounced satisfactory except the brakes, which needed adjustment.

Tests continued with an expansion of the flight envelope. On April 14th the landing gear would be retracted in-flight for the first time, allowing the Prototype 12 to ramble through the sky as it was intended to. From his viewing position on the ground, Horikoshi observed: "The airplane was flying delightfully, wildly and daringly, like a young bird which had finally found its freedom." Caught up in the drama and proving that flying touches a universal nerve, he described his reaction: "I was almost screaming, 'It's beautiful,' forgetting for a moment, I was the designer."

However, a vexing problem presented itself. The aircraft vibrated annoyingly. An analysis pointed to the phenomenon known as resonance, in which engine and airframe frequencies are the same. Experimentation with different propellers, ultimately resulting in adoption of a three-bladed propeller, and the installation of softer engine-support rubber dampers abated the issue.

The most serious problem revealed in flight tests was control response. At slow speeds, elevator response was torpid while at fast speeds it was overly sensitive. After much thought, Horikoshi devised a system of reduced stiffness in which the elevator "control cables and support system flexed slightly." This fix gave pilots the responsiveness to control inputs across the performance spectrum that met their expectations.

Approximately two years after the navy proposed the Prototype 12, Mitsubishi's fighter was designated A6M1. The "A" was the navy's code for a carrier-based fighter; the "6" reflected that this aircraft was the navy's sixth carrier-based fighter; and the "M" denoted the prime contractor Mitsubishi. A numerical suffix indicated the modification number.

The first two planes were designated A6M1. The third airframe switched to the Nakajima 940-horsepower Sakae Type 12 engine, which gave rise to the subsequent designation of A6M2. The design emphasized light weight, speed, maneuverability, and long distance. The development, which severely taxed Horikoshi and his teammates, incorporated a number of innovations related to materials, control systems, wing shape, and load limits that made the fighter a fearsome weapon against all opposing air forces in the opening rounds of World War II.

Early on September 14, 1939, a lieutenant clambered into the cockpit of the first model in the new line of fighters to deliver it to the Imperial Japanese Navy. The A6M1 rose from the dew-moistened airstrip at Kagamigahara and its pilot circled before taking up his course. "As if saying goodbye, the airplane's wings glittered in the morning sun."

Horikoshi "stood and watched until it disappeared." As happened earlier in the Prototype 12's development, emotion overwhelmed him and his fellow engineers. They were joined by the maintenance crew whose members had nursed the fighter through its teething pains. As Horikoshi described the scene, the mechanics also watched as the plane they got to know for the last two years faded into the distance on its delivery flight "with tears running down their oil-stained faces."

The Mitsubishi team had created an impressive fighter that pushed the limits to new highs. But it was precisely because the plane was treading in a little-understood corner of the performance envelope that the unpredictable occurred. On March 11, 1940, Horikoshi received the news that the second A6M1 had broken apart during a test dive at Yokosuka Naval Air Base, killing the test pilot. Just what caused the in-flight breakup mystified all concerned, potentially setting back the fighter permanently.

An investigation was convened by the navy right away. A very perceptive engineer with the Naval Aeronautical Establishment who had intimate knowledge of the aircraft's vibration issues narrowed down the root cause to the presence of an elevator flutter condition. From the wreckage it appeared that the elevator's mass balance weight, a device designed to prevent the vibrational phenomenon known as flutter, had cracked and separated along its support arm due to the stresses of repeated landings.

With the mass balance weight gone, it was theorized that the high speed encountered in the dive induced the elevator oscillation. This, in turn, caused severe airframe vibration that led to catastrophic structural failure. The investigation's conclusion was expedited and offered within a month of the accident.

Solutions included a strengthened support arm for the elevator's mass balance weight and an improved constant-speed propeller. Elevator flutter did not plague the design again. The episode attested to the sad truth that, sometimes in aeronautics, progress has rested on the greatest of personal sacrifice. Regardless, Horikoshi was haunted for the rest of his life by the death of the test pilot.

By July, in preparation for combat, production aircraft were being painted with the Rising Sun roundel. Also they received tweaks to the two cannon in the wings and the two machine guns in the nose. Anxious to get the new fighter into the Chinese theater of operations, where existing Japanese fighters were range limited, models were sent to battle before the official acceptance by the Japanese navy.

Acceptance occurred at the end of July. At that time, the fighter received its official type number and name. Since the year 1940 was 2600 in the Japanese calendar and since the military's practice was to adopt the last two digits of the Japanese year in which it accepted an aircraft into service, the fighter became known as the Type 00. The formal nomenclature was Rei-shiki Kanjo Sentoki or "Naval Type 00 Carrier Fighter." In regular usage, only a single digit was adopted in place of the two identical digits. Abbreviated this was "Rei-sen" or "Zero Fighter." The Allies assigned the code name "Zeke," but over time even the Allies referred to the fighter as the Zero.

This new weapon entered service with such superior performance over its Chinese adversaries (older Soviet fighters) that Japan's Naval Aeronautics Headquarters authorized Nakajima to produce the type under license as a means to speed up output. Under this arrangement, Mitsubishi cooperated with its main competitor. Nakajima began churning out

Zeros by September 1941, eventually accounting for 63 percent of total production.

Horikoshi's engineering team kept making improvements to address concerns based on feedback from the fighter's operational experience. A folding wing was adopted for ease of handling on aircraft carriers. Also, to cope with heavy aileron forces at high speeds, trim tabs were incorporated on the trailing edges of the ailerons.

After the installation of the aileron trim tabs, different problems began to appear during high-speed maneuvering. Incidents involving wing wrinkling and even in-flight separation of the ailerons prompted further testing. In a deliberate in-flight replication of the problems, the phenomena reappeared with fatal results. The aircraft suffered a loss of control and plummeted into the sea, killing the pilot.

Once again the cause was determined to be flutter, albeit emanating in the aileron this time rather than the elevator as before. The aileron trim tabs had substantially lowered the critical aileron flutter speed so that any Zero exceeding 370 miles per hour in a dive would be subject to structural failure. The process behind these incidents happened by means of the coupling of torsional vibration of the wing and aileron.

The potential for this problem to arise was missed in the design phase, because while the scaled-down test models were sized proportionally they lacked torsional comparability. It was only when the aircraft was flown at the edge of its performance envelope that the problem revealed itself. As happened earlier in the Zero's development, human sacrifice led to the essential breakthrough. Horikoshi was devastated by the additional loss of life in the process of perfecting his design and he took the lesson to heart.

The flawed aileron trim tab system was corrected by thickening the outer wing skin and stiffening the inner wing structure. Also, mass balance weights were added to the aileron trim tabs. Like the previous problem of elevator flutter, the problem of aileron flutter was solved with no recurrence for the remainder of the Zero's service life.

Recognizing the falloff in performance at the higher altitudes, the original Sakae 12 engine was changed out in favor of a new 1,130-horsepower Sakae 21 engine equipped with a two-stage supercharger. This caused a change in the model designation to A6M3. The redesign occurred in March 1941 with flight tests following in June. Only a modest speed improvement resulted as ways to further boost power were considered.

Emboldened by the success of the Zero's commanding performance in China, the Japanese fleet stunned the United States by catching the American outpost at Pearl Harbor off guard on December 7, 1941. From six aircraft carriers, the Japanese launched 353 aircraft of various types including Zeros. About 230 American aircraft were destroyed compared to only twenty-nine Japanese planes.

These lopsided results, crushing though they were, did not present an accurate picture of the full advantage of the Zero because the attack had been a surprise. Better insight into the Zero's superiority could be gleaned from the actions that followed shortly afterwards in the Philippines. Strikes by Japanese forces were anticipated, but frontline fighters like the Curtiss P-40 fell to the Zero in horrifying kill-loss ratios.

Continuing to deploy the Zero in the lead to achieve air superiority, air battles broke out over the Solomon Islands, Borneo, and Java. American fighters were easy prey for the long-legged and highly maneuverable Zeros. Even in dogfights against the new Spitfire over Ceylon (now Sri Lanka), the Zero's tight-turning radius gave it the upper hand. As Robert Mikesh, a former curator at the National Air and Space Museum and authority on Japanese aviation, wrote in reference to these air-to-air engagements, Japanese pilots were fond of boasting: "This is like training."

Before Japan's reversal of fortune, the sense of indomitability at the squadron level showed itself in an outlandish display by three of the leading aces in the Tainan Air Group. On May 17, 1942, Saburo Sakai, Toshio Ota, and Hiroyoshi Nishizawa joined in formation by prearrangement over the Allied air base at Port Moresby after a strafing mission. Lined up wingtip-to-wingtip, the three zoomed down in their highly maneuverable Zero fighters and yanked back up in nicely executed loops.

They repeated the aerobatic performance three times and then when Sakai saw one of his wingmen grinning and the other laughing, he signaled them to do it all over again, "swinging around in perfect formation. And still not a gun fired at us!" Later that night, the insouciant trio was summoned to the commander's office to receive an unforgettable tongue-lashing for their antics over the enemy's field. Though ordered never to engage in such "idiotic behavior" again, Sakai later wrote that he and his wingmen that day "enjoyed every minute" of their unusual demonstration flight.

Preconceptions about the Japanese, or perhaps Asians generally, as backward peoples incapable of the technological stature of Western societies lulled the Allies into complacency. There had been plenty of warning about the Zero's air combat capability from the conflict in China, but as a nonparticipant in the raging battles, the United States did not take the Zero seriously. After Japanese forces swept with lightning speed through much of the Pacific, attitudes swung the other way; the Zero took on an almost mystical quality and the successful Japanese rampage sent a chill through the American public which questioned if the Empire of the Rising Sun was invincible.

Yet even in the face of the Japanese advance, the Western mindset was still reluctant to accept that the Zero could have been an entirely indigenous Japanese creation. Because it bore a resemblance to both a 1937 Vought fighter design and the 1935 Hughes H-1 racer, wartime American commentators claimed that the Zero was a mere copy. This myth persisted for years to come, but the truth was that Jiro Horikoshi and his colleagues at Mitsubishi internally developed the design, proving that engineering brilliance knows no national or ethnic boundaries. Indeed technological breakthroughs can happen anywhere that great minds are permitted to work in accommodative environments.

Prewar American naval fighters like the Grumman Wildcat and Brewster Buffalo were not really a match for the Zero; however, if proper tactics were employed, the Wildcat had at least a fighting chance. Air tactician Claire Chennault, whose American Volunteer Group (popularly known as the Flying Tigers) had been confronting the Japanese fighter threat early on, devised a simple approach that called for his virtually obsolete Curtiss P-40 fighters to avoid dogfights and instead use their altitude advantage to dive on Zeros in onetime passes. US Navy commander John S. "Jimmy" Thach developed a variation of this technique called the Thach Weave, which involved the same diving maneuver in pairs followed by a crisscross pattern (or weave) that would enable one or the other of the two American pilots to protect his wingman should the Zero take the bait and latch onto the tail of either of the pair.

During the Battle of Midway, diversionary attacks were launched on Dutch Harbor in the Aleutian Islands. On June 3, 1942, an attacking A6M2 experienced engine trouble and its pilot made an emergency landing in the outback of Akutan Island. During rollout, the airplane flipped upside-down, killing the pilot.

Several weeks later the wrecked aircraft was retrieved and shipped to California for repair and analysis. Starting in October, the newly airworthy Zero was repainted in US markings and evaluated in flight trials with six of the leading American fighter types. The weaknesses and strengths of each when pitted against the Zero were duly noted and communicated to the pertinent frontline units.

Two years later, in June 1944, a dozen Zeros with the A6M5 designation were captured at Saipan and sent to the United States for comparison testing. This improved model was like an aged boxing champion on steroids, still capable of scoring individual knockouts and requiring respect of opponents, but facing a newer and tougher lineup. Interestingly, the same hit-and-run countertactics were advised.

The turning of the tide in the Pacific is generally attributed to the Battle of Midway. It was, indeed, a major American victory, but the ability to score the decisive blow was less a matter of air superiority and more a circumstance of fortuitous timing. The Pacific air war further shifted in the Allies' favor when the next generation of fighters arrived on the scene, starting with the Lockheed P-38 Lightning in the fall of 1942. Others that followed included the Vought Corsair and the Grumman Hellcat.

The new American fighters were generally heavier and higher-powered than the Zero. They also tended to have more protection and more guns. The Zero's performance dropped off at the higher altitudes while down low its turning advantage was retained. As the war kept grinding on, the Zero was being outgunned, outnumbered, and outclassed.

Knowing of the imperative to upgrade aircraft in wartime, Mitsubishi heeded the recommendations of pilots that the outboard sections of the A6M3's folding wings be removed and squared with fairings at the tips. The corresponding reduction in wing area of just over nine square feet contributed to improved maximum speed and slightly better maneuverability at the upper speed range. When these models were first observed by the Allies, it was thought that a whole new fighter had entered service. The fighter with the unfamiliar wing shape was given the code name "Hap" in deference to army air force General Henry H. "Hap" Arnold. Needless to say, the general did not take kindly to the enemy plane being named after him, so the code name became "Hamp." Within two months, the Allies realized that the fighter was a modified Zero and quickly went back to the existing lexicon when referring to it.

Only 343 of the square-tipped Zeros were produced. It was decided to revert back to the rounded wingtips in order to give precedence to range. However, despite 560 of this newer version of the A6M3 being manufactured, the type did not last long, having performed poorly against the newly arrived American and British fighters over Guadalcanal.

The A6M5 was the next major version to emerge. Mitsubishi sought manufacturing efficiencies to enhance the production rate and at the same time succeeded in raising the diving speed by employing heavier gauge metal for the wing skin. Also the engine's exhaust collector ring was removed; in its place, individual exhaust stacks were run straight backwards to protrude out of the aft cowl so that the rearward ejected exhaust gases could boost thrust.

This was a more competitive version of the Zero and the one built in greatest quantity with the first of 1,701 units rolling off the line in the summer of 1943. Three minor variants of this model were developed, each with a distinct designation. Modifications included further enhancement of diving speed, ammunition feed and gun upgrades, and protective measures, which included an automatic fire extinguisher system, bullet-resistant glass, and armor plate behind the pilot's seat.

It is interesting to note that up until late in the war the Japanese navy accepted the absence of protective features in its leading fighter. A conscious decision was made to proceed with the design that favored light weight and maneuverability at the expense of pilot safeguards. This fit the samurai ethos, which called for the acceptance of danger. It was only when losses became unbearable that commonsense protections were installed. Ironically, it would not be long before Zeros were used in suicide attacks.

Most improvements came with a weight penalty and more powerful engines were in short supply. The Zero, as a fighter conceived in the late 1930s, had now neared the point where its performance was being maxed out. The war was unfolding more rapidly than the design offices at the plant could keep up with.

The reversal in fortunes was not just about hardware. As mentioned, American tactics did not change appreciably, even with the introduction of the newer versions of the Zero. The steady inflow of well-trained American pilots represented a quantitative and qualitative advantage over their enemy counterparts because Japan was losing more and more of its experienced combat pilots through attrition and failed to replace them at an adequate rate.

In addition, the tightening noose around the Japanese home islands and the strategic bombing campaign's increasing intensity impacted the Japanese aircraft manufacturing industry's ability to be supplied with vital parts and raw materials. In November 1944 production of Zeros at the Nagoya plant was up to a hundred a month, but by July 1945 output fell to only fifteen. In the waning months of the war, Horikoshi complained about the lack of engineering manpower. Attempts at developing new designs were further hobbled by the government's shortsightedness, which stemmed in part from the seed of overconfidence planted during the early victories.

Mitsubishi was able to produce a follow-on to the Zero. But the J2M Raiden ("Thunderbolt" in Japanese and code-named "Jack" by the Allies) was conceived as an interceptor to protect Japan from Allied bombers. It was not a dogfighter; instead, its design prioritized speed and climb over agility. Production problems impeded the program and in the end only 470 were built.

Horikoshi worked on a true replacement for the Zero. The A7M Reppu ("Hurricane" in Japanese and code-named "Sam" by the Allies) boded ill for the Allies. On paper, the carrier-based fighter looked like a muscular Zero.

Unluckily for the Japanese, Mitsubishi and the Imperial Japanese Navy had trouble coming to terms on which engine to adopt for the promising new airframe. Horikoshi opposed the original choice, and by the time his preference was being installed the war was all but over. In the end, only eight prototypes were produced and none saw combat.

The exigencies of war combined with the wishful notion of a quick victory impeded Japan's effort to develop wholly new aircraft. Rather, the country had little choice but to focus its attention on the losing proposition of improving existing fighters like the Zero and its army counterpart, the Nakajima Ki-43 Hayabusa ("Peregrine Falcon" in Japanese and code-named "Oscar" by the Allies). These fighters, while offering a combination of winning features at the beginning of the conflict, could be improved only so much. Additionally, the Japanese aircraft industry was unable to match the output of its American opposite. Mitsubishi and Nakajima produced 10,449 of all versions of the Zero, a greater production run than any other Japanese aircraft during the war, but still short of requirements.

The ever-dwindling number of the Japanese flyers who had made the Zero's reputation as the feared predator of the Japanese fleet gradually saw the advantage of their once-dominant fighter ebb with each day as new American fighters in greater numbers reached Pacific skies. As Japan's situation grew desperate, a new tactic was employed. Starting in the fall of 1944, mass suicide attacks from the air were conducted with the Zero being used more than any other type.

These kamikaze missions usually involved the placement of a 550-pound bomb on the plane's centerline hard-point. Young, inexperienced pilots who had little chance of surviving in aerial combat by the late stages of the war were deemed expendable and were the preferred choice for these one-way attacks. With Japan facing almost certain defeat, pilots fitting the profile either volunteered for or were shamed into the kamikaze mission, some feeling that their sacrifice might reverse the glum trend and others accepting their impending death in the tradition of hara-kiri, when all is lost but one's personal honor. A sense of fatalism overshadowed this final campaign.

More experienced pilots in the latest versions of the Zero would sometimes fly cover for their doomed colleagues, attempting to ward off intercepting Hellcats that comprised the main air component of the American fleet's defensive screens. The suicide planes also had to navigate through withering antiaircraft fire from US Navy ships, but some kamikaze pilots got through. Vessels like the escort carrier USS *St. Lo* were sunk and others damaged at the Battle of Leyte Gulf in October 1944. Kamikaze attacks continued to harass the advancing US armada, notably during the invasion of Okinawa in April 1945, where some ships like the carrier USS *Bunker Hill* sustained substantial damage.

With the downswing in Japan's circumstances, the once-mighty Zero was transformed from an aggressor to a defender, from a symbol of superiority and strength to an emblem of despair and nihilism. The fighter that represented the state of the art in air-to-air combat at the outset of hostilities had been reduced to a pathetic manned missile within a mere five years. During the war Japanese technology, and to an even greater extent Japanese industry, failed to keep pace with their primary adversary.

When the war was over, Horikoshi thought "what foolish steps Japan had taken!" He blamed his country's debacle on "poor political leadership" that showed "a lack of consideration and responsibility." His meditation on the war concluded with a look to the future and the prayer: "Let intelligent leaders step forward."

•••

One of my successors as director of the National Air and Space Museum had a distinguished career in naval aviation. As a lieutenant (junior grade), Donald D. Engen flew the Curtiss SB2C Helldiver from the USS *Lexington* when the kamikaze threat raged. Don continued in the navy, rising to ever-higher positions of responsibility until retiring at the rank of vice admiral in 1978. He then enjoyed stints as an executive in private industry, a member of the National Transportation Safety Board, and the administrator of the Federal Aviation Administration before he joined the museum.

On the morning of October 25, 1944, Don's bulky dive-bomber rolled across the carrier's flight deck, building momentum for takeoff. He joined up with the other climbing aircraft. Soon enemy ships were spotted, and the attacking force, which included planes from his carrier as well as from the USS *Essex* and USS *San Jacinto*, went into action. The dozen Helldivers in Don's squadron, Bombing Nineteen, set up for runs against one of the Japanese carriers.

In the fighting, four Japanese carriers had been sent to the bottom of the sea, including the one Don had hit. It happened to be the *Zuikaku*, the carrier that had led the attack on Pearl Harbor and that five months later had crippled the first *Lexington* at the Battle of the Coral Sea, which resulted in its loss. In Don's words, it had been "the new *Lexington*'s turn to return the favor!"

As a sign of the kind of man he was, Don did not mention in his memoir that for his action that day he received the Navy Cross, one of the twenty-nine decorations he earned in the service. In 1986, forty-two years later, he received a call that was destined to rekindle memories of the day's events. As the head of the FAA, he was asked to meet a Japanese airline executive whose company had recently purchased many American airliners.

During their discussion, the Japanese executive learned that Don had served in the US Navy during World War II and that he had participated in the sinking of a Japanese carrier. Speaking through an interpreter, the executive asked which one. When Don answered the *Zuikaku*, the executive's "eyes opened wide" for that had been his ship. As they talked further, the executive sparked mutual laughter when he said that he had spent five days in the water before being rescued.

Don felt that their struggle against each other at the Battle of Leyte Gulf had created a bond between them. The upshot was that the executive had been a kamikaze pilot intent on smashing into an American vessel. War can take outlandish turns and the irony in this instance did not escape Don; by helping to sink a powerful enemy warship he saved the lives of American sailors and airmen like himself, while at the same time he also saved the life of the kamikaze pilot sworn to kill him.

CHAPTER 14

Breakthrough: Spitfire to the Rescue

In the throes of the Depression's financial crunch, the British government had imposed austerity measures that included its withdrawal of support for the 1931 Schneider Trophy seaplane race. The decision provoked an outcry from the country's aviation industry and avid enthusiasts. With little time to spare before the race, a reprieve came in the form of an unsolicited £100,000 donation from a wealthy British patron.

It is probably an exaggeration to say that the gift of Lady Lucy Houston, the widow of a shipping tycoon, assured the Spitfire's development, yet her love of country, expressed with such magnanimity, led to the completion and flight of the magnificent racing floatplane that was the direct antecedent of Britain's great fighter. Even with the infusion of funds, the British team feared it might be too late to match Italy's Macchi Castoldi M.C. 72, which was to be powered by the Fiat AS.6. However, Reginald J. Mitchell, chief designer/engineer at Supermarine Aviation Works, and Sir Henry Royce, Rolls-Royce cofounder and engineering overseer, went to work tweaking their airframe and engine, respectively.

The gleaming blue and gray Supermarine S.6B, fitted with an upgraded 2,350-horsepower Rolls-Royce R Type engine, won the Schneider race on September 13, 1931, in the absence of the expected Italian and French teams. Neither was ready in time. In the uncontested affair, Royal Air Force Flight Lieutenant John Boothman was clocked at an impressive 340.08 miles per hour.

The British, having won the race three successive times, ended it forever. Even so, shortly afterwards, Flight Lieutenant George Stainforth upped the aircraft's speed to 379.05 miles per hour. He did it again, on

September 29th, racking up a sizzling 407.5 miles per hour, a new absolute world speed record.

Between the 1929 and 1931 races, Mitchell credited the international competition as the impetus for the advances in his racing designs. Referencing the R Type engine, he wrote: "There is little doubt that this intensive engine development will have a very profound effect on our aircraft during the next few years." Supermarine's talented designer would prove to be prescient!

In the 1930s modernization was the watchword of many air forces. Although economies struggled, the need for improved performance in combat aircraft could hardly be denied. After all, in the decade's early years racing planes outran some frontline military planes.

In answer to the British Air Ministry's request for proposals for a new fighter under the F.7/30 specification, Supermarine submitted its Type 224, which first flew in February 1934. The single-seat design reflected the tug of the old and the pull of the new. It had a pudgy nose, fixed-gear fairings, an inverted gullwing, and an open cockpit. Using the problem-prone 660-horsepower steamed-cooled Rolls-Royce Goshawk engine, the plane was little more than a bridge to a more thoroughly modern fighter. The Gloster Gladiator, a sleek and powerful biplane, got the procurement nod.

In mid-1934, Mitchell moved on to a drastically different design. Backing him up, the chairman of Supermarine's parent company, Vickers Ltd., obtained authorization from his board of directors in November to spend £10,000 on the new design, now known as the Type 300. It was a strong vote of confidence by Sir Robert McLean and his colleagues on the board.

The name Spitfire had been given to the ill-fated Type 224. It was the name preferred by Sir Robert who believed the name of his company's fighter "should suggest something venomous." Unknown to Mitchell, his superiors at Supermarine had requested retention of the name for the revised model going forward in accord with Sir Robert's wishes. Reportedly, when Mitchell heard of this, he remarked that it was "just the sort of bloody silly name they would choose."

Believing that the way the RAF specification was written had boxed in the company's entry, Sir Robert opined that Mitchell could develop a world-class fighter design if freed of bureaucratically imposed constraints. Indeed, in a letter to Rolls-Royce, Sir Robert stated that Mitchell's revised design was of "a new killer fighter." Since early 1933 Rolls-Royce was engaged in the internally funded development of a new supercharged twenty-seven-liter V-twelve engine in the 1,000-horsepower class. The engine, known then as the PV-12 (for "Private Venture") would be, like its predecessors, named after a bird of prey—the Merlin.

Before his untimely death in the spring of 1933, Sir Henry had settled on key design features of the new engine. Seeking to combine the reliability of the Kestrel with the performance of the R Type, he had opted for a smaller bore than the racing engine. In doing so, he left the basis of a successful military engine.

A. G. Elliott succeeded the company's deceased cofounder as chief engineer. He worked on improving output from the initial test at 625-horsepower in the fall of 1933. Development continued for the next couple years with incremental improvements in power; by early 1936 the Merlin's design team was nearing its goal of 1,000-horsepower.

The Air Council's Air Member for Research and Development, RAF Air Marshal Hugh Dowding, was interested in seeing what British industry could produce in the way of a truly modern fighter. While air power advocates generally believed in the primacy of the bomber, he perceived the value in fighters as a critical instrument in defense of the homeland should it come under attack. In December 1934 he ordered one fighter prototype each from Supermarine and Hawker. Mitchell's Type 300 would incorporate Rolls-Royce's new Merlin C engine and feature such upgrades as an enclosed cockpit and retractable landing gear.

A year and a half later, Dowding was transferred to head the newly formed Fighter Command. At the command's headquarters at Bentley Priory, a sumptuous house on Stanmore Hill straddling the intersection of Middlesex and Hertfordshire, Dowding was known to press for the continued modernization of the fighters in the development/production pipeline. At one Stanmore conference, he memorably asked: "If Chicago gangsters can have bulletproof glass for the windows of their motorcars, why can't my pilots have it for their windscreens?" His staff chuckled, but understood what was at stake; after an initial delay, Spitfires got the strengthened glass.

During the design process, the RAF's Directorate of Armament Development and the Air Ministry's Operational Requirements Branch had concluded from testing and analysis that no less than 256 hits by .303-inch shells would be required to shoot down new all-metal bombers. Further research surmised that new bombers capable of a cruise speed of 180 miles per hour would give an interceptor a miniscule window of two seconds to fire off a scoring burst. Since then-available machine guns could fire at the rate of approximately a thousand rounds per minute, calculations showed that to be effective a fighter would need eight machine guns. Arraying many guns in the wings presented harmonization issues, but it removed worries of having to coordinate the bullet stream through the propeller arc with an interrupter mechanism. At the time, it was thought that the destructive capacity of the massed machine guns would have the most lethal effect. The theory countered the idea of a limited number of guns in line with the pilot as was the World War I convention.

The suddenly imposed requirement of eight guns doubled the number that the two companies had planned to fit in their prototypes based on the operative specification. For Sidney Camm, design chief at Hawker, this new mandate was no problem because the wings of his design, the Hurricane, had adequate thickness to accommodate the extra guns. For Mitchell at Supermarine, the added guns presented a serious challenge.

A thin cantilevered wing was integral to Mitchell's configuration, which sought to maximize speed and maneuvering performance. To sacrifice this design element would adversely affect the whole. Accordingly, he remained steadfast in preserving the thickness-to-chord ratio of 13 percent at the root with a taper to 6 percent at the tip.

The question of how to fit four extra guns, two on each side, given the determination to keep the thickness-to-chord ratio intact, became the Supermarine design team's dilemma. Mitchell's staff addressed the problem by reaching back to the wing planform used in the S.4 racing plane of 1925. They noted that transforming the prototype's planned straight tapered wing into an elliptical form, such as on the old racing plane, would expand the chord outboard of the existing gun positions, thus making room, albeit barely so, for the additional guns without disturbing the thickness-to-chord ratio.

The melodramatic 1942 movie *Spitfire*, starring Leslie Howard as Mitchell, took artistic license to extremes, especially regarding issues of the aircraft's design. The movie suggested that the choice of the elliptical wing stemmed from the desire to duplicate the flight characteristics of birds. This epiphany was reached by the actor as he observed flapping gulls through binoculars while lounging on the beach.

The film industry's pretensions aside, adoption of the elliptical wing rendered the additional benefits of reduced drag in level flight at certain altitudes and greater wing/fuselage coupling area for enhanced strength at the root. A consensus developed that the difficulties in the production of the uncommon wing shape were more than offset by the gains achieved in aerodynamics, structural integrity, and combat efficacy. On March 5, 1936, the maiden flight of the unpainted prototype, designated K5054, occurred at Eastleigh, near Supermarine's Southampton factory, with Vickers's chief test pilot, Joseph "Mutt" Summers, at the controls. From that watershed moment, the graceful lines of the elliptical wing became the signature of Britain's most alluring fighter.

Over the years, speculation arose that Mitchell had simply copied the elliptical wing that Professor Ernst Heinkel employed on his He 70, a beautifully styled passenger and mail plane that had entered service in 1934. Such conjecture was fueled by the fact that Rolls-Royce utilized one of the German aircraft as a test bed for the Merlin engine. But the Heinkel, which had a thicker elliptical wing than the Spitfire's, didn't start its test flights for the British engine supplier until three weeks after the Supermarine prototype's first flight. In any case, the hearsay about cloning the wing of the German plane was vehemently denied by one of Mitchell's top assistants.

Besides its distinctive curvature, the Spitfire's wing was notable for a single spar of multiple layers that constituted a kind of "plate web." Forward of the spar, heavy-gage Alclad covered the wing to create, in effect, a stiff torsion box. Girder ribs supported the aft wing section, which was made of thinner-gage metal. The trailing edge had split flaps and fabric-covered ailerons.

The stressed-skin fuselage was comprised of three sections. The nose was a tubular structure that enveloped the engine. The center section was of monocoque construction featuring a forward fireproof bulkhead and armor plate behind the pilot's seat. The tail section, also of monocoque construction, had a couple fuselage formers extend upward to provide structural support for an integral fin. This section was fastened to the center section by fifty-two bolts and four studs around a double frame and could be detached as a unit. Rudder and elevators were fabric covered. The tail wheel was not retractable until later models.

Another innovation was Rolls-Royce's decision to replace water with a water-ethylene glycol mix as the engine coolant. The switch would bring improved efficiency and a smaller radiator. At the same time, Dr. Frederick Meredith of the Royal Aircraft Establishment at Farnborough, one of the great centers of aviation breakthroughs, developed a ducted radiator cooling system that was streamlined and additive to the thrust quotient.

The radiator was encased in a convergent/divergent duct with all but the intake scoop buried in the aircraft's innards. The discharge air was accelerated and expelled to augment thrust, a phenomenon known as the Meredith effect. Radiator cooling, which had long been perceived as purely deleterious to performance because of unavoidable drag, could now be seen as not so debilitating. The system was subsequently adopted on the American P-51 Mustang.

The intake scoop on the Spitfire was located under the starboard wing, where a recess had been planned to accommodate a retractable auxiliary radiator for an earlier Rolls-Royce engine of the evaporative cooling type. The recess proved to be a natural spot for the fitting of the Meredith system. The oil cooler was placed in a separate protruding duct under the port wing.

During the early trials at Eastleigh, the prototype's expected true airspeed of 350 miles per hour was not attained. Instead, the aircraft fell short by a significant margin. This troubled Mitchell, for his calculations suggested that the higher speed ought to have been reached.

Mitchell commenced a top-to-bottom review of the prototype, now painted in a high-gloss pale gray/blue not unlike the colors of the famous S.6B racer. The culprit behind the lacking performance proved to be the two-bladed fixed-pitch wooden propeller. A new propeller with modified tips was hurriedly produced by Supermarine itself.

Supermarine test pilot Jeffrey Quill checked out the plane with the new propeller twenty-two days after the type's initial leap into the sky. He happily reported upon landing that he had come within 2 miles per hour of the preflight parameter. Mitchell was elated and gave his approval for the transfer of the prototype to the Fighter Flight of the Aeroplane and Armament Experimental Establishment at RAF Martlesham Heath, where military pilots would get their hands on the Spitfire for the first time as part of the vetting process.

Mutt Summers flew K5404 to the air base on May 26, 1936. RAF Flight Lieutenant Humphrey "E. J." Edwardes-Jones had been ordered to fly the new aircraft upon its arrival and to call Air Marshal Wilfrid Freeman, the new Air Member for Research and Development at the Air Council, as soon as he landed. This expedited methodology broke with the custom. At Martlesham Heath, standard procedure for newly delivered prototypes involved thorough study and special instrumentation outfitting in a process that typically entailed a week or more before an evaluation flight would even be attempted. At the time, however, Nazi Germany's aggressive posture made the Air Staff anxious for capable new fighters, and the RAF's regular protocols were adjusted to enable things to happen faster.

Edwardes-Jones received a quick briefing in the cockpit of the refueled prototype and took off on the rushed evaluation flight. The plane got a scrupulous workout. Upon return to base and entry into the traffic pattern, a peculiar circumstance was observed by the pilot. A large cross-section of base personnel gathered to glimpse at the new fighter as reflected by "the white caps of the duty cooks outside the airmen's cookhouse." The curiosity evinced by the finely sculpted, racer-like prototype at Martlesham Heath, where new types not infrequently arrived to a collective yawn, spoke volumes about how the Spitfire would excite the public and kindle a sorely needed optimism that Britain had the means to keep the threatening foe at bay.

Once back on the ground, Edwardes-Jones called London as instructed and was asked a lone question: Could the average newly trained RAF fighter pilot handle the Spitfire? The fate of the new airplane hinged, to a disproportionate degree, on one junior officer's answer. Fortunately for the defense of Britain and, one might also say, the future of the free world, Edwardes-Jones responded with a simple and emphatic "yes." After an exchange, he crowned his endorsement, saying the new aircraft was "a delight to fly." A less enthusiastic answer would not have ended the Spitfire's development, but it may have retarded the program just when there was hardly time to spare.

The unusually brisk evaluation was followed by an even more alacritous production order. On June 3, 1936, one week after the service's first flight test and before any comprehensive written analysis by the RAF, Supermarine received a production contract for 310 Spitfires, a greater quantity than for any type in Supermarine's history up to that point. The order sent executives scurrying for subcontractors who could supply the needed parts and assemblies. The Spitfire was a far more complex fighter to build than the Hurricane, which was conceived from the outset with ease of construction in mind. Delays ensued and the first production Spitfire was not delivered until nearly two years later.

Sadly, the plane's creator, the brilliant and soft-spoken Reginald J. Mitchell, would not live to see the Spitfire emerge from the production line. He had previously coped with intestinal cancer and had undergone surgery to remove a tumor in 1933. Four years later, the cancer returned and despite his utmost efforts to treat the disease by making a special trip to a cancer clinic in Vienna, he succumbed at his Southampton home on June 11, 1937.

Interestingly, in the film *Spitfire*, Mitchell's demise was attributed to overwork. Apparently, the filmmakers thought it more heroic for purposes of their wartime propaganda to show the movie's protagonist sacrificing himself through job stress rather than expiring from the recurrence of an incurable disease. Mitchell was mourned at every echelon of the RAF and by his many colleagues at Supermarine. He was forty-two years old at the time of his death.

Mitchell was succeeded as Supermarine's chief engineer by Joseph Smith, who ably fostered the Spitfire's design upgrades through successive models during the war. The issue at the moment was getting the aircraft produced in large numbers and integrated into the Royal Air Force as quickly as possible to face the growing threat from an ever more bellicose Adolf Hitler.

The British government was hoping to avert widespread conflict on the European continent, but war seemed increasingly inevitable. Starting in 1937, a network of so-called "shadow factories" was contemplated to augment production of war-related necessities. To pick up the pace of aircraft production, one of these shadow factories was contracted for through the Nuffield Organization. It was constructed at Castle Bromwich near Birmingham.

A contract was issued for a thousand Spitfires to be built at the new factory. By 1943 production at Castle Bromwich peaked with a rate of one new fighter rolling off the line on average every other hour. As a measure of the success of the plane's initial design and its ability to be upgraded in the ensuing years, system-wide production totaled 20,351 Spitfires plus 2,408 Seafires, the naval variant.

Equally impressive as the sheer quantity was the magnitude of performance improvement in the twenty-two operational marks or models manufactured through 1945. From the first prototype of 1936 to the last production model at war's end, maximum speed in level flight advanced by slightly more than 100 miles per hour and rate of climb nearly doubled from twenty-five hundred feet per minute to forty-eight hundred feet per minute. As a sign of its success, this superlative fighter entered service with the air arms of more than thirty countries during and after World War II.

The Spitfire's original hinged canopy was replaced by a sliding canopy known as the Malcolm hood which had a bulged shape to improve visibility. Other improvements over time included clipped wings to increase speed for types dedicated to low-altitude operations. On the opposite end of the altitude spectrum, some models had elongated wings and pressurized cockpits in which a Marshall blower passed in air to maintain an equivalent pressure of two pounds per square inch above the atmospheric pressure at forty thousand feet.

The first couple production Spitfires were delivered to the RAF in July 1938 and they went to work as test beds in handling trials. First delivery to an operational squadron occurred on August 4th when company test pilot Jeffrey Quill landed K9789 at Duxford and handed it over to No. 19 Squadron. The scene was indicative of what would repeat itself many times in the lead-up to war. Obsolescent fighters like Duxford's Gloster Gauntlets, open-cockpit biplanes that had entered service three years earlier, shared space on the field until phased out as newer types like the Spitfire took their place.

By July 1940, the eve of the Battle of Britain, the RAF had nineteen Spitfire squadrons spread strategically among three key fighter groups in the south and east of the country. In the months prior, Dowding had strongly resisted the temptation of British leaders to commit increasing numbers of still-scarce Spitfires to the combat raging in France. The fixed emplacements of the vaunted Maginot Line had been quickly overrun or simply circumvented by the new style of warfare that emphasized maneuver over mass. With fast-moving mechanized armor supported by air cover, Hitler's forces tore across a militarily destitute France.

Because Dowding saw the Battle of France as a lost cause, he believed that throwing more Spitfires into that futile crucible would only leave the homeland correspondingly weaker against what he was sure to be the Germans' next major campaign. For whatever it was worth, Hitler had expressed a preference to avoid destruction of the British Empire and left open the possibility of a negotiated settlement. But Churchill would have none of it. On July 17th, Hitler signed off on the invasion of Britain.

Known as Operation Sea Lion, the planned assault across the English Channel would depend on first securing the skies. Once the RAF was sufficiently weakened, the German High Command would commit more than a quarter-million ground troops to the invasion. Because conducive weather was essential, the window for the prospective invasion would remain open only through the late summer.

Hitler was emboldened by the swift collapse of much of Europe and the fact that during the Battle of France British expeditionary forces with elements of the French army had been driven back to the French coastal resort of Dunkirk. But the British people found inspiration in the miraculous deliverance of the more than three hundred thousand stranded British and French troops who were lifted off the French shore and shuttled to Britain by an improvised flotilla of boats in late May and early June. Also the air fighting over France gave the RAF confidence in the Spitfire as a match for the Messerschmitt Bf 109, the Luftwaffe's leading fighter at the time.

Two months after Dunkirk, the Germans were poised to unleash a wave of air strikes to hurt British morale and undo the RAF. Code-named *Adlerangriff* (Eagle Attack), the first strike was delayed by weather for more than a week. On August 13th, known as *Adler Tag* (Eagle Day), the opening salvo commenced with the Luftwaffe launching hundreds of bombers and fighters in loosely coordinated attacks. It was a rueful debut for the Germans, in part, because they had underestimated the value of British radar (known then as Radio Direction Finding or RDF). It was the centerpiece of the integrated air defense system that Dowding had installed with great foresight and meticulous preparation beginning in the 1930s.

The radar stations lining the British coast formed the Chain Home (though most people preferred the simpler syntax of Home Chain). Incoming Luftwaffe formations were detected over water by this phalanx of sensors, far enough away from the homeland's shore to give early warning to RAF Fighter Command. The plots gleaned from radar went first to so-called filter rooms, which in turn passed crucial data points like altitude and headings to Bentley Priory with relays to operations rooms at the various fighter group sector headquarters.

These command and control nodes were wisely dug below ground and encased in concrete. Also, with great foresight, the dedicated telephone lines that linked the diverse elements had been buried to protect them from bombardment. Early radar was unable to track inbound Luftwaffe planes once they had crossed the coast, so thirty thousand ground observers reported the findings of their optical surveillance, supplementing the radar plots.

Based on the data flow, the nearest squadrons were scrambled. While airborne, the interceptor pilots were vectored by two-way radio to the airspace deemed most likely to contain enemy attackers. It was an imaginative system, conceived and perfected by forward-thinking and highly competent individuals, which served as the model for the later, highly computerized combined air operations centers accepted as a common facet of modern Western air warfare.

Tactics called for the Hurricane to go after the comparatively slow-moving bombers while the faster and more agile Spitfire would aim for the escort fighters. On the plus side, the Spitfire was generally light on the controls and could turn inside the Messerschmitt Bf 109. Yet, the German fighter's engine was fuel-injected whereas the Merlin engine was carburetor fed, which meant that in steep dives the Spitfire could suffer fuel-flow interruption with the attendant disadvantage of temporary power loss.

On August 14th, the day after the formal start of the air war over Britain, Prime Minister Winston Churchill visited the operations room at No. 11 Group headquarters at Uxbridge, not far from London. This unit provided the primary defensive fighter force around the city. In the company of the group's commander, Air Vice Marshal Keith Park, Churchill monitored the air action, which involved "heavy fighting throughout the afternoon."

The map table, presided over by members of the Women's Auxiliary Air Force wielding rakes like croupiers at a casino, filled up with symbols indicating extensive enemy aircraft in British skies. Churchill, no stranger to combat, having participated in the last great cavalry charge at Omdurman in the late nineteenth century, was gripped by the drama that unfolded before him. He overheard the intense radio chatter of the young pilots of RAF Fighter Command as they engaged Messerschmitts. There was no guarantee of the outcome, and Churchill realized it was largely the skill and the courage of this handful of airmen that stood between the island nation and the tyranny of Nazism.

Churchill left that evening as the air combat dissipated, shaken by the prospect of such brutal combat recurring in the days ahead. On the car ride to Chequers, the prime minister's official country residence, Churchill told his aide, General Hastings Ismay, "Do not speak to me; I have never been so moved." Approximately five minutes later, he leaned forward and uttered praiseful words that became the basis of his unforgettable tribute to the pilots he so admired. On August 20th, Churchill addressed the House of Commons on the war situation, and in that long speech he expressed publicly the emotion first shared privately with General Ismay.

Referring to those he had monitored in action at Uxbridge and to their mates elsewhere in British skies, he praised "the British airmen who, undaunted by odds, unwearied in their constant challenge of mortal danger, are turning the tide of world war by their prowess and by their devotion." And then, in one of his most memorable statements of the war, which forever enshrined Fighter Command's pilots in a special place of honor, he added: "Never in the field of human conflict was so much owed by so many to so few."

Much has rightly been made of the combining of Reginald Mitchell's fighter airframe with Rolls-Royce's Merlin engine to beget the best fighter in what was arguably the most pivotal air battle of the European war. Equally important was the pairing of such an outstanding plane as the Spitfire with patriots motivated to operate it all-out for their heartfelt cause. It was a winning union, and the image of the well-proportioned Spitfire with a square-jawed RAF pilot in the cockpit became the emblem of the great air battle.

Not quite a month after his speech, Churchill returned to Uxbridge. It was September 15th, a date destined to be remembered as Battle of Britain Day. German leaders believed that their air arm's constant strikes had diminished RAF Fighter Command. This day the Luftwaffe drew on all its resources to destroy any last vestige of its opponent's fighter force to clear the way for the cross-channel invasion.

From late morning on, the Germans threw everything they had at the British defenders. From the glass-enclosed balcony, Churchill surveyed the rapidly filling map table as large formations of enemy bombers advanced and dropped their bombs, wreaking havoc on London. No. 11 Group soon deployed all its squadrons and had requested assistance from neighboring No. 12 Group. It looked as if RAF Fighter Command might be overwhelmed.

Churchill, who himself "looked grave" at the time, later wrote: "I became conscious of the anxiety of the Commander, who now stood behind his subordinate's chair. Hitherto I had watched in silence. I now asked, 'What other reserves have we?' 'There are none,' said Air Vice Marshal Park." Both sides had committed their material assets, the best equipment their designers could develop prior to the war, in the fullest

Chapter 1 *On the Wind: The Wright Brothers* by Craig Kodera

Chapter 2 *Lucky Lindy* by Stan Stokes

Chapter 3 *Bell X-1 Rocketplane Going Supersonic* (National Aeronautics and Space Administration)

Chapter 4 *North American Aviation X-15 Rocketplane Accelerating after Launch from B-52 Mothership* (National Aeronautics and Space Administration)

Chapter 5
***American Achieve-
ment*—SpaceShipOne**
by Ronald Wong

Chapter 6
***5-AT Tri-Motor Civil
Air Transport*** by Jack
Fellows © The Unicover
Corporation

Chapter 7 *DC-3* **Flagship Knoxville** by Craig Kodera

Chapter 8 *Sentimental Journey—A Lockheed Constellation Departs San Francisco* by Stan Stokes

Chapter 9 *Pan American 707* Clipper Stargazer by Mike Machat

Chapter 10
1963 Learjet 23
by Jack Fellows
© The Unicover
Corporation

Chapter 11 *A Hard Act to Follow—British Airways Concorde* by Ron Wong

Chapter 12 *The Fokker Scourge* by Stan Stokes

Chapter 13 *Imperial Japanese Navy Ace Hiroyoshi Nishizawa* by Jack Fellows

Chapter 14 *Channel Dawn—Supermarine Spitfires* by William S. Phillips
© William S. Phillips, courtesy of The Greenwich Workshop Inc.
www.greenwichworkshop.com

Chapter 15 *B-17G Flying Fortresses over Germany* (US Air Force)

Chapter 16 *SBD-5 Dauntless Dive-Bombers from the USS* Yorktown (US Navy)

Chapter 17 *P-38L Lightning over California* (US Air Force)

Chapter 18 *Major Walter Nowotny's Final Encounter with a North American P-51 Mustang* by Keith Ferris

Chapter 19 *Air Supremacist—Messerschmitt Me 262* by Ron Wong

Chapter 20 *B-47B Stratojet with Rocket Boost at Takeoff*
(National Museum of the US Air Force)

Chapter 21 *B-52H Stratofortress after Inflight Refueling* (US Air Force)

Chapter 22 *F-117A Stealth Fighter over Nellis Air Force Base, Nevada* (US Air Force)

Chapter 23 *JN-4 Early Bird at Langley* by Russell Smith

Chapter 24 *Stearman N2S-1 Kaydet* by Jack Fellows
© The Unicover Corporation

Chapter 25 *Piper's Yellow Beauty* by Sam Lyons

possible quantities their industries could produce. Now there was nothing to be done but let the opposing airmen, in the machines handed them, exert their will in the ultimate test.

Fortuitously, between the main waves of attackers, the RAF pilots had time to return to their bases, refuel, and rearm. By the time the Luftwaffe's bombers and escorts had returned, Spitfires and Hurricanes were back in the sky with vectors to intercept. The Germans failed to score the knockout blow. The Blitz would continue, but because the Luftwaffe had not achieved air superiority within the required seasonal time frame, Operation Sea Lion was postponed indefinitely. Britain would retain its independence and serve as an indispensable launch pad for US Eighth Air Force bombers starting a couple years later and as a staging area for the historic D-Day invasion in 1944.

During the Battle of Britain, the Spitfire that had flown mostly was the Mk. IA, which had the eight .303-inch Browning machine guns. By contrast, the Messerschmitt Bf 109 was equipped with two machine guns and two cannon, the latter packing a greater wallop than the Mk. IA's eight machine guns. To address this disparity, the RAF sent an experimental Mk. IB, outfitted with only two wing-mounted 20-millimeter Hispano Suiza cannon, to No. 19 Squadron. The new armament was quickly deemed unsuitable because of gun stoppages owing to the ammunition drum-feed system.

The problem was eventually resolved by improvements to the feed mechanism. In June 1940, the Castle Bromwich factory started churning out an upgraded Spitfire. The Mk. II was powered by the new Merlin XII (which ran on 100-octane fuel) and featured either a Rotol or de Havilland constant-speed propeller, which added two thousand feet to the type's service ceiling. Also, this model had an engine-driven hydraulic system for the landing gear.

Armament for the Mk. IIA consisted of the original eight machine guns whereas for the Mk. IIB it was a combination of two 20-millimeter cannon and four .303-inch machine guns. The cannon's magazines were accommodated by faired blisters in the wings, which represented an unavoidable compromise in the wings' aerodynamic streamlining. (There were various combinations of weaponry depending on the model, each one requiring an appropriately configured wing. Wing configurations were designated A, B, C, and D, based on gun packages.)

The extra weight of the cannon did not help the Mk. IIB's performance. The answer came with the introduction of the Mk. V, which incorporated the 1,250-horsepower Merlin 45 engine. Top speed of 359 miles per hour and a time-to-climb of less than fifteen minutes to thirty-five thousand feet meant the type could retain its edge against parallel improvements in enemy fighters. The Mk. V was produced in greater quantities than any other Spitfire type, with substantial numbers reaching operational squadrons in May 1941.

The most meaningful Spitfire performance improvements after the Battle of Britain came with development of the Mk. IX in 1942 and the Mk. XIV in 1943. The former, developed as an interim version based on the Mk. VC, was mated with the 1,565-horsepower Merlin 61 that provided extra power from medium altitude due to a new two-speed, two-stage supercharger. The cooling system was split with symmetrical scoops under the starboard and port wings. A new gyro gun sight was installed that dramatically improved accuracy. Also later versions of the Mk. IX had tapered fuselages with bubble canopies that enhanced visibility.

The Mk. XIV benefited from being fitted with the Rolls-Royce Griffon 65, an engine developed originally for naval aircraft, which had a larger displacement than the Merlin and could generate up to 2,375-horsepower. The aircraft's nose was lengthened with a corresponding increase in fin and rudder area. A Rotol five-bladed constant-speed propeller was installed. The design features of this mark enabled it to compete with the Fw 190 and to catch V-1 "buzz bombs" harassing the British populace late in the war.

For the British people, the iconography of the Spitfire was captured in the indomitable spirit of the brash and gutsy Douglas Robert Steuart Bader. Shortly after graduating second in his class from the Royal Air Force College at Cranwell in 1930, Bader's airmanship skills got him a slot on the RAF aerobatic team that performed at the annual flying display at RAF Hendon outside of London. But his impetuousness soon got him in trouble.

In 1931, during unauthorized low-level maneuvering, he dished out of a slow roll and his plane careened into the ground. Both his legs were amputated and the prognosis was grim. But Bader was nothing if not a fighter. He determined to walk again on artificial limbs without use of a crutch. Moreover, he vowed to fly again.

Eight years later, with war on the horizon and Britain perilously short of pilots, the RAF acceded to Bader's pleadings for a return to a fighter cockpit. During the Battle of Britain, Bader led initially skeptical squadron mates to morale-boosting success against the Luftwaffe. He demanded much of his fellow fighter pilots and even more of himself.

Brusque, intemperate, always trying to prove himself, yet never ordering an underling to do something he wouldn't do himself, the dynamic leader's "defiant character and dogmatic personality" provoked the range of human emotion from friendship and loyalty to annoyance and wrath. "He could be a right bastard at times, but we all loved him," said an airman who knew him. There could be no denying Bader's fighter pilot acumen or warrior's heart, for early on he notched twenty-two and a half air-to-air victories in both the Hurricane and Spitfire, which would rank him as the RAF's fifth highest-scoring ace of the conflict.

On August 9, 1941, he dived headlong into a melee and in the heat of battle the empennage of his Spitfire severed from the rest of the fuselage. It remains unclear if Bader's plane was felled by a collision with one of the dogfighting Bf 109s or a line of shells from enemy guns or friendly fire. When attempting to bail out, Bader's artificial right foot got trapped in the cockpit. With just six thousand feet to spare, he extricated himself. The onrushing wind and his physical exertions caused the fastener holding his right prosthesis to snap. He was sucked out into the air and floated down on his silk chute, landing in the French countryside near St. Omer.

Bader was hastened into custody. Interestingly, his German captors knew of the legless ace. Senior Luftwaffe commanders, including Adolf Galland, soon to be appointed head of Luftwaffe Fighter Command, made a point to meet the renowned airman. He was an adversary, but one whose personal story of perseverance against such overwhelming odds could hardly help but instill a sense of wonder. It was a rare moment in war when an enemy's respect tipped over for short spurts into deference—a kind of modern chivalry among knights of the air.

With Galland present, Bader was given a tour of the nearby Audembert airfield at which Bf 109s operated. Pictures of the unusual occasion were taken and, except for the differences in uniforms, one would not know that the smiling airmen were even enemies. Bader was given the unprecedented opportunity to squeeze into the cockpit of one of the Messerschmitt fighters. With a straight face, he asked if he could start the engine. Predictably, his captors, one of whom had lost a leg in World War I, declined to let him do so.

Considered insufferable by his German handlers, he was transferred to the maximum-security prison at Colditz. Even there, his tireless spirit boosted morale among his fellow prisoners. Finally, his liberation came in mid-April 1945, with the war in Europe ending early the next month and hostilities in the Pacific concluding in August.

On September15th, the fifth anniversary of Battle of Britain Day, the British government chose to commemorate the fateful air battle with a mass formation of representative aircraft. In total, three hundred RAF planes were slated to overfly London. Nominated to lead the triumphal armada through the patch of sky he knew well from his days scrambling to the city's defense as a squadron leader assigned to No. 12 Group at Duxford was the irrepressible Douglas Bader—in a glistening Spitfire.

The elliptical-winged beauty passed low over Buckingham Palace. Its finely syncopated Merlin gave off its familiar purring sound. The ceremonial flight of Britain's quintessential fighter with many other makes and models close behind was a welcome reminder of the country's mastery of the sky during the war and of the unyielding determination of its people to protect their way of life.

CHAPTER 15

Beyond the Horizon: Air Power Dreams and the Flying Fortress

The B-17 Flying Fortress advanced the transformative idea—espoused by visionary officers like Billy Mitchell and his disciples, who included Henry H. "Hap" Arnold—that air power could be decisive in war. When the time came for this modern weapon to prove itself in the crucible of hostile European skies, the four-engine beast needed modifications to both its structure and tactics, but with its courageous crews pressing on it ravaged an incorrigible enemy and buoyed the spirits of freedom-loving peoples, becoming a symbol of strength in the twentieth century's ultimate contest of good versus evil.

•••

Boeing's first really large airplanes were airliners. Notable among them was the streamlined Model 200 Monomail, introduced in 1930. As the name suggests, this was a monoplane, which represented a break from past configurations. The Monomail's long-span all-metal cantilever wing had aluminum square truss spars for strength. The aircraft also featured retractable landing gear.

A refinement, the Model 221, could carry six passengers as well as mail in upfront compartments. The pilot sat in an aft open cockpit. Based on looks alone, this beauty seemed to have great potential, but constant-speed propellers had not been perfected at the time and with only a fixed-pitch propeller the Monomail's performance fell short.

The sharp-looking Monomail led to the Model 215, a twin-engine bomber that closely resembled its commercial antecedent with open-cockpit crew positions spread out along the top of the fuselage. Boeing rightly considered this in-house development, designated the Y1B-9, a major improvement over the army's ungainly Keystone B-4A biplane, which still soldiered on as the service's standard bomber despite its World War I characteristics. The problem for Boeing was that the Glenn L. Martin Company leaped ahead with its competing bomber design.

The Martin entry, designated the B-10, was the first bomber to offer enclosed positions for all crew members. The army opted for this aircraft and gave Martin a sizable contract. Rather than throw in the towel, Boeing switched markets and developed a new airliner from its unsuccessful bomber.

The resulting aircraft was the Model 247, the first modern airliner of the post–Tri-Motor era. Introduced in 1933, the all-metal twin-engine airliner with a passenger capacity of ten became an industry sensation, setting a new level of expectation among members of the flying public. United Air Lines was the launch customer, with an order for sixty of the type.

Yet, just when things seemed so promising, fortunes took a turn for the worse. Because aeronautical technology was advancing so rapidly, the Model 247 found itself quickly eclipsed by the Douglas Aircraft Company's DC series of airliners. Compounding Boeing's plight in the quickly shifting industry environment was the US government's move to break up aviation holding companies, which in some cases had combined engine, parts, airframe, and airline companies under a single umbrella.

Boeing was part of the consortium that controlled United Air Lines. With their separation, the airline could no longer be counted on as a safe bet for future orders. Boeing faced a potentially precarious situation.

The company's first impulse was to use its existing design as the foundation for a leap back into the world of bombers. In May 1934 the army sought proposals for a heavy long-range bomber under the designation XBLR-1 (for Experimental Bomber Long-Range Number 1). Boeing scaled up its still-new airliner in drawings to beat out Martin for the contract of the bomber which later was redesignated XB-15.

The specifications required that the new bomber fly a distance of five thousand miles with a bomb load of two thousand pounds. This performance demand meant that the bomber would, indeed, be a giant of the air. The wingspan measured almost 150 feet. Four 1,000-horsepower liquid-cooled engines were to power the behemoth, but these were not ready when needed. Four 850-horsepower radial engines were installed as an alternative. Various technical issues delayed the first flight until October 1937.

Meanwhile, with meager business forcing the layoffs of eleven hundred employees in the first half of 1934, Boeing management felt pressure to drum up new contracts or risk extinction. Rather than put all its chips on either a military or civilian project, the company chose to pursue both—a new bomber and a new airliner, Models 299 and 300, respectively. The idea was to have each share as much as possible in parts, design features, and manufacturing processes to achieve an economy of scale.

On August 8th, Boeing received the formal proposal from the air corps. In the summer of 1934, Boeing's president, Claire Egtvedt, steered the company towards the preliminary design of a hoped-for new bomber. After all, the army was known to be preparing an industry competition to replace the Martin B-10. It would fit into the medium bomber classification with its size being somewhere between the twin-engine Model 247 and the huge four-engine XB-15.

The proposal contained imposing requirements: cruising speed of 220 miles per hour, maximum speed of 250 miles per hour, range of twenty-two hundred miles, endurance of ten hours, and others related to altitude, time-to-climb, engine-out performance, and payload. By the conventions of the time, twin-engine designs were expected, but Boeing leaned towards four engines to satisfy the engine-out and speed requirements. Egtvedt visited Wright Field in Dayton, Ohio, and came away with word that procurement officials would be open to a four-engine design.

The next month, Boeing's board of directors okayed going all in on the new bomber project. The company allotted $275,000, representing more than half its cash on hand. Before the prototype's completion and first flight the following year, Boeing had to scrounge up additional funds for the project. The bomber was given priority over the Model 300 airliner.

It was a gutsy decision—like betting the store—to proceed on a new bomber with scant resources and without knowing whether a contract would be forthcoming. As would be expected, the configuration of the company's XB-15, which was in-process, influenced the design of the new plane. Indeed, the Model 299 would bear more than a passing resemblance to its big brother, albeit in scaled-down form.

Luckily Boeing had talented engineers on its small design staff. Project engineer was E. Gifford Emery, who would be assisted by recent Stanford graduate Edward C. Wells. With a full-court press to create the technology demonstrator, the Model 299 was finished in less than a year.

On July 17, 1935, the aircraft was literally rolled out of the final assembly hangar at Boeing Field in Seattle. The bomber's wingspan of 103 feet and nine inches was longer than the hangar door. To remove the plane, it had to be mounted on dollies and wheeled out sideways.

In public view for the first time, Boeing's glistening new bomber designed for a crew of eight could hardly help but impress. Its streamlined all-metal construction, sturdy appearance, and sheer size as the largest land plane yet built in America (preceding the introduction of the XB-15) with a length of nearly sixty-nine feet caused quite a stir. Moreover, the bomber had five enclosed gun positions of which four were teardrop-shaped blisters on the top of the aft upper deck, in the belly, and on either side of the fuselage. The fifth was in a rotating Plexiglas nose bubble. Altogether, these defensive weapons provided overlapping cones of fire that went beyond anything yet produced.

Upon laying his eyes on the plane, a local newspaper reporter is said to have referred to it as a "flying fortress." Some accounts contend that the appellation was uttered while others point to the term's use in an article and picture caption. In any case, the nickname stuck; from then on the bomber was the Flying Fortress.

The bomber's four engines were 750-horsepower Pratt & Whitney Hornet radials. They were mounted on the massive wing, which borrowed the durable construction of the Monomail's wing. Each engine, encased in an individual nacelle with a National Advisory Committee for Aeronautics-developed cowling, turned a three-bladed eleven-and-a-half-foot-diameter Hamilton Standard constant-speed propeller.

The pilot and copilot seats were side by side. Rather than duplicating engine controls as was the custom in some twin-engine aircraft, the Boeing bomber placed a single set of engine controls between the two seats. This arrangement allowed each pilot to manipulate the same controls, one with his right hand and the other with his left hand.

The center of the fuselage was a hollowed out space for two bomb racks that could hold up to forty-eight hundred pounds of bombs. Arguably, this was the bomber's most disappointing aspect. The Consolidated B-24 Liberator and the Avro Lancaster, which came later, could carry much heavier bomb loads. Nevertheless, the air corps stood by the Flying Fortress, asserting that it would operate in large formations and that efficacy should be measured in overall effects rather than the payload capacity of a single plane.

An identifying feature of this early design was the tall and slightly swept fin, looking much like a shark's fin. The plane's rudder was decorated in the alternating red-and-white stripes common in prewar military paint schemes. Stenciled on either side of the red stripe in the center was the federal registration number, denoting this aircraft's civilian ownership, i.e., Boeing.

The Model 299's one overtly peculiar feature was the fold in the bottom of the nose. This was to accommodate a bombardier's sighting panel. Rounding out the design's modern items was retractable landing gear although both the mains and the tail wheel remained partially unshielded when raised.

Flight trials began less than two weeks after the rollout. Test pilot Leslie Tower had the privilege of taking the bomber up for its maiden flight. All went well except for a shimmy in the tail wheel during taxiing.

The army was anxious to conduct its evaluation at Wright Field, so on August 20, 1935, the Model 299 set out from Seattle to Dayton. On the flight, the aircraft averaged 233 miles per hour, a very good sign that it would satisfy the speed and distance requirements laid out by the air corps. It soon became apparent that Boeing's entry eclipsed the other bomber designs.

The Martin 146 was essentially a widened B-10. The company would go back to the drawing board and eventually develop the high-performance twin-engine B-26 Marauder. Douglas offered the DB-1, which was predicated on its DC-2 airliner, sporting a deeper fuselage to accommodate the ordnance.

While the Model 299 was clearly superior, it was also roughly double the price. This could be explained largely by the fact that the aircraft had four engines and its competitors' entries had only two engines. In the middle of the Depression, with funds scarce, the air corps would have to decide between cost and capability.

On October 30th, circumstances intervened to influence the procurement decision. As the evaluation was winding down with the Model 299 clearly in the lead, the Boeing bomber took off from Wright Field with army test pilot Major Ployer Hill in the left seat and Boeing test pilot Leslie Tower in the right seat. The plane nosed up after leaving the ground and went into an unrecoverable stall, slamming into the ground and killing the two pilots.

Enough of the wreckage was recovered intact for the accident investigation to determine the cause of the crash. The Boeing designers had devised a gust control lock to prevent the plane's control surfaces from flapping in the wind when parked on the ground. This control lock, which was manipulated from within the aircraft, had not been released prior to the flight.

It is generally accepted that this fatal accident prompted the introduction and widespread application of pilot checklists which continue to be used routinely in connection with every flight by crews around the world. Out of disaster came something worthwhile. It is probably stating the obvious to say that many lives have been saved since because of the adoption of this common pilot tool. Checklists have been imitated by a range of professionals, including surgeons undertaking complex procedures in hospital operating rooms.

For the moment, though, Boeing's ambitious plans were stymied. The army selected the Douglas DB-1, which was designated the B-18 Bolo. An order for 133 of the twin-engine bombers was issued late in the year.

Boeing had put virtually all it had into the bomber project. To be shut out of the project by the air corps would have meant almost certain collapse of the company. To the eternal relief of the company's executives, on

January 17, 1936, a contract was received for thirteen service test versions and one static test version. These aircraft, to be designated YB-17, were actually designated Y1B-17 due to the air corps' budgeting/bookkeeping system. In everyday usage, airmen referred to the bombers as B-17s.

The air corps understood that Boeing's bomber offered much more all-around capability than the smaller Douglas. Also, the Model 299's crash did not point to any design flaw but rather to a one-time human error. The small order for Boeing's new bomber represented the beginning of the military's historic association with the B-17 Flying Fortress.

With the order in hand, small though it was, Boeing embarked on the construction of a new plant at its Seattle location to correct production inefficiencies. Meanwhile, the Model 300 civil transport did not materialize; rather, a different commercial aircraft emerged. Sharing the B-17's wing among other features, the four-engine Model 307 Stratoliner entered service in 1940 as the first airliner with a pressurized cabin.

The main difference between the newly ordered bombers and the initial flying demonstrator was the switch to a more powerful set of engines. The Pratt & Whitney Hornets were replaced by the 930-horsepower Wright R-1820-39 Cyclones. This represented a significant upgrade while preserving the reliability of nine-cylinder air-cooled radial engines.

Other upgrades included improved landing gear serviceability and the addition of rubber deicer boots to the wings and horizontal stabilizers. The resulting aircraft gave air power disciples the type of fast and reasonably long-range bomber they had dreamed about. These B-17s were assigned to the 2nd Bombardment Group at Langley Field in Virginia where, in answer to critics and in pursuance of favorable publicity, they embarked on high-profile training and goodwill missions.

However, one ingredient was still missing. According to developing doctrine, the large bomber formations would succeed in their task of delivering bombs if they could operate high enough above enemy targets. To this end, the Y1B-17 originally procured for static testing was instead redesignated Y1B-17A and devoted to the flight testing of exhaust-driven turbo-superchargers.

These turbo-superchargers were fitted to the top of the nacelles as a matter of expedience. It became apparent in flight tests, however, that the installations caused turbulent airflow over the wing, making their position untenable. The solution was to relocate them on the bottom of the nacelle.

Through trial and error, the right combination of equipment and positioning was finally achieved by the spring of 1939. Benefits included a higher horsepower rating at altitude for the Y1B-17A's Wright R-1820-51 Cyclone engine. Service ceiling was increased and top speed at twenty-five thousand feet was boosted to 295 miles per hour, contrasted to the earlier model's top speed of 256 miles per hour at fourteen thousand feet. Turbo-superchargers would be standard on future B-17 orders.

The B-17 was finally ready to go into production. First in the production series was the B-17B. This model used the same engine as the Y1B-17A test model with the turbo-superchargers similarly installed. At takeoff, each engine produced an impressive 1,200-horsepower.

The most obvious improvement in the B model's design was the reworking of the nose. The odd-looking bombardier's flat-panel cutout was done away with and replaced with a more aesthetic and aerodynamic nose cone that incorporated a large flat panel within a framed structure. Also, the separate rotating Plexiglas nose gun bubble was replaced by a ball-and-socket mount that accommodated a .30-caliber machine gun.

Other changes included hydraulic brakes, a larger rudder, repositioning the direction-finder loop antenna (later changed to the football-shaped antenna), adding a pilot's observation dome to the top of the aft flight deck, and reshuffling crew positions. Thirty-nine B models were delivered through March 30, 1940. None saw combat, but remained as test beds throughout the war, validating new systems and add-ons for the later models.

At this time, the Third Reich had started its withering march across Europe, and many felt, despite strong anti-interventionist convictions, that it was only a matter of time before the hostilities enveloped America. The army air corps and the domestic aviation industry now had the action reports of allies to analyze for clues as to what might improve the combat effectiveness of existing and planned designs. In the case of the B-17, it became clear that more defensive firepower was necessary.

The B-17C was differentiated from its predecessor by the elimination of the gun blisters. At the two waist positions, flush hatches were substituted, which gave each of the gunners a pedestal-mounted gun. The overhead position was changed to a removable panel for the gun. The belly position got a large "bathtub" that contained a gun fired by an ensconced gunner concerned mainly with threats to the rear of the plane. Each of these guns was a .50-caliber machine gun while the nose retained its .30-caliber machine gun.

Engines were upgraded to the Wright R-1820-65 Cyclones, which raised top speed to well over 300 miles per hour and expanded the combat radius. The first flight of the C model occurred on July 21, 1940. This period coincided with the life-or-death struggle of Britain, as Germany had turned its attention that summer to conquering the island nation.

Although the United States remained officially neutral until being attacked, in the spring and summer of the next year it released twenty B-17Cs to the British Royal Air Force. Even with the various improvements, the aircraft, designated Fortress I's by the British, were clearly not ready for combat and did not come equipped with the top-secret Norden bombsight. Nevertheless, the British decided to employ them in a series of high-altitude raids starting with a mission against the Kriegsmarine's naval base at Wilhelmshaven on July 8, 1941.

It turned out that Messerschmitt interceptors could reach the bombers at their cruising altitude of thirty-two thousand feet. Also, high humidity and low temperatures caused certain of the bombers' systems to freeze over as well as at least one supercharger to fail. The British lost eight of the bombers in the course of two months with little to show for the attempt at high-altitude daylight bombing. The remaining Fortress I's were withdrawn from combat operations.

The failure of the new American bomber in its combat debut sent shock waves through the public back home, but the bomber advocates in the army air force (the air corps having become the army air force in April 1941) remained steadfast in their belief that the B-17 would succeed. They pointed out that although the Messerschmitt interceptors could reach the bombers at high altitude, the British did not deploy the bombers in sufficiently large formations to provide adequate self-protection. Also, it was argued that the C model, or Fortress I, would be superseded by newer models with more guns offering greater cones of defensive fire.

Lessons were learned by Allied airmen on both sides of the Atlantic. As committed as the American air officers were to their doctrine, the British took their unhappy experience with the small number of Fortress I's as a sign that daylight bombing was suicidal. Indeed, the fiasco reinforced the British view that night bombing made more sense. As British aviation historian Roger Freeman noted, the RAF was further put off by what its leaders considered the Fortress I's meager bomb load "in relation to the manning and maintenance effort."

The United States took delivery of only eighteen C models. Another forty-two were on order, but these underwent substantial changes that led to their redesignation as B-17Ds. With deliveries starting in February 1941, these aircraft had cowl flaps, twin .50-caliber machine guns in the dorsal and ventral positions, extra armor plate, and self-sealing fuel tanks. Most of the new bombers were sent to Hawaii and the Philippines during that year.

The surprise Japanese air strikes against American bases on December 7, 1941, caught a dozen B-17s tidily lined up on the apron at Hickam Field near Pearl Harbor. Separately, another dozen B-17s were inbound as the attack unfolded. All of these bombers were unarmed; one was downed and the remainder incurred damage, either from zealous anti-aircraft fire or Japanese fighters.

Hours later, the Japanese attacked Clark Field in the Philippines. Despite advance warning of the outbreak of hostilities, eighteen B-17s were destroyed. Fortuitously, one squadron was stationed elsewhere in the Philippines at the time, enabling it to fight another day.

Knowing that its mid-1930s bomber faced a capability crisis, perhaps even extinction, given the rapid pace of aeronautical advancement in the second half of the decade, Boeing had begun a meaningful overhaul of the B-17's design well before America's entry into the war. The bomber clearly needed a broader cone of defensive fire to the rear lest interceptors gang up on bomber formations from behind. The company's main focus through much of 1941 was the redesign of the tail to accommodate a defensive gun position.

Thus, the B-17E came with a tail gunner position. It was a compromise between the newest gun technology and aerodynamics. Sophisticated electrically powered gun turrets were becoming available, but the installation of such a unit in the tail would adversely affect the plane's streamlining, which was not an acceptable option.

Boeing enlarged the tail enough so that the tail gunner could half sit and half kneel in the compartment, manually operating twin .50-caliber machine guns. At the same time, the fin was scaled up to nearly four feet taller than before. Also, a sizable fin fairing was added. This tail arrangement was borrowed from the company's 307 Stratoliner in a case of a feature from a secondary design coming back to be applied to the baseline design.

Also, the clunky "bathtub" affixed to the belly was replaced by a remotely operated twin-gun turret. This installation proved to be a purely transitional step since this system relied on the gunner using a periscope in the prone position. Its impracticality led to its replacement by a modern electrically powered ball turret in the next model.

At the time, increased orders were a mixed blessing for Boeing. It wanted the extra business, but it simply lacked the capacity to meet the rising demand, especially since its futuristic B-29 bomber project consumed an inordinate amount of the company's limited resources. As early as the summer of 1940, agreements were reached with Douglas Aircraft and Lockheed's Vega Aircraft subsidiary to supplement B-17 production under license. Some of the B-17Es as well as later models were built by these manufacturers.

The American war plan called for a massive presence of heavy bombers in Britain, a staging area that offered a natural moat for a measure of security. On August 17, 1942, a month after arriving at Polebrook, not far from Cambridge, B-17Es of the 97th Bombardment Group conducted a raid on the marshalling yards at Rouen in occupied France. It was the first air strike against targets in Europe by US Army Flying Fortresses.

From that maiden mission, the greatest air armada of all time emerged. The Eighth Air Force, sometimes described as the Mighty Eighth, would gain the initiative, in concert with its RAF allies, and eventually dominate European skies. But meanwhile, the realities of the unfolding air war forced further modifications to the arriving bombers.

Early combat experience demonstrated that these new bombers were vulnerable from head-on attack. Frontal closing speeds gave the interceptors a marked advantage against the B-17s, which were most vulnerable in head-on attacks. The answer was to install more firepower in the nose, so the next model, the B-17F, had provisions for .50-caliber guns in the nose's side windows, which eventually were bulged to provide a greater field of fire for what came to be called cheek guns. Also, the original .30-caliber nose gun was replaced by a .50-caliber gun.

In fact, modifications were occurring at such an accelerated clip at this point in the war that more than four hundred changes went into the B-17F. While most of the changes were minor, the sheer volume suggested a change in model designation was warranted. The F model's most significant improvement was the switch to so-called paddle propeller blades, which increased service ceiling and speed until added weight, the perennial bane of aircraft engineers, rolled the performance numbers back. The addition of outboard fuel tanks alone increased the aircraft's weight by 6,360 pounds. The tradeoff was that range and endurance were dramatically enhanced, leading some to call the added fuel bladders "Tokyo Tanks" on the premise that they would enable long-distance raids on the Japanese capital.

By late summer 1943, production had ramped up to where the Eighth Air Force had sixteen bombardment groups operating Flying Fortresses. Smaller numbers were stationed in North Africa for a two-pronged air war against Nazi and Fascist forces in Europe. The squeeze would soon be felt by the Axis powers, but not without pain on the American side.

On August 17th, the one-year anniversary of the first American B-17 raid in Europe, 376 B-17s were sent from Eighth Air Force bases in southeast England to execute an extremely bold plan of attack on the Messerschmitt fighter factory at Regensburg and the ball-bearing plants at Schweinfurt. This was the largest assemblage of B-17s yet fielded, and hopes ran high that a major setback would be dealt to the Luftwaffe and, at the same time, that the effectiveness of precision daylight bombing would be validated. However, almost from the outset things did not go smoothly.

While the first contingent of bombers launched successfully, the second was delayed by foggy weather. This protracted gap in the timing gave the German interceptors the time they needed to land, refuel, and rearm to confront the second wave of B-17s. But even the first suffered from the scrubbing of a diversionary mission and a lack of fighter escort due to the weather.

The 100th Bomb Group, bringing up the rear of the first contingent, got the worst of the interceptors. Bombers were exploding and falling out of the sky with such dispatch that crews wondered if their group would suffer "100 percent loss." An observer in one of the B-17s remarked: "It appeared that our group was faced with annihilation." The staggering losses contributed to the group's sullen nickname, the "Bloody 100th."

The bombers that got through succeeded in damaging the targets, but the toll was sixty B-17s. This meant six hundred men went down, for each plane had a crew of ten. Moreover, many of the bombers that returned had incurred significant battle damage, requiring lengthy repairs.

Lieutenant General Ira C. Eaker, commander of Eighth Air Force at the time, later commented that the mission "was the bloodiest and most savagely fought air battle up to that time. The flight crews demonstrated a determination and courage seldom equaled and never surpassed in warfare." He added: "It set a pattern and a precedent for all bombing missions which were to follow."

In September the latest model of the Flying Fortress began to arrive at Eighth Air Force units. The only major change in the B-17G was the addition of a powered .50-caliber twin-gun Bendix chin turret operated remotely by the bombardier from his position in the nose. The new set of forward-facing guns offered additional protection against frontal attacks, which had become a favored tactic of Luftwaffe fighter pilots.

The G model was the final production variant and the one built in greatest quantity. Of the 12,731 B-17s built from start to finish, 68 percent or 8,680 were G models. All three plants built this model with Boeing's output accounting for nearly half. Eventually, Boeing produced as many as sixteen B-17s per day.

To the astonishment of still-active crews who had flown the first Schweinfurt mission, when curtains were pulled back in briefing rooms in the fall of 1943, the ball-bearing plants in the German city were back on the target list. The Eighth Air Force was returning to Schweinfurt. On October 14th the mission proceeded and, sadly, like the first, sixty B-17s were shot out of the sky—another six hundred men downed in battle. This time, adding to the dismay, battle damage assessments indicated a disappointing impact on the targets.

The losses were chilling; so many trained and skilled airmen going down on a single mission, one after the other. And, yet, the air crews never wavered or turned back; in the presence of unimaginable horrors— witnessing their buddies in the plane cruising alongside blown to smithereens—they still pressed on. Most of those aboard the bombers were barely out of high school and the officers maybe had a little college. The courage of these young Americans was boundless and it can hardly help but bring to mind Lord Tennyson's *The Charge of the Light Brigade*, the poet's stirring verse commemorating the sacrifice of six hundred of his countrymen in a cavalry charge at Balaclava in 1854.

There were other B-17 strikes that autumn against targets in Stuttgart, Bremen, Marienburg, and Munster. Some damage was inflicted on the enemy's infrastructure, e.g., at Marienburg where a Focke-Wulf factory was destroyed along with the adjoining runway. Also new technologies were being applied like H2S, a British-developed ground-scanning radar refined in the United States and known as H2X or "Mickey" to American crews.

But the bombardment groups' attrition rate on most of the raids continued to be nothing short of alarming. Sometimes thirty to forty-five bombers never returned to their home bases, on occasion representing losses of 20 percent and more. On one mission, the 100th lost all but one of its thirteen fielded B-17s. Though some of the crew members of downed planes parachuted to safety and later rejoined the war effort, most fell into the categories of killed in action, missing, or captured.

While battle-hardened crews and newly arrived replacements did not buckle, morale suffered. The question of whether or not these losses were sustainable loomed over the heads of air commanders and the bomber crews in the mission queue. Hap Arnold himself acknowledged in his postwar memoir he did not know if the United States could "keep it up." He admitted: "To this day [1949], I don't know for certain if we could have. No one does."

Naysayers in British officialdom, who had long harbored skepticism of daylight precision bombing, looked at the distressing attrition rates as vindication. As far as attrition was concerned, the absence of long-range escort fighters until late 1943 / early 1944 played a major role. Once these fighters arrived on the scene, the situation started to turn around. However, they did not completely change the attrition calculus because of Germany's stepped-up anti-aircraft defenses that included radar-directed 88-mm and 105-mm guns with a reach of up to thirty thousand feet.

Ira Eaker was replaced as Eighth Air Force commander by Major General James H. "Jimmy" Doolittle, the famous air racer and test pilot who had already distinguished himself by leading the April 1942 raid on Tokyo from the deck of a Navy aircraft carrier. Before his latest assignment, he had commanded Twelfth Air Force and then Fifteenth Air Force in North Africa and Italy. Two months after beginning his new assignment in England on January 5, 1944, he received a promotion to three-star rank.

Doolittle readily pointed out in his autobiography that as he assumed his new position larger external fuel tanks were arriving, which greatly extended the range of existing P-47 Thunderbolts. Also, long-range fighters, the P-38 Lightning and P-51 Mustang, began to reach England in meaningful numbers. Perhaps equally as important, Doolittle changed escort tactics.

When Doolittle paid a visit to his fighter commander, Major General William E. "Bill" Kepner, he noticed a sign on the office wall that read: "THE FIRST DUTY OF THE EIGHTH AIR FORCE FIGHTERS IS TO BRING THE BOMBERS BACK ALIVE." Doolittle, whose flying experience had included fighters, was piqued. He told Kepner to replace that sign with one that read: "THE FIRST DUTY OF THE EIGHTH AIR FORCE FIGHTERS IS TO DESTROY GERMAN FIGHTERS." It was a marked change in strategy, which was not universally embraced, but Doolittle believed for the rest of his life that his policy of "ultimate pursuit" was the correct one.

The tide of the air war finally started to shift in February 1944. In the final year of the European war, missions of the B-17s as well as the B-24s had a cumulative effect on the Nazi war machine, wearing it down slowly but surely. Oil supplies became scarce, transportation slowed to a crawl, and the attrition suffered by German forces was harder to replenish.

The B-17 Flying Fortress was an instrument of total war. By war's end, it and the other heavy bombers, most notably the B-29 Superfortress, pummeled cities, turning whole blocks into piles of rubble. The bombing's effect on the will of the enemy is still debated. No doubt there were Germans who remained defiant, wanting to avenge the destruction to their homeland. At the same time, the core of the Third Reich had been drained, and when Allied leaders proclaimed V-E Day on May 8, 1945, opposition was minimal.

During its three years of combat, the Eighth Air Force reported 43,742 bomber crewmen and fighter pilots killed or missing in action. It lost 4,456 bombers in the air war. This enormous depletion of personnel and equipment was not forgotten by those whose casualties were lessened by the airmen's sacrifice.

In April 1945 Schweinfurt fell to the 42nd Infantry Division, known as the "Rainbow Division." A large Nazi flag was lowered from a flagpole in the city and, as a token of appreciation from the American troops who knew of the strenuous efforts to vitiate the city's strategic targets from the air in advance of their ground offensive, it was sent to the 305th Bombardment Group, one of the groups hit hard in the second Schweinfurt raid nearly two years earlier. When the flag was held up, with its specious swastika in full view of the group's personnel assembled in a hangar at their base near Chelveston in Northamptonshire, a message from their grateful infantry cohorts was read: "To the Eighth Air Force. The Rainbow has revenged your losses at Schweinfurt!"

•••

When hostilities ceased, Jimmy Doolittle authorized thirty thousand ground personnel under his command to be flown over Germany "to see with their own eyes what they had helped to bring about." The view was stark; a pastoral vista had been systematically transformed into a veritable moonscape, an unnerving tableau representative of how monstrous bombers like the B-17 could be if applied businesslike by forces incited to righteous indignation. It was also, in its disfiguring frightfulness, an affirmation of air power's ability, in coordination with land and naval forces, to coerce malefactors into submission.

The best known of the breed is the *Memphis Belle*, the B-17F that William Wyler made the focus of his 1944 documentary of the same name. Assigned to the 91st Bombardment Group, the bomber became one of the first to complete twenty-five combat missions. Having met their quota, the pilot, Robert K. Morgan, and his crew were sent back to the United States for a tour that raised funds for war bonds.

The aircraft's nickname derived from Morgan's sweetheart, Margaret Polk, who lived in Memphis, Tennessee. The romance soon cooled. But affection for the *Memphis Belle* has lived on.

For years the city that is the bomber's namesake publicly displayed the relic. It became too much of a challenge after weather, vandalism, and inadequate funds left the *Memphis Belle* subject to an uncertain future. In 2005 the bomber went into a comprehensive restoration at the National Museum of the US Air Force where, when finished, it will occupy a prominent display space as one of the Dayton, Ohio, museum's celebrated artifacts.

In his remaining years, Ira Eaker, who had subsequently served as commander of the Mediterranean Allied Air Forces and then chief of the air staff, seized every opportunity to perpetuate the history of the aircraft and those who operated it. When a group of civic leaders in the City of Memphis invited him to attend their May 17, 1987, dedication of the new memorial pavilion for what they hoped would be the permanent home of the *Memphis Belle*, the general's deteriorating health forced him to decline. But he sent a letter which was read at the occasion.

The letter's words could have been addressed to not only those who flew the *Memphis Belle*, but "those thousands of other airmen and ground crews who took the battle to the enemy." The general's tribute made a fitting epitaph for all who participated in the historic air campaign: "Let us in particular salute those airmen who gave their lives in carrying out this mission. The *Memphis Belle* shall remain a living memorial to their brave deeds four decades ago and a reminder to present and future generations of Americans of the need to remain vigilant and strong in the preservation of freedom."

CHAPTER 16

In the Nick of Time: Mr. Heinemann's Dauntless Dive-Bomber

Gustave Henry Edward Heinemann was born in Saginaw, Michigan, on March 14, 1908, to parents of German and Swiss ancestry. Displaying the stubbornness at an early age for which he would become well known, he insisted that his first teacher call him Ed. Against the teacher's repeated protestations, the intransigent schoolboy persisted and from then on he was Ed Heinemann.

This pesky youngster from a family of modest means showed a surprising aptitude for mechanics. Starting at age five, he built toy canoes and miniature sailboats. He also proved to be an inveterate tinkerer with things around the house.

In 1915 the Heinemann family left Saginaw for the promise of a milder climate in California's Sacramento Valley. During that year's Panama Pacific International Exposition in San Francisco, Ed's mother and father took their seven-year-old son to the city's waterfront where the colorful event was in full swing. Along the decorative shoreline, Ed got his initial exposure to the world of airplanes when, as part of the exposition's ceremonies, celebrated aviators Lincoln Beachey and Art Smith performed an awesome routine in aircraft with a skeletal framework. The flyers made a lasting impression.

The following year, on Ed's birthday, the grandfather who still resided in Saginaw gave Ed a toy biplane. Ed cherished the gift. From that point, airplanes transfixed him.

Ed's family moved to Los Angeles in 1916 where his father found employment as a furniture company foreman. When school let out, Ed spent afternoons with the neighborhood boys at an automotive speedway that seconded as an airport. Arriving and departing aircraft titillated the young onlookers.

One of the flyers Ed got to know was the pioneering Neta Snook. As a pilot, she represented the new vanguard of female flyers and garnered her own measure of fame as Amelia Earhart's flight instructor. Ed lent Neta a hand whenever she needed her biplane trainer, a Curtiss Jenny, pushed in or out of its hangar.

Cognizant of their son's mechanical aptitude, Ed's family enrolled him in the Manual Arts High School of Los Angeles, known then for its vocational curriculum. The specialized public school counted Jimmy Doolittle among its distinguished alumni. The talents Ed had exhibited outside of school began to blossom with the trades-oriented coursework.

In his spare time, Ed built a working radio from discarded wires and assorted debris. This homebuilt contraption enabled him to be the first on his block to learn of President Warren Harding's death. Ed also built a motorboat which he skippered up and down the Southern California coast.

As recounted in his autobiography (cowritten with Rosario Rausa), he excelled most when he took pencil to paper and recreated machinery in precise cutaway drawings. His drafting teacher at Manual Arts High, August Flam, saw this prodigious capacity and encouraged Ed to pursue technical drafting. Also, because Ed was tremendously self-motivated, he devoured stacks of books and sheaves of articles on engineering and science that were not on the school's required reading list.

By 1925 Ed had earned most of the credits required for graduation, but he was anxious to get out into the world and apply himself. With his drafting teacher at first expressing dismay but then giving his blessing, Ed dropped out of school at the height of the Roaring Twenties. His lack of a diploma didn't faze him; he boldly sought employment at a number of companies, with Douglas Aircraft as his first choice.

The firm had been formed in the back of a Los Angeles barber shop by Donald Douglas, an engineer with a degree from the Massachusetts Institute of Technology. In 1921, the year after its founding, Ed witnessed the maiden flight of the Cloudster, the company's first aircraft designed for the ambitious goal of flying nonstop across the country. According to former company employee and historian Wilbur H. Morrison, Ed "was particularly impressed by Douglas's youth, and how nice he was in answering his countless questions."

With a recommendation from his drafting teacher, Ed's wish for a job at Douglas came true in 1926. It was an invigorating time at the company. The manufacturer still rode the wave of favorable publicity for having supplied the army air service with the reliable if plodding biplanes that had been the first aircraft to circumnavigate the globe two years earlier.

Because of the company's growth, offices were relocated to larger quarters, a converted movie studio in Santa Monica. When Ed crossed the threshold, the company's administrative and engineering roster overflowed with existing and evolving industry luminaries. A nonpareil amalgam of top-notch aeronautical minds occupied the building.

Besides company founder Donald Douglas, the group included James H. "Dutch" Kindelberger, who later headed North American Aviation; John K. "Jack" Northrop, who founded his own corporation that survives as a major force in aerospace technology; and Gerald "Gerry" Vultee, whose company was eventually swallowed by industry giant General Dynamics. Ed and his coworkers in the old studio constituted a prestigious nucleus of aviation talent the likes of which probably won't be assembled under one roof ever again. Ed realized how lucky he was to be a part of this illustrious team.

Economic realities intervened, however, and in 1927, at the age of only eighteen, Ed was laid off from his $21-a-week draftsman job. He went to work briefly for a small aircraft manufacturer and then, in 1928, he joined California businessman G. E. Moreland's aircraft company, rising to chief engineer at the ripe age of twenty-one. While there, Ed designed his first airplane from scratch.

It was a fabric-covered two-place open-cockpit trainer with a parasol wing, called simply the Moreland Trainer. The diminutive craft, with an impressive cruising speed of approximately 150 miles per hour, was designed for the military. But its introduction in late 1929, which coincided with the onset of the Depression, undid the otherwise promising biplane virtually before it got off the ground.

Entrepreneurially inclined Jack Northrop remained undeterred by the economic headwinds and during 1932 he brought Ed into his new venture, based in Inglewood, California. While working for the friend he had met at Douglas Aircraft, Ed benefited from exposure to Northrop's revolutionary Alpha, Beta, and Gamma series of sport, mail, and racing aircraft which had begun with the Alpha's introduction in 1929. These futuristic all-metal monoplanes with cantilevered wings and enclosed cockpits represented a considerable leap from the wood-and-fabric planes common in the 1920s.

Northrop's bold product line, which fused Art Deco styling with the science of aerodynamics, aroused the public's interest in aviation. The shimmering airplanes exuded speed, style, and comfort. Some of the period's most dashing and daring aerial swashbucklers, like Frank Hawks and Lincoln Ellsworth, flew the Northrop brand for their record-setting and exploratory adventures. Other Northrop projects at the time included military pursuit and light bombing planes.

However, the controlling interest in Northrop's entity was held by Donald Douglas. Wanting a greater measure of independence, Northrop severed the tie in 1938. He would be free to pursue, among other ideas, his long-held concept of a flying wing.

At this critical juncture, in which one of the industry's greatest names chose to go it alone by splitting off from one of the industry's other great names, Ed had to decide if he would join the new freestanding enterprise or stay with his first employer. Ed had gained valuable experience under Jack Northrop, who he considered a designer *par excellence*. To continue working with such a visionary in an emergent startup was a powerful lure, to be sure, but Ed demurred; he had recently married and there were practical considerations associated with matrimony.

Being a risk-taker in the creation of modern airplanes was not only acceptable but expected. Yet, as a husband trying to make ends meet in a downturned economy, one's livelihood had to take precedence. In a fateful decision, Ed stayed at Douglas Aircraft, where he grew and thrived over the next twenty-four years, figuratively carving notches in the sky as one of the most successful and prolific aircraft designers of all time.

•••

The dilemma for carrier aviation was how to put effective bomb loads on targets using airplanes that were small and light because of the inescapable constraints imposed by mobile flight decks. One of the answers was development of dive-bombing. The planes built expressly for the mission wouldn't be able to carry bombs with anywhere near the capacity of land-based bombers, but the precision achievable from the delivery method would, in theory, compensate for the reduced explosive tonnage.

In 1934 the Navy's Bureau of Aeronautics sought to modernize its fledgling carrier air component with competitions for a fighter, scout bomber, dive-bomber, and torpedo/horizontal bomber. In the dive-bomber category, Northrop's XBT-1 emerged as the clear favorite, with Vought offering a credible but ultimately underperforming design that ended up being purchased in small numbers as the SB2U-1 Vindicator. The Northrop design evolved from the company's line of civilian monoplanes that had already made their mark.

The navy liked the experimental design and ordered fifty-four production aircraft, designated the BT-1. However, as soon as the new aircraft reached carrier squadrons in 1937, deficiencies became apparent. Control authority wasn't quite up to snuff and the landing gear did not fully retract, contributing to speed retardation.

Learning from the fielded aircraft, Ed came up with the XBT-2 in 1938. Modifications of the earlier design included a different rudder, improved aileron system, fully retractable main landing gear, and a more powerful engine—the 1,000-hp Wright R-1820-32 Cyclone. The wing incorporated "letterbox" slots to delay aerodynamic stall, which gave the dive-bomber much better handling characteristics in slow-speed flight, which is critical for carrier landings. At the other end of the performance spectrum, the new variant, with its many changes, could boast a 35-miles-per-hour advantage in top speed over the BT-1. Ed's design was truly distinct from that of his mentor.

The navy's Bureau of Aeronautics recognized the refined dive-bomber's potential. Yet this was just as the Northrop-Douglas alliance was at its breakpoint. In April 1939 the nod went to Douglas, which received a contract for 144 aircraft under the designation SBD (for Scout Bomber Douglas).

For the next five years, Douglas produced six production models of the SBD, from the SBD-1 through the SBD-6. Only fairly minor changes were made along the way, attesting to the validity of Ed's underlying design. A total of 5,936 were delivered to the US military, which made the dive-bomber the second most numerous aircraft to roll out of Douglas plants during the war; first was the military transport version of the DC-3.

About 80 percent of the Douglas dive-bomber output, representing 4,923 aircraft, went to the navy and Marine Corps. The army air force had prioritized its heavy bombers, which, of course, were made for horizontal bombing. Nevertheless, the army appreciated the value of dive-bombing and ordered 1,013 of the new dive-bomber. The army dive-bombers carried the designation A-24 and were built at the Douglas plant in Tulsa, Oklahoma.

In keeping with a popular custom in the lead-up to World War II, Douglas planes were given names that started with a "D." Following the company's Devastator torpedo bomber, the name Dauntless fit right in. The army had its own ideas for names, and so its version of the dive-bomber was called the Banshee—not for the speed but the purported screeching sound made when the plane went into a dive.

At a time when much of America shunned the thought of intervention, Ed Heinemann was mindful of the escalating war abroad. Imbued with impressive leadership skills, he drove his army of engineers and draftsmen at the Douglas Aircraft plant in El Segundo with an infectious sense of purpose. Even his wife at the time pitched in by typing manuscripts of the pilot manual. With this foresight and initiative, the aircraft's introduction gave the United States a technological edge and valuable time for training to prepare for the inevitable major sea-based confrontation with the emboldened Japanese, who sought to solidify their position in the Pacific following the surprise attack on Pearl Harbor.

The Dauntless could deliver its ordnance with unprecedented accuracy. The key was the plane's ability to maintain stability as it bore down directly on the target in a steep dive. Pilots liked the aircraft's control responsiveness, a surprising performance characteristic given its gross weight of over five tons. The dive-bomber carried either a single thousand-pound bomb slung under the fuselage (sometimes augmented by two hundred-pound bombs) or two five-hundred-pound bombs, a substantial munitions load for a naval attack aircraft of the period.

Starting with the third production model, the SBD-3, pilots had two fixed forward-firing .50-caliber machine guns at their disposal. For protection, an aft-facing gunner in a rear seat operated free-swiveling dual .30-caliber machine guns. All but the first Dauntless production models had a fuel capacity that gave them an effective sea duty range of fourteen hundred miles. The Dauntless, like every subsequent naval combat aircraft with the Douglas nameplate in the Heinemann era, was bolstered by a built-in ruggedness, for Ed knew that the demanding environment of carrier operations required no less.

In June 1940 the first operational SBD models began rolling off the assembly line, and about six months later they startled everyone involved in producing and flying them by showing fatigue cracks at their wing roots. This wasn't supposed to happen to such a sturdy plane and the unexplained weakness in the aircraft's structure threatened to undo the whole production run. Ed rushed to solve the mystery.

Late that year, Ed showed up with sacks full of parts and tools at the airfield in Guantanamo Bay, Cuba, where a marine squadron was flying the new dive-bombers. Taking charge is the way he cured problems. Earlier, when the XBT-1 had exhibited serious tail flutter on its first flight, Ed went up with test pilot Vance Breese on the very next hop to figure out the solution, which resulted in the "Swiss cheese" dive flaps, perforated surfaces along the wing's trailing-edge to ensure stability in a dive.

To ascertain the source of the wing-root fatigue cracks, Ed felt that he needed photographs of the airplanes during their landings. At first, the squadron's skipper cried out that taking pictures was unacceptable since the dive-bombers were classified. Cooler heads prevailed after it was explained that the designer looking at pictures of the airplane he created wouldn't imperil national security.

Characteristically, Ed didn't assign an assistant or ask an enlisted marine to perform the perfunctory job of picture taking. Instead, he stretched out belly-down adjacent to the runway, near the touchdown point, clutching a Leica he had brought with him. He snapped away as a Dauntless went around the pattern doing touch-and-goes. Almost sixty exposures later and after assiduously scrutinizing the resultant prints, Ed identified the culprit.

The main landing gear struts were compressing to the stops every time a Dauntless touched down with the high sink rate typical for carrier landings. The pressure from repeated landings of this type produced wrinkling known as "oil-canning" on the wing root fairings. Having determined the cause, the solution was fairly simple.

Ed proposed drilling access holes at the weak spots, inserting stiffeners, and then riveting them to the airframes. The improvised fix involved having twenty of the heaviest marines at the airfield stand on the outboard section of the wings to induce just enough upward movement at the root to get at the space into which the stiffeners were wedged.

The marines were satisfied with the on-site adjustment, Douglas Aircraft's reputation for reliability was preserved, and Ed made it home for Christmas. Already manufactured SBDs were similarly modified and the aircraft still under construction had stiffeners installed at the factory. The Dauntlesses were ready. Less than a year later, America was at war.

•••

Following the Japanese attack on Pearl Harbor, its mastermind, Admiral Isoroku Yamamoto, mounted a major Pacific offensive aimed at tiny Midway atoll located 1,140 miles northwest of Honolulu. With the benefit of superior intelligence, the US Navy's Pacific Fleet commander, Admiral Chester Nimitz, dispatched three aircraft carriers to waters off Midway. They represented the centerpieces of Task Forces 16 and 17, which were to spring an ambush on the approaching Japanese fleet.

On the morning of June 4, 1942, intrepid US Navy flyers, intent on proving themselves against the virtually unscathed naval forces of Imperial

Japan, received the command to man their planes. They clambered into the cockpits of the dive-bombers, torpedo planes, and fighters arrayed on the flight decks, with no way of knowing just how momentous would be the day's events. The immediate task was to pinpoint the Japanese Carrier Striking Force, which was complicated by the plot from a PBY patrol plane being a few hours old.

The *Hornet* launched its TBD (for "Torpedo Bomber Douglas") Devastator torpedo planes first, allowing its faster SBDs and Wildcat fighters to catch up. However, visual contact between the two groupings was lost when the low-flying Devastators were obscured by overhanging clouds. VT-8's Lieutenant Commander John Waldron picked up low-level cues that led him and his squadron's fifteen torpedo planes to the enemy ships while the higher-flying aircraft stuck to the originally reported coordinates.

Waldron's squadron skimmed over the water, making a beeline for the Japanese ships that loomed ahead. But the lethargic Devastators were hopelessly outdated, plodding planes that in this case suffered the added disadvantage of no fighter escort. They were sitting ducks for anti-aircraft batteries and interceptors. Only one of the Devastators even got close enough to drop its torpedo.

All of Torpedo Eight's aircraft were lost and Waldron himself was never seen again. Meanwhile, the Dauntlesses and Wildcats from the *Hornet* failed to sight the enemy armada. Frustrated and running low on fuel, the dive-bomber air crews and fighter pilots turned back to their ship or took up a course for the nearer Midway.

In what looked like it might be shaping up as another wartime debacle for America, Devastators from the *Enterprise* soon entered the fray. They were subjected to the same intense fire. Most were hit and went down. Before the tide of battle would shift, things got even worse.

Roughly fourteen miles southeast of the Japanese force, the dozen Devastators of *Yorktown*'s VT-3 were intercepted by a formation of Zeros. Fighter escort was to be provided by Wildcats under the leadership of Lieutenant Commander Jimmy Thach, an aggressive and highly regarded fighter pilot. Unfortunately, he had been ordered to take only six planes up. When the melee started, he and his squadron mates were consumed with saving themselves and unable to come to the aid of their carrier's besieged torpedo planes. For all the patriotic fervor riding in the TBDs that morning, the antiquated aircraft did not stand a chance.

The navy's hopes rested on the Dauntlesses. The models built to that point were the SBD-1, -2, and -3. When Task Forces 16 and 17 sailed out of Pearl Harbor, the three US carriers had 112 of these new planes. But after attrition through mishaps, fuel starvation, prior engagements, navigational miscues, maintenance issues, and the holding of some in reserve, only forty-seven now hovered in sight of the Carrier Striking Force. Four of the dive-bombers belonging to VB-3 experienced premature bomb release over the open waters due to someone cross-wiring the arming and release switches on their newer SBD-3 models, which left just forty-three planes able to drop bombs.

When Lieutenant Commander Max Leslie brought the seventeen SBDs of Bombing Three from the *Yorktown* into the battle from the southeast, he didn't realize that dive-bombers from the *Enterprise* were entering the scene from the south. At the time, Leslie was also unaware of the horrible fate that had befallen Torpedo Three below the clouds. From fourteen thousand feet, he saw three of the Japanese carriers. One with a bright red sun emblazoned on its flight deck stood out; he knew the time was ripe to strike. All his squadron's SBDs would attack the same ship as a means to ensure destruction.

Leslie signaled his men to peel off in a sequenced dive-bombing run by patting the top of his helmet with his hands in the universal sign language of pilots that means "I've got control; follow my lead." One after the other, the Dauntlesses rolled sideways and sped nose-down, concentrating on the carrier that had the veritable bull's-eye improbably painted on an apt aim point. Even though Leslie was one of the squadron's pilots to have prematurely released his bomb, he went first into the dive, partly because it was expected of the C.O. and partly because he could still use his forward-firing machine guns to take out anti-aircraft batteries for the benefit of his comrades, who were fast to follow him.

Leading the larger strike component of two SBD squadrons from the *Enterprise* was the carrier air group commander, or CAG, Lieutenant Commander Clarence Wade McClusky. His decision to fly a disciplined search pattern and his luck in spotting a lone Japanese destroyer arguably did more to reverse the fortunes of the battle than anything else that day. The destroyer, which had broken off from the Japanese Carrier Striking Force to chase an American submarine, steamed back towards its sister ships, unwittingly leading the bulk of the battle's remaining navy dive-bombers to their desired targets.

As soon as McClusky was over one of four Japanese carriers sighted by his flight, he radioed his wingman to follow him down on the closest carrier, which prompted confusion by initiating the dive-bombing runs of VS-6's Dauntlesses and most of VB-6's as well. This wasn't how it was supposed to happen; twenty-five dive-bombers joined in an attack on a single ship, leaving only five SBDs to go after one of the other carriers. Watching this confused scene unfold, Lieutenant Dick Best, commander of Bombing Six, maintained his skeleton formation in the direction of the next closest carrier. He radioed the four other pilots, "Don't let this carrier escape."

When the downsized contingent of Dauntlesses was aligned at fifteen thousand feet above the ship, Best rolled into a dive knowing that he and his few squadron mates who followed had no margin for error. If they failed to hit the enemy carrier it would steam away, perhaps never offering itself as such an ideal target again. He rode his SBD down until he was as sure as he could be that his bomb would ram into the ship's flight deck, like waiting to see the whites in the enemy's eyes. At no more than a thousand feet he pickled off the bomb, then pulled up and banked away, craning back to see the carrier erupting in flames. Another two planes scored on their runs. The three-to-five bombing ratio was the best of the day.

The Dauntlesses from *Enterprise* and *Yorktown* had arrived on scene as their star-crossed torpedo bomber brethren were being decimated just above the waterline in brave but futile straight-in attacks. The lumbering Devastator torpedo planes were disastrously out-of-date, fodder to be eaten alive by the combined fire of Japanese ships and fighters. If any silver lining offset the slaughter at the waterline, a modern Pickett's charge, it was that the Japanese concentrated on the low-altitude fracas and remained oblivious to the thunder about to descend from high above.

Only anemic anti-aircraft fire filled the sky and nary a Japanese Zero launched to intercept the diving SBDs. The flight decks of the enemy carriers were crammed with aircraft being refueled and rearmed. The fortuitous conditions for the attacking Dauntlesses enhanced their destructive effect and their survivability at the same time.

The air assault had lasted a mere four minutes. In that scant span of time, the carriers *Akagi*, *Kaga*, and *Soryu* were removed from the fight. The *Hiryu* eluded the attackers for the moment, but was shattered and sent to the bottom later on by diving Dauntlesses.

The destruction of four Japanese carriers represented an enormous loss for the Empire of the Rising Sun. It was not without a price, though. In the afternoon of June 4th, just a couple hours before the *Hiryu* was blown out of the water, her planes seriously damaged the *Yorktown*. Three days later, a Japanese submarine finished off the limping US carrier, which marked the end of the Battle of Midway.

What transpired was the most consequential battle at sea of the entire war, perhaps of the century, and some say since Trafalgar. Except for the morale-boosting Doolittle Raid and the revolutionizing Battle of the Coral Sea, both of which had been militarily indecisive, the Allies had known only setbacks in the Pacific to that time and the news on other fronts wasn't promising. At a strategic crossroads in the vast ocean, Ed Heinemann's paradoxically beautiful yet lethal Dauntlesses set upon the heart of the Japanese Carrier Striking Force and won.

For the first time on the high seas, America had attained a decisive victory through air power. In the Battle of Midway, Japan suffered a major blow that was at once a profound deficit from which it never fully recovered. The American triumph blocked Japan from gaining control of the Pacific and paved the way for the defeat of the aspiring Asian hegemon.

The character of the air campaign in the Pacific and elsewhere had been cast. For the remainder of the war, the Douglas dive-bombers would repeat the successful engagement profile shown at Midway. The Dauntlesses immortalized their name in battles at places like Guadalcanal, the Eastern Solomons, and Santa Cruz. The biggest of the war's five carrier battles came two years after Midway in the Philippine Sea.

Task Force 58, a massive conglomeration of American naval might, waded amid the Marianas, not far off the shores of Guam, Saipan, and Tinian, seeking to deprive the Japanese of the use of the airstrips on the islands while also keeping an eye out for enemy carriers. On June 19, 1944, Task Force fighters engaged Japanese aircraft and got the better of them. But the exact whereabouts of the Japanese carriers remained unknown. It was feared that if the enemy ships were not soon sighted they would slip away. In hopes of catching them, the Task Force made a solid 20 knots on a westerly course.

Prospects improved on June 20th when a Grumman TBF Avenger spotted the elusive Japanese fleet in the early evening. However, the Task Force commander, Vice Admiral Marc Andrew "Pete" Mitscher, then faced the kind of classically hard decision that weighs on officers at the battle front. Plots put the enemy 237 miles away, near the maximum operational range of the navy's combined aerial strike packages. Remaining daylight hours were scarce, which compounded the dilemma.

Barely skipping a beat, the aggressive Mitscher said in his trademark laconic style: "Launch 'em." He had commanded the *Hornet* at Midway and this was an opportunity to avenge the massacre of Torpedo Eight. As many as seven Japanese carriers were within range, and 216 planes from Task Force 58 headed out to intercept them. Twenty-seven Dauntlesses were in the strike package.

Damage inflicted on the distant Japanese fleet during the engagement had disappointed the participating US airmen. Most of the enemy ships escaped and, before the night was over, roughly half of the navy's attacking aircraft went down, some because of hostile fire but more owing to fuel exhaustion during the 270-mile return flight. Yet, the Japanese force was reduced to six carriers. More telling was that only thirty-five airworthy planes were left aboard those carriers. For most intents and purposes, Japan's once-menacing carrier operations ceased to be a meaningful factor from that point.

Ironically, how the mission ended became the most memorable part of the whole exercise and an enduring example of valor in naval aviation history. As feared, darkness had enveloped the many ships of Task Force 58 before the carrier-based planes returned. Doctrine forbade the illumination of ships at night in waters where the enemy, especially its submarines, might be lurking.

All hands aboard the ships arrayed at sea anxiously awaited the decision of their commander, especially as the distant rumble of radial engines would soon fill the night sky. On the one hand, would the admiral dare to violate protocol and endanger the carriers and their support vessels? Or, on the other hand, would the admiral expose the flyers coming back from a harrowing assignment to extraordinary jeopardy?

With no time to spare, word spread from the flagship *Lexington*. Admiral Mitscher, himself the thirty-third naval aviator and the recipient of the Navy Cross for his role in the first attempt to cross the Atlantic by air in 1919, issued the order: "Turn on the lights." Suddenly, Task Force 58 lit up its corner of the Philippine Sea.

The carrier-bound SBDs and the battle's other surviving aircraft would have a place to recover if their fuel supplies didn't run out first. The magnificent gesture saved lives and exemplified the bond among men of the air. One of the pilots held in reserve described it from his carrier: "To hell with the Japs around us. Our pilots were not to be expendable."

The SBD's replacement, the Curtiss SB2C Helldiver, was bigger with enhanced performance. But those improvements were mostly incremental and offset by a litany of quirks that made the Helldiver suspect in the minds of some of the air crews who operated it. Its combat debut at Rabaul in November 1943 was a year late. Success in operating the Helldiver depended on how well squadrons managed its idiosyncrasies.

Helldivers superseded Dauntlesses throughout the remainder of the war, but a shrinking number of forward-deployed SBDs remained and continued to fight on until the war ended. The Douglas dive-bombers' longevity, which extended from before Pearl Harbor to post–VJ Day, was a distinction not shared by any other naval attack aircraft. A grizzled veteran of the Pacific air war who had flown both the Helldiver and the Dauntless reminisced years later: "The SB2C was of little improvement on the SBD . . . the SBD would be my choice."

It is said that by war's end the Douglas dive-bombers had sunk more enemy vessels than any other aircraft. Eighteen enemy warships met their end at the hand of Dauntlesses, including six Japanese aircraft carriers in

1942 alone. In all, SBDs finished off more than three hundred thousand tons of enemy shipping.

When America had nothing else to hold the line against an existential aggressor storming across the Pacific, a barely adequate quantity of Dauntlesses arrived on scene in the nick of time. In the absence of precision guidance, the dive-bombing techniques honed by navy and marine aviators made the SBD a fearsome weapon. In the words of naval aviation historian Barrett Tillman, the Douglas dive-bomber was "A classic aircraft in both design and utilization [that] performed its mission supremely well. . . . [Its] contribution to winning the Pacific war was unexcelled by any other American or Allied aircraft."

However, for everything that went into preparing the SBDs for combat, including the training and eagerness of the young pilots and gunners/radiomen, it was unknown how the virgin airplanes would perform as they entered all-out air war over remote stretches of open ocean for the first time. Indeed, the plane's top speed was pegged at a mere 250 miles an hour (217 knots), which prompted some to refer to the SBD half-disparagingly as "slow but deadly." Battles can be great levelers. Unanticipated variables and the inevitable fog of war can interfere with the best-laid plans and negate the finest attributes of combatants and their machines.

Even Ed Heinemann humbly admitted years later that he had no idea how significant his dive-bombing platform would be. In retrospect, with the SBD's wartime accomplishments a matter of historical record, the type's designer stated with characteristic succinctness that his creation "turned out to be the right plane at the right place for the right war."

•••

Ed Heinemann's design solidified the association of the Douglas brand with carrier operations, especially the attack side. Though Ed's star was rising at the burgeoning airframe manufacturer, he was not one to grab headlines. Instead, he spread the credit for the Dauntless among members of his design and engineering staff. It was a practice he repeated often over the next couple of decades, as his prolific output continued to influence concepts of air power.

While Ed flourished under wartime pressures, he didn't forget the mentor who had backed him during his youth. The wartime crunch caused an insatiable demand for skilled draftsmen and Ed hired August Flam, his high school drafting teacher. As a summer temp at the El Segundo plant, the older man plied the trade he had so ably imparted to his prized student.

High on Ed's list of teammates was a configuration engineer and design illustrator of uncommon depth who also shared a burning passion for all things aeronautical. Robert Grant Smith had joined the company in 1936 and was known by his first two initials. As the war raged and deadlines compressed, R.G. had become Ed's go-to guy, his trusted right-hand man.

Ed was the idea man. He would conjure up a shape and describe it to his friend. Next, R.G. drew the airplane much as a portrait would be pieced together by a forensic artist from the description of an eyewitness to a crime. The visages that Ed related verbally to R.G. invariably came out looking terrific on R.G.'s sketchpad. In more than one instance, the artwork went a long way towards persuading navy procurement officials to approve funding for a Heinemann concept.

The key to the duo's success seemed to be that they didn't know what the limits were. Their dreams ran to infinity; anything was possible. Long afterwards, R.G. used to explain the spirit of those invigorating years by saying: "Ed and I were having so much fun designing airplanes, we didn't know that we were making history."

At a banquet in 1987, Ed turned to me and opined, with a twinkle in his eye, that the old-line companies had grown into bloated bureaucracies. It was an ode to a splendid time long gone, rendered as a tender lament. In contrast to the halcyon days when men like Donald Douglas called the shots on little more than uncanny intuition, committees of techies came to dominate from workstations networked to a bank of mainframe computers whose preprogrammed databases began to coldly proscribe the realm of the realizable.

During his maturation as a designer, Ed's imprint became increasingly conspicuous. The Heinemann credo could be summarized in an expression he was fond of repeating about one of his twin-engine bomber designs during the war: It lacked frills, but got the job done. The premise underlying virtually all of his combat designs was that aircraft systems must be easy to understand, readily serviceable, and simple to use. Also, their structures must be a pillar of strength, able to withstand the grueling punishment often experienced in the heat of battle.

The salutary effects of Ed's designs caused him to be lavished with heartfelt tributes. In the 1960s Ed visited a naval air station where a squadron was equipped with his Skyraider, a single-engine bomber that he considered the sequel to the Dauntless. The aviators' wives formed a moving line at a reception for Ed and began to kiss him one by one. The squadron commander's wife explained that she and her peers wanted to express their thanks for his sturdy airplane that they were confident would bring their husbands home from battle.

•••

The seven-story glass and steel atrium of the National Naval Aviation Museum in Pensacola, Florida, is graced by four highly polished jets spawned by Ed Heinemann's creative genius. Suspended from the ceiling in a dramatic diving diamond formation, the aircraft are painted in the shiny blue and gold scheme of the Blue Angels. The navy's air demonstration team flew the delta-wing light attack plane from 1974 to 1986.

In a gallery not far from the suspended formation is another of the great designer's airplanes. Set on the wooden planks of a simulated World War II-era carrier deck is a real-life SBD-2 Dauntless, Bureau of Aeronautics number 2016. Delivered to the government a year before Pearl Harbor was attacked, the dive-bomber was parked at Ford Field on December 7, 1941, and managed to survive the bombs falling around it.

Six months later the SBD was on Midway Island. It was one of sixteen marine Dauntlesses that went after the *Hiryu* on June 4th. Despite heavy enemy fire, the pilot nosed his aircraft down and held it on the target until just eight hundred feet above the ship. Only then did he release the bomb and pull away. On the flight back to Midway, interceptors were in hot pursuit, wounding the SBD's gunner, severing the pilot's throat communications cord, and knocking out the aircraft's hydraulic system.

The pilot made a one-wheel landing on the island's airstrip. The dive-bomber had been riddled by 219 bullets, but got its crew back to base. For their heroism, the pilot received the Navy Cross and the gunner received the Distinguished Flying Cross.

The Dauntless was repaired, but being an early model it did not go back into combat. Instead, it was assigned to the Glenview Naval Air Station near Chicago where it served as a trainer for student aviators seeking carrier qualification by landing aboard a couple of special-purpose carriers in Lake Michigan. On June 11, 1943, something went awry while on approach and the SBD ditched in the water. The student pilot was rescued, but the aircraft sank to the bottom of the lake where it lay for more than a half century.

In 1994 it was resurrected from the drink. After a painstaking seven-year restoration, the museum put the historic Dauntless on public display. It is the only surviving Dauntless known to have flown in the Battle of Midway, a relic that commemorates a pivotal moment in history when the forces of freedom prevailed against long odds to reverse the course of war when further slippage was no longer tenable.

In its elegant simplicity, the museum's precious dive-bomber is a tribute to those who flew and maintained it, as well as to the person who conceived it and his coworkers who built it. In the natural light that bathes the artifact of epic battles, the modest warplane evinces the glory of hard-fought victory for a noble cause. Visitors who amble through the gallery can be seen pausing to gaze at the old SBD, perhaps imagining the few minutes in tense skies of long ago when America's finest patriots, at the controls of machines like this shining example, reclaimed the future for democracy.

•••

Subsequent introduction of stealth, precision munitions, satellite links, and drones would seem to nullify Ed's foundational principle of keeping combat systems simple. Indeed, in the Persian Gulf war of 1991, the year that Ed died, the war's air campaign represented a turning point in the conduct of air warfare. The advantage redounded to the side that dominated the electronic environment through expensive and sophisticated means. However, would-be revisionists should recall that in the short but intense air campaign, free Kuwaiti Air Force pilots fought to liberate their country, to regain its sovereignty in smoke-filled skies, flying one of Ed's designs, the A-4 Skyhawk—Heinemann's Hot Rod—the straightforward attack jet that had first flown thirty-seven years earlier.

Technology changes with time. The latest military aircraft, loaded with high-tech gadgetry, didn't magically appear. Rather they grew from the arable plateaus formed by talented innovators who came before. Few have laid groundwork as fertile as the high school dropout from Saginaw.

The open air above was his bailiwick, and he inhabited it with impressive creations like his quintessential Dauntless dive-bomber. Neither the empyrean nor the way people see it would ever be the same. That is the immutable inheritance conferred by Ed Heinemann, trailblazer of the sky.

CHAPTER 17

Fork-Tailed Devil: Lightning Strikes

In 1937 Lockheed Aircraft Corporation was a reborn airframe manufacturer cautiously navigating the shaky economy of the Depression years, trying to establish a foothold in both the commercial airline and military markets. At the time, the air corps had assessed the looming threats abroad and concluded that it needed a plane that would represent an order of magnitude beyond anything yet produced. Because of Lockheed's recognized expertise, it was invited along with five other industry players to enter a competition for the high-altitude interceptor.

Specifications in air corps Design Competition X-608 were nothing if not demanding. The new plane was required to have a minimum true airspeed of 360 miles per hour at altitude and the ability to climb to twenty thousand feet within six minutes. Something radical was needed, and the big brains on Lockheed's design team were just right to answer the call.

Chief engineer Hall Hibbard and his young assistant, Clarence L. "Kelly" Johnson, worked in tandem, devising prospective solutions with configurations so unusual they could hardly help but prompt skepticism. Johnson drew six different designs. All were twin-engine concepts, but each had a distinctive layout. Two of them incorporated the engines in the fuselage with shaft-driven, wing-mounted propellers, either tractor style or the pusher type. One design placed a massive pod between twin booms with a push-pull engine arrangement.

The design plucked from this creative reservoir was the now-familiar twin-boom shape with an engine mounted in the nacelle of each. Propellers turned in opposite directions (the left turned clockwise and the right turned counterclockwise as viewed from behind) which negated the common left-turning tendency produced by propeller torque effect in single-engine planes. The pilot sat under a bubble canopy in a nacelle sandwiched between the booms with all the firepower concentrated in the nose.

Propulsion was one of the project's biggest challenges because the highest-thrust engine available at the time was the General Motors Allison V-1710-C twelve-cylinder, liquid-cooled engine with a potential of 1,150-horsepower. To maintain power at higher altitudes, the engines were coupled with General Electric turbo-superchargers, though these proved to be problematic. The Lightning was about one and a half times the size of a typical single-engine fighter; its added mass led to a gross weight of 15,416, more than double the leading army fighter of the late 1930s.

The wing was slender and tapered. Span was fifty-two feet. The considerable length and meager chord rendered a very high-aspect ratio. The plane's roll rate was inhibited, but then the P-38 was perceived as a platform that would swoop down on its prey at high velocity from superior altitude, theoretically obviating the need for maneuverability. Eventually, production models were built with a hydraulic boost mechanism to improve roll rate.

The aircraft was a paragon of technical advancement. It was of all-metal construction, even the control surfaces. Instead of the generally accepted tail wheel configuration, the P-38 sported a more pilot-friendly tricycle landing gear. Fowler flaps from the outboard ailerons across the trailing edge of the center wing section offered much improved slow-speed handling characteristics for good control on landings. Streamlining involved the application of butt joints and flush riveting.

In the baseline model the nose was an awesome gun nest. Weaponry consisted of a 20-mm cannon positioned in the center with four .50-caliber machine guns filling the space on top and to the sides. The P-38's nose-mounted guns fired in parallel streams directly in line with the pilot, which was in contrast to most other fighters whose wing-mounted guns fired in angled streams, requiring the pilot to estimate the point of convergence. Also, as a harbinger of the design concept known now as modularity, the nose could house things other than guns, for example, cameras and even a Norden bombsight operated by an onboard bombardier. Accordingly, the platform had a rich service life through the entirety of World War II, with 10,037 produced in eighteen distinct models.

Liking what Lockheed had proposed, the air corps issued Contract 9974 on June 23, 1937, authorizing a lone XP-38. Construction on the aircraft began in July 1938 and was finished in December. In the early morning of New Year's Day 1939, the disassembled test article was trucked under cover to nearby March Field. First flight commenced on January 27th.

Lieutenant Benjamin Kelsey ran the plane through its paces. While it had some quirks, the XP generally met expectations. On February 11, after only five hours total flight time, the new plane took off for Wright Field in Ohio with one stop at Amarillo, Texas. Chief of the air corps Major General Henry H. "Hap" Arnold greeted Kelsey upon landing at Wright Field. The general was pleased with the en route true airspeed at cruise power that had averaged an impressive 360 miles per hour, which translated into a ground speed of 400 miles per hour.

Arnold wanted Kelsey to keep going all the way to the East Coast to set a transcontinental speed record that would demonstrate the technological leadership of the air corps and the domestic aviation industry. Such a flight, it was believed, would support the case for increased air corps funding. Everything went fine on the final leg of the flight until just before the end.

On descent into Long Island's Mitchel Field, the XP's carburetors started to ice up. When Kelsey needed extra power to make the runway, the engines responded anemically and unevenly. With no alternative but to set the disabled plane down in a forced landing, it came to rest on the grounds of the Cold Stream Golf Course in Hempstead.

The aircraft was a total loss, but thankfully Kelsey survived uninjured. Although the wreck of the sole test plane slowed development, the crash did not otherwise impede project progress, for Washington decision makers understood that the aircraft was fundamentally sound, having traversed the country in an elapsed time of seven hours, forty-three minutes and thereby coming within twenty minutes of smashing the world record set by Howard Hughes in a racing plane conceived expressly for that purpose. Less than sixty days later, Lockheed received an order for thirteen YP-38 prototypes.

Teething problems delayed the first flight of the YP until September 16, 1940. However, the performance estimates were so striking that orders for production models had been received not just from the air corps but from the British Royal Air Force and the French Armée de l'Air. In June, 1940, when France fell, the British assumed their ally's order.

Though little known now, the first production P-38s went by the name Atlanta. The RAF felt Lightning was a more appropriate name despite serious performance limitations encountered with the early models. In October 1941, both Lockheed and the newly renamed army air force adopted Lightning as the official nickname. Ironically, the Air Ministry cancelled its order for 667 Lightnings five months later.

Part of the YPs testing entailed a series of high-altitude dives. In May 1941 it was discovered that control authority was lost at high speed until reentering denser air at lower altitudes. The problem was traced to tail buffeting and compressibility.

Mistaking the former for tail flutter, external balancers were installed on the elevator. The real problem was later accurately diagnosed as tail buffeting. It was relatively easily rectified by adding wing fillets where the wing joined the pilot-carrying center nacelle.

The latter difficulty was a more vexing issue for the design team. Compressibility had not yet been extensively studied, but it was theorized that the P-38, being so fast in dives, must have encountered shock waves as it neared the speed of sound. Test pilots Jimmie Mattern, Milo Burcham, and Ralph Virden conducted the dive tests.

In an attempt to address the lack of control in such a flight profile, spring-loaded servo tabs were installed on the elevator's trailing edge. Sadly, while this add-on device enabled greater pilot control input, the additional stress during pullout was prone to cause the tail to rip apart. On November 4, 1941, the lesson was learned the hard way when Virden pulled to exit a 535-miles-per-hour dive. The servo-tab-equipped P-38 suffered the catastrophic tail failure, resulting in the pilot's death.

Lockheed engineer Ward Beman developed a solution, which involved the installation of a small electrically operated dive brake under each wing. These surfaces counteracted the pronounced nose-down pitching tendency brought on by compressibility. Regrettably, this fix was not achieved until February 1943 when more than half the total P-38 production had already been completed and delivered.

The silver lining was that many of the planes had not been sent overseas but were retained stateside for training. For the models operating in Europe, aftermarket kits were packaged for field installation. Unfortunately, the convoy ship carrying the kits was sunk by a stalking German U-boat. In the absence of remedial kits, a dive speed limitation was imposed on the deployed P-38s. Meanwhile, the dive brake modification started to appear on production planes near the end of the J model output in June 1944.

Because of the P-38's far-reaching innovations, peculiarities encountered during initial operations put the plane at risk of being discredited by the very pilots assigned to fly it. Idiosyncrasies are not uncommon when new technologies enter operational use for the first time, and diffidence on the part of operators in the field is to be expected. Frontline pilots on the early production models had doubts about the radical fighter, especially its handling characteristics when an engine would quit.

Lockheed made a concerted effort to allay the concerns of army aviators. Company test pilots traveled to air bases, dramatically demonstrating the one-engine flight envelope. Memorable performances were executed at low level in front of airmen aligned along runways by accomplished Lockheed test pilot and daring air racer Tony LeVier. Presaging the air show routine many years later of well-known P-38 owner/performer Lefty Gardner, the twin-boom fighter would be flipped upside down and back upright with a single engine running. The breathtaking displays helped to instill confidence and rebuild morale where it mattered most.

In the design offices and on the factory floor, improvements kept coming. In mid-1944, the Lightning's capability reached a new level with the production of the last 210 P-38Js. These aircraft incorporated the lessons learned since the rollout of the XP-38 four and a half years earlier.

The maturing of the underlying design brought dive brakes, aileron boost, enhanced cockpit heating, electrical system circuit breakers, and a sufficient intercooler system. Models along the way had already added such improvements as maneuvering flaps, flat bulletproof windshield, evolved engines, and more reliable supercharging. The final production model was the P-38L, essentially a late "J" model except for more powerful Allison V-1710-111/-113 engines delivering 1,475-horsepower with a war emergency rating of 1,600-horsepower at 28,700 feet. However, the extra power was tempered by five hundred pounds of added weight. Production of P-38s throughout the war finally came to an end when the last of 3,810 "L" models rolled out in August 1945.

The army was intrigued by the idea of night fighters. Accordingly, in 1944, Lockheed used knowledge gained from radar installations performed as field modifications to develop the "M" model based on the "L" airframe. The P-38M had a stepped-up seat for the radar operator behind the pilot and the AN/APS-6 radar was placed in a specially designed radome affixed to the bottom of the nose. Flight tests, which began on February 5, 1945, showed that this plane could achieve faster speeds than the much-delayed Northrop P-61, a purpose-built night fighter. Sporting a glossy black motif, the small number of converted P-38M night fighters came too late for wartime use.

Except for 113 Lightnings assembled by Consolidated-Vultee, Lockheed itself assembled the huge number of fighters. As a sign of the company's ramped-up production, its covered manufacturing floor space expanded from 1.6 million square feet at the end of 1940 to 7.7 million square feet by the middle of 1943. Correspondingly, the workforce grew during that period from nearly seventeen thousand to ninety-one thousand. Many were women, who took up the slack caused by men going to war.

As America converted from a peacetime footing, field commanders cried out for more of the modern combat planes. To meet the increased demand, sometimes construction exceeded factory capacity and planes were wheeled outside for final assembly. As advances were made, modifications occurred along the assembly lines to accommodate the improvements. Production peaked in 1944 with the rollout of 4,186 P-38s in that year alone.

The company, based in Burbank, California, was acutely aware of security concerns since defense-related facilities on the West Coast were thought to be vulnerable in the wake of the surprise attack on Pearl Harbor. As a protective measure, California's airplane factories were draped in camouflage netting that, when viewed from above, resembled pastoral landscapes embellished with clumps of trees, fake ranch houses, and fencing. The contrived scenery was worthy of Hollywood's set decoration experts like those at the Warner Brothers studio, a Burbank neighbor.

•••

With America fully drawn into World War II, the army air force scrambled to produce not only the weapons to achieve victory but also the means to transport them to the fields of battle. Because cargo ships were subject to U-boat attacks, external fuel tanks were quickly developed for P-38s to enable flights across the Atlantic. In summer 1942 the 1st Fighter Group's P-38Fs made the crossing from Maine to England with stops in Labrador, Greenland, Iceland, and Scotland.

It was a major feat, considering that the first solo flight across the ocean occurred just fifteen years earlier. To ensure proper navigation, the fighters flew in four-ship formations trailing a B-17E. A contingent of P-38s laid over in Iceland to provide temporary air cover in concert with a P-40C squadron already assigned to protect Icelandic skies.

On August 14th a P-38F piloted by Lieutenant Elza E. Shaham was prowling over the island nation when he spotted a Focke-Wulf Fw 200 Condor patrol bomber and dived on it with guns blazing. Some accounts report that one of the air defense P-40s fired and struck the Luftwaffe aircraft too. In any case, the encounter represented America's first air-to-air victory in the European theater. It proved to be the first in a long string for the Lightnings, which were destined to live up to their name by unleashing powerful bolts from above.

Once in England, the 1st Fighter Group flew training and patrol missions along with the newly arrived 14th Fighter Group as part of the quickly growing Eighth Air Force. No contact was made with enemy aircraft, but that was to change in the autumn when these units and the 82nd Fighter Group received orders to transition to Twelfth Air Force to participate in Operation Torch, the invasion of North Africa. On the way to the Bay of Biscay, Lightnings of the 82nd downed a couple Junkers Ju 88s.

In November the P-38s went into action escorting B-17s to a Luftwaffe airfield at Tunis. At this point P-38s usually flew ground strafing missions, hitting dug-in positions and tanks. Despite challenging desert conditions and inadequate numbers to cover the vast expanse of northwest Africa, the three groups developed a comfort level with their planes that contributed greatly to eventual Allied air superiority.

In late 1942 two Lightning groups expressly outfitted for reconnaissance arrived in Africa. The 3rd Photo Reconnaissance Group was commanded by Elliot Roosevelt, the president's son. Flying the F-4 and the F-5A, the group's pilots relied on speed for protection since the aircraft were unarmed.

Despite being a big fighter, the Lightning could compete effectively in turning dogfights with both the Luftwaffe's Bf 109s and Fw 190s. The Germans came to respect the impressive maneuverability and immense firepower of the P-38. The Lockheed fighters and other Allied aircraft were particularly effective in robbing the Axis powers of their airlift. Formations of enemy transports resupplying the vaunted *Afrika Korps* made easy prey.

The campaign drew to a close on May 13, 1943, with the German and Italian surrender. One Luftwaffe pilot surrendering to Allied soldiers in Tunisia appeared hysterical as he pointed towards the sky. He kept repeating *"der Gablesschwanz Teull."* It was a reference to the P-38 that embodied the frightfulness of being on the receiving end of its concentrated guns. The translation—"the fork-tailed devil"—proved to be an apt description that enjoyed staying power among aviation enthusiasts. World War I pursuit pilot and future air force chief of staff General Carl Spaatz said that the Lightning was "in a class by itself."

Even before this victory, Allied units looked to stepping stones across the Mediterranean. Enemy positions on the islands of Pantelleria, Lampedusa, and Sicily were targeted. The P-38 made an effective dive-bomber. Also, skip-bombing techniques were employed to get at sites ensconced in the sides of elevated terrain.

Little more than a month after the invasion of Sicily commenced on July 10th, the island fell and attention turned to the Italian mainland. For the time being, P-38s continued their ground-attack role. However, on

November 1st the three in-theater P-38 fighter groups were transferred from Twelfth Air Force to Fifteenth Air Force. Suddenly, the missions switched to mainly bomber escort. Proving the efficacy of the aircraft and their pilots, the groups had already amassed so many air-to-air shoot-downs that they could boast no less than thirty-seven aces.

As a sign of the war's progress, in February 1944 Fifteenth Air Force's P-38s started escorting bombers on raids all the way to southern Germany. In April the fighters escorted bombers on raids to the oil refinery at Ploesti, Romania. Air defenses were intense and bomber attrition was high.

On July 10th forty-six P-38s of the 82nd Fighter Group went to Ploesti, not as escorts but as dive-bombers with each carrying a thousand-pound bomb. A slightly larger contingent of 1st Fighter Group P-38s led the way as advance escorts for their comrades in arms. Close to the refinery, the 82nd's Lightnings pulled up from treetop level, gained altitude, and then dived down on their targets. Hits were scored, but on the way back swarms of enemy interceptors attacked. Both sides lost more than twenty planes in the ensuing dogfights. It was a high price to pay, and it discouraged the use of fighters for strategic bombardment.

The absence of Lightnings in Eighth Air Force was addressed when P-38Hs of the 55th Fighter Group arrived at Nuthampstead in Hertfordshire in September 1943. Conversion to P-38Js occurred a couple months later. Notably, on March 3, 1944, the 55th had the distinction of being the first fighter unit to escort bombers to Berlin and back, a thirteen hundred-mile endurance run. The next month it operated the bombardier-carrying Droop Snoot version of the J model, which enabled level bombing from high altitude by other Lightnings.

Eighth Air Force got more P-38s when the 20th, 364th, and 479th Fighter Groups arrived in late 1943 and early 1944. Flying tactical rather than strategic missions were the P-38s of Ninth Air Force operated by the 474th, 367th, and 370th Fighter Groups. In the European theater various issues arose with the P-38 that made pilots and commanders question its desirability. Lieutenant General Jimmy Doolittle, Eighth Air Force commander, chose to replace the type with longer-range P-51 Mustangs and highly durable P-47 Thunderbolts, so that by VE Day only the 474th still operated the twin-boom fighter.

The P-38's teething problems affected the way some frontline fighter pilots perceived the radical aircraft. At high altitude, where temperatures could sink to a bone-chilling -60 degrees Fahrenheit, the plane's cockpit heating system simply didn't put out enough warm air to abate the cold. Additionally, the windshield would frost over, frustrating shivering pilots.

The turbo-superchargers were problematic at high altitude. Moisture condensed and iced up, playing havoc with pressure-sensor readings. During descent, excess manifold pressure put the engines in jeopardy. Difficulties in the intercooler operation could cause engine failure as well.

Colonel Hubert A. "Hub" Zemke, an ace and fighter group commander, flew the Thunderbolt, Lightning, and Mustang in combat, and had as good a basis to compare the fighters as anyone. He was critical of the P-38's twin-engine configuration, saying that one of the Allison engines was prone to conk out and thereby necessitate the second one to get the pilot back to base. He preferred the P-47's Pratt & Whitney Double Wasp air-cooled radial engine which could take heavy punishment from enemy fire and keep on going, unlike the P-38's Allison liquid-cooled engines that were certain to seize up if the coolant line was hit. Also he much preferred the P-47 in a dive for there was no speed limitation as with the P-38 during his time in the type.

The P-38's war against Japan started in response to the enemy's invasion of Attu and Kiska in the Aleutians in June 1942. To cover America's western flank, early-model Lightnings were rushed to Alaska to hold the line even though they were not considered combat ready. The 54th Fighter Squadron's newly modified P-38Es, with the capability of carrying external fuel tanks, arrived on scene soon afterwards.

Thus equipped, the fighters were able to patrol long stretches of the twelve hundred-mile island chain. The other three squadrons of the 343rd Fighter Group did not receive a full complement of P-38s. These squadrons operated a mix of P-38s and P-40s.

The Lightning's initial air-to-air victories were scored near Atka on August 4th when Lieutenants Kenneth W. Ambrose and Stanley A. Long, flying out of Umnak, each downed large Japanese flying boats. Not many enemy fighters were encountered in the Aleutians. By July 1943 Japanese forces were driven from Attu and Kiska.

It was said that the greatest challenge to the 54th Fighter Squadron and all of Eleventh Air Force was the weather. Indeed, the inhospitable climate took its toll. Nevertheless, starting in 1944 the 343rd Fighter Group pressed attacks in the Kurile Islands which continued until Japan surrendered.

The P-38 made its name as an outstanding fighter farther south in the Pacific where conditions and circumstances finally allowed the plane's attributes to flourish. Major General George Kenney, Fifth Air Force commander, recognized the type's potential and in the early going repeatedly requested more Lightnings. He wanted the aircraft to be able to attack Japanese fighter formations from on top, a forte not shared by his P-39s and P-40s, which were better suited to attacking bomber planes at the lower altitudes.

As hurriedly as the factory produced P-38s, it was initially not fast enough to satisfy the need in the Pacific. Lightnings possessed long legs which answered the distance requirements of Pacific missions. Also the twin-engine configuration provided a measure of redundancy which was welcomed by the pilots flying for hours over vast stretches of ocean or heavily forested jungles. Similarly, P-38 pilots in Tenth and Fourteenth Air Forces operating in the China-Burma-India theater appreciated the second engine on flights over equally foreboding jungles and unforgiving mountainous terrain.

The first Lightnings to reach the Pacific were P-38Es converted to the F-4 reconnaissance configuration with four K-17 cameras packed in the nose normally occupied by machine guns and cannon. Missions started on April 16, 1942. Major Karl Polifka led the 8th Photographic Squadron, known as the "Eight Balls," first from Melbourne, Australia, and later from Port Moresby, New Guinea. In the summer of 1942 his unit's reconnaissance routes crossed Rabaul and tracked back to Lae and Salamaua.

It was demanding work; the planes were unarmed and the only escape from prowling interceptors came from inherent speed and an unusual cerulean camouflage scheme. Polifka's overflights of enemy outposts "unarmed and unafraid" set the standard for reconnaissance pilots who followed in every combat theater. The enormous volume of photographic material added immeasurably to the Allies' understanding of Japanese positions and movements, giving commanders raw data necessary for informed decision making.

What many consider the most audacious P-38 mission of the war occurred on April 18, 1943. Navy cryptographers had determined that on that date the mastermind of the Pearl Harbor attack, Admiral Isoroku Yamamoto, would be flying from Rabaul to Ballale airfield on Shortland Island as part of an inspection tour. He would be in a Mitsubishi G4M1 Betty bomber-transport accompanied by another Betty with six Zeros as escorts.

Senior American leadership authorized the assassination of the vilified enemy naval officer. P-38s were selected to do the job because they were the only fighters in the Pacific theater capable of flying the five hundred-mile route to the intercept point. Major John W. Mitchell of the 339th Fighter Squadron was placed in charge of the mission. The assignment called for extraordinary precision in planning and implementation.

A combination of sixteen P-38Fs and P-38Gs from the 18th and 347th Fighter Groups of Thirteenth Air Force set out from Henderson Field on Guadalcanal with both 165- and 310-gallon external fuel tanks. The aircraft skimmed over the open water in an attempt to evade enemy fighters. Timing was amazingly accurate, for at 09:34 hours, one minute from the scheduled intercept and thirty-five miles off of Ballale, the Lightnings' radios crackled, "Bogeys eleven o'clock high."

The American fighters climbed for the advantage and then pounced on the formation. Both Bettys were sent down in flames and several Zeros were claimed. Only one of the P-38s was downed in the melee.

For years a debate has raged over who shot down Yamamoto's bomber-transport. Captain Thomas G. Lanphier, Jr., was first to claim the feat and for some time he was believed to have been rightfully credited. However, Lieutenant Rex Barber always felt that he had downed the admiral's plane. In subsequent years, accumulated evidence has suggested that Barber may have fired the fatal shots after all. In the end there may never be definitive proof to resolve the long-running controversy.

In a curious historical twist, the airman associated with stretching distance through adept fuel management on his record-breaking solo transatlantic flight stopped to visit and fly with forward-deployed P-38 pilots, who daily faced the challenge of squeezing every last mile of range out of their fighters. Charles Lindbergh, as an old air reservist, had yearned for a flying billet in the air war once America formally joined in the fighting, but his prewar anti-interventionist rhetoric made him a pariah in the eyes of President Roosevelt, who rejected the legendary pilot's requests for a new commission. Not willing to accept no for an answer, Lindbergh found his ticket to the front as a civilian technical representative of United Aircraft Corporation.

From June through August 1944, Lindbergh flew with the 475th Fighter Group, commanded by the third-ranking P-38 ace, Colonel Charles H. MacDonald. Having been obsessed with the science of fuel efficiency during his distinguished flying career, Lindbergh observed that the combat pilots' cruise technique wasted precious fuel. On his mission of July 1st, he returned to base after six hours and fifty minutes of flight with 210 gallons of fuel still in his P-38's tanks. He counseled that by adjusting rpm down and manifold pressure up, a slow cruise speed could result in an endurance of nine hours. At first scoffed at by critics who thought such a cruise technique would foul the spark plugs and overheat the engines, actual practice bore out the recommendation.

Civilians were not to fly on combat missions, but Lindbergh wrangled his way into the cockpit of combat-bound P-38s by asserting he had to do it as the only way to fulfill his job as a technical representative of a leading manufacturer. On July 28th he was part of MacDonald's flight of eight Lightnings. Two Mitsubishi Ki-51 Sonias were encountered over Elpaputih Bay off Ceram Island in the Dutch East Indies. In the ensuing dogfight, Lindbergh scored and sent one of the Japanese planes crashing into the sea.

In the Pacific air war, Lightnings shot down 1,358 enemy aircraft, which was a greater number than any other US fighter. More than a hundred pilots in the Pacific theater became aces flying the P-38. Among these were America's two highest-scoring aces of all time, Major Thomas B. McGuire, with thirty-eight victories, and Major Richard I. Bong, with forty victories.

Bong's victories were tallied up from late 1942 through late 1944. As his score rose, he was assigned to staff duties, but took advantage of his position to "freelance" on combat missions. Starting in January 1944 he emblazoned the likeness of his sweetheart and future wife, Marge Vattendahl, on the nose of his P-38. The young Midwesterner was said to be fun-loving and mild-mannered on the ground, but when he went aloft in his fighter he turned relentless in his dozens of dogfights.

In many ways, Bong personified the American fighter pilot. He grew up on a farm in Poplar, Wisconsin, and was drawn to planes at an early age. Before deploying overseas, he buzzed a homemaker's clothesline, swept low over San Francisco's Market Street, and by some accounts slipped under the Golden Gate Bridge. He was reprimanded by Major General George Kenney, who later acknowledged that such gung-ho airmen were the type of pilot the country needed in the unfolding war. In the ultimate irony, it was Kenney, as commander of Far East Air Forces, who little more than two years after disciplining the hotshot fighter jock, recommended Bong for the Medal of Honor. General Douglas MacArthur personally awarded the medal to the rapidly matured twenty-four-year-old.

Most of the Lightnings provided to the Allies during the war were the reconnaissance variants, F-4s and F-5s. Notably, the Free French Groupe de Reconnaissance II/33 in North Africa operated F-5s while attached to the American Twelfth Air Force. One of the French unit's pilots was famed author and air mail pioneer Antoine de Saint-Exupery, who had left the comfort of New York's literary salons to rejoin the fight to liberate his country. On July 31, 1944, he launched on a photographic mission from Bastia, Corsica, and went missing off the southern coast of France. Tragically, like the young prince in his well-known children's book, he was never to be seen again. However, he left an indelible mark on those who he had touched under the wing of his aircraft.

CHAPTER 18

The Perfect Blend: Curvaceous Airframe Plus Powerful Engine Equals the Mustang

The British government's burning need for more fighters on the eve of its defense of the homeland gave birth to the Mustang, lending credence to the aphorism "Necessity is the mother of invention." Since Adolf Hitler's rise to power in 1933, Germany had been transformed into an armed state with vast military resources that eclipsed those of Britain. By May 1940 German forces had rampaged through much of continental Europe and the dragon's fire would next be disgorged across the English Channel.

To meet the imminent challenge, the island nation's factories were churning out Hurricanes and Spitfires as fast as possible. But the indigenous industry had only so much capacity. Against this backdrop, the British Purchasing Commission visited the United States on a buying spree to try to plug the gap.

Complicating the issue, the United States at the time did not have a fighter capable of matching the Messerschmitt Bf 109 or, for that matter, the new Supermarine Spitfire. Given the situation, Britain aimed to satisfy its numerical requirements with the best fighter it could acquire, even if it was inferior to the enemy's primary fighter and its own latest fighter. With France on the precipice, Britain was poised to take delivery of the Curtiss-Wright Hawk 75 fighters that the French had on order. These were export versions of the already obsolete radial-engine P-36 Hawks.

Additionally, France expected to receive an improved version of the Curtiss fighter that incorporated the Allison V-12 liquid-cooled engine. Known as the Hawk 81A, this was an export version of the P-40

Warhawk. Britain acquired 471 of these, calling them Tomahawks. The British also bought 560 of an improved version, the Hawk 87A, which they called Kittyhawks.

The problem was that, even before these orders were finalized, Curtiss's capacity to produce the large number of planes then under contract with both foreign governments and the US Army Air Corps precluded timely delivery. It would take 120 days to clear the backlog to begin producing the newly ordered British planes. Seeking an alternate source to build the Curtiss fighters under license, the British Purchasing Commission turned to North American Aviation.

Company executives welcomed the entreaty from the British as an opening to a major opportunity. Rather than simply acceding to build a competitor's existing fighter, which underperformed extant enemy designs, the company proposed a brand-new fighter with superior performance. This was a brash move, especially considering that the company had not produced a fighter in its short history.

In its favor, North American Aviation had already sold the British its highly regarded training aircraft. Moreover, the company's president, James H. "Dutch" Kindelberger, and vice president / general manager, John Leland "Lee" Atwood, were impressive industry figures. Kindelberger had attended Carnegie Institute of Technology and served as chief engineer at Douglas Aircraft. Atwood had earned an engineering degree from the University of Texas and, like his boss, had previously worked at Douglas Aircraft. This was a company going places, led by capable men who British officials were comfortable working with.

Convincing preliminary drawings and weight estimates were presented to the commission. A contract for 320 of these fighters was signed on May 29, 1940. Internally, the project was known as the NA-73. The British, exercising their prerogative as the purchaser, initially chose Apache as the name for their prospective new fighter but soon switched it to Mustang, not knowing then how indelible that choice would become. Because the Curtiss delivery would have taken 120 days, the commission gave North American Aviation an identical timeline in which to deliver the first flyable example of its ambitious clean-sheet design.

Overall engineering responsibility was vested in the company's chief engineer, Raymond H. Rice, while the job of design went to Edgar Schmued. Pressure to meet the deadline was intense, prompting Schmued and his teammates to burn the midnight oil and devote their weekends to bringing the new fighter to fruition. Schmued had long fancied such an assignment.

Curiously enough, as the late aviation museum archivist and biographer Ray Wagner has written, Schmued was born in Germany and emigrated to the United States only ten years before the outbreak of war and the start of his work on the Mustang. From his birthplace in Hornbach, the family moved to the more populous city of Landsberg where Schmued's father, a dentist, reestablished his practice with the hopes of servicing a larger clientele. During a family outing when Schmued was eight years old, he heard a noise above and looked up to see an airplane for the first time—a Wright biplane making its way from Berlin to Russia. He later recounted that the sight of the biplane made "a tremendous impression" on him and that he had "decided, right then and there, that this was for me. This was going to be my life."

Growing up, he was not a good student. Rather than focusing on his coursework, he fixated on aviation and what he termed "technical developments." His father nurtured an understanding of machinery and complemented the steady reading of books borrowed from a local library with purchases of books on aviation subject matter.

College was out of Schmued's reach, even if he had earned good grades, because his family lacked the requisite financial resources. The young man set out to educate himself in the disciplines relevant to being an aircraft designer. He studied college-level texts on his own and went to work for an engine manufacturer, where a two-year stint imparted the ground-up basics of using machinery to produce complex equipment, including the know-how behind hand-forging.

During World War I, he skirted the German draft because he had retained the Austrian citizenship handed down from his father. He turned seventeen in the last year of the war and was believed to have served out that year as a mechanic with the Austro-Hungarian Flying Service. Back at home after the war, he sought to build his first airplane using a small Anzani engine obtained by his father.

Under the strict terms of the peace accord, his aircraft was prohibited and the Allies confiscated it. Despite the ban on aircraft building, his desire to create marketable planes never waned. Meanwhile, his mechanical aptitude was put to good use by an automobile parts maker outside of Hamburg. By his twenty-third birthday, he had been granted five patents for a variety of automotive devices.

Because Germany's post–World War I economy faltered amid hyperinflation, in 1925 Schmued decided to seek greener pastures by moving to Brazil, where his two brothers had already settled. His dream of finding a wealthy Brazilian to support his plane building did not materialize. Rather, to support himself, he became a mechanic at a General Motors dealership in the South American country. A company executive spotted his abilities and before long he was invited to join the company in the United States.

A coveted entry visa was granted, and in 1930 the thirty-year-old sailed to America, full of hopes for transforming his incessant airplane drawings into tangible flying machines. Since General Motors had bought a controlling interest in Fokker Aircraft the year before, Schmued was assigned to the plane maker's New Jersey factory. A six-month night school course in English boosted his language proficiency.

Unfortunately, the timing to affiliate with the aircraft manufacturer could hardly have been worse. The company, which had been renamed General Aviation Corporation, fell on hard times from the double whammy of the lingering effects of the Depression and headlines announcing the March 31, 1931, fatal crash of a Fokker airliner carrying University of Notre Dame football coach Knute Rockne. Before the end of the year, the New Jersey factory was shuttered. Operations were downsized and transferred to a plant in Dundalk, Maryland.

For the next couple years, General Aviation bided its time, working on a few projects that did not amount to much in economic terms. A Fokker-inspired army observation plane and a small airliner kept Schmued busy as a project engineer and manager, respectively, but those aircraft quickly faded in the difficult marketplace of the early 1930s. Change came in June 1934 with the passage of the Air Mail Act, which, among other things, separated aircraft manufacturers from mail-carrying airlines as a means to foster competition.

The legislation disentangled the holding company whose tentacles extended to General Aviation. North American Aviation had been established as a holding company by investment banker Clement M. Keys in 1928. It continued to gobble up an eclectic potpourri of plane makers and commercial air transport companies through the early 1930s. Then, in 1933, General Motors bought a 30 percent interest in North American Aviation.

After the new law was enacted, General Motors reorganized North American Aviation as an autonomous operating company. Renowned corporate troubleshooter Ernest R. Breech was appointed chairman of this nearly moribund shell company, and his move to install Dutch Kindelberger and Lee Atwood as the company's top day-to-day managers was a stroke of brilliance. The reorganization came as the company's fortunes hit rock bottom, employment having shrunk from a peak of thirteen hundred just a few years earlier to only two hundred. The company's new leaders had exciting plans up their sleeves.

Although technically not a new company, North American Aviation came to life as an operating entity in 1934. Recognizing the value of cultivating a distinct identity, a company-wide contest was held to see who could come up with a logo design to best represent the fledgling manufacturer. Edgar Schmued entered a triangular shape with each letter from North American Aviation's "NAA" acronym occupying a corner of the triangle and an eagle's profile in the middle with its wing turned down to symbolize the most powerful moment of the flapping cycle, as if to say the lift of the company's airplanes derives from the strength of an eagle's wing. Schmued's submission was chosen as the company's official emblem.

Embodying the workforce's spirit, this NAA imprimatur subsequently decorated the blueprints and/or the data plates of the company's many storied platforms, from its AT-6 advanced trainers that taught a generation of military aviators how to fly to the B-25 Mitchell medium bomber that carried Lieutenant Colonel Jimmy Doolittle and his fellow

Raiders to Tokyo, and from the X-15 rocketplane that nibbled at the edge of space to the Apollo command module that transported humankind literally to the moon. For his enduring artwork that won the company's logo design contest, Schmued received the first-place prize of twenty-five dollars. Awarded in the mid-1930s, it was, as a colleague later remarked, "Big bucks in those days."

Dutch Kindelberger decided that the company's future lay in military aircraft, so that is where the company's efforts were directed. Early projects included the monoplane trainer and an all-metal, single-engine observation plane, both for the army. Another change at the company was its move to Southern California for the good year-round flying weather and the advantages attendant with the growing local economy.

The company set up shop on a twenty-acre site on the east side of Mines Field, later to become Los Angeles International Airport. The new building was located at the intersection of Imperial Highway and Aviation Boulevard in the suburb of Inglewood. Schmued shared a small second-floor office with three others.

When the Mustang order came in, Schmued immersed himself in the project with equal measures of enthusiasm and perfectionism. He was assisted by a team that Dutch Kindelberger allowed him to handpick. The men he chose were "desperately wanting to build a fighter." His vision for the fighter showed itself when he told the company's chief structures engineer: "I want smooth surfaces." Indeed, the resulting fuselage had compound curves and flush skin joints. Also, the Mustang had to be easy to construct because wartime needs were anticipated to generate orders for large quantities.

Aiming to have production aircraft rolling out of the factory in a year, he knew time was precious. He devised a schedule that called for the prototype to be completed in only a hundred days. As it turned out, getting to the first flight would require twenty-eight hundred detailed drawings and 41,880 engineering man-hours.

One of the reasons the design team proceeded confidently on such a demanding schedule was that Schmued had conceived important subassemblies on his own, dating back as far as five years earlier in the hope of one day having a project like the Mustang on his drafting table. When opportunity finally came knocking, he was prepared with layouts of the cockpit, engine, guns, etc. It was like fitting generic pieces into a customized puzzle.

Interestingly enough, in 1939 the company had assigned Schmued to design a primary trainer in hopes of dominating the overall trainer market. Schmued had a flyable example ready in a mere thirty-nine days. Designated the NA-35, the aircraft was an all-metal, low-wing design with tandem seating for two in open cockpits. It was powered by a 150-horsepower inline air-cooled Menasco engine, which contributed to streamlining of the frontal cross-section.

The trainer's prospects did not appear promising given the already crowded field. In addition, the company's other work was very demanding. Under the circumstances, the trainer project was sold to Lockheed's Vega Division where it went dormant because of the government's reluctance to buy all-metal trainers at a time when it feared aluminum might become scarce. Although nothing came of the NA-35, Schmued later wrote how some of the little trainer's components found their way into his next and most famous design.

To break from the mold and offer a truly superior fighter, the design team knew it had to innovate. They scrapped the original plan to use a conventional airfoil when the National Advisory Committee for Aeronautics (NACA) presented promising data on the laminar-flow airfoil. The company's young aerodynamicist Edward Horkey, a recent Caltech graduate, saw the potential for this new wing shape.

Looking conventional enough from above, the wing's leading and trailing edges were straight with a simple chord-wise taper from 104 inches at the roots to fifty inches at the tips. However, as viewed in cross-section, the wing had the appearance of two symmetrical crescents joined together. A typical wing is thickest near the leading edge, but in the case of the laminar-flow wing the thickest point is much farther aft.

By means of this aerodynamic sleight of hand, boundary-layer air adheres to the wing slightly longer than is otherwise the case. This lower-drag design provides better efficiency which translates into longer endurance and faster speeds. These qualities contributed greatly to making the Mustang a world-beater among piston-powered fighters.

At the time the North American Aviation engineers were considering the radical new wing shape, it was not clear if the laminar-flow airfoil would work as well in the real world as theoretical studies suggested. To confirm the hypothesis, wind tunnel tests were conducted at Horkey's alma mater. These were supplemented by tests in the larger wind tunnel at the University of Washington.

Another notable design feature was the radiator scoop's placement on the lower aft section of the fuselage. This rearward placement ensured that the aircraft's aerodynamics would not be muddled. Also the radiator ducting took advantage of the breakthrough made in the mid-1930s by F. W. Meredith of the Royal Aircraft Establishment at Farnborough in England.

By channeling the heated air that passes through the radiator into a narrowed exhaust duct, it was possible to actually create thrust. This side benefit of the Mustang's radiator system partially offset the protruding scoop's drag. Known as the Meredith effect, this countervailing of engine-cooling drag enhanced the Mustang's performance.

Despite the hurdles associated with the major new technologies incorporated in the airframe, the prototype was rolled out in 117 days, just a little more than two weeks past the ambitious internal deadline and still three days ahead of the commission's timeline. Unfortunately, Allison did not have an engine ready for installation at that time because the engine company's personnel did not believe that an airframe could be constructed from scratch in such a short interval. Frustrated to have the gleaming all-metal NA-73X on the ramp with no engine, North American Aviation's representative at Allison's Indianapolis, Indiana, plant was told: "Don't come home without an engine."

The engine, a 1,150-horsepower V-1710-39, was delivered eighteen days later. About a month afterwards, on October 26, 1940, the fighter was taken aloft by Vance Breese, an experienced test pilot contracted by a number of manufacturers for sometimes nail-biting first flights. The aircraft performed in keeping with expectations.

On November 20th another contract pilot, Paul Balfour, took the NA-73X up for a series of speed runs. On the third pass, the engine quit. The powerless aircraft was too distant to glide back to the airport, so Balfour alighted on a bean field. Because it was freshly plowed, the extended main landing gear dug into the topsoil, causing the prototype to flip, tail over nose. Though the plane sustained heavy damage, Balfour was not seriously hurt.

The accident investigation revealed that Balfour had simply forgotten to switch to the reserve fuel tank, thus starving the engine of fuel. Schmued and his colleagues were relieved that the aircraft was faultless. The flight test program continued with the next plane in line, the first production model.

By August 1941, Mustang Mk I's were being crated and shipped to England. The Royal Air Force's initial reaction to its newest fighter was mixed. On the one hand, the plane was faster than the Spitfire Mk V and could fly twice the distance. Yet, on the other hand, the Mustang's thrust-to-weight ratio left something to be desired. Its non-supercharged Allison engine did not enable a comparable climb rate or good performance at higher altitudes.

The army air corps tested the fourth and tenth aircraft off the production line. The army's view of the new fighter paralleled that of the Royal Air Force. This led the army to favor a dive-bombing variant to be outfitted with dive brakes and bomb racks. Eventually, this type was given the designation A-36 and the name Apache.

The problem of how to solve this otherwise outstanding fighter's lackluster performance during climb-out and at higher altitudes continued to frustrate the Allied air arms on both sides of the Atlantic until the idea percolated that the Rolls-Royce Merlin engine, with its two-stage supercharger and greater horsepower, could be substituted for the Allison engine. One of those advocating the switch was Major Tommy Hitchcock, the air attaché in the American Embassy in London.

If Hollywood ever gets around to making the epic on the P-51's development, Hitchcock's life could easily be a featured storyline. Indeed, his friend F. Scott Fitzgerald used him as the model for characters in his novels. He left the comfort of high society to join the Lafayette Flying Corps during World War I. Shot down and captured, he escaped. After the war he completed his education at Harvard and Oxford. Following in his father's tradition, he became a leading polo player and sportsman.

In early 1942 Hitchcock wrote about "cross-breeding" the Mustang's airframe with the Merlin 61 engine. Notably, Rolls-Royce test pilot Ron Harker did likewise. The British proceeded first, flight testing a Merlin-powered Mustang in the fall of 1942. In the United States a similarly converted Mustang flew about six weeks later that fall. Performance expectations were confirmed. The marriage of the Mustang with the Merlin transformed a decent fighter into a great fighter.

Interestingly Packard Motors was already building Merlin engines under license at its plant in Detroit. These American-built engines would go into the Mustangs then being produced, the P-51Bs at North American Aviation's Inglewood plant and the P-51Cs at a new Dallas, Texas plant. There were no meaningful differences between the two designations other than manufacturing location.

The most successful version was the P-51D. This model's Plexiglas bubble canopy replaced the razorback design of the earlier models. The new canopy gave pilots an unobstructed view in all directions, greatly enhancing situational awareness. The D model also received two additional wing-mounted .50-caliber machine guns, bringing the total to six. The addition of these guns made the already deadly Mustang an even more lethal platform.

To improve lateral stability, this new model got a dorsal fin fairing. The added surface area helped to cut down on the fighter's dangerous tendency to depart violently from controlled flight when at low speeds. The P-51D is the most common model flying today.

Arguably the Mustang's greatest wartime contribution was as an escort fighter. In 1943 US daylight bombing missions to targets like the aircraft factories at Regensburg and the ball-bearing plants at Schweinfurt had Spitfire and Thunderbolt escorts only part of the way. Bomber losses were staggering and not sustainable. The Mustangs with their longer legs changed the equation dramatically.

Starting in early 1944 Mustangs could be equipped with seventy-five-gallon drop tanks, which permitted escort missions all the way to Berlin. Later 108-gallon drop tanks became available, further expanding range. Before the war, air doctrine held that tight formations of heavy bombers would be able to defend themselves with concentrated cones of fire from the large numbers of guns arrayed in the formation.

This theory did not pan out in practice. The closing speeds of enemy interceptors were so great and the variety of attack angles in the open sky so vast that aerial gunners aboard the bombers often had slim pickings. The disastrous consequences of unescorted heavy bombers caused theorists to modify operating principles. Prewar theory caught up to actual air combat experience, in which the relative positions of bomber and fighter were reversed. Suddenly the fighter could claim primacy over the bomber, and the Merlin-powered P-51 came on the scene none too soon.

A special place in the operational history of the P-51 is occupied by the all-black 332nd Fighter Group. Known as the Red Tails because of the bright red tail markings that decorated their Mustangs, these fighter pilots received plaudits for their fierce protection of B-17 and B-24 bombers of Fifteenth Air Force. Notable among their many escort missions was the one to Berlin on March 24, 1945.

This mission clocked in at sixteen hundred miles—the longest attempted by Fifteenth Air Force. The target was the Daimler-Benz tank factory. Fifty-four Mustangs of the 332nd participated in the mission. Most of the group's Mustangs rendezvoused with B-17s of the 5th Bomb Wing. The Red Tails were to hand off the bombers to another fighter group as the formation neared Berlin, but when the other group was late the 332nd stuck with the bombers.

Shortly afterwards, the bombers came under attack by twenty-five interceptors, mostly Me 262s, the newly developed jets that were substantially faster than any piston plane. Unfazed, the Red Tails plunged into action. In the ensuing dogfights, the 332nd's pilots downed no less than three of the jets. For "outstanding performance and extraordinary heroism" on this grueling mission, the 332nd was awarded the Distinguished Unit Citation.

The genesis of this exceptional fighter group goes back to the Tuskegee Institute in rural Alabama where in 1941 the air corps set up a segregated flight training program to allow African Americans to fly US military aircraft for the first time. Because all of the program's graduates received their air corps silver wings at this location, the pilots (and ultimately everyone associated with the program) came to be known as the Tuskegee Airmen. Selected to lead this unique unit into battle was Benjamin O. Davis, Jr., the son of the army's first black general and himself the first black graduate of West Point in the twentieth century.

Ben, Jr., who I was honored to know, carried himself with an impeccable military bearing. He was a no-nonsense, spit-and-polish officer who demanded nothing but the best of his men. He knew all eyes were on his unit and that more than a few in the higher echelons in the army air force did not want the black flyers to succeed. A lesser commander would have caved under the intense pressure, but he remained steadfast, guiding his fellow black aviators to the double victory against the enemies of totalitarianism abroad and racism at home.

The 332nd's reputation for defense of bomber formations grew to the point where bomber groups began calling with increasing frequency for the Red Tails to be their escorts. Davis capitalized on the 332nd's popularity by repainting the nose of his fighter with the words "By Request." Following in his father's footsteps, he became the first black general in the air force.

When I headed the National Air and Space Museum, I encouraged a new exhibit called Black Wings, which for the first time in our galleries told the story of the important contributions of African Americans to the history of aviation. When the exhibit opened on September 23, 1982, it was greeted with much acclaim, and in the years that have followed, the interest in the subject has mushroomed to where there are now permanent exhibits like Black Wings at air museums around the country.

Looking back on the groundbreaking exhibit, it strikes me as how essential the P-51 was to the success of the Tuskegee Airmen and, conversely, how advantageous it was for the P-51's reputation to have had the Tuskegee Airmen among its pilots. One of the special aspects of the original Black Wings exhibit is that the curators found photographs of mostly little-known pioneers in black aviation and displayed them on the same wall panels with the more widely recognized personages like Benjamin O. Davis, Jr. What I wrote then about these brave flyers remains just as true now: "Those in search of models for the youth of today could scarcely find a better set than the black men and women who fought for the right to fly."

Mustangs are best remembered for their service in the European theater of operations, but they also played a vital role in other theaters. Starting in the summer of 1943, Mustangs and their dive-bombing counterparts, the Apaches, began flying combat missions in China. As in Europe, as time passed the more effective models reached Asian air bases.

The same basic guidance was given to the pilots of the newer Mustangs as had been given to the pilots of earlier models and, for that matter, the old P-40 Warhawks. The pilots were warned not to get into a turning contest with the light and highly maneuverable Japanese Zero. Instead, tactics called for pilots to use the Mustang's speed advantage to make a lone diving pass on the enemy fighter and then keep going.

With the Allies closing in around the Japanese home islands, heavy bombers, including the new Boeing B-29 Superfortress, staged at Guam, Saipan, and Tinian for long-range raids. Large numbers of Mustangs operated from closer-in islands like Okinawa to provide fighter escort. The fighters would rendezvous with the bomber formations in overwhelming displays of force, eventually leading to only minimal air-to-air opposition.

The P-51D was followed by other models, among them the P-51K. Built at the Dallas plant, it had a different make and model of propeller than the P-51D. The P-51H was a major reconfiguration of the Mustang. It weighed six hundred pounds less than the D model, was powered by an up-rated engine, and sported a longer fuselage with taller vertical tail surfaces. Only several hundred were built because production came so late in World War II.

Some Mustangs were converted into photoreconnaissance versions with the designation F-6, later changed to RF-51. North American Aviation built a total of 16,241 P-51s. The most numerous were the D models.

By far the strangest outgrowth of the standard Mustang was the P-82 Twin Mustang. War planners wanted a very long-range escort fighter and figured the logical way to achieve it was to take the fuselage of the existing top-line long-range fighter and combine it with a virtually identical one on a common wing and horizontal stabilizer. Conceived during World

War II, the aircraft did not enter the operational inventory until 1948. It saw service, but was withdrawn in 1953. Only 223 were built.

Korea was the Mustang's next war. The fighters had been redesignated F-51s. They played a critical role early in the conflict, holding off North Korean forces as they marched south.

The World War II-vintage planes were not a match for the newer jets and ended up being assigned mainly to ground attack and close air support missions. The Mustangs could be effective in these roles, but they were terribly vulnerable to concentrated ground fire and especially to deliberately set flak traps. In the United States F-51s were commonly found in Air National Guard units until replaced by jets later in the 1950s.

•••

It is interesting to look back over the years to see how engineering departments have changed. When I was a young officer in the Strategic Air Command, a visit to major military airframe manufacturers like North American Aviation and Boeing revealed huge florescent-lit rooms that seemed to extend for acres, each filled with the huge desks required to create blueprint plans. Manning each desk was a young to middle-aged male, clothed in a white button-downed shirt and subdued tie.

The rooms were oddly immobile—everyone was intent on the drawing before him. And the word "him" is used advisedly, for once you passed the receptionist, you saw no more women. The curious thing was the silence—no phones jingling, no conversations going on, just the hard, unrelenting work of applying each of their individual skills to the project.

The loudest noise was the click of the slide rule as they worked out the numbers for the new project. It sounds like a dismal scene but it was just the opposite. These were engineers excited to be working on new products, the results of which, they knew, might be decisive in warfare. One of the most prominent in my memory was Edgar Schmued.

I had the privilege of meeting him only briefly, but recall clearly that my first reaction was concern about his somewhat fierce look. However, he flashed a smile that lit up his face, and made me very comfortable. He was clearly a capable and busy man, so I decided that it would be unfair to take advantage of his friendliness by taking up his time. I have regretted this ever since because there were so many questions I would have asked him.

The legend of the P-51 has only grown since World War II. The surviving Mustangs are in many ways the ultimate collectibles. Nicely restored examples can fetch a few million dollars, which, needless to say, is a price that the original wartime pilots and even Edgar Schmued could hardly have imagined in their wildest dreams.

Yet because of the Mustang's history as one of the premier instruments in the defense of freedom in some of the greatest air battles ever fought, today's well-heeled owners are typically humbled by the encounters they have with the aged airmen who tamed the hostile skies in the magnificent fighter. What I have observed over the last few decades as the so-called warbird movement has blossomed is that the owners of these aircraft know deep down that they aren't really the owners. Most realize that they are but the stewards of these gems, privileged to "borrow" them from the original flyers whose valiant deeds gave meaning to the planes and burnished the reputation that awes us.

As stewards they maintain the beautiful artifacts in immaculate condition for display at air shows, fly-ins, and air races, keeping alive the inestimable stories of heroism in the sky. And when the time comes for the inevitable transfer, the fighters will likely pass by means of the unwritten but widely accepted custom to another set of stewards who, like their forbears, would be expected to perpetuate and share these exemplary tokens of history for their generation and, if the pattern repeats itself, the next and the next after that. Mustang preservationists of the early 1980s, especially in Southern California, were fortunate to have the airplane's chief designer make the rounds of the show circuit.

Though hard to believe, Schmued had never flown in his famous airplane until a pilot took him up in a modified two-seat version at a 1981 gathering to celebrate the Mustang's forty-first anniversary at the Chino, California, airport. The designer was in his eighties by then and enjoying the limelight that came with being introduced at aviation events as the man who spawned the Mustang. It is hard to know who got the bigger thrill, the designer being hailed in the midst of shiny examples of the aircraft that had quickly evolved from the sketches on his drafting table four decades earlier or the jolly flyers, huddled by their planes, who chanced upon the individual whose genius enabled their treasured hours soaring above the clouds in the most enchanting of flying machines.

Yet as the Mustang's creator knew so well from his experience, glory is fleeting. In the mid-1930s, during the cross-country drive with his family to North American Aviation's new headquarters in California, with hopes riding high for life in the Golden State, a collision with another vehicle killed his first wife. In the early 1950s office politics at North American Aviation took a nasty turn, which cast a pall over his ability to add to his many rewarding professional accomplishments and caused him to resign after twenty-two years at the company, three years short of qualifying for a pension.

On June 1, 1985, almost forty-five years to the day that the British Purchasing Commission placed its bet for a superior new fighter on a designer who had never completed a fighter, Edgar Schmued died quietly at his home north of San Diego. In accordance with the family's wishes, arrangements were made to scatter his ashes over the Pacific Ocean from one of his cherished Mustangs. Prominent air racing pilot Clay Lacy, who was then flying a Mustang, organized like-minded and similarly equipped pilots to join in a formation.

Two weeks after Schmued's death, six P-51s led by Lacy (and trailed by an F-86 Sabre) set out to honor the man who had created the wings on which they rode. But before crossing the shoreline and heading out to sea, they aimed for a certain intersection in the meandering grid of Los Angeles. When they approached Inglewood, they swooped down low.

For a few moments airliners were cleared from the airspace around busy LAX, the old Mines Field. The tribute formation came barreling in, the strumming of finely tuned Merlin engines reverberating off the site of the North American Aviation factory at Imperial and Aviation. What remained of the designer who had drawn the Mustang in the building's second-floor office now flashed overhead. Soon the ashes would be devoured by the ocean and Edgar Schmued would be gone forever. But for the pilots in the formation and the larger aviation community, the legacy of the Mustang designer was bound to live on, vibrant and inspiring, as long as his resplendent fighter continued to occupy a place in the sky.

CHAPTER 19

German Jet: The Messerschmitt Me 262 Ushers in a New Age

An assistant to the Third Reich's Armaments Minister, Albert Speer, called it a "savior weapon." Indeed, a few years into World War II, with the strategic tide showing signs of shifting from the Axis to the Allies, much was riding on the radical new aircraft that originated at Willy Messerschmitt's Augsburg factory. Unlike any operational fighter the world had seen, this was a propellerless plane that, if successful, promised to revolutionize air warfare.

From his first flight in the Me 262 on May 22, 1943, General-leutnant Adolf Galland, the Luftwaffe's young and charismatic *General der Jagdflieger* (chief of Fighter Command), felt excitement and relief. He was excited by the German jet's unsurpassed performance which afforded previously unimagined combat potential, and he was relieved by the knowledge that his Luftwaffe fighter squadrons were in line to possess a superior weapon that might compensate for Germany's inability to match the industrial output of its main enemies. But, as so often happens in war, expectations did not pan out quite as hoped.

Galland, known as Dolfo to his friends, had volunteered for duty with the Condor Legion during the Spanish Civil War. Flying Heinkel He 51 biplanes, he was part of the German vanguard that used the battleground in Spain as a kind of laboratory to test equipment and tactics that would be honed for application during World War II. Later, he flew fighter missions in the invasions of Poland and France, where, in the latter theater, he began to accumulate a long string of air-to-air victories. During the

Battle of Britain, he was awarded the Knight's Cross and promoted to Kommodore of JG 26.

Flying the Bf 109 in skies rich with dogfighting opportunity, Galland's tally continued to rise, so that by November 1941 he had scored a prodigious ninety-seven victories. The same month, his friend Werner Molders, *General der Jagdflieger*, died in a plane crash. Because of Dolfo's airmanship, warrior spirit, and leadership skills, he was tapped to fill the position. It was a meteoric rise for the twenty-nine year-old fighter pilot. He harbored reservations about the job, though, because it came with the proviso that he would not be permitted to fly in combat and because, as he put it, he did not want to be "tied to a desk job." In early 1942, for his earlier exploits as a frontline air commander, he was awarded the Knight's Cross with Diamonds, Germany's highest military decoration.

Dolfo was a powerful personality, one who kept his emotions under absolute control whatever the circumstances. He was extremely gracious, with an aristocratic manner that charmed all, especially women who happened to be present. I came to know him fairly well over a period of ten years, entertaining him at the National Air and Space Museum and in my home. He responded with equal courtesy when I went to Germany.

It was interesting to observe how carefully he maintained both his political and his fighter-pilot persona over an extended period of time. As a former senior officer in the Luftwaffe, he was always careful about separating his personal ideas from his work for Germany when it was a Nazi state. It was very evident that he had difficulty reconciling his personal pride in the men and equipment of the Luftwaffe with their employment in Adolf Hitler's service. There was a natural reluctance on his part to criticize the Luftwaffe in which he had operated so effectively and during which time he had lost so many of his friends in combat.

He recognized that people generally felt that a man in his position must necessarily have known of the Nazi crimes committed against Jews, Soviet prisoners of war, and others. He was essentially in a no-win position—an officer of the "old school" in an air force that was part of a military enterprise usurped by a pathological misfit and used in unacceptable ways to fulfill a demonic vision. Like millions of native Germans who found themselves swept up in the convulsions stirred by Hitler's machinations, he would never be able to sever himself completely from the link to the horrors perpetrated by the evil regime. Within this macrocosm of perfidy, however, Dolfo was a military aviator and an officer in the pseudo-Prussian style trying, along with cohorts, to perform his duty in accordance with an unwritten but identifiable code of honor.

He did not take well to being deskbound as a staff officer, a circumstance compounded by the internecine intrigue of the Nazi hierarchy. By January 1945, as Germany's wartime prospects were fading, he had a falling out with Reichsmarschall Herman Goering who had the SS place him under house arrest. Although Dolfo and Hitler had mutually frustrated each other, the Fuhrer overrode the arrest order, releasing the ground-tethered fighter pilot to fly in a new squadron equipped with the Me 262.

No longer burdened by the nugatory staff position, which had involved pushing back against incompetence and corruption, Dolfo was at last freed to be a flyer again. At such a late stage in the war, with the impending catastrophe all but unstoppable, he and those in his fighter unit were not seeking to "give to the war the much-quoted 'turn'" nor to show fealty to unworthy leaders like Goering and Hitler. Rather, to return to the sky—to a squadron—was to share the bond of fellow airmen who clung to a notion of patriotic duty, terribly flawed though it was, and to fly this exotic new machine. As Dolfo expressed the sentiment, "The magic word 'jet' had brought us together to experience once more *die grosse Fliegerei*" ("the great flying").

In February, Dolfo took command of the new squadron, Jagderverband 44, at Brandenburg-Briest. Only a little over two hundred Me 262s of the 1,433 built would attain operational status, but JV 44 received its apportionment. While being formed, word of this unit spread throughout the Luftwaffe and pilots were drawn to it like a magnet. As Dolfo later wrote, "Many reported without consent or transfer orders."

Most who joined the squadron had been flying combat missions since the war started. All had been wounded. Indeed, three of the squadron's officers came directly from the hospital. No less than ten of JV 44's pilots had been awarded the Knight's Cross. This high military decoration was, in Galland's words, "the badge of our unit."

The experience of the squadron's pilots was reflected in the disproportionate weighting to the higher ranks: one lieutenant general, two colonels, one lieutenant colonel, three majors, five captains, eight lieutenants, and approximately an equal number of second lieutenants. It was an extraordinary array of military flying talent: Major Gerd Barkhorn (301 victories), Major Walter Krupinski (197 victories), Oberst Johannes Steinhoff (176 victories), Oberst Guenther Luetzow (108 victories), Major Erich Hohagen (57 victories), and, of course, their leader and friend, Dolfo (97 victories).

This was Germany's fighter "dream team," a cadre of the country's best practitioners of the art of air-to-air warfare. The squadron was the Richthofen Circus, the Lafayette Escadrille, the Flying Tigers, and Top Gun all rolled into one. JV 44 was the elite of the elite!

Many of these officers, like Dolfo himself, had burned bridges and fallen out of favor with their superiors for infractions that today we would equate to political incorrectness. For that reason, JV 44 was offhandedly referred to as the "Squadron of Malcontents." Sometimes, in honor of its leader, the squadron was called "Kommando Galland." Yet, one sobriquet has stuck through the passage of time. It truly captures the essence of this astonishingly gifted unit: the "Squadron of the *Experten*."

The squadron's fighter plane was no less extraordinary than the squadron's men aching to take it into action. The Me 262 could fly faster than the Allies' top-of-the-line propeller-driven fighters (and by some accounts, depending on altitude and maneuvering scenario, the speed advantage exceeded 100 miles per hour). Moreover, in the war's closing days, a new and deadly air-launched munition was fielded. The 50-mm R4M rocket was fired in salvos of a dozen at a time from under the Me 262's wing and because of its explosive power sent anything it touched flaming to the ground.

With just four weeks left until the collapse of the Third Reich, JV 44 finally finished training up its pilots and began operations from Munich-Riem. Operating conditions were marginal since the Allies were closing in from three sides and bombing raids on the airfield occurred with increasing frequency. Dolfo and his men got in the habit of diving into foxholes dug on the airfield's grounds. The jets were camouflaged and hidden in surrounding foliage immediately after every mission.

Dolfo continued to lead and racked up seven more victories, bringing his tally to 104. On April 25th, he encountered sixteen B-26 Marauders in a close formation. At a distance of six hundred yards, he launched all two dozen R4M rockets from under both wings within half a second. The fusillade saturated the formation and caused one of the bombers to burst into flames immediately upon contact. Another bomber had sections of its starboard tail surfaces and wing blown away, sending it into an irretrievable spiral.

The next day another Marauder formation appeared. But this time, in his excitement, the air combat veteran forgot to release the second safety catch required to fire the rockets. He reverted to his four 30-mm cannon and scored some hits on two of the bombers.

While fixating on a damage assessment of the second B-26 he had hit, an escorting Mustang caught him off guard. Machine gun rounds smashed into his jet, tearing off parts of an engine, knocking out his instruments, and wounding him in the knee. Limping back to base, a ground-strafing P-47 Thunderbolt tried to finish off Dolfo's Me 262. With no choice but to proceed with the landing of the stricken jet, Dolfo barely managed to stop before running out of runway. He then crawled out of the cockpit and scurried to a nearby bomb crater for shelter until a ground crewman drove up in a tractor to whisk him out of harm's way.

Dolfo's knee wound necessitated a cast; the war was over for him as it soon would be for his colleagues. The airfield was no longer secure. The jets were transferred to Salzburg where advancing Allied forces rendered the Squadron of the Experten defenseless on May 3rd.

Between his last two missions, Dolfo gathered his pilots together and told them: "Militarily speaking the war is lost. Even our action here cannot change anything. . . . I shall continue to fight, because operating with the Me 262 has got hold of me, because I am proud to belong to the last fighter pilots of the German Luftwaffe. . . . Only those who feel the same are to go on flying with me." Like a captain of a sinking vessel on the high seas, estranged from the political honchos far removed from the roiling waters, Dolfo sought honor by going down with the ship, surrounded by his like-minded mates.

After the war, he reflected with the benefit of hindsight on his time at the controls of the world's first operational jet fighter and on his being in the company of fellow "experts." He wrote glowingly of the Me 262. He commented on the inauspicious timing of that futuristic airplane's entry into service: "It does not bear thinking about what we could have done had we had those jet fighters, 3-cm. [30-mm] quick-firing cannons, and 5-cm. [50-mm] rockets years ago—before our war potential had been smashed, before indescribable misery had come over Germany through the raids. We dared not think about it. Now we could do nothing but fly and fight and do our duty as fighter pilots to the last."

Yet the unavoidable question raised by the Me 262 was what effect it might have had if Reichsmarschall Herman Goering had not interfered with the production and development of advanced concepts, including the jet engine, in 1940. Wallowing in the successes of the Luftwaffe and the Wehrmacht on all fronts, Goering caused delays in the development of the jet engine and other key weapons, so that more resources could be devoted to consumer goods. It is almost certain that these decisions were not the result of investigations and recommendations from key players in the military and industry.

Rather they were an expression of Goering's enormous ego and his desire to curry favor with the public. This, and his penchant for making intuitive decisions, probably set the jet engine program back by at least one year. In turn, this prevented Germany from achieving the air superiority needed to prevent an Allied invasion of Europe in 1944.

As previously noted, Dolfo's postwar recollections walk an unsteady line between his desire to disassociate himself from the top Nazis and his desire to have the effectiveness of the Luftwaffe and his own contributions to that effectiveness fully recognized. There is absolutely no evidence that Dolfo failed to do his utmost for the Luftwaffe, even after he had recognized the sordid, immoral, and ultimately fatal fate of Germany as it followed the illegal path of Hitler's policies. As with so many German officers, he had to struggle to rationalize his nationalistic patriotism and his analysis of Nazi Germany's politics. A single but very convincing example of this is his recognition of the qualities and potential of the Me 262. Despite any reservations he may have had at the time about the

Nazis, he nonetheless called for an immediate emphasis on and priority for the Me 262 at the expense of other vital fighter programs, including many variants of the Me 109 and Me 209.

One has to understand and discount the political considerations that he claimed in the postwar years. Here he was, a ninety-seven-victory ace leading the German fighter effort and he is suddenly presented with the Messerschmitt Me 262. It exploits the new jet technology, offering a measure of superiority over competing Allied fighters. The Me 262 gave other advantages as well, including being easier to maintain, requiring fuel that was less expensive and more available than conventional aviation gasoline, and offering German pilots an opportunity to accept or refuse combat as they wished.

The vast improvement of performance resident in the Me 262 makes it not unreasonable to state that had the German aircraft and engine industry been allowed to proceed without the interference so arbitrarily imposed by Goering in 1940, the Luftwaffe would have been able to prevent the Allied invasion of Europe in 1944. The effects of this development might well have caused the Soviet Union to make a separate peace with Germany that would have eliminated the possibility of an Allied invasion for some time. The most obvious change in the conduct of the war would have been that the first atomic bombs would not have been dropped on Hiroshima and Nagasaki, but rather upon Berlin and Munich. The political repercussions of this switch in nuclear targets would have echoed down through the decades, with absolutely unpredictable effects on what became in time the Cold War.

•••

Ernest Heinkel was an ambitious German businessman. In the mid-1930s, he wanted his aircraft manufacturing company to expand its offerings and he believed designs with a speed advantage would gain a foothold in the market. The way to do it, Heinkel theorized, was to develop an in-house engine-building capability much as his competitor Hugo Junkers had done.

Heinkel's interest was piqued when his friend, Professor R. W. Pohl of the University of Goettingen, recommended a young researcher of a radical propulsion concept. Majoring in applied physics and aerodynamics, postgraduate student Hans-Joachim Pabst von Ohain had already received patents on a turbojet engine using a centrifugal compressor. Von Ohain was delighted to join Heinkel's company because its backing gave him the means to turn his ideas into a working jet engine.

After a successful static test of an experimental jet engine in March 1937, the company proceeded to develop a flying demonstrator. Designated the Heinkel He 178, the small aircraft was fitted with the eleven hundred-pound thrust HeS-3b engine. On August 27, 1939, Flugkapitan Erich Warsitz rode the jet into the sky above the airfield at Marienehe for what was the first flight of its kind.

It should be mentioned that contemporaneous with von Ohain's developmental work, British Royal Air Force Flying Officer Frank Whittle had independently conceived a jet engine, though of notably different design. Whittle's engine was installed in the Gloster E 28/39 and flew for the first time on May 15, 1941. Had the British Air Ministry not given short shrift to Whittle's invention when it initially emerged earlier in the 1930s, Britain may have been first to fly a jet. During the war, the United States had to make up for even more lost ground, relying heavily on the Whittle engine.

From the mid-1930s, the German Air Ministry sought to spur development of cutting-edge propulsion systems—both jets and rockets. To this end, a variety of companies received contracts for ramjets, pulsejets, and turbine engines, while others received inquiries regarding development of enabling airframes. In 1938 the Reichsluftfahrtministerium (RLM) asked Robert Lusser, head of Messerschmitt's project bureau, if his company would produce a study of a twin-engine fighter based on the BMW axial-flow turbojet then under development.

Not wanting to be left behind in the face of Heinkel's progress on a jet, Messerschmitt moved forward on a design. The project was designated P. 1065. Employing an egalitarian approach, decisions were made by a committee in which Woldemar Voigt played a central role as the soon-to-be new head of the company's project bureau. The jet plane was truly a clean-sheet design as there was no model as a basis. The committee proposed an all-metal, low-wing cantilever monoplane which, in theory, could achieve a maximum speed of 560 miles per hour.

Because multiengine piston planes mounted their engines on the wings, the Messerschmitt team reasoned that such placement would make the most sense for the jet engines. However, rather than mounting the engines integrally with the wing to maximize streamlining as had been contemplated at the outset, it was wisely decided for flexibility's sake that under-wing nacelles would be the better way to go.

The wing was too thin to accommodate the retractable landing gear. The solution was to adopt a fuselage in the shape of a triangle as viewed head-on. This gave the aircraft its distinctive shark-like appearance, which added to its aesthetics and mystique. Also, a tail-wheel configuration was adopted, as that was the convention at the time. When this proved to be problematical, a tricycle arrangement was substituted in its place.

Messerschmitt engineers realized that though their jet plane would be faster than any piston-powered plane, it had a practical limit because at the higher speeds the drag curve steepened prohibitively. On the plus side, the extra power of the jet engines permitted the carriage of more fuel and four nose-mounted 30-mm cannon. This standard armament contributed to the aircraft's reputation as an awesome fighter.

As often happens in the developmental process, there were changes in the distribution of the aircraft's weight, which caused the center of gravity to become untenable. In a word, the Me 262 was nose-heavy. A quick and dirty solution was devised: the originally planned straight wing would have a sweepback outboard of the nacelles. Later, the wing's entire leading edge was swept back eighteen and a half degrees, giving the plane an arrow shape. Fortuitously, this sweep delayed compressibility, which contributed to the higher-than-otherwise critical Mach number of 0.86.

In mid-May 1940, Messerschmitt shared its design with the RLM. At this point, the German High Command was basking in battlefield successes and would soon consummate further conquests in Western Europe. Interest appertaining to the project slackened off. Nevertheless, the company received a contract for three prototypes.

Of course, crucial to the success of the aircraft were the jet engines themselves. The BMW 003 engine underperformed in bench testing, which alarmed Messerschmitt's design team. With the jet engines delayed, Messerschmitt decided to equip its first prototype with a single

Junkers Jumo 210G piston-powered engine in the nose. The propeller-driven test aircraft, Me 262 V1, would provide baseline flight data.

On April 18, 1941, Flugkapitan Fritz Wendel successfully flew the test platform. Flight trials showed this piston-powered, propeller-driven hybrid reaching speeds in excess of the Bf 109, proving its aerodynamic edge. Pleased with the progress, in July the RLM ordered five test articles and twenty preproduction planes.

Later that year, BMW finally delivered the long-awaited 003 jet engines to Messerschmitt. The engines were installed in the previously flown platform, and as a precaution, the piston engine and propeller were retained in the nose. On March 26, 1942, Wendel lifted off from Augsburg in this oddly configured aircraft.

The aircraft's takeoff roll was long and slow because of the weight of the jet engines and their anemic thrust. At an altitude of only 165 feet, the port engine flamed out followed by the starboard engine. Later analysis showed that the compressor blades broke in both jet engines. Disaster was narrowly averted when Wendel rammed the piston engine's throttle to the stop. He managed to nurse the floundering plane back to the runway.

The near-fatal performance of the jet engines meant that BMW would have to completely redesign the 003. The only viable alternative for Messerschmitt at this juncture was to turn to the competing power plant being developed by Junkers Motorenbau (Jumo for short). Austrian engineer Anselm Franz had been busy since the fall of 1939 developing what would become the Jumo 004.

In late 1941 the 004A preproduction model generated an impressive twenty-two hundred pounds of thrust in a static test run, eclipsing all other designs. However, this model was too heavy to be practical. Other concerns included the short span between overhauls as parts wore out quickly under the unusually high stresses.

Franz and his colleagues went to great lengths to finesse the 004 into a workable engine. The first production model, the 004B-1, experienced vibration failures in the turbine buckets, but rather than give up, a professional musician was engaged. His "perfect pitch" in conjunction with his violin bow determined the natural frequencies of individual blades in an assembled turbine wheel. Aided by the fine tuning, engineers tapered the blades ever so modestly to increase their natural frequency which, combined with a reduction in the engine's rpm from 9,000 to 8,700, solved the vibration problem.

The third prototype, Me 262 V3, was to be used for the first pure jet flight in the test program. The size of the 004 required enlarging the aircraft's nacelles. Fin and rudder surface area had to be increased to compensate for the adjustments to the nacelles.

On July 18, 1942, Wendel got the aircraft into the air, but not without difficulty. The aircraft was still configured with a tail wheel at this time and the elevators were ineffective until the tail rose off the ground during the takeoff roll. This is when the design team realized that switching to tricycle gear would be necessary.

Also the early flights revealed that the partial wing sweep caused airflow problems when banking. This was corrected by thickening the inboard section of the wing and extending the angle of sweep all the way to the root. Messerschmitt had designed leading-edge slats for the Bf 109 wing, and did the same for the Me 262, which improved lift by 30 percent.

Hitler observed a demonstration of the Me 262 on November 26, 1943. He considered this impressive new weapon to be the means to potentially penetrate the curtain of Allied fighters and to strike Allied ground positions in the invasion that he felt certain would be launched soon. Production of the jet was prioritized, but by preference of the Fuhrer, it was to be configured and employed as a bomber, not a fighter. The formal declaration was issued shortly after D-Day, on June 8, 1944. This was madness, the equivalent of pressing down on the accelerator with one foot to get as many Me 262s delivered as soon as possible while applying heavy brake with the other foot by using the jet counterproductively.

Continuing engine problems caused further delays, however, and the first Me 262s with the Jumo 004B-1 engine began arriving in the Luftwaffe's hands in small quantities in June. The Messerschmitt staff reluctantly complied with Hitler's dictate, all the while urging a reversal of the policy. Finally, in November, the directive was rescinded. The Me 262 could be the fighter it was always meant to be.

In the short time that the aircraft was in production, many variants came into being, but in limited numbers. These included the two-seat Me

262B for training and a night-fighter modification of the B, designated Me 262B-la/U1. The two main variants were the fighter type known as the Schwalbe or Swallow and the Hitler-inspired bomber variant known as the Sturmvogel or Stormbird. For all its advantages, the world's first operational jet fighter, regardless of variant, was plagued by a flagrantly deficient training system and an inadequately developed tactics doctrine.

Germany was increasingly desperate and this new aircraft, despite not being ready for combat, was thrown into the fray for there was nothing to lose. The Allies' first recorded sighting of the Me 262 in full interceptor mode came from an RAF Mosquito crew on a reconnaissance mission over Munich on July 25, 1944. The British airmen had to use all their skill and the high performance of their plane to dodge the tail-hugging jet.

The Allies were alarmed because the Mosquito could fly higher than the enemy's propeller planes and outrun them too. The fact that the feared German jet had finally been fielded and that it proved to be so speedy and nimble meant that no Allied aircraft would be safe. From that incident until the end of the war, the ears of Allied intelligence perked up when there were indications of the jet's deployment.

Back on July 18, 1944, Hauptmann Werner Thierfelder, the head of the Me 262 test unit, died in the crash of one of the jets due to an engine malfunction. Dolfo chose Major Walter Nowotny, one of Germany's highest-scoring aces, to take command of the fighter unit that sprang from the test unit. Nowotny was well known to the German public because of his air combat successes and seemed the natural choice to lead the first Me 262 combat unit, known as Kommando Nowotny.

Nowotny had made a name for himself shooting down three planes over the Baltic Sea in 1941. His Bf 109 had been damaged, which forced him to ditch in the water. He managed to inflate his dinghy and then, in the course of a three-day odyssey, to use his hands to paddle to land. The next year, he was promoted to command I./JG 54, the highly effective and well-known Green Hearts. He was twenty-one years old at the time.

During 1943 Nowotny's air victories reached a then-unprecedented level of 250. He became the youngest pilot ever to receive the Knight's Cross with Diamonds. Yet even youthful enthusiasm combined with an impeccable résumé and a superior plane would not be enough to prevail against the staggering odds in the closing months of the European war.

Allied fighter pilots had learned that the German jet was most vulnerable during takeoff and landing as it would be flying at low speed. Tactics called for attacks on the Me 262 airfields during which it was hoped the jets could be attacked in the pattern or, even better, while still parked. For its part, the Luftwaffe began to employ the long-nosed Fw 190s as escorts for the Me 262s during these vulnerable interludes.

Nowotny made strides in proving the worth of the Schwalbe, but it was simply too late. British and American fighters swarmed the remaining German bases. Also, when escorting bomber formations, the Allied fighters used their lopsided numbers to gang up on the jets. On November 8, 1944, Nowotny's Me 262 was hit and seen streaking almost straight down out of the clouds, impacting the ground and exploding in flames. Dolfo eulogized Nowotny as "an excellent officer."

Shortly after the young ace's death, the unit was withdrawn. It had scored twenty-two confirmed victories against losses of twenty-six of its own aircraft. The crushing results made clear that it was only a matter of time before the final blow would be struck.

The great potential of the Me 262 was never fulfilled. In the context of the immediate battle space, the warplane's material impact was negligible; it ended up being little more than a compelling historical footnote. Yet the jet was a revolutionary machine, its real meaning contained in what it presaged for the future of military and commercial aviation.

CHAPTER 20

An Implausible Romance: Warm Feelings on a Cold War B-47 Bomber

Almost everyone has a memory of particular warmth from the past. It might be a first pet, a first car, a first romance, but it brings a feeling of comfort, or perhaps even of regret, but unforgettable nonetheless. My own remembrances make this truly an "implausible romance" for they are of a killing machine designed to decimate whole nations in a single strike, and which managed to kill far more of its crew members in peacetime than can be justified.

Yet there it is. I recall my years flying the Boeing B-47 Stratojet bomber with the greatest possible affection, for its startling innovative appearance and performance, for the positive effect it had upon the United States Air Force, and for what it did for me before, during, and after every flight.

While many surviving B-47 aircrew members recall the aircraft, I doubt if all or even most feel as I do. Many were hotshot young cadets just graduated from flying school, intent on flying fighter planes, and found themselves suddenly drafted into copilot duty on the "Stratojet," as we *never* called it. Others regarded it as just another milestone in their career progression. For those interested, there is a fine group, the B-47 Association, which does an excellent job preserving the legacy of the aircraft.

As noted, my feelings for the aircraft stem from multiple sources. The first was the heady exhilaration of moving from the staid but reliable Boeing B-50 (a B-29 upgraded structurally and equipped with more powerful engines) to the B-47. The second was that I was flying that aircraft in a remarkable war plan that provided absolute assurance that the fearsome Soviet Union would not start a nuclear war. (A personal note on the war plan: In the B-50, we were tasked to fly to Tula, about two hundred miles southeast of Moscow, drop our nuclear bombs on the city of two hundred thousand, then do a 180-degree turn, fly until our fuel ran out, then bail out over the Ukraine and "try to find a friendly native." In the B-47 we were tasked with the same mission, but after the drop we were to fly to Stockholm and land.) The third was an awareness of the quality of personnel who flew and maintained the aircraft and were uniformly dedicated, first-rate people. Finally, there were the sheer aesthetics of flying a beautiful machine that demanded the most from you at every moment, from preflight to takeoff to the mission to landing and a debriefing. Anything less than your best effort at all times could result in disaster—and it did for too many people.

A question about morality arises immediately. Is it really right to be enamored of an aircraft whose only mission was to drop nuclear weapons on an enemy city and destroy it utterly? In today's politically correct atmosphere and with the Soviet Union gone, the answer would be no. (Even though we should remember that Russia's nuclear power is now in the hands of Vladimir Putin, whose admitted ambition to emulate Catherine the Great has encompassed nibbling on Ukraine.) But in those early years of the B-47, extending from 1951 through, say, 1964, the answer was—and is—unequivocally yes. We were faced with a huge superpower capable of overrunning Europe and subduing even Great Britain in a matter of weeks, and able to penetrate the US air defenses on one-way nuclear missions in a matter of hours. It was a Cold War only because the United States kept it cold rather than hot, and it did it initially with the fantastic Strategic Air Command (SAC). This became the most powerful force in the history of the world, and was created by the world's greatest—and most wrongfully vilified—air commander, General Curtis E. LeMay.

National Security Council document NSC 162/2 of October 30, 1953, called for inflicting massive retaliatory damage on any attack by having tremendous offensive striking power. LeMay directed SAC's unprecedented peacetime growth in strength and proficiency. From 1951 to 1957, SAC blossomed from twelve to 1,285 B-47s and from one B-47 medium bomb wing to twenty-eight, each wing with forty-five aircraft.

Being part of that expansion contributes to my being enamored. Although it sounds as gritty and hot and uncomfortable as it was, there was a visceral, intimidating, horrifying sense of awe in rolling out in a line of beautiful B-47s, one of forty-five at my 93rd Bomb Wing, aware that in the bomb bay was death to millions. That awareness was enhanced by the knowledge that at perhaps fifteen other SAC bases the same massive reprisal was in progress—and that meant there would *not* be a war by the traditional meaning of the word. At that moment, something like six hundred B-47 aircraft would be preparing to enter the Soviet Union from several directions and utterly destroy it. Most telling of all, those B-47s would have killed the Soviet leaders, which made them very reluctant to go to war at all. It is one thing to have several hundred thousand soldiers under your command killed by pressing a button. It is quite another to effectively commit suicide with the same button press.

Above and beyond the nation-saving, war-making capability of the B-47, there were the sheer aesthetics of its design, the amazing flying characteristics, and the utter satisfaction of completing a demanding mission.

Aesthetics

Few aircraft have had so ugly a series of prototype designs proposed for it as the B-47. If you examine the first attempts of Boeing engineers to use the newly introduced jet engine, you wonder what they could have been thinking. They stuck the new jets like boutonnieres at every point on thick, ugly fuselage and wing positions, moving from one unsightly mess to another.

Yet after four years of intensive development the gorgeous XB-47A made its first flight on December 17, 1947, one of two prototypes built under a $10 million contract. It was the product of Boeing expertise and the information engineer George Schairer garnered from captured German data on swept wings and high-speed flight. The prototype was so radical that one of its primary engineers, Holden Withington, told me that as he watched it taxi out for its first takeoff, he was still not certain that it would fly. Yet it was undeniably beautiful, and grew even more so in refined developments of dedicated electronic aircraft.

The XB-47 featured slender shoulder-mounted wings that were swept at thirty-five degrees, as was the horizontal stabilizer. A huge bubble canopy housed the fighter-like cockpit that sat the pilot and copilot/gunner in tandem. The navigator/bombardier/radar operator was tucked away in the nose, beneath the clanging in-flight refueling receptacle. In later models he had no outside visibility at all. Initially there were no ejection seats, but later the aircraft commander and pilot positions received upward firing seats, while the radar observer's seat fired downward. (Our radar observer, a fine man named John Rosene, always used to ask just before takeoff that if anything went wrong, would we kindly roll the airplane a bit to one side, so he wouldn't fire himself into the ground.)

A unique four-wheel bicycle landing gear positioned the aircraft in permanent takeoff position. General Electric J47-GE-25 turbojet engines of seventy-two hundred pounds of thrust were used. In a configuration that would become common for large jet aircraft, pod-like nacelles held the engines a safe distance from the wing, which added the benefits of minimizing airflow disruption and improving the mechanics' ease of access. Two engines were clustered in each inboard nacelle, with an outer nacelle containing one engine and a retractable tip-gear designed to keep the flexible wing on a heavily loaded aircraft from touching the ground. The engines were powerful for their time, but inadequate for the aircraft, especially in hot weather or at high-altitude landing fields. The air force continually added mission requirements, which grew the maximum takeoff weight from 125,000 to 206,000 pounds.

The selection of the ultra-thin wing created both structural and aerodynamic problems. It had to be built with great strength to withstand huge deflections, as much as seventeen feet in flight. But it was also flexible chord-wise, so that at speeds above 425 knots, the ailerons acted as a tab, twisting the wings rather than inducing a bank. At 456 knots, the ailerons were totally ineffective, and the control wheel could not be budged from side to side. In turbulent weather I had watched the wing seem to curl up and over in a violent rumba rhythm that seemed certain to jettison the engines.

All of these features, as troublesome as some were, made the B-47 into a stunningly good-looking aircraft, especially to a young first lieutenant flying a B-50. I had literally to fight to become a copilot in the aircraft because I lacked the stated minimum qualifying flying hours. It took some doing, including pounding my fist on the squadron adjutant's desk, but in 1954 I was assigned to training at McConnell Air Force Base, Kansas, during the hottest summer on record. Flying was officially cancelled when cockpit temperatures of aircraft on the ramp reached 145 degrees!

At McConnell I quickly discovered that flying the aircraft at approach and landing speeds was demanding because the jet engines were so slow to accelerate. A drogue parachute was used to allow approach and landings to be made with the engines still carrying enough power to enable rapid throttle movement. After landing, a thirty-two-foot brake parachute and antiskid brakes stopped the aircraft. Everything was new, everything was different and demanding. In short, everything was wonderful.

The Toll

The cost in crew members was staggering by today's standards. From 1953 to 1959, B-47s suffered 296 major accidents and 242 fatalities. This was an era when the World War II aphorism "you have to expect losses" remained a philosophy. The two most costly years were 1957 and 1958. In 1957 there were twenty-four crashes that cost sixty-three lives. In 1958 there were twenty-five aircraft crashes and fifty-eight fatalities. Can you imagine what today's media would have to say about the air force losing two bomber aircraft per month for two years?

The vast majority of crashes were attributed to human error, with pilots assigned the principal blame. There were many reasons for this. The three-man crew flew a vastly more complicated aircraft than the ten-man crews of the B-29 or B-50. It was easy for any of the crew members, particularly the aircraft commander, to have their attention diverted momentarily from the task of flying the aircraft. This was especially true on missions that sometimes ran as long as twenty-four hours.

Yet attention to flight control was absolutely critical. Crew coordination was essential, but could be easily disrupted when an emergency occurred during critical areas of flight.

The extremely clean lines of the B-47 enabled both its performance and its problems. A pilot concentrating on a new situation—course change, a sudden red light, radio instructions, anything—might let his attention wander for a few seconds and find himself banking in a dive that pushed his speed to a point where recovery was impossible. This proved to be a frequent scenario during instrument flight. Where the B-50s of the time might let down in an instrument approach from a holding point in leisurely thousand-foot increments, the B-47 descended at a hell-for-leather six thousand-foot-per-minute rate that sometimes led to lethal miscalculations. And these led to the major complaint about the B-47: It killed too many people, not in the enemy's camp, but its crew members.

The B-47 required much closer attention than previous aircraft to preflight planning, fuel distribution, trim settings, and airspeed control. It was deceptively easy to fly but extremely precise operation was required during takeoff, in-flight refueling, instrument flight, and landing. This became even more important with the introduction of new tactics that included higher takeoff weights, minimum interval takeoffs, three-ship cells for in-flight refueling, tankers with marginal performance, and operation from alternate airfields.

Using the Boeing KC-97s as refueling aircraft caused many problems. The KC-97 could not fly fast enough to keep the B-47 from stalling when it had a full load of fuel. It had to be put into a descent to maintain enough speed so that the bomber did not stall. Operating with the KC-97 was particularly difficult for the three B-47 cells, especially at night or in weather.

Other factors intervened as well. After October 1, 1957, SAC sought to keep one-third of its bombers and tankers on alert, with weapons loaded and the crews ready for takeoff within fifteen minutes. Extra demands were imposed by "Reflex Action" operations that required ninety-day overseas tours.

The concept of low-level flight as a tactic to avoid Soviet radar was intended to decrease B-47 losses in wartime. The B-47 was to enter Russian airspace at low altitude and near the target pull up into what was called the LABS (Low Altitude Bombing System) maneuver. In this the B-47 entered a half loop at maximum speed, automatically released its bomb at a predetermined point, then rolled out at the top in an Immelmann turn at a frighteningly low airspeed. It then dived away from the target to regain speed. There were several other "toss bombing techniques"—all dangerous. In the "Pop-Up" maneuver, the B-47 would fly in at 425 knots indicated airspeed until about sixty seconds prior to "bombs away." It would then climb to thirty-five hundred feet above the ground, level off, drop the parachute-retarded bomb, and make an immediate turn to escape.

The general strain on the aircraft structures caused by the stress of atmospheric turbulence at low altitudes was exacerbated by a higher tempo of operations. This required more frequent refueling missions and increased numbers of takeoffs and landings.

The majority of accidents occurred to crews in which the aircraft commander was a reserve officer with a relatively high total of flying hours but only a relatively small amount of time in the B-47. In addition, the records show that both pilots usually had a limited amount of instrument and night flying time. The pilot was all too often a young first lieutenant, usually with less than five hundred hours total time and perhaps fifty hours in the B-47. Time and again, the accident board concluded that the primary cause was operator error in which faulty technique "allowed the aircraft to get into a position from which they were unable to recover."

Many of the accidents occurred on takeoff, all with a chillingly similar pattern. The high gross weight takeoffs appeared to be normal until a few seconds after liftoff. Then a wing dipped, the runway was struck, and the aircraft crashed and burned. Analysis revealed that a loss of power (engine failure, failure of water injection) induced yaw. The B-47 would enter a stall, and a crash became unavoidable. Takeoff crashes also resulted from incorrect preflight planning. In one instance, the aircraft commander failed to include the weight of twenty-two hundred gallons of external fuel in his calculations, rotated too soon, stalled, and crashed. In another, the use of an outdated manual led to setting the elevator trim incorrectly, with the same rotation, stall, and crash sequence.

The year 1958 had an almost equally dismal record which reached a crescendo in March, when six aircraft disintegrated while flying low-altitude missions. Two of the aircraft were very low-time B-47Es, one with 1,419 hours and the other with only 1,265 hours. Of the six crashes, four were directly attributable to structural fatigue failure. These crashes served notice that flaws might show up in any B-47, whatever its flying time. The B-47 was planned to serve as SAC's primary weapon until 1965, but concern grew that it might have to be phased out prematurely. Further, concern developed that the fatigue problem might reoccur in the B-52 and subsequent aircraft.

SAC reacted in April by limiting the B-47 to 310 knots indicated airspeed and 1.5-g maneuvers. Low-level flying was banned, gross weight could not exceed 185,000 pounds with external tanks, and banks were limited to thirty degrees. Restrictions were placed on flight through turbulent air, stalls, and touch-and-go landings. Specific limits were placed on refueling practices. Aircraft were to be carefully inspected for cracks indicating fatigue.

On May 29 the primary fix was issued, Technical Order 1B-47-1019, which provided the kits necessary to reinforce the wing root. All three contractors and the Air Materiel Command worked on what became known as the Milk Bottle Program. The name derived from the large milk-bottle-shaped pins used to fasten the wings to the fuselage. Eventually 1,622 B-47s received this modification by January 1959, at a cost of $62 million. Additional fatigue problems appeared later, especially in the upper fuselage longerons, but for the most part, B-47s were cleared for flight.

Although the response to the emergency was ultimately successful, the results were not immediate. Despite a dramatic slash in flight hours to 150,238 in 1958, twenty-two more B-47s were destroyed. It was not until 1960 that the corrective efforts began to have effect. As the B-52 grew in numbers, economics dictated the phase out of the B-47, and by 1966, only sixteen RB-47s were operating.

The B-47 experience had been a sobering one. SAC training and flying-safety procedures were vastly improved as the B-52 became the principal bomber. But extra-high performance remained costly, as the beautiful but accident-prone Convair B-58 Hustler would prove.

CHAPTER 21

The Best Bargain in Military History: The Big Ugly

In the late 1940s, when the concept of the B-52 began to be an issue, it was natural that the emergent missileers and the established bomber pilots should clash on it. Air force innovator Bernard Schreiver strongly supported the creation of the intercontinental ballistic missile force, which still defends our nation, while his former commander, General Curtis LeMay, pressed for increasing emphasis on replacing the B-47 fleet with a smaller fleet of more efficient B-52s.

Schriever, in one brilliant confrontation, presented the argument that the equivalent of the proposed B-52 fleet could be achieved if the B-47 was reequipped with four of the Pratt & Whitney J57 engines. LeMay, all too aware of the probability of budget-induced limitations on B-47 flight hours, argued in his usual forceful way for the adoption of the B-52.

In the end, as in most cases, LeMay won the argument and Boeing was given the go-ahead for mass production of the B-52, which had made its first flight in 1952. The first two aircraft were fitted with the tandem seating and streamlined canopy similar to that of the B-47, but LeMay rightfully insisted that the plane be redesigned with the two pilots sitting side by side, able to communicate with motions and gestures, and to provide more direct assistance if called upon.

No one, including LeMay himself, could have ever forecast the subsequent fantastic history of the B-52. Just its existence imposed an almost impossible demand for defense by potential enemies. The jet-powered heavy bomber demonstrated its ability by globe-circling trips to show the flag around the world, all the while retaining an unprecedented capacity for nuclear destruction.

From its first flight to the present day, the B-52 has projected American air power around the world. Fortunately, it was never required to use its nuclear capability in anger, but it has used its massive conventional bombing strength in myriad battles. Further, it has updated its capability by providing a perfect platform for the launch of missiles.

To an ex-B-50 pilot, the B-47 was like a sports car, while the B-52 performed like a truck. One essential advantage was the crosswind landing system, which made it possible to use the huge aircraft on days when there was a stiff crosswind component. When heavily loaded, one could see the "wings start to fly" long before the wheels were ready to leave the ground. All in all, the B-52 was a remarkable airplane, more advanced than any other bomber when it appeared, and versatile enough to still be in frontline service more than sixty years after its first flight.

The combination of the B-52 and the nuclear weapon creates an unimaginable force that can never be captured in film or on television. Dropping a live nuclear weapon at night from the B-52 is absolutely awesome. From 1958 to 1960, I had the privilege of assignment to the 4925th Test Group (Atomic) at Kirtland Air Force Base in New Mexico, with the official duty title of "nuclear test pilot." The 4925th conducted many of the major nuclear tests over the years and had an amazingly talented group of pilots, radar observers, and bombardiers assigned to it. Our missions were much easier than the typical Strategic Air Command (SAC) training mission and much shorter as well. Ordinarily, a six-hour mission featured an actual drop of a (non-nuclear) test bomb over the Salton Sea in Southern California, followed by electronic bomb runs on a number of cities.

The majority of the flying was done to establish the procedures for the conduct of dropping live nuclear weapons in a test area so that the maximum amount of information could be obtained from the minimum number of drops, and with the minimum radiation contamination. It involved drops from "as low as you dare" (which for me was probably fifty feet off the ground) to about fifty-two thousand feet. This was the maximum altitude our early-model B-52s could reach and required wearing an uncomfortable early pressure suit.

The B-52 was used in the last series of airborne nuclear tests in 1962. Typically conducted in the designated zone near Christmas Island, the B-52 would make a number of practice runs against the target. As many as one hundred other aircraft would be in the air to gather data covering the flight and, more importantly, to capture the subsequent explosion of the nuclear weapon from every possible angle. This included size, brilliance, radiation, accuracy, and more. The bomber would also be carefully monitored from the ground, inch by inch, as it burst through the black night sky.

It would then complete its "live" run, which was spectacular. A parachute-retarded nuclear bomb allowed the bomber to fly straight ahead after the drop. The first indication of detonation would be a quiver on the Mach meter as the first wave accelerated past the aircraft. The next indication would be when the light from the exploding bomb quite literally turned the night into day, the entirety of the heavens came alight brighter than the sun. The blast lit up the hemisphere as far as anyone could see, and the light was not like a flashbulb; it endured for moments before collapsing back upon itself into the dark night. I well recall that our radar navigator, a man noted for his accuracy but not his philosophy, remarked that "every head of state should see a nuclear explosion in person—it would make them realize just how powerful the weapons are."

You heave a sigh of relief—a successful mission, one less to do, and no harm done to anyone! Now, some five decades after these tests, the B-52 labors on, not dropping nuclear weapons (but some with the capability still to do so). Instead, the venerable warplane serves as the workhorse carpet-bombing threat that can meet any emergency on any continent at a moment's notice. It's an old aircraft—in some instances the B-52 has been flown by the grandsons of the men who first flew it—but it is still going strong and will be around for at least another three or four decades. It has become not only the best and most useful bomber, but the least expensive to use because of its longevity—the best bargain in military history.

•••

The B-52 is a mainstay of the US bomber fleet. Though officially named the Stratofortress, the subsonic bomber is more often called the BUFF for Big Ugly Fat Fellow (while in less pristine jargon the last word is replaced by an alliterative expletive). The only model still flying is the B-52H. A total of 102 H models were built as the concluding segment of a production run that aggregated 744 aircraft.

The last B-52 rolled off the assembly line in October 1962. Virtually all crew members who currently fly aboard the bomber were born after it was built. The aircraft has undergone extensive structural modifications and avionics upgrades during its extended service life, keeping it an effective platform well into the twenty-first century. The miracle of its adaptability goes back to its development.

By the end of World War II, the jet engine was a reality that the air force sought to exploit in its emergent bombers. The problem was that the early jet engines failed to provide the blend of high thrust and efficient fuel consumption necessary to carry a heavily laden bomber great distances, as the air force requirement mandated. Not surprisingly, the first post–World War II heavy bomber was the mixed propulsion B-36 Peacemaker, which had a combination of propeller-driven and pure jet engines that were variously "turning and burning."

Boeing had conceived a scaled-up version of its B-29/B-50 with six turboprops. Meanwhile, though, Boeing was developing the XB-47, a futuristic medium bomber with swept wings and four jet engines mounted in cluster pods. Because of the thrust limitation, fifth and sixth jet engines were added in individual pods on either side near the wingtips. The promising possibilities of this jet-powered medium bomber led some on the Boeing design team to suggest that the heavy bomber should be similarly configured with pure jets rather than turboprops.

The imperative for a long-range strategic bomber was heightened in June 1948 when the Soviet Union blockaded the Western sectors of Berlin. It became clear that the United States would need a modern heavy-bomber force to counter the threat posed by the rising tensions of the Cold War. Against this backdrop of increased urgency, work on the B-52 continued with a heightened sense of purpose.

The air force procurement officer on the project, Colonel Pete Warden, was open to the idea of a pure jet design, but he wanted the turboprop configuration to remain a consideration. There are varying accounts of what happened next, but in general the story goes that on a Friday in mid-October 1948, Boeing's top designers and aerodynamicists—Ed Wells, George Schairer, Bob Withington, Vaughan Blumenthal, Art Carlsen, and Maynard Pennell—met with Colonel Warden at Wright-Patterson Air Force Base in Ohio.

Reportedly Colonel Warden told the men at that point that a pure jet design was the way to go after all, but that the configuration they had presented was deficient for it would hold back the bomber's speed. They needed a greater angle of sweep, closer to that of the B-47, and more engines than the six adopted for the B-47. The Boeing team regrouped in a room at Dayton's Van Cleve Hotel and worked nonstop through the weekend, sparing no effort to create the definitive design. They even obtained balsa wood from a local hobby shop to sculpt a model of their proposed heavy bomber.

First thing Monday morning the team showed up in Colonel Warden's office with the model fittingly decorated in air force colors. Also, they submitted a thirty-three-page report revealing performance, engineering, production, and cost details that represented the culmination of their extraordinary exertions over the weekend. The wing was swept thirty-five degrees and the aircraft was to be powered by eight engines mounted in four under-wing pods of two engines each.

Though it defied the odds, the design thrashed out that weekend by the team from Seattle proved to be an engineering marvel. The design that derived from such improbable circumstances led to the B-52, which profoundly affected the balance of power for the generation to come and remains a bulwark of American might.

As indicated, maiden flight occurred less than four years later, on April 15, 1952. Lead test pilot was the flamboyant Tex Johnston, Boeing's choice to take the helm on this important foray. The flight lasted nearly three hours as Tex and his copilot, Air Force Lieutenant Colonel Guy Townsend, got the feel of the new plane.

It was soon determined that the bubble-type canopy under which the pilot and copilot were seated in tandem should be changed to a more conventional bomber flight deck layout with side-by-side seating. Landing gear consisted of bicycle-type twin-row trucks of two wheels each spaced along the length of the lower fuselage. Innovatively, the wheels could pivot to remain in line with the runway as the aircraft crabbed at an angle in a crosswind. Lithe outrigger gear at the wingtips kept the fuel-laden wings from drooping to the ground and scraping against the taxiway/runway pavement.

A wing with a high angle of incidence permitted rotation while the aircraft was still positioned horizontally. Auxiliary power for the many power requirements in the massive airframe came from a bleed-air system driving small turbines. The original Pratt & Whitney J57 turbojets, which produced eighty-seven hundred pounds of thrust, were accompanied by deafening howls and black smoke trails. Reflecting the myriad improvements to the aircraft over its amazingly long time in service is the fact that today's Pratt & Whitney TF-33 turbofan engines are rated at nearly double the thrust level of the bomber's earliest engines.

The first combat-capable version was the B-52B, which achieved readiness in June 1955. The first large production run was of the B-52D. Some of the D models were constructed at Boeing's Wichita, Kansas, plant, supplementing the Seattle output. The most numerous model was the B-52G. All G models were produced in Wichita.

The G model moved the tail gunner position forward to a monitoring screen for the automated four .50-caliber machine guns. The aircraft could accommodate the then-new AGM-28 Hound Dog standoff cruise missiles on two inboard wing pylons. A shortened tail fin graphically changed the side-view profile. Also the fuel tanks were made an integral part of the wing which allowed for structural strengthening.

The final model was the B-52H, also built exclusively at the Wichita plant. Notably, it received an engine upgrade that not only boosted thrust, but improved consumption to where a 30 percent increase in unrefueled range was possible. The machine guns in the tail were replaced by the Vulcan gun system with six 20-mm cannon. Today's crews consist of five: the aircraft commander, pilot, and electronic warfare officer (seated in the upper flight deck where there is a fourth seat available for an instructor), radar navigator, and navigator (seated on the lower flight deck); all six positions have ejection seats.

The B-52 was a key asset of Strategic Air Command. The bomber frequently flew long-range high-altitude missions in preparation for a nuclear counterstrike against the Soviet Union. However, with the rise of a sophisticated surface-to-air missile threat, doctrine shifted and the bombers started to fly low-level missions as a means to avoid radar detection. The increased flying in thicker and more turbulent air near the ground necessitated structural upgrades to the B-52 fleet.

Under the hard-charging SAC commander, Curtis LeMay, B-52 flight and maintenance crews were forged into an exceptionally professional fighting force. SAC operated with great regimentation. It was an organization that exemplified the virtues of discipline and teamwork.

Largely because of the finely honed skills of SAC's personnel and the unparalleled efficacy of its bombers, Soviet leaders did not dare to tap the tripwire. The certainty of catastrophic consequences prevented the Cold War from erupting into a shooting war. SAC's motto of "Peace through strength" provided an epigrammatic description of the winning strategy. Without a single bomb being dropped in anger, the generational contest ended in a euphoric moment at the wall in Berlin where it had symbolically begun.

It was in the unlikely airspace over the jungles of Vietnam that the B-52 got its baptism of fire. Raids started on June 18, 1965. B-52Fs flying from Andersen Air Force Base in Guam ranged over preselected sites in South Vietnam where the Viet Cong were thought to be operating. The bombing campaign, characterized by long flights and questionable effects, ensued for years under the code name Arc Light. As the war dragged on, some missions were flown out of the much closer U Tapao Air Base in Thailand.

Frustration reached the boiling point in late 1972 when North Vietnam would not negotiate in earnest at the Paris Peace Talks. Massive raids were ordered to jump-start the stalled diplomacy. For eleven days in December, the skies over North Vietnam reverberated with the roar of waves of B-52s. Hanoi and Haiphong, the North's two major cities, were targeted like never before.

Because the airspace was more heavily defended than any other in the history of air warfare up to that time, B-52 losses were considerable. The array of top-line Soviet surface-to-air missile batteries caused an attrition rate of 7 percent after the first three nights of bombing. Tactics employed in the bombing campaign, known as Linebacker II, were flawed and contributed to the toll. Changes were implemented and SAM positions were targeted with renewed vigor, which improved the situation.

The relentless pounding, in coordination with other air force and navy attack aircraft, had a substantial impact. Not only did the North Vietnamese take up negotiations again in Paris, but the North's military leaders along with a large portion of the North's population were deeply shaken. It was revealed years afterwards that officials in the North had doubted their ability to continue resisting because of Linebacker II's devastation.

Interestingly, SAM defenses had been depleted, which meant that the skies would have been virtually open to US bombers had raids continued. When the constraining rules of engagement had been lifted by US policymakers, measurable results were evidenced. All of this has caused some analysts to wonder what outcome might have been achieved if such ferocious air strikes had been unleashed early in the war.

For nearly the next two decades, the B-52 force refocused on the Cold War. Crews remained on alert in scramble huts near their bombers, ready to launch retaliatory strikes on a moment's notice. The nuclear-armed B-52s were a main component of the nuclear triad which still includes them as part of the bomber component along with land-based ICBMs and submarine-launched ballistic missiles.

When the Iron Curtain finally came crumbling down on November 9, 1989, there was but a brief sigh of relief for US airmen. In 1990 Kuwait, a small and vulnerable country rich in oil reserves, had been overrun by its belligerent neighbor to the north. In conjunction with a large coalition of international partners, US air strikes were ordered against Iraq in early 1991.

In the opening phase of Operation Desert Storm, seven B-52s from Barksdale Air Force Base in Louisiana embarked on a mission to Saudi airspace where they employed Conventional Air Launched Cruise Missiles (CALCMs) against designated targets in Iraq. The bombers then returned to their home base in what was the most distant bomb run in history up to that time. The nonstop mission involved multiple air refuelings and lasted a grueling thirty-five hours.

Isolated carpet bombing was successful in compelling Iraqi troops to abandon their positions and surrender. B-52s delivered more than twenty-seven thousand tons of bombs. In little more than a month of aerial bombardment and a matter of only a few days of land warfare, Kuwaiti sovereignty was restored.

The following year, with the Cold War lapsing into faded memories, the air force was restructured to better contend with new global challenges. Strategic Air Command was inactivated; its B-52s were transferred to the newly established Air Combat Command. In the post-Soviet era, with no strong-fisted global power imposing its will in forgotten corners of the world, long-simmering ethnic divisions broke out in the Balkans.

In the spring of 1999, Operation Allied Force commenced against Serbian forces to stop so-called ethnic cleansing against Albanian and Muslim majorities in Yugoslavia's Kosovo province. B-52s staged for sorties at RAF Fairford in England. These operations initially involved use of CALCMs and soon entailed gravity bombs. The ethnic cleansing at first accelerated, but as the bombing ramped up, the Serbian forces stood down and a peace agreement was signed on June 9th.

Any thought of mothballing the fleet of aging bombers ended on September 11, 2001. Jihadi terrorists hijacked four domestic US airliners. Two were rammed into the twin towers of the World Trade Center and one was flown into the side of the Pentagon. Passengers were aroused on the fourth airliner, and after a fight for control it slammed into a field near Shanksville, Pennsylvania.

Nearly three thousand people were killed. Most of the victims were civilians. The horrifying acts prompted a military response less than a month later. As Operation Enduring Freedom unfolded, B-52s and other bombers aided the takedown of Afghanistan's Taliban government and the scattering of the al-Qaeda terrorist organization's key leaders. In addition to bombs, B-52s dropped propaganda leaflets.

With radicalized elements in the Middle East seemingly intent on obtaining weapons of mass destruction, fears grew in Western capitals that Iraqi dictator Saddam Hussein may have developed such weapons. Though the suspicions were later determined to be unfounded, the United States decided once and for all to remove Saddam from power. It was not emphasized in the rationale for the invasion, but policymakers considered humanitarian grounds to be a basis for the intervention given Saddam's brutality. Also it was thought that Saddam's removal might cause a new, more hopeful dynamic to take root in the troubled region.

B-52s played a role in Operation Iraqi Freedom, which got under-way the night of March 20, 2003. Flying from Fairford and the island of Diego Garcia, the B-52s pummeled Iraqi forces with a variety of ordnance. The air campaign persisted for eighteen days until Saddam's regime was toppled.

The bomber has proven to be a versatile delivery platform. It can be configured for the full range of bomber/attack missions, including nuclear strikes, conventional saturation bombing, and surgical blows. Before the air force had deployed a large number of Predator/Reaper unmanned aerial vehicles to the conflict in Southwest Asia, the B-52H served as a kind of close air support aircraft, loitering high above the battlefield for long dura-tions and launching precision-guided weapons as directed by ground troops.

Concerns over the integrity of the US nuclear arsenal arose when a succession of troubling incidents demonstrated that oversight and proper handling were deficient. A number of senior officials, including both the air force secretary and chief of staff, were replaced. A new organization was established to renew the high levels of safety, security, and effective-ness that nuclear weapons warrant and that were manifest during the time of the vaunted Strategic Air Command.

Air Force Global Strike Command was activated on August 7, 2009, to assume this important responsibility. The B-52 fleet, the sole B-2 wing, and the three remaining ICBM wings came under its purview at that time. On October 1, 2015, the two B-1 wings, which are no longer nuclear capable, transferred from Air Combat Command to Global Strike Com-mand, placing all of the country's long-range heavy bombers under the same command structure.

A current focus is on the Pacific Rim, as China flexes its new-found muscle and the irascible North Korean regime continues to make mis-chief. B-52Hs are currently rotated on a virtual permanent basis at Andersen Air Force Base in Guam. With air tanker support, this outpost in the Pacific gives the bombers a springboard to reach points in Asia.

There are sixty-five combat-coded B-52s left in active duty (split between Barksdale Air Force Base in Louisiana and Minot Air Force Base in North Dakota). Eleven are in the reserves at Barksdale. A roughly similar number of combat-coded B-1s is in the operational inventory and nineteen B-2s remain combat coded. The total heavy-bomber count today is exceedingly small by historical standards. Because these bombers have precision strike capability, substantially fewer airframes are required to hit a given target set. Yet the fact that so few comprise the force means that there is hardly any margin for attrition.

Despite its age, the B-52 has continued to demonstrate its worth. Both the air force and prime contractor Boeing see the old bomber soldiering on for years to come. Indeed, an air force study has projected that the B-52H can remain a viable military platform through 2044, and Boeing has indicated that the aircraft can keep flying through 2060, based on a structural service life of eighty thousand hours. If the latter comes true, B-52s—the actual airframes of the models currently flying—will achieve an operational span of ninety-nine years!

One modernization idea was to swap out the B-52's eight aging engines with four engines of the type used on either the Lockheed C-5 cargo plane or the Boeing 757 airliner. This would have led to significantly reduced maintenance and higher fuel efficiency, but was rejected because of the estimated time and cost to integrate the aerodynamics-changing retrofit. Instead, attention focused on the possibility of doing an engine-for-engine swap so that the aircraft's configuration would remain essentially unchanged.

Under this proposal, the replacements would be off-the-shelf engines used on regional airliners or high-end business jets, offering better maintainability, sustainability, and performance. From an environmental standpoint these engines would be drastically less polluting and much quieter. Also additional thrust would permit the carriage of a heavier payload. Pratt & Whitney, manufacturer of the bomber's decades-old TF33 engines, advocates upgrading them through targeted design changes, which it claims would be the lowest-cost solution.

Beyond modifications to keep the B-52 viable as a flying machine, extensive avionics and weapons upgrades continue to be implemented to enhance the aircraft as a combat platform. One of the more important programs is the coming replacement of the B-52's outdated APQ-166 radar. Meanwhile, phased installation of the Combat Network Communications Technology (CONECT) is occurring to integrate the bomber into network-centric operations. With the addition of the Link 16 data link, the B-52 will have an unmatched ability for secure communication with other mission aircraft.

Whereas in the past, human-to-human communication via voice was necessary, it will be possible for vital data to be transmitted machine to machine. This technology will simplify and speed up the transfer of target coordinates to the B-52 from ground-based tactical air controllers. By eliminating tasks in the data transfer process, the so-called kill chain will be compressed and there will be less probability of flawed data entry.

The B-52 dropped the thirty thousand-pound GBU-57A/B Massive Ordnance Penetrator (MOP) in tests. Though currently qualified to be carried only by the B-2, this huge bomb can slice through two hundred feet of earth before detonating its five thousand-pound conventional warhead. The MOP would probably be used against Iran's deeply buried high-value nuclear program sites if the already strained relations between the United States and the Islamic republic take a turn for the worse.

Separately, installations of an upgraded rotary launcher have begun. Along with an electrical power system enhancement, this will give the B-52 the ability to carry large numbers of the precision Joint Air-to-Surface Standoff Missile (JASSM) internally. Also in the works is the follow-on cruise missile, known as the Long-Range Standoff (LRSO) weapon, which will eventually equip the B-52.

With further modifications and upgrades in the years to come, some current crew members speculate that the B-52 will be around long enough for their children and maybe even their grandchildren to fly it. Little could Boeing's design team have known during the drawn-out weekend at the Van Cleve Hotel, sketching configurations, running numbers, and fashioning a balsa wood model that their labors would yield such a long-lived warplane. The air force has already stated that it expects the B-52 Stratofortress to complement the next bomber, the B-21 Raider, when it enters service, scheduled for the mid-2020s.

CHAPTER 22

Stealth: The Black World's
F-117 Nighthawk

Modern stealth is largely the outgrowth of Middle East air warfare. In the opening days of the 1973 Yom Kippur War, Israel's last major conventional war, Soviet-supplied surface-to-air missiles (SAMs) strategically positioned around key Egyptian targets knocked down Israeli combat planes at an alarming rate. Things got so bad that it looked like the theretofore invincible Israeli Air Force would not be able to sustain the attrition rate, leaving the Jewish state vulnerable to the whim of Arab leaders who almost without exception clamored brazenly for annihilation.

To prevent the unthinkable from happening, the Nixon administration initiated an urgent airlift to resupply Israel's rapidly depleting stock of weaponry. Israel regained its footing after having been caught off guard in the surprise attack on the holiest day of the Jewish calendar. The uneasy status quo of the seemingly endless standoff between Israel and its neighboring states soon resumed. But for Western air-power analysts, it was clear that existing technology and doctrine would have to change.

A Pentagon study of the situation concluded that if Soviet and Warsaw Pact forces went up against America and its Western allies in a non-nuclear confrontation in Eastern Europe, where the equipment and training on both sides were essentially of the same caliber of the participants in the Yom Kippur War, US air assets would be all but wiped out within a mere seventeen days. This frightening prospect prompted the Defense Department to seek a solution in a hurry. By the mid-1970s a top-secret program was gearing up to develop stealth as the silver bullet to defeat the Soviet Union's dire SAM threat.

In 1974 the Defense Advanced Research Projects Agency (DARPA) invited five well-known aerospace contractors to participate in a hush-hush program code-named Project Harvey to develop an aircraft with low observables across various spectra, starting with radar and including infrared, optical, and acoustic. (The project's name derived from the 1950 Jimmy Stewart movie that featured an invisible rabbit named Harvey.) Since Lockheed had not built a fighter since its 1950s-vintage F-104 Starfighter, the company was not among the five invitees. Nevertheless, the company's Skunk Works unit got wind of the program and its leader, thermodynamics specialist Ben Rich, used his contacts to get a foot in the door. The Skunk Works had to obtain permission from the CIA before informing DARPA of its success in reducing the radar cross-sections of its spy planes.

By the time of Lockheed's entry into the program, McDonnell Douglas and Northrop had already received small contracts for preliminary studies. But the math and radar wizards at the Skunk Works are the ones who broke the intellectual lock to the treasure chest of modern stealth, the kind of cloaking that could make a full-size fighter aircraft the equivalent of a tiny speck in electromagnetic terms. Point man was Denys Overholser, a thirty-six year-old who gave new meaning to the word geek. He was assisted by octogenarian Bill Schroeder, the Skunk Works' sage on radar reflectivity, who came out of retirement expressly for the project.

The breakthrough came when Overholser realized that an obscure technical paper written by Pyotr Ufimtsev, a Soviet expert, contained the means to make an airplane virtually undetectable or untrackable by radar. What Overholser gleaned from the dense content of the paper, which had been translated into English by Air Force Systems Command's Foreign Technology Division in 1971, was not apparent to the paper's author. This represented an incredible irony: An American aerospace giant would use the gist of a scientific report that emanated from the Soviet Union to develop advanced technology that would leapfrog the Soviet military.

In February 1975 Dick Scherrer joined the Skunk Works to head the design team for this revolutionary aircraft. In a matter of weeks following the breakthrough, the team presented a sketch of their stealth concept. Its shape, as envisaged from the overhead perspective, resembled a diamond or, more precisely, an Indian arrowhead. Sarcastically, it was called the "Hopeless Diamond." If it would work, as the in-house sorcerers had calculated, using not slide rules but sophisticated computer programs, then the Skunk Works would be on the road to shaking up air warfare in ways more profound than its game-changing U-2 and SR-71.

Almost from the start, it seemed the effort might quickly be snuffed out—and by an unlikely transgressor. Clarence L. "Kelly" Johnson, the longtime Lockheed designer who founded the Skunk Works, had retired, but the Burbank, California, facility was stamped with his imprint and the iron-willed taskmaster kept an office onsite which he visited every week. His advice was sought regularly by the old hands who had spent part of their careers working with the man who many considered the industry's towering figure. So it was jarring to the team behind the new stealth configuration that Johnson declared his skepticism.

Noted for his bluntness, Johnson marched into his handpicked successor's office shortly after perusing the rendering of the Hopeless Diamond, and without warning, he literally kicked an unawares Ben Rich in the rump. In his memoir, cowritten with Leo Janos nearly twenty years later, Rich still remembered the incident because the wallop had not only stunned him but was "hard too." Johnson's strong hands then scrunched the Skunk Works' project proposal into a wad. Continuing to fume, he then tossed it to the floor. Without losing his rhythm, he blurted out a vulgarity laced barrage at Rich, concluding: "This crap will never get off the ground."

Any other executive would be fired, probably on the spot, for such aggressive and demeaning behavior in the workplace. But this was Kelly Johnson, the arm-wrestling brawler from northern Michigan who even competitors had to acknowledge was a design genius with a talent for delivering cutting-edge aircraft under budget and ahead of schedule. The secret developmental projects unit he had established at Lockheed during World War II to produce the P-80 Shooting Star, America's first operational jet fighter, had become the envy of the industry, a model for all organizations seeking to spur innovation, and a symbol of the American can-do spirit.

Much of his success could be credited to his "14 Points," the rules he laid down for his coworkers as Chief Skunk. These tenets he espoused with religious fervor and enforced as if they were the Ten Commandments. Some of the points, paraphrased: Keep personnel headcount at the minimum necessary; monitor costs carefully; trust between the company and its customers is everything; job performance matters and compensation should be tied to it; keep security tight. His mantra was captured best in his tart exhortation to employees: "Be quick, be quiet, be on time."

Johnson hovered over the Skunk Works like an in-your-face emperor. He was always demanding, and usually right, on technical questions. With a combination of professional excellence, a fire in the belly to get things to work, a prodigious imagination, and a domineering personality, he was the embodiment of the Skunk Works. Rich wrote in his memoir that Johnson's "personality and character were branded on everything we did." Attempts at imitation in later years, whether at Lockheed or the many other organizations that have sought to pattern themselves after the famed workshop / think tank, have usually fallen short. There was only one Kelly Johnson.

Johnson believed, as was common in aviation design circles, that an airplane will fly as good as its aesthetics suggest—a nicely styled aircraft with clean lines will fly well and one looking lumpish will disappoint in the air. Rich and his colleagues went along with that idea, but in their stealth concept the primary concern was avoidance of detection so that the design driver became low observables rather than aerodynamics. This gave the concept an odd appearance—like the coupling of a medieval suit of armor with a Lego-like toy plane in the shape of a diamond as seen from above. Johnson did not care about the extenuating circumstance; stealth notwithstanding, a diamond shape represented too much of a compromise in flying performance. He was not swayed that the old cliché about looking right to fly right could be violated.

A mock-up of the Hopeless Diamond was set to be tested in an electromagnetic chamber against a mock-up of the Skunk Works' little manta ray-configured D-21 drone. Developed as a mini spy platform, the drone was considered the stealthiest aircraft that the Skunk Works had produced up to that point. Johnson had been integrally involved in its evolution.

Perhaps Johnson's complaints about the Hopeless Diamond were rooted in part in his pride in the D-21 and the natural desire to not see one's invention upstaged. He continued to argue that it was a fool's errand to pursue the new, oddly shaped stealth concept. Johnson went so far as to bet his friend Rich a symbolic quarter that the Hopeless Diamond would fail to have a smaller radar cross-section in the technical comparison with the D-21. Not one to mince words, Johnson expressed his dim view of the Hopeless Diamond's supposed benign radar cross-section by blurting out: "Theoretical claptrap, Ben."

The test occurred on September 14, 1975. To Johnson's chagrin and Rich's relief, the diamond shape was "a thousand times stealthier" than the D-21. Rich collected on the one-quarter bet, which was "in some ways even more satisfying than winning the Irish Sweepstakes." As he flung the coin to Rich, Johnson cryptically remarked: "Don't spend it until you see the damned thing fly."

A further test of the mock-up mounted atop a pedestal at an outdoor test range confirmed the earlier test's findings. In fact, the mock-up had such a minimal radar cross-section that it failed to register at all on the range's detection equipment, baffling the monitoring technician. Suddenly, though, a radar return was picked up in the control booth. It turned out to be radar energy bouncing off a crow that dropped out of the sky to nest on the mock-up. An excited Rich knew then that his risky bet on a full-blown stealth design had been validated and that his team had generated the basis for domination of air warfare into the foreseeable future.

DARPA liked what it saw. The competition was narrowed down to just Northrop and Lockheed in what became the Experimental Survivable Test (XST) program. Both companies had used computer modeling to arrive at their configurations, which surpassed what any other aerospace contractors could offer in the way of stealthy concepts in the mid-1970s. In comprehensive evaluations of the competing mock-ups at the air force's radar target scatter test range at White Sands, New Mexico, the Skunk Works' design won easily.

Northrop's design was remarkably similar in general appearance to the Skunk Works' entry, and DARPA was sufficiently impressed with it that Northrop was encouraged to continue its low-observables studies. The company's XST design evolved into the Tacit Blue technology demonstrator that was variously called the Whale or the Flying Bathtub, for its odd appearance. The aircraft was flown in secret in 1984 and 1985 as a part of the Pentagon's Black World. While advancing stealth technology, it also incorporated a sophisticated Hughes radar which was designed to detect ground movement. Tacit Blue's success contributed to the development of Northrop's B-2 stealth bomber and E-8 Joint-STARS ground surveillance aircraft.

In April 1976 the Skunk Works received a contract for two flying demonstrators to prove the feasibility of marrying stealth to an airframe which could operate effectively as a tactical aircraft. The program was code-named Have Blue. The aircraft were assembled at the Skunk Works' Burbank facility, under the same roof as earlier trailblazing planes like the U-2.

Have Blue was highly classified and yet constrained by the tight budget environment of the 1970s. Off-the-shelf parts were used as much as possible, and these were delivered by circuitous means as a way to mask their intended purpose. Each aircraft had two General Electric J85 non-afterburning engines that were scrounged up from the navy's T-2 Buckeye trainer inventory. Ben Rich, who thrived on cracking jokes, later quipped that the engines were by GE but the body was by Houdini.

The two single-seat aircraft, referred to as Blue 01 and Blue 02, featured the basic design elements that would become hallmarks of the production models—an external shape dominated by facetted panels, a pointy nose, a modified delta wing with a dramatic sweep, and two canted fins. The first platform was equipped with a sensor-laden nose boom and an externally mounted spin chute, since its main objective was to determine handling qualities. The second platform did not have these items as it was to verify the stealth qualities.

Because of compromised aerodynamics dictated by the primary concern to minimize radar cross-section, the aircraft needed a fly-by-wire flight control system. To ensure its integrity the system was quad-redundant. It turned out that the configuration lent itself to nose-up pitching tendencies, which were balanced by a two-piece tail-mounted flap known as the platypus. Control surfaces consisted of elevons and the fins, which were all-moving.

To start flight trials, Blue 01 was disassembled and loaded into an air force C-5 cargo plane. On November 16, 1977, it was ferried from Burbank to Area 51, the ultrasecret test range in the remote Nevada desert that had been selected by Kelly Johnson and Lockheed test pilot Tony LeVier back in the 1950s as the ideal location for flight testing the most highly classified aircraft. At Area 51, Blue 01 was reassembled and started flying on November 30th.

On May 4, 1978, after two dozen flights, Blue 01 suffered a landing accident. Company test pilot Bill Park was injured but survived. Despite the loss of the first demonstrator, the data gained during the flights left no doubt that the design was airworthy. Blue 02 started its flight test program in July. Flights continued for a year, proving the platform's stealthiness. On July 11, 1979, during one of its last scheduled flights shortly before reaching the formal end of the test syllabus, the aircraft lost hydraulic pressure in an engine fire. Air force major Norman Dyson ejected safely.

Although both demonstrators were wrecked due to in-flight anomalies, the program was considered a success since the test objectives had been achieved. Have Blue demonstrated that a stealth aircraft was possible. The focus then changed to weaponizing the platform.

A sign that Pentagon officials considered the Soviet SAM threat a clear and present danger was the fact that the Skunk Works received an unprecedented production contract while the Have Blue flight tests were still occurring. Under the code name Senior Trend, the Skunk Works was to produce five full-scale developmental aircraft and twenty operational models. The fighter was assigned the designation F-117A, deliberately out of the air force's White World sequencing, to preserve the program's anonymity. Payload of the stealth aircraft would be limited, so to be effective it needed a precision munitions delivery system. Success would depend on the ability to integrate that system with the exotic airframe.

A full-scale wooden mock-up was assembled at Burbank in 1979. The mock-up gave engineers a practical means to work out design details.

Plans were made for flight test to be conducted by a joint contractor / air force test organization at Area 51.

An ambitious production calendar was adopted with first flight of the full-scale developmental aircraft planned for July 1980. However, the state-of-the-art design presented novel challenges in the manufacturing process. First flight occurred at Area 51 on June 18, 1981, but before the landing gear could be retracted the aircraft was recalled because of over-heating in the engine exhaust system.

A more serious problem arose on the second flight thirteen days later. When the landing gear was retracted shortly after takeoff, the plane started to yaw. This phenomenon was attributed to a lack of fin surface area. The solution was to retrofit the few airframes already manufactured with larger fins and to adjust assembly-line construction accordingly. Counterintuitively, the larger fin area helped to lower the radar cross-section.

The incident led to the aircraft being tagged the "Wobblin' Goblin." Somehow the derisive appellation leaked out of the Black World. As a result, many people incorrectly believed that the instability of these early stealth aircraft doomed the production lot to poor handling characteristics.

The full-scale developmental aircraft were used to test the various systems from avionics to low observables and from navigation to weapons targeting. It became clear that the original date for initial operational capability, of March 1982, would slip because of a combination of integration and manufacturing complications. These challenges were formidable, given the revolutionary nature of the aircraft, but the Skunk Works took it all in stride and pressed ahead when any other organization at the time would likely have been overwhelmed.

The point of the plane was to minimize and deflect radar energy. The computing power available when the F-117 was conceived in the 1970s could go only so far in modeling the stealth design. This led to the airframe having a facetted fuselage and a wing with a sweep of sixty-seven and a half degrees.

In addition to the shape being optimized for a low radar cross-section, the materials used on the aircraft's surface had properties to reduce radar reflectivity. Originally, the Skunk Works used a radar-absorbent material (RAM) known as BX210, which was glued on in sheets. Each application was tantamount to a custom job, which made the process prohibitively expensive. Worse was that the adhesive could loosen if exposed to hydraulic fluid and other liquids.

A substitute was quickly developed, which was applied by hand sprayer. In 1984 a further improvement came in the form of BX199, which was sprayed on robotically to ensure consistent coatings on the multiple airframe panels. The aircraft's nose-mounted infrared acquisition and designation system presented its own low-observable hurdles. How could the system pass infrared and laser energy through an aperture but remain impervious to radar?

After considering a few different possibilities, Alan Brown, the Skunk Works' F-117 program manager, developed a fine-wire screen of stainless steel as an interim solution. Interestingly, two apertures were necessary, one in the topside of the nose and another in the bottom of the nose to accommodate a forward-looking infrared turret and a downward-looking infrared turret, respectively. A normal targeting pod would allow for a wide field of view, but in a stealth aircraft the protrusions of a pod had to be avoided.

The F-117 was powered by two General Electric F404 non-afterburning turbofan engines. Exhaust ducting to rectangular slotted exit nozzles was aimed at lowering both the infrared and radar signatures. In return for the contribution to low observables, the engines paid the penalty of a 15 percent decrease in maximum thrust to 9,040 pounds per engine. Importantly, the engine inlets were located atop the wing to shelter them from ground radars. An angled grid over each inlet acted as a facetted surface to deflect radar energy, plus the grid was coated with RAM.

Unlike a conventional fighter with an air-to-air capability, the F-117 was a dedicated ground attack platform. Its doctrinal predicate was the opening up of hostile airspace to subsequent waves of conventional warplanes. In other words, this newfangled fighter would use its unique protective outer shell to slip through sophisticated air defenses and bust open the "barn door" to enable the so-called "bomb trucks" to come storming through to wreak havoc on selected targets.

The only weapons available to the F-117 were carried in two relatively compact weapons bays in the aircraft's belly. They were released by separate trapezes in each bay. A typical weapons load consisted of two two-thousand-pound guided bombs like the GBU-27 equipped with a Paveway III laser guidance kit.

Almost from the beginning of the Black World's stealth program, rumors swirled in the aviation community about sightings of an odd-looking jet optimized for stealth. The speculation was put to rest on August 22, 1980, when Defense Secretary Harold Brown announced "a major technological advance" involving stealth that would enable the country to build aircraft immune from the danger posed by then-existing air defenses. The decision to go public before the first full-scale developmental aircraft had flown raised eyebrows among people in the know.

President Jimmy Carter was in the midst of a hotly contested reelection campaign in which challenger Ronald Reagan had decried cutbacks in force structure. Reagan singled out the cancellation of the B-1 bomber and promised to restart the factory. For his part, Brown defended his announcement, pointing to increasing leaks of the aircraft's existence as well as the need to expand the number of people working on the burgeoning stealth program.

Still, no one outside the Black World had a clue what this covert aircraft looked like. At the Edwards Air Force Base open houses in the mid-1980s, some clever airmen roped off a section of the static display ramp and posted a sign that read "Stealth Fighter." It was a gag, as though to say the plane's stealthiness succeeds so well that it is invisible to the naked eye.

In 1986 well-known plastic model builder Testors released a 1/48-scale model of its conception of the mystery plane. Looking as if it had been patterned after Lockheed's familiar SR-71, it was dubbed the F-19 Stealth Fighter, based on the most recent assigned fighter designations of F-16 (for General Dynamics's Fighting Falcon) and F/A-18 (for McDonnell Douglas's Hornet). Reportedly the kit sold seven hundred thousand copies, the highest number for any plastic model kit in history.

Two years later, the public would realize that the Testors's configuration was terribly wrong. Based on new, authoritative information, the plastic model's designation was as way off as its shape. On November 10,

1988, the Pentagon released a fuzzy photograph of the F-117A, giving a first look at the much-discussed but never-before-seen aircraft.

Importantly, the revelation allowed the F-117s of the 4450th Tactical Group to start flying in the daytime at the Tonopah Test Range in Nevada. While the aircraft would only be used in combat during the night to maximize cloaking, the night-only flying that had been mandated up until then had caused ongoing problems with pilots and ground crews. Unnatural circadian rhythms and disrupted family life had turned the flying job into a grind. Moreover, during this period in the 1980s, the couple of fatal accidents involving Nighthawks, as F-117s were nicknamed, may have been caused, in part, because of the fatigue associated with the night-flying protocol.

The F-117's combat debut sowed doubt about its prowess. An international imbroglio was triggered in May 1989 when Panamanian strongman Manuel Noriega rejected the results of his country's election, making it clear that he refused to let go of power. In a snub to the United Sates, which had long ties to the Central American nation, Noriega accepted military aid from traditional American antagonists like Cuba's Fidel Castro.

Tensions were further heightened by the possibility that Noriega might attempt to restrict passage of United States and allied ships through the Panama Canal. Another factor compounding the situation was that Noriega had been indicted by US courts for laundering drug money. President George H. W. Bush decided to act when a US serviceman was killed and another taken into custody.

In the wee hours of December 20th, a couple Nighthawks that had been en route from Tonopah via five aerial refuelings dropped one GBU-27 each in a field adjacent to barracks of the Sixth and Seventh Rifle Companies of the Panamanian Defense Forces at Rio Hato. The idea was to stun and disorient Noriega's forces. Observers questioned the use of America's most advanced planes, given that there was no sophisticated air defense system to take down. However, US planners felt it made sense to use aircraft known to have a night-precision strike capability. In addition, President Bush insisted that every resource of the nation be put to work in support of American troops on the ground.

Much confusion accompanied the mission, which was initially to include an attack on two Noriega residences until it was determined that the notorious dictator had abandoned them. The two bombs dropped by the Nighthawks did not land exactly where intended and their value in any case was dubious because the Panamanian troops were not asleep, as had been expected. On January 3, 1990, Noriega was arrested and flown to the United States where a trial resulted in his incarceration. Panama returned to normalcy with the duly-elected government assuming office. The desired outcome was achieved, but the Nighthawk's role had been minor and left people scratching their heads about whether this highly touted combat plane would live up to all the hype surrounding it.

The doubts were erased at 02:51 hours Baghdad time on January 17, 1991. Lieutenant Colonel Greg Feest, the same pilot who had dropped the first bomb in Operation Just Cause, did likewise in Operation Desert Storm. Flying the same F-117A he had flown on the Panama mission, this time he went after a high-value communications bunker which linked perimeter radars with Iraqi air defense headquarters. He released one of his two thousand-pound laser-guided bombs and reported that he saw "the bomb go through the cross-hairs and penetrate the bunker," blowing the doors off.

The Iraqi capital suddenly lit up with anti-aircraft tracers and flares. Soon video of the wild scene was streamed live on cable news around the world. Like the other Nighthawk pilots flying missions in the dark of that early morning, Feest did not know if his aircraft's inherent stealth would protect him in what was inarguably the most heavily defended airspace in the history of war.

The fact that all the F-117s made it back to Saudi Arabia later in the morning was a testament to the Skunk Works. A 100 percent retrieval of attacking planes under even a fraction of such intense fire was unheard of. Over the next forty-three nights, forty-one Nighthawks carried out 1,247 sorties and not only were none lost but reports claimed the jets returned without a scratch.

A further sign of the success of the Nighthawks was that they inflicted a disproportionate share of damage on targets struck from the air, given their small percentage of the coalition's total sorties, even if not the one-to-forty ratio originally cited. By one analysis, the stealth aircraft had a hit rate of 75 to 80 percent. This estimate encountered a good deal of skepticism, but even if cut in half the percentage was still high by historical measures.

The black jets had paid off in a big way. Because of their stealth and precision, just eight Nighthawks supported by two air tankers achieved the battle space effect of a traditional attack package consisting of over thirty strike fighters and more than forty support aircraft. Not only did this differential in combat packages represent an equipment cost savings of $5 billion, but with the employment of the stealth alternative only eight service personnel—the F-117 pilots—would be in harm's way versus the dozens at risk if the customary strike package were used. The air tasking calculus had turned completely around; instead of trying to decide how many planes it would take to destroy a target, planners were deciding how many targets to assign to a strike package.

In addition to stealth aircraft and precision munitions, the new hardware of Desert Storm's air campaign included space-based assets (which enabled exceptional communication, navigation, and targeting). Combining and coordinating these elements contributed greatly to the takedown of Iraqi defenses and the liberation of Kuwait, which occurred after only three days of ground fighting. Precision was on its way to being a standard feature of air warfare. Importantly, the modern technology was coupled with an evolving doctrine that called for attacking high-value targets like command-and-control nodes, radar sites, operational headquarters, central communications facilities, etc. In this way the enemy would be directionless, its frontline troops would be without air defense and cut off from their leadership. With the head of the "snake" severed from the body, the carcass could be finished off with relative ease. It could be said that the F-117 was partly the consequence of this doctrinal mindset and partly its inspiration.

Still, weapons makers have yet to produce a totally unassailable platform. Even the creators of the world's first true stealth aircraft never claimed their invention was infallible. The point was driven home on the night of March 27, 1999.

As part of Operation Allied Force, the United States and other NATO members were attempting to coerce Serbian leader Slobodan Milosevic into a peaceful resolution of the hostilities in Kosovo. An F-117 of Hollo-man Air Force Base's 49th Fighter Wing, piloted by Lieutenant Colonel Darrell P. Zelko, call sign Vega 31, had just released two GBU-27s on a heavily defended air defense node south of Belgrade. After apparently scoring direct hits on his target, Zelko turned sharply away and began to think about the flight back to Aviano Air Base in northern Italy.

Cruising at twenty-six thousand feet, he got as far as twenty miles northwest of Belgrade when two SA-3 radar-guided surface-to-air missiles came rushing up at his aircraft. One whizzed by terrifyingly close. The second exploded, ripping off a large section of the port wing and throwing the remaining hulk into a violent roll.

Fighting negative g-forces, Zelko was able to activate his ejection system. His parachute canopy blossomed and he floated down. In the next seven hours he evaded capture using techniques imparted during survival training. He was whisked away by US Air Force Special Opera-tions forces who executed a heart-pounding rescue.

Much remains classified regarding the F-117 shoot down, but some information has emerged. It appears that the Yugoslav 3rd Missile Bat-talion of the 250th Air Defense Missile Brigade, which launched the damaging salvo, had played its hand exceedingly well, as if in the ultimate high-stakes poker game. Under the command of Lieutenant Colonel Zoltan Dani, the air defense crew changed its position on the ground rather than remain a stationary target. Also it stayed off frequency as much as possible to avoid being a source for US HARM anti-radar mis-siles. These tactics are likely to have derived from lessons learned through failed SAM engagements earlier in the decade.

It is believed Serbian agents may have been planted in crowds gathered around Aviano Air Base, noting takeoff times. If so, the F-117 departures would have been relayed to the air defense units lying in wait. Moreover, Dani is said to have extracted position clues from eavesdropping on the unencrypted radio transmissions between that night's F-117s (Zelko's jet was one in a strike package of eight) and an AWACS command aircraft.

Contributing further, the black jets' routing by some accounts exactly replicated itself from the beginning of the air campaign four days ear-lier. This alone would have given a savvy air defense crew a slice of sky to concentrate on. Assuming that routes were not changed on a nightly basis, then F-117 mission planning reflected complacency, the sense that stealth by itself was an adequate shield when, in actuality, tactical insouciance can cause an alert opponent to quickly seize the initiative, turn the tables, and gain the advantage.

As the first stealth design matured, it appears that its facetted surfaces and early RAM were subject to budding counter-stealth techniques, including the use of lower frequencies which exploit surface wave effects. To compensate, mission profiles were thought to include active-jamming escorts. Reports indicated that electronic countermeasures were to be incorporated in Vega 31's strike package by means of the participation of US Navy EA-6B Prowlers, but these jamming aircraft were withdrawn to provide cover for a later B-2 mission. Whatever caused the loss of Vega 31, no F-117 was ever lost in combat again.

In the early morning hours of March 20, 2003, F-117s returned to Iraqi skies with lethal intent. This time the United States sought to depose Iraq's dictator, Saddam Hussein, fearing he had stockpiled weapons of mass destruction. The original invasion plan was preempted by intelligence suggesting that Saddam and other high-ranking Iraqi officials were lodging at the Dora Farms bunker complex southwest of Baghdad.

A mission to target the bigwigs was quickly drawn up during the night. The mission's two F-117 pilots, operating out of Al Udeid Air Base in Qatar, had barely enough time to execute their assignment before sunrise. Despite dropping their bombs (newer EBGU-27s equipped with GPS and inertial guidance for use in cloud conditions) on the given coordinates, Saddam was not present. The failure drove home the point that in the era of precision-guided bombs mission outcomes are largely dependent on intelligence inputs.

In the ensuing air campaign, not a single Iraqi fighter rose to challenge the US air armada. Saddam's air commanders had learned the futility of going up against an air and space colossus. The memory of the 1991 blowout was still fresh.

In Operation Iraqi Freedom, the US coalition achieved mastery of the air in eighteen days. Nighthawks flew only eighty-two sorties. Already weakened from the pounding administered a dozen years earlier, Iraqi air defenses crumbled relatively quickly so that conventional ground-attack aircraft had free reign to work down the target list. By this time, precision-strike capability was much more prevalent among air force combat planes generally, which enabled greater battlefield effects in less time.

The Nighthawks did not fly combat again. By December 2005, the Lockheed F-22 Raptors had reached initial operational capability. The new multirole air dominance fighters feature the next generation of passive stealth technology as reflected in their blended shaping. They can sweep the sky clean of any current or foreseeable enemy fighter while at the same time delivering the kind of bomb load carried by the older F-117s.

In April 2008 the F-117s were retired. However, they have remained in flyable storage in climate-controlled hangars at the Tonopah Test Range in Nevada. From time to time, a few of the aircraft are flown to retain flight proficiency in the type and to practice a return to service should the Nighthawks be recalled to flight status.

Their future disposition is not certain. On the one hand, proposed language in a 2016 defense funding bill sought to repeal the provision that required they be kept in flyable storage. If this happened, the aircraft would likely be transferred to outdoor storage at Davis-Monthan Air Force Base in Arizona, known as the "boneyard," where the blistering sun would despoil their low-observables coatings, making them all but useless as stealth aircraft. On the other hand, in November 2016, Air Force General Herbert J. "Hawk" Carlisle, at the time head of Air Combat Command, stated that he had thought about bringing some F-117s out of storage to be used as so-called "Red Air" aggressor aircraft in adversary training for the pilots of fifth-generation fighters, the F-22s and F-35s.

During its couple decades of operational service, the F-117A was so successful that foes downed only one with a so-called "golden BB." Yet the success manifested by the US military's advanced technologies has fomented a new and frustrating disparity. Hardcore and fanatical enemies have adapted. Reverting to simple, cheap, and homemade weapons employed with messianic fervor, these adversaries have answered the high-tech brawn with an acute version of asymmetric warfare.

Second-generation stealth aircraft have been used in the ongoing war against the Islamic extremists. But the uneven matchup, conventional against unconventional, has been frustrating for the traditionalists who have been stymied by the practitioners of this hybrid form of conflict. Zealots, who lack a single manned warplane let alone a multimillion-dollar state-of-the-art stealth fighter, have been able to prolong their fight indefinitely and even expand their reach.

The very supremacy of high-tech weapons of the late twentieth century and beyond has, in an ironic twist, led not to counter-weapons per se but to an opposing modus operandi that exploits the traditionalists' ingrained weakness, leading to the enfeeblement if not outright impotence of the qualitative advantage. This is not because of any flaw embedded in the technologies or any lack of heroism on the part of the operators; quite the contrary. The technologically handicapped side is fighting devoid of any moral constraint under the rubric of total war. By contrast, Western militaries have eschewed any construct of total war since World War II.

It is true that wars are sometimes won by superior weaponry. But matters of conviction and ethos have a role in determining the results of combat. The Western powers' unsatisfying results on the contemporary battlefield should serve as a reminder that the annals of armed conflict are replete with examples where willpower has taken precedence over firepower.

In war, possession of the qualitative advantage, even if coupled with superior numbers and astonishing bravery, does not necessarily deliver triumph. There is an elusive ingredient behind the secret to victory. As General George S. Patton, Jr. wrote, "It lurks invisible in that vitalizing spark, intangible, yet evident as the lightning—the warrior soul."

Section 4

Fun Flying: Trainer/Sport Platforms

CHAPTER 23

Empowering Flight and Barnstormer Dreams: The Fanciful and Fabled Jenny

To me the Curtiss Jenny is an early incarnation of the Boeing Stearman. Both gave faithful service as two-seat open-cockpit biplane military trainers and then quite naturally flowered into long-lived, crowd-pleasing stunt planes, the preferred show platforms of audacious barnstormers and their wing-walking compadres. Because the Jenny came first, its burden was higher.

With a maximum speed of 75 miles per hour and an endurance of barely more than two hours in its ultimate form, the Jenny did not earn its reputation in the usual way with speed or distance records. Instead, the wood-and-fabric aircraft, though temperamental, offered its operators a measure of unaccustomed serviceability. And in the eye of many if not most beholders, whether student flyers or air-meet spectators, this flying machine possessed proper proportioning, the look of a light training plane naturally evolved—it was the template, the archetype, the standard specimen for the genre.

The inception of the Jenny can be traced to a few years after Glenn Curtiss's company began supplying trainers to the US Army. By 1912 the Curtiss Aeroplane Company of Hammondsport, New York, sought to replace its antiquated pusher land planes with a more modern tractor-style configuration, encouraged by the army, which was anxious to remedy a rash of flying training accidents. The pusher layout had been a Curtiss hallmark dating back to the 1908 pushers *June Bug* and *Silver Dart*. These were research "aerodromes" sponsored by Alexander Graham Bell's Aerial Experiment Association, with Curtiss serving as director of experiments.

The association was dissolved in early 1909, having achieved its goal of developing viable aircraft (which followed the Wright brothers' success at Kitty Hawk by six years). Later in 1909 Curtiss began producing his own pusher designs in Hammondsport. Some of these gained considerable fame. In a specially powered model, Glenn Curtiss himself won the 1909 Gordon Bennett Cup at Reims, France. The next year he piloted his *Hudson Flyer* in a highly publicized flight to become the first person to cover the 156-mile distance between Albany and New York City by air.

In 1910 it was a Curtiss pusher flown by Eugene Ely that became the first aircraft to successfully launch from a ship, the cruiser USS *Birmingham* as it lay in anchor off the Virginia coast. The following year, Ely scored another first by landing his pusher on a specially constructed deck on the cruiser USS *Pennsylvania* in San Francisco Bay. Widespread notoriety came with the public displays of daring exhibition pilot Lincoln Beachey in a Curtiss pusher modified for aerobatic maneuvering.

In 1914, the year that the army grounded all its pusher trainers, Curtiss produced the Model J, which was the company's first successful tractor land plane (also tested as a floatplane). It was designed for Curtiss by B. Douglas Thomas, an Englishman who had worked on tractor types at Sopwith and Avro in Britain. Glenn Curtiss personally lacked experience with tractor types, which explains why he had enticed Thomas to join him in making this major transition for the company.

The Model J was a tandem two-seat biplane employing a French Eiffel 36 airfoil and powered by a 90-horsepower Curtiss OX engine. First flown in the spring, the aircraft was adjudged to have decent flying qualities. The army bought two.

Thomas designed a sister ship known as the Model N. This aircraft was very similar to the Model J in basic layout, but it used a different airfoil and the ailerons were located between the wings. Later the ailerons were repositioned in the more conventional location along the trailing edge of the outboard section of the upper wings. The other notable difference was the Model N's 100-horsepower Curtiss OXX engine.

The army liked what it saw in these two biplanes. In December 1914 small numbers of the Model J were ordered with certain features borrowed from the Model N. This amalgamation of the best of the two models led to the memorable JN series, which historian Peter Bowers and others have rightly called "immortal." As historians are also quick to point out, the name Jenny refers to no lady; rather the name is a "phonetic corruption" of the joined "J" and "N" letters.

Curiously enough, there was no JN-1. It was decided to skip to the JN-2 designation because of the peculiar way the type was arrived at through the meshing of two distinct models. Soon after its introduction, the JN-2 became the first US aircraft to be deployed on tactical missions in foreign airspace.

Starting in March 1916, Army General John J. Pershing led American troops on what was called a "punitive expedition" into Mexico in search of Pancho Villa, the firebrand whose paramilitary forces had left Americans dead in a cross-border raid. The First Aero Squadron operated eight JN-2s to provide reconnaissance. Although the men and their aircraft gave all they had, a combination of high elevations, extreme temperatures, and strained logistics impeded the air operations.

Next in the series was the JN-3, which incorporated some meaningful improvements. First, this new model had a longer-span upper wing. Second, the outdated aileron shoulder-yoke control system was replaced by a control wheel. Britain, which by now was embroiled in World War I, ordered the type to augment its flight training. To accommodate its foreign customer, Curtiss opened a plant in Toronto.

In July 1916 the first JN-4 rolled out of the factory. This model bore only minor changes to the JN-3. Refinements continued through the JN-4A, JN-4B, and JN-4C. It is worth noting that the Canadian version of the JN-4 was autonomously developed and assigned the designation JN-4(Can).

In the United States, the Canadian-built aircraft was nicknamed the Canuck. It incorporated a major improvement. A control stick substituted for the JN-3's control wheel. Reportedly production of this well-regarded Canadian JN-4 totaled 1,347.

It is worth noting that the army bought a small number of Twin JN observation planes in 1916 and 1917. These twin-engine aircraft were scaled-up versions of the newly developed JN-4. Although the configuration freed up the nose for an observer, overall performance was not enhanced by the addition of an engine. No further orders were placed for this offshoot of the baseline trainer.

The JN series reached a milestone when the JN-4D appeared in June 1917, shortly after the United States had entered World War I. This new version was powered by the 90-horsepower Curtiss OX-5 engine and incorporated the Canadian version's control stick. The aircraft had cutouts in both the upper wing's center section trailing edge and the lower wing's inner trailing edges to enhance the pilot's visibility. With war a reality for America, the need for pilots increased dramatically and trainer production went into full gear.

The Curtiss factory in Hammondsport was unable to keep pace. The company established a new plant in the bustling industrial metropolis of Buffalo, only about a hundred miles farther upstate, where it already had some manufacturing operations. The new plant, which cost $4 million and covered a seventy-one-acre footprint, was the largest airplane production facility in the world at the time.

Even with the new capacity, which came on line in July 1917, the company was forced to share JN-4D production with six other manufacturers from St. Louis to San Francisco. During the war, the army took delivery of 6,070 Jennies, of which nearly half, 2,812, were the JN-4D. This model and its Canadian equivalent were the aircraft most associated with postwar barnstorming.

The army continued to refine its proven trainer both during and after the war. New models were developed that upped engine power. The JN-4H and JN-6H replaced the 90-horsepower OX-5 engine with the 150-horsepower American-built French Hispano-Suiza engine. Variants of these models were used for numerous special purposes, including bomber and gunnery training with bomb racks and a flexible aft-mounted gun, respectively. Some late-model Jennies were even converted into ambulance ships, able to carry a single litter in an enclosure behind the pilot.

The final trainer version was the JNS (for "JN Standardized"), which basically combined the features of the JN-4H and JN-6H models, although with a variety of different engines in the 150- to 180-horsepower class. At war's end, aviation had made enormous strides and the army knew its primary trainer's days were numbered. By the mid-1920s, the new Consolidated PT-1 was on track to supplant the Jenny.

In 1927 the army retired its remaining JN trainers. The type had done its job, but the replacement platform provided better performance and enhanced safety. It was in keeping with the spirit of the reorganization that occurred the year before when the air service had become the air corps.

It has been said that during World War I 90 percent of American airmen got their primary training in a Jenny. This is perhaps the greatest testament to the type. It also meant that following the war, as the trainer became available as surplus equipment, there would be large numbers of ex-military pilots ready to step into the cockpit of the plane they knew well. This abundant biplane was poised to introduce a large swath of the public to the wonders of flight in a burst of barnstorming across the country.

Rather than flooding the postwar civilian market directly, the US government accepted industry offers for the trainers, which in most cases had been worn down from heavy use. Curtiss bought back two thousand Jennies at only thirteen cents on the dollar. After overhauling the planes, the company claimed in advertising that they were as good as new. In 1919 these aircraft were listed at $4,000 apiece, which represented a modest discount from the original pricing to the army during the war.

Prices gradually worked their way down as both Canadian models and British versions started to reach the market. The planes were expensive for individual buyers, whether novices who harbored dreams of learning to fly or veterans who planned to go into business as aerial performers. The alternative of buying brand-new trainers or sport planes was simply out of the question for most potential buyers because of prohibitively high sticker prices.

By the mid- to late-1920s, the market for the venerable trainers softened. Operators had begun to sell their Jennies to other operators, and depending on engine and airframe condition, the planes could go for a few hundred dollars or fetch as little as fifty dollars. By then, a rash of mishaps and a new regulatory scheme spoiled the market's appetite.

The aviation epoch that had been defined largely by the ubiquity of the Jenny faded into the past, but stories of those who had lived as vagabonds of the air were handed down through word of mouth. As the late aviation writer Martin Caidin learned doing research for his book *Barnstorming*, not everyone accepts the romanticized depiction of the gypsy pilots of the Golden Age of Flight. One doubter told him: "The lot of them sound like hot-rodders with oily clothes and goggles, and a jolting whiskey breath. I mean *bums*. So their flying was great. Okay. But did any of them ever amount to a damn?"

Martin answered by relating the experience of one of the barnstormers, a young pilot who was mostly self-taught and in search of adventure after paying $500 in April 1923 for a disassembled JN-4 in Alabama. Once it was put back together, he headed west to Oklahoma and then veered north, selling rides along the way, until reaching his boyhood home of Little Falls, Minnesota, in June. He seized the opportunity to demonstrate the war-surplus biplane to the farmhands he had known as a coworker while growing up.

He successfully fought off the gremlins that plagued his Jenny as he hopped across Minnesota during the summer of 1923. It was a time when cow pastures substituted for airport runways and when out of necessity the flyers had to be their own mechanics. By the time he arrived at the International Air Races at St. Louis' Lambert Field in October, he was discouraged because of his failure to make ends meet. He decided to join the US Air Service, but before reporting, he embarked in the fall on one last aerial fling, a foray down south with a student of his in a haggard Canuck.

The encounters were priceless. An example was landing low on fuel in the public square of a Texas hamlet where hospitable townsfolk poured out to gaze at the biplane that had literally dropped from the sky. The "excited schoolmarm" even excused her students for the occasion as if the barnstormers were modern Pied Pipers.

Amid travails, the trip continued until "the Canuck sagged wearily in the savage heat" of the Texas desert, impaling itself on a towering Spanish bayonet cactus. It was time to bid a bittersweet farewell to the world of barnstorming and report to the army for flight training. Martin saved the identity of the "young pilot" until the end. "Oh, yes. His name: Charles A. Lindbergh."

Having soloed in a Jenny and then having crisscrossed swaths of the country in one, the lanky young barnstormer got even more time in the type, a JN-4H, as part of his army flight training in 1924. Despite its obvious limitations, Lindbergh always had a soft spot in his heart for the trainer. About it, he said: "It is doubtful whether a better training ship will ever be built. . . . Jennies were underpowered . . . somewhat tricky . . . splintered badly when they crashed . . . but when a cadet learned to fly one . . . he was just about capable of flying anything on wings with a reasonable degree of safety."

The late Frank Tallman, who in his prime was called the "King of Stunt Pilots," knew the Jenny well. His first flight in the type occurred in the early 1920s when, as a toddler, he flew on his father's lap. He got to fly one himself when he was fresh out of the navy at the end of World War II.

Given the Jenny's ample wingspan of more than forty-three feet and its many struts and wires, he learned that when you do a preflight walk-around of "the old girl you can start at breakfast, and if you are careful you can finish in time for an early dinner." Flying over the open road at normal cruise speed, you would see cars pass underneath you. According to Tallman, the controls had a "stretching rubber band-like quality" that took some getting used to. There was also a time lapse between control inputs and the response in control surface movement, so you had to be patient before the plane got around to pointing in the direction you had commanded it.

A Jenny with a Hispano-Suiza engine was preferred. The extra horsepower over the basic Curtiss OX-5 engine made a tremendous difference in load-carrying capacity, rate of climb, and forward speed. Jennies outfitted with the Hisso, as the Hispano-Suiza engine was abbreviated, could easily execute the garden variety of aerobatics. However, higher cost and scant availability consigned many barnstormers to the lighter-powered models.

Another choice was between the American-built Jenny and the Canadian-built Canuck. All else being equal, the Canuck usually got the nod because each of its wings had two ailerons, which enabled a crisper control response. There was one more possibility that presented itself to the barnstormers.

A competing two-seat trainer produced by the Standard Aero Corporation of Plainfield, New Jersey, was a dead ringer for the Jenny. The Standard J-1, which reputedly had better aerodynamics than the Jenny, might have eaten into Curtiss's wartime trainer contracts except for the plane's unreliable 100-horsepower Hall-Scott A-7A engine which, compounding its operational difficulties, proved to be a fire hazard. In the postwar era, Hall-Scott engines were switched out for Hissos, which made the Standard a highly desirable choice.

As a primary trainer, the Jenny was built to teach the fundamentals of airmanship. Therefore, it had about as spartan an assortment of instruments as one would expect: just five. To monitor the engine, there was a tachometer, oil pressure gauge, and owing to the OX-5 being a water-cooled engine, a water temperature indicator (mounted on a cabane strut above the windscreen). Flight instrumentation included an altimeter and an airspeed indicator (fastened to a port wing strut) that was "the size of a porthole on the *Queen Mary*."

The Jenny landed like any of the next generation of light planes in the Taylorcraft or Cub category except that it had a wooden tailskid instead of a tail wheel. That feature was common in aircraft of World War I vintage. What it meant was that you had to operate it off of grass fields, in which case the tailskid helped to slow down the plane during landing rollout, an important factor, given that the plane came with no brakes. The plane's immense drag did a lot to slow it down too, making it possible to land at uncommonly short fields.

At modern airports where the few remaining Jennies fly in air shows, the planes are typically towed over the paved taxiways using a dolly under the tailskid. When in the vicinity of the takeoff and landing area, most often the grassy strips adjoining concrete runways, the planes are disconnected from the tug. Because the type is sensitive to crosswinds, Jenny pilots have been known to take off and land in the grass perpendicular to the hard surfaces.

After World War II the old trainer was already quite the antique and invariably aviators gawked at it whenever the opportunity presented itself. Tallman wrote about his time ferrying a newly purchased Jenny from St. Louis to Chicago on a chilly day at eight thousand feet. Lo and behold, a Constellation airliner on the same route spotted it from behind and descended down to the biplane's altitude, circling it with "passengers waving from every window." Tallman was left feeling "as exposed as a man taking a shower in Central Park."

When talking about Jennies back in the Golden Age, reminiscent barnstormers would say: "What it took to fly was gas and guts." Representative of the early barnstormers was Floyd Hurtial Rodgers, a Texan who went by the aeronautically inspired nickname of "Slats." He was a lovable rogue who variously risked his life in rickety planes in dubious weather and his freedom on flights smuggling whiskey across the border from Mexico.

At air shows he excelled at swooping down low in front of the audience, touching the ground with his wheels, and then pulling up into a loop. Based out of Love Field in Dallas, Slats wrote: "I figured what the crowd loved was noise and low flying. It worked even if I did get gravel in my face sometimes from my own prop wash."

Show pilots kept refining their routines and adding drama to their performances to draw ever larger audiences. Parachute jumpers and wing walkers joined the show. In some ways, the Jenny was tailor-made for the new phenomenon of wing walking. The biplane was festooned with a patchwork of wing struts and bracing wires as well as wingtip skid bows and king-posts on top of the upper wing—all convenient grip points for the performers hanging on in flight.

Over open spaces at state fairs, spectators were mesmerized by the sight of these daredevils transferring from one Jenny to the next. Clutching a piece of the aircraft's structure and holding on for dear life in the pounding slipstream, if all went according to plan, the wing walker managed to hoist him- or herself onto the other plane's wing. It was heart-stopping to watch because it truly involved a death-defying feat.

The more charismatic aerial artisans were inevitably called to Hollywood. The movie companies wanted to capture the thrilling stunts on film to reach audiences of millions. Notable among flyers wooed by the studios was Ormer Leslie Locklear, who had the looks and demeanor of a leading man.

Locklear's flight maneuvers in *The Great Air Robbery* were breathtaking to moviegoers. The flying sequences established a new bar for the film industry. Unfortunately Locklear did not survive long in his new profession of Hollywood stunt pilot. In a climatic night scene for another film, he dived from three thousand feet in a Jenny specially equipped with bright flares, and as he pulled up at two thousand feet the plane stalled and spun into the ground.

Flying accidents resulting in injury or death were not uncommon in the barnstorming era, and over time the cumulative effect alarmed the public. Some of the flying was unforgivably reckless, plus operators faced no constraints on modifications they wished to make to their aircraft. The barnstorming community's freewheeling ways were destined to end with the passage of the Air Commerce Act of 1926.

Starting the next year, the Aeronautics Branch of the Department of Commerce clamped down on the previously unregulated flyers. It would no longer be possible for self-taught and unlicensed flyers to sell rides and stage air shows. Governmental oversight, approvals, certifications, etc., would now hold sway. The onset of the Depression at the end of the decade was a further encumbrance.

Frank Tallman said that the barnstormers who flew the Jenny possessed "iron nerves and enormous skill." He summed up the period with the account of an old-time Jenny pilot who had just finished a treacherous midair transfer and was approached by a young journalist inquiring what most frightened him. "He thought for a moment and then replied, 'Starvation!'"

CHAPTER 24

The Man Is the Machine: Lloyd Stearman and the Fabulous Biplane He Inspired

Sometimes the little things reveal the most about a person's character.

On June 9, 1930, one of the aviation industry's leading lights dictated a letter of recommendation for his company's seventeen-year-old office boy.

In his nine months on the job, the adolescent had run errands, including a mail drop at the Wichita, Kansas, post office in the boss's shiny new Packard sedan. "Don't crack it up," cautioned the boss when he handed over the keys. On another occasion, the boss asked his helper to oil his swivel chair which had a nagging squeak.

The letter was succinct and unambiguous in its praise for the "alert, wide awake young man." It further described the teen as "courteous, conscientious and honest."

An imposing winged globe with a big "S" inscribed in it decorated the stationery's masthead. Below the four simple and direct sentences of unreserved endorsement were the signature lines: "Very truly yours, THE STEARMAN AIRCRAFT CO., Lloyd Stearman, President."

The fastidious office boy, Marvin Michael, ultimately took three educational sabbaticals that culminated in his earning a master's degree in aeronautical engineering. He went to work for Boeing, the eventual parent company of Stearman Aircraft. After more than three decades at the company, Michael retired as an engineering test pilot.

Lloyd Carlton Stearman and his early business associates knew the value of a helping hand, an ardent word of support, a hard-earned break.

In 1920, at age twenty-two, Lloyd read a newspaper advertisement for a position at E. M. "Matty" Laird's airplane company in Wichita. Lloyd, a native Kansan, wasted no time in applying, for he knew by then that his heart was in aviation.

Up to that point in his life, Lloyd hadn't had much luck completing what he had started. His civil engineering studies at Kansas State Agricultural College were interrupted by his enlistment in the navy when America entered World War I. Similarly, his naval flight training in the Curtiss N-9 flying boat concluded prematurely when the war ended. Moreover, his one-year stint as an apprenticing architect at a firm in Wichita seemed to be going nowhere.

Laird recognized underlying qualities in the young Lloyd Stearman and hired him to perform a range of drafting and engineering duties. Little did anyone know in those budding days that once in this groove Lloyd's course would lead eventually to his banding together with various aggregations of extraordinarily talented aviation trailblazers. Nor could anyone have foreseen then that the dusty little prairie town to which the scant but growing cadre of air-minded visionaries gravitated would become the "air capital of the world" much as Detroit ripened into the automobile capital.

An eyewitness to the maiden flight of Matty Laird's plane remarked that its lissome motion through the air resembled the poise of a swallow in flight. Without hesitation, Laird thereupon dropped the prosaic name of Tractor that he had given the two-place biplane and rechristened it the Swallow. Production of the new aircraft proceeded apace, bolstered by the mechanical prowess Lloyd possessed as a result of the knowledge passed on by his father who was a commercial contractor. As a measure of his determination, Lloyd completed his flight instruction at this time in one of the very planes he was helping to build.

Three and a half years after Matty Laird founded his company, he departed due to a dispute with his patron, local oil tycoon and pilot Jacob Moellendick. Lloyd, who had been one of Laird's protégés, was promoted to chief engineer of the renamed Swallow Airplane Manufacturing Company. Lloyd's knack for design soon led to the New Swallow. This aircraft was a significant upgrade of the baseline product.

The New Swallow was also meaningfully differentiated from the multitude of war-surplus Jennys in that it was configured to carry three people, had only two wing struts per side instead of four, and featured a fully enclosed 90-horsepower liquid-cooled Curtiss OX-5 engine. Publicity for the highly regarded plane was enhanced by impressive exhibition flights made by Walter Beech, a transplanted Tennessean who had been hired as a part-time demonstration pilot only a year after Lloyd started working for the company.

The chief engineer and the demonstration pilot jointly calculated that if the aircraft's wood innards were replaced by tubular steel, durability and performance would vastly improve. However, Moellendick was put off by the heretical idea, not least because of the relatively recent investment he had made in woodworking machinery for the factory. In the face of Moellendick's intransigence, Beech and Stearman sought backing for a new company.

By the end of 1924 the two frustrated men had made the rounds and persuaded several people to support their venture. One was a much admired self-taught pilot who had been entertaining crowds at air shows across the prairie landscape for a dozen years. Interestingly, that pilot had reputedly flown the first plane that Lloyd had ever seen when he was growing up in Harper, Kansas. More recently, one of Lloyd's New Swallows had been purchased and flown by the pilot, Clyde Cessna.

In early 1925, in a convergence of aviation eminences rarely replicated in the industry's long and consequential history, Lloyd Stearman, Walter Beech, Clyde Cessna, and assorted other partners established the Travel Air Manufacturing Company in the back room of a Wichita milling plant. Cognizant of his greatest strength, Lloyd retained his post as chief engineer in the new company.

Lloyd stayed at Travel Air for not quite two years, but in that time he fathered the Travel Air A, BW, 2000/3000/4000 series of biplanes and the Type 5000 cabin monoplane. These models represented a technological progression and exuded a handsome proportionality. The biplane lineup included some models that sported unusual upper wing elephant-ear ailerons.

Aesthetics were matched by practical attributes. Indeed, in 1926 a Travel Air won the Second Annual Ford Reliability Tour. The same year, another Travel Air set a new cross-country record—just thirty-one hours from coast to coast. Most memorably, on August 16-17, 1927, Art Goebel and William V. Davis won the Dole Race with a twenty-six-hour flight that spanned the twenty-four hundred miles from Oakland, California, to Oahu, Hawaii, in a Travel Air 5000 dubbed the *Woolaroc*.

Yet amid the triumphs, tragedy beset the up-and-coming designer/ engineer. After a flight test of a Model A on August 13, 1926, Lloyd was taxiing to a hangar at Wichita's municipal airport when a collision occurred. The aircraft's propeller struck local businessman George Theis, Jr., injuring him fatally.

Lloyd had eyeballed the airport grounds from the cockpit, but simply didn't see the man who parked his car close to the aircraft right-of-way and then stepped out inattentively. Lloyd was heartbroken and extremely apologetic. In the end, the deadly occurrence was deemed an accident.

In October 1926 Lloyd moved to Venice, California. He was drawn by the desire to start his own company in the perennially good flying weather and favorable business environment then endemic to the Golden State. As aviation historian Edward H. Phillips pointed out in his account of Stearman business ventures, Lloyd was further motivated by Santa Monica-based Travel Air dealer Fred Hoyt who, along with his partner, George Lyle, invested with Lloyd to form the first company to bear the Stearman name.

As his own boss, Lloyd was free to pursue his promising design concepts. The quixotic innovator's dreams blossomed into a line of aircraft that represented a leap into the modern realm. The first of his new C series biplanes had a substantial and stately profile.

A distinctively squared vertical stabilizer and rudder became a Stearman compositional hallmark. Advances included wheel brakes and hydraulic shock absorbers in a fixed undercarriage. Additionally the main landing gear legs were positioned to give a wide stance.

The biplane's wings had differing spans. In this sesquiwing configuration, the top wing was considerably longer than the lower wing. The C series is perhaps best remembered for its later variants that used progressively more powerful air-cooled radial engines.

Despite its outstanding products, the company was inadequately capitalized. Under the circumstances, in 1927 Lloyd was enticed to return to Wichita. Generous financing was offered by Walter Innes, Jr., a former business partner. Lloyd's company, still with his name on the marquis, moved into a large facility north of town.

The stylish Stearman biplanes that had originated in California spawned the M-2 and C-4A/4C mail planes and the LT-1 passenger plane. These were in the same class as the regal Douglas M-4, Pitcairn Mailwing, and Boeing Model 40. Few aircraft evoked a sense of the Golden Age as consummately as the commercial biplanes.

Their pilots flew from an open cockpit situated along the aft fuselage while passengers and/or mail remained ensconced in a commodious forward cabin. The designs constituted the aerial equivalents of the period's chauffeur-driven Rolls-Royce and Dusenberg limousines. Paradoxically Lloyd, who was described at the time by a Wichita newspaper as "modest and unassuming," had helped to glamourize aviation.

The company's success prompted its takeover by the huge United Aircraft & Transport syndicate. Under the new ownership Lloyd remained president of his company, but the transaction had occurred ominously on August 4, 1929, less than three months prior to the stock market collapse which reverberated from Wall Street to Main Street and represented the onset of the Depression.

At first the giant holding company was undeterred. With its backing, the Stearman subsidiary proceeded with a major expansion in Wichita. Operations were relocated to a factory that doubled the floor space of the existing facility.

However, production receded unavoidably due to the faltering economy. Lloyd pressed forward with his latest design, the Model 6 Cloudboy, which factored in the transformation of the marketplace. The new aircraft would lack the grandeur of Lloyd's designs of the immediate past. Necessity decreed a bare-bones two-seater to serve as an entry-level aircraft, equally suitable for the novice and the aspirant.

The Cloudboy was conceived as an inexpensive-to-build aircraft, using off-the-shelf materials and components in a straightforward biplane configuration that manifested elegance in its simplicity. Lloyd's new aircraft also preserved the admirable Stearman tradition of ruggedness and adaptability with possible future growth in engine size, weight, and horsepower.

Because of the drop-off in civilian sales, the company looked to the military as an important potential source for new orders. In 1930 the army air corps embarked on a quest for a new trainer to replace its Consolidated PT-3. Not coincidentally, that same year the Cloudboy flew for the first time.

A couple Cloudboys, designated XPT-912, were evaluated at Wright Field in Dayton, Ohio. By the end of the year, Lloyd's design had sufficiently whetted the service's appetite that a contract was issued for four additional aircraft, with the designation YPT-9, to conduct further testing. The company did not receive the hoped-for production contract, but the Cloudboy military trainer prototype was a crucial step towards development of the fabled Stearman primary trainer.

In any case, Lloyd felt crimped because he no longer called the shots at his company which now was but one entity in a sprawling conglomerate. For a while he concentrated on his forte of research and development, but by summer 1931 his entrepreneurial impulses prevailed. He left Wichita once again for the seemingly greener pastures of Southern California.

In another confluence of aviation wizards, Lloyd teamed with Walter T. Varney, an airline executive whose company had previously bought Stearman planes, and Robert E. Gross, a prominent aviation financier. They had their eyes on Lockheed Aircraft Company, which was part of the failed Detroit Aircraft Corporation. Though Lockheed was mired in the bankruptcy of its corporate parent, it had a sparkling record as a maker of cutting-edge aircraft that found favor with some of the era's most daring pilots.

On June 6, 1932, the three businessmen, along with other investors, bought Lockheed for the sum of $40,000. (Yes, for less than today's cost of an F-22 wheel strut, Lloyd Stearman and his associates bought the whole company.) The bankruptcy judge reportedly said, "I sure hope you fellows know what you're doing."

Meanwhile, back in Wichita, the Stearman Aircraft Company was being run by its new president, Julius E. Schaefer. One of the priorities was to apply the lessons learned in the company's loss of the army trainer competition and offer a winning design for the next round of acquisitions. Three company engineers, Mac Short, Harold W. Zipp, and J. Jack Clark, logically took Lloyd's Cloudboy drawings and used them as the predicate for their design work.

Among the changes they incorporated in Lloyd's original layout were a cantilevered landing gear and installation of ailerons on the lower wings only. Wingtips and tail surfaces were no longer square but round. For ease of production, they stuck with the idea of using readily available materials.

The fuselage was formed by a tubular steel frame. Wings were made of wood ribs and spars. Cotton-linen fabric was stretched over most of the fuselage, wings, and tail surfaces. What emerged from the drafting tables was the Model 70. The company's chief test pilot, Deed Levy, flew the plane to Wright Field for trials.

The Stearman trainer type was well regarded by the military pilots who tested it, but one problem stood out. When stalled, the Model 70 just slumped in the air. The pilots opined that for the aircraft to be an effective primary trainer it would have to have a more definitive break when stalled.

Also it would have to be more responsive to control inputs in both spin entry and recovery. Eventually these concerns were addressed by the insertion of stall-spin strips in the leading edges of the lower wings. The wings' narrower camber changed the airflow at high angles of attack, which produced the desired effect.

An order for forty-one of a slightly altered version, known as the Model 73, was placed by the navy and designated the NS-1. The first aircraft was delivered in December 1934. The door to military sales had been opened.

It was an eventful time for the company because a radical restructuring of the corporate parent was mandated under antitrust laws enacted that year. The United Aircraft & Transport empire was split into pieces.

The Stearman unit was apportioned to the newly freestanding Boeing Aircraft Company.

Once this corporate upheaval played out, management and design personnel at the Stearman operation in Wichita turned their attention to capitalizing on the navy's trainer acquisition by trying to persuade the army to do likewise. The Model 73 was minimally modified, with changes to both the landing gear and the wing. This refined aircraft was designated the Model X75 and later simply the Model 75.

The army liked the aircraft and committed to order a significant quantity. However, funding shortages delayed purchase of production models until fiscal 1936. The initial batch of twenty-six trainers had the 220-horsepower nine-cylinder Lycoming R-680-5 radial engine. The army designated this primary trainer the PT-13.

Thus, a legend was born. The Model 75 in its various military designations came to occupy a place of honor in the chronicle of flight. The type is believed to have taught more American cadets how to fly during World War II than any other primary trainer. The many airworthy examples today serve as a ubiquitous bridge to aviation's glorious past.

With war clouds on the horizon, government leaders recognized the dire need for more military pilots. Resultantly, trainer production was dramatically ramped up. In the late 1930s and early 1940s, the Stearman assembly lines in Wichita were humming. An astounding 8,585 Stearman trainers were built, more than any other American biplane. (Spare parts for the equivalent of another 1,761 aircraft were produced.) Most aircraft went to the US military services, but their universally recognized virtues as a training platform made them popular with numerous foreign air forces.

At Randolph Field in San Antonio, Texas, the Naval Air Station in Pensacola, Florida, and other military flight training locations around the country, the Model 75 filled the skies, preparing cadets to fly in the greatest aerial armada ever amassed. Notable students who received training in the Model 75 included members of the Women's Air Force Service Pilots, the first females to fly US military aircraft. African Americans who later were celebrated as the Tuskegee Airmen also learned to fly at the controls of the splendid biplane.

Dozens of fighter aces and even *Mercury* astronaut John Glenn got instruction in the Stearman trainer's open cockpit. And in the frigid skies of the upper Midwest, George Herbert Walker Bush, bundled in a full fleece-lined leather flying outfit and far removed from the trappings of the White House that he would experience much later in a different kind of government service, felt the invigorating rush of air against his face aboard the Stearman as a rite of passage to the rarefied domain of military flyers.

The army purchased four production versions, mostly the PT-13 and PT-17, with the main difference between models being the engine type. Concern that Lycoming would not be able to keep pace with the manufacture of airframes caused the army to order the Continental R-670 engine as a substitute. Aircraft with this 220-horsepower seven-cylinder radial engine were designated PT-17. Navy equivalents of the PT-13 were the N2S-2 and N2S-5; its equivalents of the PT-17 were the N2S-1, N2S-3, and N2S-4.

Paint schemes were a modeler's delight. Prewar army trainers had regulation blue fuselage and orange-yellow wings. The rudder was festooned in patriotic "candy cane" or "barber pole" stripes that alternated between red and white. Navy training biplanes in those early years were painted orange-yellow all over to ensure visibility. In 1942 the official paint schemes for primary trainers of both services transitioned to an overall silver shade. By then, many of the trainers had already been built and they were not repainted unless repair or maintenance reasons required that their fabric covering be replaced.

The company adopted "Kaydet" as the trainer's official sobriquet. In time, army brass embraced the nickname. For its part, the navy was known for its casual usage of the term "Yellow Peril" which applied equally to the variants of the N2S and the navy's indigenously produced N3N biplane trainer. Yet pilots and their flight line colleagues have a strong independent streak and the sanctioned monikers didn't ring true; they came across as either stolid or facile.

Students, instructors, and mechanics referred to the formidable biplane trainer by its pedigree—Stearman. The usage spread and has survived through post–World War II generations to the present. In fact when an aviation neophyte visits an airport these days and is lucky enough to see a colorfully decorated wartime training biplane coasting overhead, some old wag on the ground, if asked, will invariably identify the antique by saying, "Oh, that's a Stearman." There could hardly be a more fitting tribute to the man whose design genius inspired the airplane that epitomizes silk-scarf flying.

As for the career path of Lloyd Stearman, he became Lockheed's president at thirty-four years of age, in 1932. He brought with him a concept for an all-metal twin-engine transport, which during the early to mid-1930s was developed into the Model 10 Electra. In the process, Lockheed was stumped as to how the aircraft's stability problems could be rectified.

A brash University of Michigan aeronautical engineering student named Clarence L. "Kelly" Johnson determined through wind tunnel testing that a split tail was the solution. Refashioned accordingly, the Electra hatched many follow-on configurations, eventually morphing into a patrol bomber that sold in quantity to the British later in the decade. The deal secured Lockheed's place as a major player in the aviation industry.

Lloyd left Lockheed in 1936. A succession of jobs followed. For a while he partnered with Dean Hammond to redesign the twin-boom pusher Hammond Model Y light plane under the new Stearman-Hammond banner. Sales of the new model were anemic so in 1938 Lloyd moved yet again. For the duration of the war, he was employed as an aviation engineer at the Harvey Machine Company, which produced engine cowlings for military planes.

In 1945 Lloyd set out to harness the old magic he had ignited years before. He established the Stearman Engineering Company in California and channeled his energies into the design of a purpose-built crop duster. Ironically it wasn't able to compete with the aircraft that already bore his name, the Model 75. A spate of army and navy Stearman trainers inundated the postwar civilian market at incredibly low government surplus prices. The tried and true biplanes made incomparable agricultural applicators.

Rather than resist the obvious and overwhelming tide, Lloyd spent a short time modifying the former primary trainers for spraying and dusting work. He even designed metal wings as a replacement for the standard wood-and-fabric wings. That led to a job at an agricultural implement manufacturer.

As would be expected, Lloyd yearned to get back into the aviation business. One day in 1955 he walked into the employment office at Lockheed, then headquartered in Burbank, California. The story goes that he filled out an application as would anyone coming in off the street. The form included a question about past employment at Lockheed. Lloyd marked the "Yes" box. The subsequent question pertained to former position. Lloyd, not a man of many words, filled in the blank line with his old job title: "President."

For the next thirteen years Lloyd worked as an engineer for the company he once headed. One of his assignments involved work on the needle-nosed F-104 Starfighter, a Mach 2 interceptor conceived and masterminded by the same Kelly Johnson of Electra redesign fame. By the time Lloyd retired from Lockheed in 1968, the industry he had helped to cultivate looked beyond the sky to the heavens. It was a remarkable genesis from open-cockpit flying over the windswept prairies of Kansas to enabling sleek jets to nibble at the edge of space.

Lloyd and his wife, Virtle Ethyl, had two children. Son William was a naval officer in the Pacific during World War II. With advanced degrees in international affairs, he went into the Foreign Service and served both behind the Iron Curtain and in Vietnam. For seventeen years, he worked in the White House as a member of the National Security Council staff, including time as an assistant to secretary of state Henry Kissinger. Daughter Marilyn married and had five children. One of them, Patrick, learned to fly and not surprisingly developed a soft spot for the planes originated by his grandfather.

Ever the restive dreamer, Lloyd continued to pursue his concept for a crop-dusting airplane during retirement in Los Angeles. He even formed the Stearman Aircraft Corporation, the last aviation company with his name on it, for his desire to create and build winged wonders would never die. But Lloyd's plane-making days were over and the cancer that had weakened him finally took its toll. He passed away on April 3, 1975.

On their way to keeping the flame of liberty shimmering, many World War II airmen rode the wings of the biplane whose classic lines were influenced by Lloyd Stearman. Only some of the trainers leaving the Wichita factory had manufacturer plates with the Stearman name etched on them, for in the late summer of 1941 it became Boeing's practice to refer to its Stearman unit as the Wichita Division. Nevertheless, the end users—the people who flew and maintained the aircraft—branded the product as they saw fit.

Today, in the absence of a multimillion-dollar marketing campaign or a "customer loyalty" program touted by a sports superstar, the brand hasn't been diluted. Rather, with the passage of time, it has solidified. Conjoining the man with the machine seems natural, even destined, for there could hardly be a better way to immortalize the name of the aviation pioneer whose vision fostered the venerable airplane.

To fly the Stearman is to connect with the spirit of an exalted yore. The cockpits are not hollow but overflow with timeless memories of good flights and happy landings. The wings don't weary but hold the wind for climbs to where the birds flutter free. With each ascent, the charmed ship nurtures camaraderie among the souls privileged to soar in its solid yet airy frame and burnishes its namesake's enduring and proud legacy.

CHAPTER 25

Magic: How the Piper Cub
Spread the Dream of Flight

It was an early spring day in 1963. The breaking dawn bared a dew-moistened landscape under a clarion sky. Seizing the fortuity, Mom and Dad acceded to my longstanding wish for an airplane ride. That brisk morning they drove me to a grass airstrip nestled in an outlying suburb of Cleveland.

The field was strewn with airworthy Piper Cubs, the classic all-yellow J-3 models with feisty four-cylinder 65-horsepower engines. High-time Cubs, identifiable by their oil-splattered fuselages, were for sale at the bargain price of $600. Less worn Cubs, whose fabric retained the factory-fresh lemony sheen, were offered for the princely sum of $1,000.

The telltale smell of butyrate dope and burnt fuel, the sweet aroma unique to airports, wafted in the air. Once in a while, one of the high-wing taildraggers taxied into position. When its engine revved up from a gentle putt-putt to a high-pitched raspy buzz, the plane sped down the emerald carpet of freshly sprouted grass and rose skyward. The transition from ground to air, the act of soaring aloft, seemed to be the singular response to an irresistible summons. Better even than the gazelles that run wild on the vast stretches of the Serengeti, the machines skittering on the grass entered the more expansive domain of the air, their occupants perhaps beckoned by expectations of release from earthly burdens.

At age twelve, I harbored aspirations of flying high and fast, like my heroes the *Mercury* astronauts whose forays into the new frontier of space had begun just two years earlier. Cape Canaveral was their portal to the heavens, but for at least a couple of the original seven space travelers the genesis of their remarkable journeys was a small airfield near their childhood homes. My nascent aerial odyssey was about to assume a similar pedigree at the charming if unadorned Chagrin Falls Airport.

The grass was green, the sky was blue, and in every direction one turned there were the agile yellow ships ready to sail on voyages of self-discovery. The airport's verdant landscape and tinny hangars evoked the perfect aura for my maiden flight. Everyone on the field, from the mechanics in grease-stained coveralls to my uniformed instructor pilot, appeared to be devoid of the conceits and affectations experienced elsewhere; instead, they projected a sense of high purpose, a desire to do something grand, not for material reward but for the satisfaction that appertained to the doing itself. In my eyes, these otherwise common men were noblemen.

•••

The miracle of the Piper Cub was that it made the sky accessible to whoever hankered to flirt with the clouds. In a way, the remarkable airplane's evolution started in 1911 when an adolescent by the name of Clarence Gilbert Taylor witnessed Calbraith Perry Rodgers amble by in a garishly decorated Wright B biplane dubbed the *Vin Fiz.* The flimsy and mishap-prone crate was participating in a much publicized contest to be the first to fly across the country and to do so in less than thirty days.

From the time of that sighting, C. G. Taylor, as the teenager would later be known, was intent on building his own planes. By 1927 he was designing light planes with his brother Gordon in their hometown of Rochester, New York. The first design was a two-place, high-wing configuration called the Chummy because of its snug side-by-side seating.

In 1929 the brothers were lured to Bradford, Pennsylvania, by city development officials and private investors. Among the financial backers in the Taylor Brothers Aircraft Company was William T. Piper, a member of a local farm family. Mr. Piper had served in the army during World War I and subsequently earned a mechanical engineering degree from Harvard. He had interests in oil and real estate but, oddly enough, no background in aviation.

Timing could hardly have been worse, since the stock market collapse occurred in the autumn, portending hard times. In 1931 overhead costs in the face of declining sales made bankruptcy unavoidable. The only buyer for the assets was Mr. Piper, who paid $761 to become sole owner. The surviving entity's name was shortened to Taylor Aircraft Company.

Hopes for the struggling business rode on C. G. Taylor's latest design, the E-2. This was a refinement of prior designs that sought to appeal to flying schools as a light and economical tandem-seat trainer. The E-2 was formally named the Cub and the models that rolled out of the factory had the name emblazoned on the fin.

Conflicting accounts continue to muddle the story of how the name was adopted and who conceived it. It is certainly true that success has many claimants for there were at least several company employees, an advertising executive, and an airport manager who asserted paternity. Regardless of its provenance, the name took on legendary status, eventually encompassing not just the more than thirty thousand single-engine light planes of similar configuration built by Taylor/Piper in succeeding years but virtually every plane subsequently produced that bore a resemblance to the Taylor design. Cub became synonymous with light planes as did Lear with corporate jets.

Despite its aerodynamic profile and light weight, the plane was dreadfully underpowered. That changed when Continental Motors developed the A-40 four-cylinder, horizontally opposed engine. This light 37-horsepower engine had been the missing link and, once incorporated into the Cub, it changed the company's fortunes and the course of history. To be sure, teething problems plagued the new engine, but once the bugs were ironed out, the airplane's sales surged.

In 1933 a newly graduated engineer from Rutgers University showed up looking for work. Walter Corey Jamouneau was hired as an unpaid apprentice, the only employee on the factory floor with a college degree. He proved to be a jack-of-all-trades, excelling at manufacturing, sales, and design. With Piper's encouragement, he significantly redesigned the Taylor E-2.

Because of the extensive changes, a new model designation was required. The company decided on J-2, which led to the belief, long accepted in aviation lore, that the young engineer whose surname began with the letter "J" was recognized by an eternally grateful corporate hierarchy. More likely, the company simply stuck with its existing designation system which had already reached the letter "H." According to this view, the company skipped over the letter "I" to avoid confusing it with the number "1."

The J-2 received certification on February 14, 1936, and was marketed as the New Cub. However, not all had been going smoothly in the executive echelon. Taylor wasn't able to countenance his design being tinkered with. Moreover, he fundamentally disagreed with Piper over the business plan, which called for selling a higher volume of planes at lower prices. The discord reached an impasse and Taylor left the company in December 1935. He moved to Alliance, Ohio, where he made highly regarded side-by-side two-seaters under the Taylorcraft banner.

The Bradford factory had served the company well, but it was rife with fire hazards. It erupted into flames late on March 16, 1937, and was left a smoldering hulk. Luckily, no one was injured and fifteen airplanes were moved to safety.

By summer, operations and personnel began moving to an abandoned hundred thousand-square-foot silk mill in Lock Haven, Pennsylvania, eighty-five miles from Bradford. Roads, rail lines, and the Susquehanna River made the Lock Haven plant readily accessible by conventional means. Importantly, the city had offered to construct a two thousand-foot hard-surface runway as an incentive for the company's relocation.

In the face of the company's many challenges, Jamouneau was charged with further improving the Cub. He replaced the tailskid with a tail wheel, flight instruments were added to the panel, a higher grade of steel tubing was used to accommodate larger engines, and seat cushions were installed for increased comfort. This variant of the Cub was designated the J-3.

The first of these iconic models was rolled out in the autumn of 1937. It sported what became the familiar all-yellow paint scheme highlighted by black stripes along the sides of the fuselage as well as the teddy bear emblem on the fin. As aviation historian Carroll V. Glines pointed out in his chronicle of the Cub, the shade of yellow brightened after World War II when butyrate dope was used for finishing instead of nitrate.

In November that same year, the company opted to change its name to avoid confusion with C. G. Taylor's new firm. William Piper had labored to make ends meet through the hard times, even foregoing a salary for part of the troubled decade. It was only logical that the company's name should be Piper Aircraft Corporation.

By the end of 1940, with war clouds on the horizon, Cubs were churned out of the expanded Lock Haven factory at a rate of 125 a week. During the global conflict, Piper Cubs played meaningful roles, notably as army liaison airplanes with the designation L-4. Among various duties, they served as aerial ambulances, artillery spotters, and VIP transports. Moreover, Piper boasted that four of every five US military pilots during the war had received their introductory flight instruction in the company's airplanes.

After the war, surplus Cubs flooded the market. Also, tricycle-gear designs were catching on as a popular alternative to the traditional tail-wheel configuration. Production of the ubiquitous Cub ceased in 1947, though a considerably beefed-up look-alike, known as the PA-18 Super Cub, was introduced in 1949 for utility-type operations.

The Cub had had an amazing run. Records indicate that 22,206 civil variants and 8,197 military variants were built. The most numerous model was the J-3 with a total of 9,782 completed. For decades after the assembly line stopped making Cubs, flight schools continued to use them to give a generation of aspiring flyers their first taste of the air.

Because the Cub was so economical and relatively easy to fly, it was an everyman's plane, a great democratizer of the flying community. Lots of Cubs on the ramp meant you could count on a culture of egalitarianism at the airfield. The Cub was unquestionably the Model T of the air. Today Cubs are collector's items, often exquisitely restored and valued at many times their original factory price, magnificent relics of a time fondly remembered by aging pilots.

In the hopeful aftermath of World War II, Mr. Piper penned an autobiographical book that talked up the business of general aviation. America was back to work and at peace. The future seemed limitless.

The book's concluding paragraph embodied that optimistic outlook as Mr. Piper laid out his deep convictions about light-plane flying and the people who do it. He stated that "a healthy personal plane industry is of great material and social value to the United States. The private pilot serves as one of the most effective instruments of goodwill." Amen!

•••

The Cub that would provide my ride had taxied up. I shook hands with the pilot, M. R. Smith, and bid a temporary adieu to my parents. It must have been a special day for them too, a culmination of sorts.

Mom had grown up on the periphery of the Cleveland Municipal Airport (now Hopkins International) during the interwar years, known as the Golden Age of Flight. She scaled the airport fence Labor Day weekends throughout the 1930s and beheld the National Air Races, arguably the greatest aviation spectacles of all time. She later went to work as a ticket agent at that very airport.

She met my father there following his service in the army air force during World War II as a desk-bound sergeant at a couple of air bases. The two of them knew well from experience that extraordinary things can happen at airports. Now their son would know it too.

I buckled into the back seat of N98029. Without fanfare, Mr. Smith switched on the Cub's engine. He hollered to me over the cacophony to cup, not grip, the control stick with my right hand, motioning as he spoke, and to place my feet over the rudder pedals. I would follow his inputs on the controls.

Through the Cub's side window, I caught a glimpse of Mom and Dad. I waved, but my attention quickly shifted back to the airplane. The Cub taxied far more bumpily than I had imagined. This was it, though, the nonpareil event, the lissome ship about to lift its eager passenger on its high-spread wings into its exalted realm.

We had taxied a long ways, to be able to take off into the wind. The waddling S-turns across the field enabled a slow-motion survey of the whole airstrip, a chance to absorb the scene from the privileged vantage point reserved only for those in an airplane's cockpit. I was in sync with the resplendent and invigorating gateway to my dreams. This was the most magical place in the world.

The noise was louder inside the Cub than out as we clattered down that rough-hewn runway, throttle full open. Before I knew it, we were airborne and climbing. We leveled off soon because it didn't make sense to go high during a fifteen-minute orientation flight.

With the throttle reduced, the hum of the engine subsided and the rush of air became aurally dominant. The horizon defined our relationship to the globe, which wended beneath us at a crawl. We were one with the sky, like a vessel floating on gentle ocean currents, more skiff than speedboat.

My nervousness was more than balanced by the sense of adventure. Mr. Smith turned his head to check on me. He saw a twelve-year-old transfixed by the sight-picture and beaming with joy.

With steady hand, Mr. Smith performed gentle turns left and right. He told me to coordinate stick and rudder, to feel the airplane. Yes, it was rudimentary, the first building block of airmanship, but I was flying.

The world wasn't so big anymore; it could be tamed. I was, briefly, the master of my fate, an individualist empowered to exercise a newfound independence and ride the wind in whatever direction my heart deemed desirable. Dreaming to fly led to the act of flying and that, in turn, caused me to discover the dream of flight, which is the dream that anything is possible.

The quaint airport where I was initiated into the milieu of flyers has long since given way to the vagaries of real estate development. Where once Piper Cubs gathered momentum in dashes for the sky, homes now predominate in the archetypical grid work of late twentieth-century American subdivisions. According to a data base search, the faithful airplane, good old N98029, was eventually stricken from the federal registry, its assorted parts perhaps languishing forgotten and forlorn in someone's barn, awaiting either the brusque consignment of the junkman or the affectionate rejuvenation of the restorer.

Regardless of the Cub's disposition, the flight in that beautiful little unassuming ship lives on where it matters most. In the precious minutes that I sailed on its lemon-colored wings, the kingdom of the sky was revealed and it touched my soul. So no matter what airplane has been handy since, I feel that each time I rumble down a grass strip, raise the tail wheel, and ease back on the stick to ascend, I am reentering that distinctive and everlasting domain of the Cub.

INDEX

Rentschler, Frederick B., 11
Rhodes, Jeffrey P., viii
Rice, Raymond H., 247
Rich, Ben, 295–98
Rickenbacker, Edward V.
 ("Eddie"), 104–5, 159–60
Ridley, Jack L. ("Jackie"), 25–27
The Right Stuff (movie), 31
Robertson Aircraft, 67
Rockne, Knute, 158
Rodgers, Calbraith Perry, 335
Roosevelt, Elliot, 238
Roosevelt, Franklin D., 243
Royal Australian Air Force, 84
Royal Canadian Air Force, 84
Royce, Sir Henry, 178, 180
Russell, Jack, 26, 30
Rutan, Burt, vii–viii, xii–xxi,
 48–49, 53, 55. *See also*
 SpaceShipOne
Rutan, Dick, 48
Rutan Model 76 Voyager
 (aircraft), vii
Ryan, T. Claude, 10
Ryan Company, 14–15
Ryan NYP. *See Spirit of St. Louis*
 (airplane)

S
Saint-Exupery, Antoine de, 244
Sakai, Saburo, 170
Sanger, Eugen, 35
Saulnier, Raymond, 152
SB2C Helldiver (Curtiss-Wright),
 176, 225

SB2U-1 Vindicator
 (Vought), 216
SBD Dauntless, xi, 217–26,
 228–29
Scaled Composites, vii, 48–54
Schaefer, Julius E., 328
Schairer, George, 276, 286
Scherrer, Dick, 295
Schmued, Edgar, 247–51, 253,
 258–60
Schneider, Franz, 156
Schroeder, Bill, 295
Seafire [Spitfire variant]
 (Supermarine), 186
September 11 terrorist
 attacks, 290
Servanty, Lucien, 133
7A Champ (Aeronca), xx
Seversky Aircraft Company, 164
Shima, Katsuzo, 166
Short, Mac, 328
Showa Hikoki Kogyo (Japanese
 manufacturer), 84
Sidey, Hugh, 112–13
Siegler Corporation, 121
Sikorsky, Igor, 12–13
Silver Dart/Aerodrome #4
 (AEA), 312–13
Skylab Orbital Workshop, 10
Smith, Cyrus R., 80
Smith, Joseph, 185
Smith, M. R., 339–40
Smith, Robert Grant
 ("R. G."), 227
Smith, Russell, v

ABOUT THE AUTHORS

Walter J. Boyne is the former director of the Smithsonian Institution's National Air and Space Museum and the Chairman Emeritus of the National Aeronautic Association. He accumulated more than 5,000 flight hours in a variety of US Air Force aircraft, including the Boeing B-52 Stratofortress as a nuclear test pilot with Air Force Systems Command. Colonel Boyne has written over seventy aviation-related books including bestsellers on both the *New York Times* fiction and nonfiction lists. Colonel Boyne holds degrees from the University of Pittsburgh and the University of California at Berkeley.

In 2007, he was inducted into the National Aviation Hall of Fame, joining approximately 270 of the most famous names in global aviation. In 2011, he was inducted into the American Combat Airman Hall of Fame for his service during the Vietnam War. In 2014, he received the Major General I. B. Holley Award from the Air Force Historical Foundation for contributions to the preservation of Air Force history. He is also a member of the French Society de l'Air et de l'Espace.

Colonel Boyne is one of the most frequently-televised authorities in highly-rated aerospace programming of the Discovery and History Channels. He continues to be a much sought-after on-air expert for domestic and international television productions. Colonel Boyne wrote a regular column on historic airplanes for the Air Force Association's *Air Force* magazine.

Philip Handleman is President of Handleman Filmworks, an Emmy-winning independent production company. Mr. Handleman's still photography graces the US postage stamps that commemorate the fiftieth anniversaries of the Air Force and the Air Force Academy, with print runs of 45 million and 60 million, respectively. He is a longtime pilot who currently owns and flies a World War II–vintage Stearman biplane. He has written twenty-two aviation-related books and maintains one of the world's largest aviation libraries at his private airport. Mr. Handleman graduated from Washington University and completed the Executive

Academy at the University of Michigan's Graduate School of Business Administration.

Mr. Handleman is the recipient of the 2008 Harriet Quimby Award from the Michigan Aviation Hall of Fame for contributions to aviation art and literature. In 2010, he received the Combs Gates Award from the National Aviation Hall of Fame for contributions to the preservation of America's air and space heritage. He has also been recognized by the Tuskegee Airmen National Historical Museum with its Outstanding Achievement Award and its Lifetime Distinguished Achievement Award. For his advocacy of Selfridge Air National Guard Base, the National Guard Association of Michigan presented him with an Honorary Life Membership.

Known as a staunch aviation advocate, Mr. Handleman fostered changes in federal aviation statutes that enhance nondiscriminatory regulation in the national airspace system. His articles have appeared in many aviation publications like *Aviation History* magazine. He has also contributed to a wide range of non-aviation publications, including the *Wall Street Journal*, *USA Today*, and the *Los Angeles Times*.